HUNGARY

ROMANIA

WESTERN SLAVONIA

EASTERN SLAVONIA

Danube R.

Horgos

VOJVODINA

Vukovar

Sava R.

Novi Sad

Bosanski Brod

Keraterm

Banja Luka

Brcko

Belgrade

Danube R.

OSNIA AND HERZEGOVINA

Tuzla

Drina R.

var

Jajce

Kakanj

Zvornik

S E R B I A

Srebrenica

Area of detail

Sarajevo

Pale

Goražde

Užice

Nis

HERZEGOVINA

Mostar

Kursumilja

PALMATIA

MONTENEGRO

Pristina

BULGARIA

Sofia

Dubrovnik

Podgorica

KOSOVO

Yugoslavia prior to 1991

Kms.

0 ————— 75

Miles

75

Shkoder

Kukes

Skopje

A D R I A T I C   S E A

Durres

Tirana

MACEDONIA

A L B A N I A

G R E E C E

Ioannina

CORFU

© A·Karl / J·Kemp, 2003

WAR HOSPITAL

WAR HOSPITAL

A TRUE STORY OF SURGERY
AND SURVIVAL

Sheri Fink, M.D.

PublicAffairs
New York

Book design by Jane Raese
Text set in 12-point Spectrum

Library of Congress Cataloging-in-Publication Data
Fink, Sheri.
War hospital : a true story of surgery and survival / Sheri Fink.
p. cm.
Includes bibliographical references and index.
ISBN 1-58648-113-4
1. Yugoslav War, 1991–1995—Medical care—Bosnia and Hercegovina—Srebrenica.
2. Disaster medicine—Bosnia and Hercegovina—Srebrenica.
3. Emergency medical services—Bosnia and Hercegovina—Srebrenica. I. Title.
DR1313.7.M43F56 2003
949'.703—dc21
2003046624

FIRST EDITION

1 3 5 7 9 10 8 6 4 2

To my parents and grandparents

and the doctors and nurses of eastern Bosnia

Medical ethics in time of armed conflict

is identical to medical ethics in time of peace . . .

The primary obligation of the physician is his professional duty;

in performing his professional duty,

the physician's supreme guide is his conscience.

The primary task of the medical professional

is to preserve health and save life.

—Regulations in Time of Armed Conflict,
World Medical Association, 1956, 1957, 1983

The doctor's fundamental role is

to alleviate the distress of his or her fellow men,

and no motive, whether personal, collective or political

shall prevail against this higher purpose.

—The Declaration of Tokyo,
World Medical Association, 1975

CONTENTS

PART I: BROTHERHOOD AND UNITY

PART II: THE BLOOD OF WARRIORS

MAPS

CAST OF CHARACTERS

Alić, Ejub, 32 (AH-leetch, Ey-yoob)—Physician at Srebrenica (SREB-
rehn-eet-sa) war hospital, separated from his wife and young son.
Born in a small village and worked as an internal medicine resident in
Bosnia before the war. Heavyset, with a round face, a good sense of
humor, and a weakness for plum brandy.

Dachy, Eric, 30 (Dah-shee)—Head of the Doctors Without Borders
mission in Belgrade, Serbia. Responsible for aid to eastern Bosnia.
Belgian family practitioner. Passionate and outspoken. Wears a
trademark black leather jacket and ponytail.

Dautbašić, Fatima, 26 (dah-UTE-bah-sheetch, fah-TEE-mah)—
Physician at Srebrenica war hospital. Family practitioner before the
war. Girlfriend of Dr. Ilijaz Pilav. Has long, dark hair, beautiful eyes,
and a high-pitched laugh.

Lazić, Boro, 27 (LAH-zeetch, BOE-roe)—Physician with Bosnian Serb
forces across the front lines from Srebrenica. Friends with several
Srebrenica doctors and nurses before the war. Slender, with light
brown hair, blue-green eyes, and a boyish face.

Mujkanović, Nedret, 31 (mooy-KAHN-oh-veetch, NED-reht)—
Surgical resident who volunteered to walk to Srebrenica across
enemy territory in August 1993. Handsome, with an athletic build, a
clean-shaven face, and a highly charismatic, if temperamental,
personality.

Pilav, Ilijaz, 28 (PEE-lahv, ILL-ee-ahz)—Physician at Srebrenica war
hospital. Born in a small village near Dr. Ejub Alić. Worked as a
general physician before the war. Boyfriend of Dr. Fatima Dautbašić.
A tall, gaunt, and unassuming man with a scraggly beard and
mustache.

PROLOGUE

THE SURGEON SHOWED UP wearing gym clothes. We met in the smoke-filled interior of one of Bosnia's best hotel cafés, where, gesturing, drawing, and occasionally lifting his tall, athletic frame from his seat to underline a point, he told me the story that had made him famous. It began with his hike across twenty-five miles of enemy territory to reach the besieged eastern Bosnian town of Srebrenica. There, along with a small band of village doctors, most barely out of medical school and not one a surgeon, he ministered to the medical needs of 50,000 people. Rudimentary equipment and the lack of electricity, running water, and often anesthetics were just the beginning of the hardships. These doctors and nurses were visited by nearly every imaginable affliction of modern war.

The handsome, dark-haired doctor regaled me for two full days, interrupting our conversation only to greet well-wishers, who called him by his first name, "Dr. Nedret." His casual dress reflected confidence and charisma befitting a man who embarks on a journey knowing that it can lead to one of only two endpoints: martyrdom or magnificence. Nedret told me a story of triumph and tragedy, heroism and human weakness, of friendship and love surviving against all odds in a climate of anger and vengeance. All this took place in the town of Srebrenica, which, attacked in the presence of U.N. soldiers, became a central testing ground for U.S.-European relations, NATO's post–Cold War significance, and what U.S. President George Bush senior dubbed "the new world order."

WHAT LED ME TO Dr. Nedret Mujkanović (and later his less hyperbolic but equally impressive fellow doctors of Srebrenica) was a conference on "Medicine, War, and Peace" that I attended my final year as a medical student. The winter conference took place in an unheated Bosnian medical school auditorium beneath blown-out windows, unrepaired two years after the war. One by one, doctors, nurses, and aid workers related wartime experiences that had pitted their personal struggle for survival against their duty to practice medicine.

Those stories led me to reflect on my previous conception of war medicine. The popular culture depicts war as a rite of passage, a proving ground for the famous surgeon-pioneers, and a culture medium for history's greatest medical advances. The words of a British physician from the turn of the last century epitomize this view: "How large and various is the experience of the battlefield and how fertile the blood of warriors in the rearing of good surgeons." This cheery quotation graces the preface to NATO's official war surgery handbook and is so well-known that it was repeated to me by a war doctor in Bosnia (who attributed it, interestingly, to a Russian).

But even the peacetime practice of medicine in the most technically advanced country of the world sometimes crushes doctors' personal lives and professional development. Years of rigorous, all-consuming training, unreasonable hours, sleep deprivation, pressure to be superhuman and perfectionistic, and repeated exposure to life-and-death dilemmas often dehumanize doctors and lead them to burn out and neglect their own health and well-being. Having known American doctors who committed suicide, abused drugs, or made serious mistakes under the pressures of normal medical practice, I wondered whether a "fertile rearing" was really what the Bosnian war doctors had experienced. I returned to Bosnia the following year to find out.

Those first two days I spent with the war surgeon, Dr. Nedret, offered nothing to contradict and much to support my initial, romantic notions. War had left him an optimist. It gave him plenty of chances to hone technical skills, devise ingenious adaptations to seemingly impossible situations, and perform uplifting, sustaining, purposeful work in bleak and tragic circumstances. As I probed deeper and met more doctors who'd worked in Srebrenica, though, I learned that the constant grind of not only living through war, but also treating its most severely affected victims, led some lifesavers to hopelessness, despair, and even criminal activity.

Medicine and the war in Bosnia, I discovered, were intricately intertwined. In Bosnia, doctors, aid workers, and patients, in spite of their "protected" status under international law, became the earliest and among the most regular targets of war. Conversely, several physicians instigated and led the war's campaigns of "ethnic cleansing" and geno-cide. And finally, at times aid efforts paradoxically stood in the way of more decisive actions to bring peace and were used as shameful cover for international failure and inaction on diplomatic and military fronts. It took the killing of most of Srebrenica's adult male population, the largest massacre on European soil in nearly half a century, to move the powerful nations of the world to action.

———

THE STORY OF SREBRENICA AND ITS DOCTORS so impressed me that I spent the next four and a half years pursuing its details. What happened when doctors—community leaders used to having the power to fix things—realized that bandaging patients' wounds did nothing to ad-dress the root causes of their suffering? Were the ethics of medicine in wartime truly identical to the ethics established for peacetime? Did the international conventions protecting and governing the practice of medicine and delivery of aid need updating in this post–Cold War–type conflict? These were some of the questions I set out to answer. Because enemy forces had overtaken the town, including the hospital, dispersing or killing all of its medical workers and patients, my work involved combing Bosnia and the world for survivors and sneaking around Sre-brenica's abandoned hospital in pursuit of a story that gripped me ever more tightly.

What I found in Bosnia was a story of individual doctors that high-lighted, clarified, and personalized a war so many people outside found confusing and that offered insights into larger questions about how "reg-ular people" with no conscious desire to fight (with, in fact, a sacred pledge to sustain life) were caught up and participated in war. I chose to reconstruct a narrative from the perspective of several doctors—Bos-nian Muslim, Bosnian Serb, and international from Doctors Without Borders—whose individual backgrounds, personalities, and beliefs led them into and out of the war zone at various times, responding in very different ways to the challenges that faced them. What linked them, be-sides the three-story Srebrenica Hospital building, was their confronta-tion, at least once, with that ultimate doctors' dilemma—whether to serve their patients or save themselves.

These individuals offered hundreds of hours of their time, recalling in great detail the most difficult days of their lives. I was most surprised by the extent to which their work influenced the war itself. Doctors mixed medicine with advocacy, community organizing, and politics. Some—with the painful conviction that they could save more lives by taking lives—shook off their white coats, picked up guns, and turned themselves into fighters. Here is their story.

PART ONE

BROTHERHOOD AND UNITY

There was a time when meadow, grove, and stream,

The earth, and every common sight,

To me did seem

Apparell'd in celestial light,

The glory and the freshness of a dream.

It is not now as it hath been of yore;—

Turn wheresoe'er I may,

By night or day,

The things which I have seen I now can see no more.

—**William Wordsworth** (1770–1850)
Ode, Intimations of Immortality
from Recollections of Early Childhood

For men to plunge headlong into an undertaking of vast change,

they must be intensely discontented yet not destitute,

and they must have the feeling that by the possession of

some potent doctrine, infallible leader or some new technique

they have access to a source of irresistible power.

—**Eric Hoffer,** *The True Believer*

1

FIRST DO NO HARM

THE NURSE'S HANDS FLUTTER AROUND THE PATIENT, but the doctor just stands and stares. He squeezes his right fist around the white cloth he used to dry his hands, crushing it, and then opens his hand, finger by finger. Squeezes. Then opens.

A technician bending over the patient straightens, wiping his bare hands on his white coat. Another leans over to fillet the patient's blue jeans with a pair of scissors.

Summer sunlight floods through the large, wood-trimmed window and pools on the patient's right leg. The knee looks normal. But the swollen, blotchy skin below it leads to a foot mummified in layers of bloodstained, torn bed sheets. The medical technicians begin unwinding the improvised bandage.

Dressed in a white gown, round face and brown sideburns capped by a blue paper hat, thirty-two-year-old Dr. Ejub Alić stands back from the table. A man taping the operation with a camera powered by a car battery softly begins to narrate. It is July 17, 1992, at 2:50 P.M. The hospital in Srebrenica, Bosnia, closed for the first three months of war, reopened only five days ago. And Ejub, a pediatrics resident accustomed to treating kids' sore throats and earaches, is being asked to amputate a young man's leg. He watches the nurse pull off the last cloth strip, baring the full, damning evidence of the injury to everyone's eyes and nostrils. An exploding mine has bitten off the bottom of the foot and left two flaps of skin yawning around the patient's missing heel. During the time it took for the patient's family to get him here, arranging for a horse and cart and driving through a dozen miles of mountainous territory partly held by the enemy, bacteria have digested the remains into a tangle of blackened sinews.

There is no monitor here, but Ejub doesn't need one to tell him that the heart of this patient—not much more than a boy, really, twenty

3

years old, lying on the orange cot still in his jeans and beige T-shirt—is beating quickly. Blood loss, fever, raw fear. The patient's well-defined muscles evince the three months he's spent hefting a rifle and ammunition around the hilly, forested, some would say backward, border country of eastern Bosnia. When war exploded on the eve of Bosnia's independence from Yugoslavia and Serb nationalist forces quickly took control of two-thirds of the republic's territory, this young Muslim man picked up a hunting rifle and fought to protect his family's village east of Srebrenica. So far he has helped save its citizens from the fate suffered by thousands of Muslims throughout Bosnia—deportations, imprisonment in concentration camps, executions, and massacres.

The young man's pallor gives him a weakly appearance. He has curled his left arm to his chest, as if bracing himself, and on his wrist, a large, steel-colored watch ticks away the time. Someone has draped a small towel over his eyes, shielding him from the sight of what will come.

A nurse bends over the leg and shaves it with bare hands and a serious expression, ignoring the putrid smell. A tendril of dark hair escapes her blue cloth cap and curls beneath the birthmark on her left cheek. When she finishes, Ejub repeats her work, picking up the razor and inching it up from the blue, livid ankle to the pink, healthy thigh, postponing the inevitable moment when his scalpel will meet skin. Neither he nor any of the handful of doctors who have, over the past few days, made their way from islands of neighboring "free" Bosnian territory to the town of Srebrenica has experience as a surgeon. Ejub cannot recall surgery ever having been performed in this small, Spartan hospital, where women used to come to give birth before the war. No, Ejub is no surgeon, has never aspired to be a surgeon. Although he has talent for fine manual work—he practices woodcarving—his short, chubby fingers make performing even some non-surgical medical procedures difficult. But now he has war experience, having worked as the sole doctor in a nearby Muslim village that was isolated for the war's first three months. Here, there is no one any better qualified than he, and if he doesn't try to do something, this young man will most certainly die.

Ejub drops the razor into a beaker full of hydrogen peroxide. Used in the production of rockets and torpedoes, paper, chemicals, and car batteries, here in the operating room it serves as a sterilizer. Some townspeople found a cache of the liquid treasure at the abandoned battery factory up the road. Others diluted it with water purified in fifty-liter vats used, in better times, for distilling plum brandy. War is full of such small, absurd ironies. A 3 percent solution oxidizes bacteria to death without harming human tissue. If Ejub didn't have it, he'd be stuck in American Civil War–like conditions. One out of three amputation patients used to die from infection or blood loss. Sterile technique, shown to prevent infection by Joseph Lister in 1865, catapulted survival rates and stood as one of two great surgical advances of the century. Ejub calls hydrogen peroxide "Bosnia's greatest war hero." Little jokes like this keep him going.

At the moment, Ejub isn't smiling. The ability to sterilize equipment and apply an antiseptic puts him only one foot into the nineteenth century. The century's other great discovery—general anesthesia—is not something Ejub has to offer his patients. All he has are two syringes of precious local anesthetic swiped from the town's abandoned dental clinic. They lie in a silver pan before him. Ejub knows how to use the anesthetic to numb the skin, but not to prevent pain in deep structures such as bone. When he thinks of the fact that the injured foot connects to a conscious human being, he wonders whether it would be better, in some cosmic sense, not to operate. Not long ago, when faced with his first amputation, he felt so powerless that he prayed to God for the suffering patient to die before he began. And—regardless of the fact that he's trapped in what some people are calling a "religious" war—Ejub does not even believe in God.

To counter his paralysis, Ejub steers his mind away from the patient and toward the wound. He forces himself to sit down beside the low-standing cot and take up his instruments: a pair of pincer-like forceps in one hand, for gripping skin, and a scalpel in the other. He holds the blade like a pencil and inscribes a semicircle in the skin of the swollen, dusky lower leg. This is his first mistake.

The patient, knee propped up on a folded blanket, remains still, silent. Ejub stares at the leg as he works, face impassive, deepening the incision, bowing flesh with his scalpel as if playing a violin. The world has constricted to the leg, the leg and the job he has to do, like a piece of wood he needs to whittle into shape.

He has no assistant to expose tissue according to the display he needs, or to scan for blood vessels and, fingers dancing a delicate ballet with his, tie them off in silence. Instead, he has the help of an older pediatrician who is even less adept at surgery, the recently appointed director of the war hospital, Dr. Avdo Hasanović. The bulbous-nosed doctor seats himself on a stool across from Ejub, takes up the other of Srebrenica's only two scalpels, and begins to stab at the patient's calf as the nurse struggles to hold it steady.

The two doctors work separately, trying to complete the surgery more quickly and thus minimize pain and the dangerous blood loss that could lead to shock and death. The patient has already bled a great deal from his wound, and, with no blood bags and no electricity to run a refrigerator for transfusion products, they cannot give him a transfusion.

The patient groans—just once. He has barely flinched or bled, and Ejub has overlooked what this means: He is cutting dead tissue. Fragments of the exploding mine have seared the patient's blood vessels, starving the lower leg of vital blood supply. If the doctors complete the amputation here, gangrene and infection will creep up and ultimately kill the young man.

Ejub scrutinizes the leg.

"A little higher," he pronounces and points to a spot. He looks to the older doctor, who nods his agreement.

Starting at this point, Ejub slides his knife down, splitting the skin just as the nurse slit open the pant leg. The flesh drops to either side as he cuts.

After some poking and probing, the other physician picks up the task and begins to slice upward. The nurse can barely keep up with him, untying and retying the rubber catheter being used as a tourniquet, higher and higher, swabbing with disinfectant, injecting with anesthetic, her escaped curl of hair nearly brushing the patient's bloated skin, her bare fingers flirting with the scalpel.

Now the skin incision has been extended to its new, higher position. The two doctors resume cutting toward bone. Each stroke of their scalpels takes them deeper, away from numbed skin and tiny capillaries and closer to large nerves and arteries. A loud "Ohhhh!" escapes the patient.

The doctors intensify their work. Ejub's scalpel nears the anterior tibial artery. Its caliber measures approximately a quarter of an inch and it contains blood pressurized by every pulse of the heart to roughly 120 mm of mercury or two pounds per square inch. Normally, surgeons defuse the vessel, gently lifting it away from the surrounding tissue and tying it in two places with lengths of absorbable, string-like suture. Only then do they cut it.

But Ejub, rushing, has little suture or experience. He slices through the artery.

The doctors fumble to stop the bleeding with the rubber tourniquet, retying it tightly around the patient's leg, hoping that the external pressure will overwhelm the blood vessel's internal pressure, giving the blood in the vessel time to clot. To compound the force, Ejub grips the leg tightly between his hands.

The patient moans.

The other doctor presses down on the patient's knee with his left hand to steady it, forceps dangling from his fingers. With his right hand he saws and saws with his scalpel. The edge of the blade slices through a dense network of nerve endings in the membrane around the bone, the periosteum. The patient yells.

Ejub presses his fingers hard against the skin to close off the broken artery. For now he blocks out his emotions and tries to focus, but the shutter of his mind snaps and his brain can't help being exposed to the horror. Still, he reaches for the *zhaga*, a "p"-shaped saw designed for cutting metal, not bone. The man with the camera stops recording the operation. Soon the worst part is over and somehow the young patient survives. The operation is done, and all Ejub wants is a cigarette.

The doctor peels off his gloves, pulls off his gown, and doffs his blue cap. He walks out of the operating room and down the dark hallway, pushes open a wooden door, enters a vestibule, and exits the hospital through its back door. He walks down its steep driveway and turns left onto the main street.

Hills lurch up around him, casting evening shadows on the road. He strides uphill, past old homes that once had terra-cotta tile roofs. Shrapnel marks splatter some façades; others are destroyed, skins burned off, just skeleton masonry remaining. Brick chimneys trace jagged silhouettes against the sky. The roofless hulks are like open dollhouses. He knows the people who lived in these houses, can recite them by name as he walks up the street—Begić, Delić, Fazlić . . .

A child of the mountainous villages just south of Srebrenica, Ejub has never liked living in a valley. Even when he first arrived in Srebrenica to work as a doctor six years ago, six years before the war, he felt trapped.

Now men sow the hills with mines instead of corn, wheat, oat, and to-bacco seeds. They drop explosive-filled shells into mortars and let them fly. Every missile that comes whizzing out of these hills, bursting into hot metal fragments, reminds him of his vulnerability. His body, too, can be pierced like Swiss cheese. And who would take care of his wounds?

Ejub, a nominal Muslim, had liked his Serb neighbors, and they had liked him. He has his own way of rationalizing why people who like each other have begun to fight. War is like a marriage squabble. Sometimes you get into an argument with your wife, and you realize, somewhere along the way, that you might have been wrong, but then it is too late to go back and admit it. You keep on fighting. In war, there are times you wish there weren't a quarrel and that you could go back to the begin-ning, but you can't because blood has been spilled and, almost by natural law, it goes on and on and you have to defend yourself. That is how he makes sense of it, if any sense can be made of it at all.

He reaches his orange brick apartment building and enters the door on the west side. He goes to sleep in his marriage bed. Like every night for three months since the fighting started, no matter where he sleeps or for how long, he dreams about the wife and son he sent away for safety.

He awakens gripped with the fear of death and the certainty that he will be killed before seeing them again. Perhaps sleep is where the oper-ating room images develop, where gruesome photos from the surgeries he's done stack up. He lies in bed and prays for a replacement to come.

FOR DIFFERENT REASONS, the commanders of the ad hoc troops defend-ing the territory around Srebrenica also want a qualified surgeon to take over the makeshift operating theater. Medicine is a war weapon. The presence of six doctors on six islands of land around Srebrenica has cor-related with their successful defense.

Now that the islands have been connected, five of the six doctors have come together in a central place, forming the Srebrenica war hospital and temporarily boosting morale among soldiers and civilians. Amputa-tions take place in the hospital room rather than on the kitchen tables or living room floors of village houses where they did the first three months of war.

For a while, just knowing that a doctor stands behind them has kept up the defenders' morale. But in many ways, medical care is still in the Middle Ages. A head, chest, or stomach wound means near-certain death. As more soldiers realize this and lose the will to fight, their commanders believe, there is more of a chance that Serb forces will succeed in expelling the Muslims from their land, "ethnic cleansing."

The nearest big city controlled by Bosnian government forces—Tuzla—lies only fifty miles away but a world apart, inaccessible beyond miles of enemy territory and minefields. With no working telephones, making a link with that outside world means finding the man who used to run the amateur radio club and outfitting one of his ham radios with a car battery.

When the amateur radio operator makes a connection, he speaks slowly and clearly:

"In Srebrenica, we are running out of medical supplies."

"We are in desperate need of a surgeon here."

"People are dying of injuries that could be treated."

The people who hear these words pass them on to Bosnian radio, where the message is broadcast into the homes of Bosnia's biggest cities, where it sticks in the memory of a self-styled war surgeon named Dr. Nedret Mujkanović.

The radio operator's plea also makes its way into the ears of local translators who work for the United Nations in the Bosnian capital, who tell their international bosses about the situation, who pass the information to other aid workers, who pass the word to a particularly strong-willed Belgian doctor named Eric Dachy, who works for an aid group called Doctors Without Borders.

2

ERIC

For Dr. Eric Dachy, Srebrenica sounds like salvation. By the summer of 1992, the thirty-year-old Belgian generalist has arrived upon some of the most brutal scenes of the wars of Yugoslavia's dissolution, but always after the fact, when nothing is left to do but offer succor to the survivors. The fact that an island of non-Serbs is holding out in eastern Bosnia means there is still a place to intervene before the worst occurs.

Over his past eight months as regional director of Doctors Without Borders, Eric has come to be considered, by dull U.N. functionaries and the few unenthusiastic aid workers in Belgrade, Serbia, the capital of what remains of Yugoslavia, as "our best example of local color." With his keen mind, unorthodox appearance, and steady-burning pilot flame of outrage at injustice, Eric has made his mark. When he strides into co-ordination meetings chronically late in his black leather jacket, uncut brown hair stuffed back in a ponytail, looking as if he's been up all night, the others can almost hear a Harley-Davidson roaring behind him. But his teen rebel appearance belies a mature sensibility.

Eric doesn't need the meetings, the others agree. The meetings need him. He seems to grasp what it is taking others, even those older and more experienced at this work, much longer to figure out. For one thing, they aren't in the tropics. The malaria pills the aid workers dump here are a useless source of medical waste. This population, older and with more chronic diseases than most recent refugee populations, needs its blood pressure pills, diabetes medications, and dialysis fluids. If the agencies are serious about restoring dignity to these refugees, they need to start providing soap, toothpaste, shampoo, and other items for personal hygiene, regardless of the fact that aid workers in poorer countries have to fight for enough syringes to immunize children.

But even this doesn't seem to be enough anymore in light of the horrors Eric has witnessed. Increasingly, he challenges his colleagues with the idea that the real issue isn't how to provide humanitarian aid, but how to stop the war. The nightmares he has seen these past months have made him question everything—the value of life, the principles that can be defended here, and the impact of his presence as a humanitarian aid worker. He searches for a corner of this war where what he can provide will be truly needed.

Sometimes he wonders how the hell he landed in this violent place and why the hell he stays here. Religion, which motivates so many others who go out in the world to "help," has nothing to do with it. In fact, Eric's upper-middle-class parents in Brussels, Belgium, raised him as an atheist in the predominantly Roman Catholic country. On the one hand, atheism has led him to take a rational approach to the world rather than a moralistic one. On the other hand, Eric's father, a lawyer whom he loved and revered, instilled in him a hunger for justice.

Eric isn't a stranger to conflict. Angry voices echoed through his childhood home. Growing up in the tumultuous 1960s with two older siblings acting out their adolescent rebellions, well-behaved and high-achieving Eric didn't draw too much attention from his parents. Family quarrels helped Eric hone his skills in argumentation and critical thinking and heightened his desire for justice, but he hated the fights and hated the splintering relationships between people he loved. Fed up, he left home at age seventeen to attend college and live with a girlfriend. He harbored dreams of putting everyone back together again, giving each of them what they deserved to make them happy, stop blaming one other, and be friends again. A half year later, on Eric's eighteenth birthday, his father died suddenly. Eric's plan to mend the family went into hibernation.

Eric struggled through medical school and then opened a general practice in his suburban Brussels apartment, but found his work less than stimulating. He dawdled through the post-graduate training needed for full physician certification, dabbled in learning psychoanalysis, and filled out his nights and his gut at Brussels bars.

What captivated him in the late 1980s was news of the changing international order. When the Berlin Wall fell, symbolizing an end to the conflict between east and west, he expected world peace to break out. Instead came the 1991 Gulf War. He wasn't a pacifist, but he opposed it, believing that Iraqi leader Saddam Hussein's foray into Kuwait could be stopped by other means.

One day Eric stood up from his TV set and decided to do something to help the war's victims. He made an appointment at the Brussels office of Doctors Without Borders and asked to be sent to Baghdad. When they told him they didn't work there, he deemed them a bunch of fraidy-cat "wankers" and went home. That was it. He'd considered it just one afternoon. But two weeks later, someone from the aid organization called him back. Kurds were fleeing Iraqi air strikes in long columns toward the north. They needed assistance. Could Eric go?

He went, not knowing much at all about the organization that the French-speaking call by the acronym MSF, for *Médecins Sans Frontières*. He knew them only by their poster campaigns, which proclaimed, "We didn't study medicine to cure imaginary patients." Eric interpreted this to mean that they got things done for people in need and challenged prevailing attitudes. He liked those who "shook the tree" a little bit.

MSF had been born kicking and screaming its way out of the Red Cross in Biafra, Nigeria, in the late 1960s. As Nigerian forces brutally squelched a secessionist struggle, a group of young French Red Cross doctors arrived to find famine sweeping across the rebel-controlled area. The doctors could do nothing to help. Hands tied by the International Committee of the Red Cross's strict operating procedures (based on international conventions not yet updated to cover internal armed conflict), the doctors could not deliver crucial food supplies to rebel areas without the consent of the official government. The Nigerians weren't willing to give it. Even worse, as evidence of genocide against the Biafrans grew, the Red Cross kept silent. This infuriated the French doctors. Thirty years earlier, Red Cross officials had failed to speak out about the mass deportations they documented during the Holocaust. That inaction had led some progressive intellectuals to discredit the very concept of humanitarianism. "The ethics of the Red Cross," one ranted in a criticism of Camus's *The Plague*, "are solely valid in a world where violence against mankind comes only from eruptions, floods, crickets or rats. And not from men."

The French doctors in Biafra seemed to agree. They revolted and broke their International Red Cross pledge to "abstain from all communications and comments on its mission." They accused the Nigerian government of genocide and the Red Cross of failing to provide aid as famine ravaged the region. After leaving the Red Cross, they founded the group that would, in 1971, become MSF.

MSF took the rigid, law-based approach of the Red Cross and bent it. Staying at work night after night, red-rimmed eyes burning with conviction and the smoke of dozens of cigarettes, its founders crafted a new philosophy of humanitarianism: MSF would go wherever people suffered, regardless of political or military boundaries, with or without permission. Aid workers would bear public witness to outrages, from human rights violations to the blocking of humanitarian relief.

Although some came to consider the typical MSF volunteer an adventurer or, in the words of a former MSF worker, a "naïve, Schweitzer-like individual, who seeks to change the world through medical skills and goodwill," the idea of humanitarian doctors who went where needed, blind to all obstacles, and spoke out about what they saw, took off in the public imagination.

"The age of the 'French doctors' rapidly replaced that of heroes in the mould of Che Guevara—the latter more romantic, undoubtedly, but disqualified by reason of their enthusiasm for gulags," wrote Rony Brauman, president of MSF-France, in the early 1990s. "The humanitarian volunteer, a new, newsworthy figure, neither statesman nor guerrilla, but half-amateur and half-expert, began to appear at the flashpoints which light up the progress of history ... the victim and his rescuer have become one of the totems of our age."

By the late 1970s, the world began catching up. The 1977 Second Additional Protocol to the 1949 Geneva Conventions—the modern version of humanitarian law aimed to protect civilians, the injured, and other noncombatants from the effects of war—authorized humanitarian assistance even in internal armed conflicts, situations increasingly common after World War II. Dozens of similar groups, known as nongovernmental organizations or "NGOs," formed around the world, an alphabet soup that included IMC (International Medical Corps) in the United States and MDM (the French acronym for Doctors of the World) in France. They recruited doctors and other experts to volunteer for varying amounts of time—from a few weeks to a few years—providing medical or technical assistance to those in need. Each had its own philosophies and strengths; MSF specialized in acute conflict and disaster assistance.

When Eric Dachy went to MSF in 1991 it was the beginning of what cultural critic David Rieff dubbed the "era of the NGOs." Governments and funding agencies increasingly chose non-governmental organizations to implement aid programs because of their efficiency compared with large, intergovernmental organizations such as the United Nations. More importantly, the "right to intervene" to alleviate human suffering, which MSF co-founder Dr. Bernard Kouchner dubbed *droit d'ingérence*, was perched to leap from operating principle of humanitarians to foreign policy of nations.

In April 1991, MSF assigned Eric to the border of Iraq and Turkey to respond to one of the largest and fastest refugee outflows in recent history. Saddam Hussein's forces' brutal suppression of a Kurdish uprising in the wake of the Gulf War sent up to 2 million Iraqi Kurds fleeing northward toward Turkey and Iran. Making an unprecedented linkage, United Nations Security Council Resolution 688 labeled Iraqi "repression" a "threat to international peace and security" and insisted that Iraq allow humanitarian organizations to assist the displaced. Kouchner, who had left MSF and become a French government minister for health and humanitarian action, helped draft the historic resolution.

A U.S.-led thirteen-nation coalition force then created a "safety zone" in northern Iraq, allowing aid workers to operate and Kurdish refugees to return home. Operation Provide Comfort erased the thick line between military and humanitarian work and so marked a new development in the discipline of humanitarian aid. Groups such as MSF, the United Nations High Commissioner for Refugees (UNHCR), and the Red Cross worked in cooperation with coalition troops. Kouchner championed state involvement in aid delivery, arguing that humanitarian intervention was inherently political and NGOs were too weak to accomplish their objectives when opposed by controlling powers. More traditional humanitarians, though, argued that states' intentions could not be purely humanitarian and worried that involvement with the military would undermine their own neutral status.

Eric Dachy packed his bags quite unaware of and uninterested in any philosophy of humanitarianism. He joined MSF because he wanted to do "something altruistic" for the Kurds. As a physician bored with the sprained ankles and tummyaches of suburban general practice, he was simply looking for the chance to treat and even cure patients with serious health problems. He arrived in Üzümlü, a muddy, hilly border village full of mountain views, Kurdish refugees, and cholera, and spent the next three months treating hundreds of very sick and shell-shocked patients with a combination of medicine and psychotherapy. He marveled at how instantly useful he felt as a doctor. His boredom vanished.

Eric returned to Belgium and told MSF he wanted to do it again. He closed his medical practice and awaited his next assignment. It came quickly. Labeled an expert after just three months in the exigent world of aid work—with its ever-shifting cadre of workers, never quite enough of them, never quite as well-trained or experienced as they should be—MSF sent him to central Africa to help the government of Chad fight cholera.

He had a disappointing three months. The government strictly prohibited him from treating patients or improving the curative programs he found inadequate, and Eric grew angry and disillusioned. He discharged his fury in a letter to MSF headquarters in Brussels, but after finishing his mission he readied himself to go out again. He wanted to help people in need. He had learned that aid work wasn't perfect, but he still believed in MSF, and MSF, because it valued strong opinions and new ideas, still believed in him.

The hot tropical sun still fresh on his skin, he awoke one morning in November 1991 to a call from MSF, this time to go to Yugoslavia. "For a few weeks," the voice on the phone said. "Can you leave immediately?"

The next morning at MSF's Brussels headquarters, Eric was briefed on his mission. He knew almost nothing about Yugoslavia, a disintegrating, post-Communist Eastern European country. After World War II, the Partisan hero Josip Broz "Tito" had gathered six Balkan republics together into the Yugoslav Federation: Serbia, Croatia, Bosnia-Herzegovina, Slovenia, Macedonia, and Montenegro. The ethno-religious makeup of each republic was different, but this "Land of the South Slavs" was mainly populated by closely related Slavic peoples who had converted at various points in the history of empires to Orthodox Christianity (Serbs, Montenegrins, and Macedonians), Catholicism (Croats and Slovenians), and Islam (Bosnian Muslims), along with significant populations of ethnic Albanians, Hungarians, Jews, and others.

Tito tolerated no divisiveness between the groups, which had fought bitterly, but also had traditions of peaceful coexistence. Some believed this served to sew up a dirty wound—it left dangerous emotions festering within hearts and in families, infecting new generations at dinner tables, rather than allowing the grievances to be aired and cleared in the larger society. Others believed that covering up the past was the best way to move forward in peace for groups of people so geographically intermixed that they obviously had to coexist. For a long while it worked. The younger generations, especially city residents, ignored the past and stopped caring about what ethnicity or religion they were supposed to be.

Tito died in 1980 without leaving a successor, and the fairly prosperous country backslid into the worldwide recession. Serb intellectuals, voicing sentiments forbidden during Tito's rule, began complaining that Serbs, the most numerous group in Yugoslavia, lacked power commensurate with their numbers and were in some areas "endangered."

A Serb politician, Slobodan Milošević, found that appealing to Serb nationalist sentiment won him support and the leadership of the Serbian Communist Party. Through various tactics, he came to control half of the votes in the Yugoslav federal government, where the leaders of the six republics and two autonomous provinces now shared power. Multi-party elections in other republics brought nationalists of other ethnicities to office who opposed Serbia's domination. After holding referendums, the republics of Croatia and Slovenia declared independence from Yugoslavia on June 25, 1991. Slovenia quickly resisted intimidation by the Yugoslav army, but Croatia had a significant Serb minority who feared they would lose power and suffer violence in a newly independent nationalist Croatian state. The Serbs' fears were fanned by both Croat provocations and a media blitz of nationalist Serb propaganda. Croatia disintegrated into war between pro-independence Croatian forces and a combined force of Yugoslav National Army and Serb irregular units.

"We have no dog in this fight," said the U.S. Secretary of State, and, for the first time since World War II, the United States stepped back and left responsibility for an issue with significant security implications to the European Community, which failed to stop the fighting. In September, the United Nations imposed an arms embargo on all of Yugoslav territory. This served to favor the Serb-dominated Yugoslav army—the sixth largest in Europe—which had stockpiles of weapons and its own strong armaments industry.

Eric's mission was to evacuate war-injured patients who were huddled in the basement of a hospital in a Croatian city, Vukovar, that was being held under siege by the Yugoslav National Army and Serb irregulars.

Several weeks earlier, in mid-October, an MSF representative based in the Croatian capital, Zagreb, had struck a deal between Yugoslav and Croatian rebel forces for evacuation of Vukovar's injured patients. On the way out of Vukovar with the first group of 109 critically injured patients, the twelve-vehicle MSF convoy fell under a shower of mortar fire. Later a land mine exploded, maiming two MSF nurses, on a road the convoy had been directed to take by the Yugoslav National Army. MSF's leaders had unknowingly participated in a plan that linked the organization's access to the hospital with the safe passage of Yugoslav forces from an army barracks in Croatia. The incident shocked the MSF workers, who had never before experienced being targets. And being lied to.

More than fifty other wounded patients were still waiting to be evacuated from the bombarded hospital, which had no running water or stable source of electricity. Eric was being dispatched to the capital of Yugoslavia—Belgrade, Serbia. Far from the area of conflict, he'd be working to convince high-ranking Yugoslav Army officers to allow MSF to complete the evacuation.

He arrived two days later and took time to familiarize himself with the warm, autumnal capital, noting the proud and handsome features of its residents. He strolled along wide boulevards flanked by ugly, socialist-style buildings and turned onto small sylvan streets lined with old square houses capped by terra-cotta tiles. He visited the city's central park where the Sava and Danube rivers meet, overlooked by an ancient fortress, Kalemegdan, where Serbs were trapped by marauding Turks, a perpetual reminder of hundreds of years of hated Ottoman rule and the inspiration for epic poems about Serbians' mythic suffering. The next day he awoke early and rolled out of Belgrade in an old Lada sedan, heading northwest toward Vukovar. The Russian antique belonged to the only driver Eric's translator could find whose hunger for money surpassed his fear of driving into an artillery barrage. Confident, inexperienced, and armed only with good intentions, Eric fully expected to enter the besieged city to assess the medical situation. But, after more than fifty miles and several police checkpoints, Serb soldiers stopped the car at a sign marked "*ratna zona.*" War zone.

The soldiers refused to let them proceed.

"Impossible. Far too dangerous," they said, which struck Eric as ironic because, after all, the danger came from the soldiers themselves. He stepped out of his car and listened to the boom of heavy guns, feeling each detonation shake the ground and echo in his belly.

Having failed to break the siege lines, he visited a few nearby health clinics and rode back to Belgrade in the dark. That night he couldn't sleep. He sat in an old armchair by the window of his room, facing the moonlit garden. He closed his eyes and thought of Vukovar, thoughts he would record in a chronicle of his experiences:

What if chance had led me to be born there? Would I have had the wherewithal to escape in time? I'm not sure. I can easily imagine having chosen to remain, having refused to believe that everything was going to hell. Now, I, too, would be a prisoner, trapped under bombardment with thousands of others.

Damn it, he would get them out. He'd do everything in his power to get them out, like a fireman carrying people out of a burning house. This, he decided, would be his mission. His only mission. MSF's mission, too. This was a cause that would be worth any trouble, any difficulty he'd have to bear.

He no longer considered himself a humanitarian as he had in Iraq and Chad. Here, in this place of extreme violence and sophisticated hospitals full of experienced surgeons and nurses, there was no space for a good-willed doctor with basic medical knowledge. No space at all. Here, he would have to become an activist.

His anxiety evaporated, replaced by a calm serenity. He believed his life had just changed. It had taken a direction.

Over the following weeks, the sun disappeared from the Belgrade sky and the temperature sank. Every day Eric and an MSF administrator tried to gain official access papers to Vukovar, hoping to negotiate a ceasefire, bring medical supplies to the hospital, and carry out the planned evacuation. They chased from one government office to another where Communist-style apparatchiks happily clinked glasses of the plum brandy they kept in their cabinets, but refused to so much as direct them to those in charge of access to the *ratna zona*. At last a functionary offered the name of a top general, but they never made it past his secretary. After numerous office visits and phone calls, they garnered only a threat: Call once again and I'll toss you in prison. Delegates of the International Committee of the Red Cross (ICRC) faced similar frustrations in their negotiations for access to Vukovar.

In late October, as conflict had broadened throughout the Republic of

Croatia, the U.N. secretary-general again designated the United Nations High Commissioner for Refugees, UNHCR, as the "lead agency" to coordinate humanitarian assistance in an internal conflict zone. Because the UNHCR had managed the large aid effort in northern Iraq earlier in the year, it was the obvious agency to task with the difficult and unfamiliar job of providing aid to besieged or displaced people who, because they hadn't crossed international borders, lacked the official status of refugees.

Eric Dachy, though, had already realized that aid was a secondary concern to the people in Vukovar. Radio news reported intense shelling of civilian areas. Even the hospital had been hit. Noncombatants were suffering and dying because they were being targeted.

When UNHCR Belgrade convened a meeting of aid workers from the principal international organizations, Eric led the charge. He was a doctor, not a politician or a top-ranking U.N. official. But, like his MSF forebears who had witnessed the failed aid operations in Biafra, he burned to take control of the situation and make it right. And he believed that through MSF he could.

"This massacre should be stopped!" he cried out at the meeting, sure that his colleagues would agree.

But a representative from the ICRC blithely pointed out that the granddaddy of humanitarianism, the founder of the Red Cross himself, Henri Dunant, had done his good deeds for the wounded on the battlefield of Solferino, Italy, *after* the battle was over.

The others concurred. Perhaps they had been around the block once too often and grown accustomed to war's outrages. As humanitarians, international law gave them the duty and right to improve the lot of civilians and other noncombatants in conflicts. They were doing their best to achieve this. They could not stop the war or enforce the international laws that prohibit the disproportionate targeting of civilians during wartime. That was a task for states, not aid workers.

Eric wondered whether he lived in the same world as these fatalists who shrugged and asked, "What more can we do?" How could they be so unconcerned? He left the meeting feeling alone in the urgency of his worry for the estimated 15,000 to 20,000 civilians trapped in Vukovar.

On November 5, 1991, the presidents of Yugoslavia's six republics signed the Hague Statement on Respect of Humanitarian Principles. In it, the leaders agreed that "wounded and ill persons must be helped and protected in all circumstances, all arrested persons, and notably combatants who have surrendered, must be treated with humanity," and they promised "unconditional support for the action of the ICRC in favour of the victims."

The shelling and bombardment of Vukovar's civilians, however, continued. Neither MSF nor the ICRC gained permission to aid the wounded. Less than two weeks after the humanitarian declaration, on November 18, 1991, Vukovar fell to the Yugoslav National Army and to local Serb nationalist soldiers. Eric Dachy raced to get there, and not only to deliver the needed medical supplies. The spirited director of Vukovar's hospital had become a hero of the Croatian resistance. Journalists broadcast her descriptions of suffering at the hospital as it was repeatedly targeted by heavy artillery and critical supplies such as anesthetics ran dry. Eric had an inkling that as an international, his presence might protect her and her colleagues from attacks of vengeance.

Despite his efforts, soldiers stymied him for an additional two days before promising to let him through on the morning of November 20. He left at dawn for Vukovar with a colleague and a translator. At the last military checkpoint before the city, he came across a frantic International Red Cross worker, arriving after the battle, like his predecessor, Henri Dunant, but looking mightily distressed. Gesturing wildly as he spoke to a group of soldiers at the checkpoint, he barely seemed to notice Eric. After a delay, soldiers permitted the MSF and Red Cross teams to cross the checkpoint and drive toward the city. In a few miles, a tapestry of destruction that rivaled Guernica unfolded.

Eric peered out at the city around him. It looked like the moon. So desolate. Even the air seemed to be afraid of what had happened.

He bumped along the pitted road, sandwiched between ruined buildings perforated by thousands of bullets, ripped by shells. Empty window frames jutted at strange angles, an occasional curl of smoke the only movement inside, an occasional red glow of fire the only color. Gray, broken trees leaned over the road, branches splayed at odd angles, their few dead leaves unsettled by the breeze. Dog and pig carcasses littered the ground next to cars flattened by tanks.

It seemed surreal to Eric. This, he thought, was a city in the middle of civilization, in the middle of Europe! It was completely destroyed.

They drove slowly in silence. Eric noticed the body of a small man wearing a cap, curled up on the side of the road as if he was asleep. For a moment, he allowed himself to imagine the man's fight for life under siege, to wonder who he was, how he died, and why he put on his hat today. Eric wished they could stop, wake him up, and tell him that his suffering was over.

At the hospital, Serb militiamen stood outside wearing long beards in the style—Eric was informed—of Chetniks, World War II anti-Croat, anti-Communist fighters loyal to the Serb king, themselves emulating Serb warriors who fought against the Ottomans. Eric noticed shell craters on the exterior of the hospital, and when he went inside, he found its upper floors deserted. Patients huddled in the basement and several anti-atomic shelters, for two months the only usable parts of a hospital constantly under fire. In spite of the conditions, the medical staff had somehow managed to keep the patients' bandages clean.

The ICRC had reached agreement with the Yugoslav National Army and Croatian authorities to "neutralize" the hospital—take control of it as a protected object under international law—and undertake an evacuation. But the previous evening, soldiers had removed the aid workers from the hospital and begun to evacuate the patients themselves. Eric looked around for doctors and nurses, but saw none. Someone told him Serb soldiers had arrested the medical workers after accusing them of experimenting on Serb patients. Eric sent his translator to ask the patients what they had seen and heard. The translator returned and whispered that soldiers had earlier arrested and taken away dozens of those sheltering in the hospital.

"You may find fresh dead bodies in the back of the hospital," the Red Cross delegate told him. But Eric didn't feel he was there to risk his life collecting crime evidence—his job was to help the living.

Eric watched soldiers manhandle bedridden patients, pulling those with fractured limbs out of their beds and depositing them onto the seats of buses supposedly bound for hospitals in Croatia and Serbia. Faced with dozens of menacing soldiers, Eric felt unable to protest the nature of the evacuation and resolved to register a complaint with the army later.

A group of the Yugoslav soldiers, perhaps eager to remove a witness, lured Eric away from the hospital with a story that Serb babies had been killed by Croats in a nearby suburb. "Why is everyone so concerned about the Croats?" they goaded Eric. "What about the Serbs? Show some impartiality."

Their appeal worked. Eric and his translator returned to their car and followed a shiny Mercedes toward the supposed crime site. A few miles outside of Vukovar, the car took off without them.

Meanwhile, back in Vukovar, the nervous Red Cross representative protested the military takeover of the hospital, cornering a dark-haired, mustachioed Yugoslav National Army major named Veselin Šljivančanin in front of a TV camera.

The tall officer glared down at the pipsqueak Red Cross delegate as if he were an ingrate.

"It's a shame for you to behave this way toward me," the officer chastised him. "I gave you everything you asked for."

The same camera found the Red Cross delegate later, brandishing a copy of the previous day's agreement. In a tremulous voice rent with dramatic pauses, he read it point by point, frequently enunciating his words.

"*No weapons were allowed in neutralized zone! . . .*"

"The compound and the hospital should have been clearly marked by *Red Crosses . . .*"

". . . the Croatian authorities and the JNA will give *all necessary collaboration to the ICRC . . .*"

"Now gentlemen," he said, to the woman and several men gathered around him, "you are witness, as I am, the present situation. Ahem."

"As you may notice," he continued a few moments later, "the International Committee of the Red Cross is completely unable to perform the task that was entrusted to it by the parties and cannot be in any way responsible for what has been happening early on this morning and now."

What that was, exactly, he could not say. He did not flinch as the sound of an explosion underscored his ominous statement.

Several journalists later sought out the Yugoslav Army officer for an explanation.

"I am very proud that I am commander of these soldiers," he said through a translator as a gaggle of young uniformed men stood behind him stifling giggles like fifth-graders trying to keep poker faces. The officer accused the Red Cross representatives of wanting to control both Vukovar and the Yugoslav Army, and he questioned the neutrality of the humanitarians because "they have never given us the help in food or medicines for *our* soldiers, *our* people."

The sight of a commanding officer whose forces had pounded the hell out of a city of roughly 20,000 civilians just days before requesting pity for his soldiers was almost farcical. So, too, was the sight of the strung-out ICRC representative insisting on the observance of numbered rules and international laws and red-crossed white flags, while being so clearly impotent in the face of actual events. And Eric Dachy, who had labored so long and hard to enter Vukovar and care for its injured civilians, had been suckered into a wild goose chase out of town.

Comical, if it weren't for the fact that at that very moment, 200 or more of those hauled away from the hospital that morning were being taken by Serb paramilitary and Yugoslav army soldiers to a farm called Ovčara, two and a half miles southeast of Vukovar. There, they were forced to run a gantlet, beaten, driven in groups to a dirt field, shot, and their bodies buried by bulldozer in a mass grave.

These were the first mass killings of the war. They were atrocities for which the cocky Major Šljivančanin and three of his associates would later be indicted by an international war crimes tribunal for crimes against humanity. News of the incidents spread amongst Yugoslavia's doctors, patients, and civilians, robbing them of their trust in hospitals as safe places.

The experience of Vukovar devastated Eric Dachy. It taught him the character of the war. It made him swear that somewhere else he'd find a way to intervene before the worst occurred.

WITH VUKOVAR NEARLY EMPTY and his MSF mission a failure, Eric thought of leaving the Balkans, but the war in Croatia continued to spread, and a visit home to Belgium at the start of December changed his mind. At a friend's birthday party, he found he could only think of Yugoslavia. Many people he knew and liked approached to ask him, "Hey, how is it there?" but their eyes glazed before the end of his answers. He was furious about what was happening in the middle of Europe, and people back home didn't seem to realize it. He knew his friends, polite as they were, weren't really interested.

He went to the MSF office in Brussels to discuss some things MSF might do to publicize the situation and the impotence of the European Community to stop the conflict. One idea was to place a huge ticker in front of European Community headquarters depicting the rising number of victims of the war similar to the ticker in New York City showing the rising U.S. national deficit. Another more radical idea was to stage a mock hostage situation at the airport to symbolize MSF's utter revulsion over the situation. Still, when Eric was asked to give a radio interview, he was briefed by MSF's communications director not to take sides and expressly forbidden to call for international military action to end the conflict. As a humanitarian, he could only describe what he'd witnessed and let the listeners make their own decisions.

Brussels, his old world, seemed unreal and artificial. For some reason he couldn't quite verbalize, he felt drawn to the war zone. Nothing matched its intensity or reality. It felt strangely like home.

Eric returned to Belgrade and spent the winter bringing medical aid to places where war disrupted normal supply routes. In January, Croatia was recognized as an independent country and in February, peace dawned on the horizon. Both Serbs and Croats agreed on the deployment of the second largest international peacekeeping force in history. The 12,000 U.N. peacekeepers from more than thirty nations, led by an Indian general, were to supervise a ceasefire, disarm Serb militias, and oversee the withdrawal of the Yugoslav National Army from Croatia. The operation's command headquarters would be in the neighboring Yugoslav Republic of Bosnia-Herzegovina and the troops would be known as the United Nations Protection Force or UNPROFOR.

Eric settled into his job that winter, making needs assessments of war-displaced populations, helping rehabilitate a health center serving the elderly in a Serb-held suburb of Vukovar, and supporting existing medical structures with donations of medicines and basic surgical equipment. He purchased some personal items to make Belgrade homier. He went shopping for a winter jacket, and the one that caught his eye was black leather, with a silver zipper set to the side. Before he spotted it, the biker's jacket was probably destined to be an elytron on the back of one of the Belgrade paramilitary toughs who roared around town after service in Croatia, suspiciously flush with cash.

Eric took the leather between his fingers. It felt thick, like elephant hide. He tried it on. Encased in the sturdy, supple jacket, he felt protected. He bought it, along with a few suit jackets, in an effort to "refine" his image after noticing that most people in Belgrade, unlike him, didn't slouch around in tennis shoes and T-shirts. However, the leather jacket, which he wore like a talisman, only served to heighten his already conspicuous appearance and attract the bemused attention of his colleagues.

On a Sunday afternoon in the first week in April, Eric sat in his living room watching live television coverage of a peace protest in Bosnia, another republic that was breaking off from Yugoslavia. Eric had visited Bosnia numerous times and the people in the multiethnic republic always insisted, "We won't fight here." But lately that had changed. "If we fight here," someone told him, "it will be worse than Lebanon."

When he visited a few days ago, the roads were studded with checkpoints, the evenings were disturbed by shelling and gunfire, and the word on the street was, "It's going to be soon." He passed through a city, Bijeljina, where Serb troops had recently taken control. Frightened-appearing Muslim men were gathered on the sidewalks, and they told Eric they were trying to prove they didn't have weapons. At the hospital, the former director, a Muslim replaced the previous day by a Serb, whispered that the mortuary was full—executions.

The previous month, Bosnians passed a referendum to leave Yugoslavia and—although the vast majority of Serbs boycotted the vote—on March 6, Bosnian President Alija Izetbegović had declared Bosnia-Herzegovina an independent and sovereign state. Just as in Croatia, nationalist leaders rallied Bosnia's Serbs against becoming a minority in a newly independent country. Beginning April 1, Serb paramilitary groups opposed to Bosnia's independence occupied ethnically mixed Bosnian cities such as Bijeljina, Zvornik, and Foća, murdering some non-Serbs and triggering the flight of the non-Serb populations.

Thousands of marchers were now gathered in the capital, Sarajevo, taking a stand against interethnic distrust and trying to prevent the outbreak of all-out war. Eric heard shots ring out and watched as the camera panned to some felled marchers. People looked panicky. Then Eric saw something that amazed him—the protesters refused to flee. They stood steady and raised their fists toward the killers, howling in indignation. Eric felt his throat tighten. A medical student on the peace march was killed. The flames of war leapt up to consume Bosnia.

3

ILIJAZ

THAT SAME FIRST WEEK OF APRIL 1992, Dr. Ilijaz Pilav, a twenty-eight-year-old general practitioner at the Srebrenica health clinic, also sat glued to his television set, watching images of a reality he had, until then, failed to imagine. With small, intense eyes beneath thick, worried brows, he took in news of the violence kicking up in nearby towns, hopping like a tornado toward Srebrenica. In spite of the dissolution of Yugoslavia and the fighting in Croatia, the possibility of war in Bosnia had merely tickled the edge of his conscious mind, a mind more focused on personal concerns and a major family illness.

These days, Ilijaz often made the half-hour drive to his boyhood home, guiding his new, white Yugo south on the main road out of Srebrenica, then west into the hills to the tiny rural village of Gladovići. Despite years of city living and a professional education, Ilijaz's countrified appearance clung to him.

His family raised livestock and grew vegetables and fruit on a hillside that inched down to the Drina River canyon, the natural border between the Yugoslav republics of Bosnia and Serbia. As a young boy, his typical day began with the crowing of roosters. From the windows of the family's two-story house, Ilijaz would peer across the blue river to the biggest mountain in western Serbia, Tara, tracing the road that zigzagged from a height of more than 4,200 feet down the face of one of its peaks toward the Perućac hydroelectric dam.

The crisp, fresh air filled with the lowing of cows and the yodels loosed by villagers. His mother labored in the kitchen, stooping over a table to roll thin leaves of dough that she layered into pans to bake meat pies called *burek* or, when guests appeared, swiveling the handle of a copper coffee grinder in her lap, elbows akimbo. His father worked the land with his older brothers, angling groundward to chop wood, harvest crops, pitch hay, and slash the tall grasses. Ilijaz, the baby of the family, watched and begged to wield the scythe.

"You're too little!" they cried as they shooed him.

When he asked what he could do to help, they told him to stay out of the way. So Ilijaz found other children to lead in games. He picked fights when he thought he had good cause, learned to read and write by looking over the shoulder of a school-aged friend, and gamboled through the woods and meadows.

At day's end, the waning sun flooded the land with light, gilding the cornstalks and tree branches, illuminating the haystacks and brushing the bends of the river with red. Light still dappled the plains on the Drina's opposite bank after evening shade had blanketed Gladovići. A lick of fog sometimes advanced and covered the village with a ghostly glow. Later, separated from his birthplace forever, it would seem to Ilijaz that winters in Gladovići never felt cold and summers shimmered with more sunshine than anywhere else.

The idyll ended when he entered school. The schoolhouse walls and the daily commitments impinged on Ilijaz's freedom, and he burst out to do his homework in the light of the open sky. Accidents of fate had guided his destiny from birth when his parents named him "Ilijas," but the clerk writing the birth certificate misheard and wrote down "Ilijaz." School was no different. His fate changed when a first-grade teacher failed to pick him for her class of "best" students. He started studying harder, resolving to disprove the teacher's pessimistic forecast.

His father encouraged his studies and hoped, without pushing him, that he would become a doctor. He also taught him about God, called Allah, and their religion, Islam, stressing that it counseled respect not only for himself and his own people—all of Gladovići's 500 or so inhabitants were Bosnian Muslim—but also those who practiced other religions.

Ilijaz mostly ignored religion, focusing instead on his studies. When he finished primary school as one of the top students, there was nowhere to go but out. The hillside villages had no high school, so his father sent him to live with a sister and study in Srebrenica, a city of 6,000. Ilijaz missed nature. He missed his parents. Still, he did well in math and physics and planned to become an electrical engineer. A few days after high school graduation, he and a group of classmates traveled to Bosnia's capital to enroll at the University of Sarajevo. The thought of living in

Bosnia's biggest city filled the small-town teenagers with excitement. The university departments were spread around the unfamiliar city, and Ilijaz stopped a police officer to ask for directions to the school of engineering.

"Oooohhh," the officer said, "engineering is all the way in Lukavica, seven and a half miles from here."

Ilijaz certainly had not come to the big city to spend four years in a suburb. That moment he ruled out a career in engineering.

"What department is closest to here?" Ilijaz asked the policeman.

The man put a finger to his mouth and thought for a second.

"The medical school's over there." He pointed up a hill. Ilijaz thanked him.

What was a doctor? Ilijaz barely knew. He'd had only a few brushes with the type. He remembered vaccination day at school, when he'd sneaked out of line after watching white-coated adults stick needles into children's arms. He'd considered their actions an injustice, and leaving was his form of protest. Only once, when he'd had a sore throat, had he met a doctor face to face—Sabit Begić, a pale man in a white coat that blended with the colorless walls that surrounded him. Ilijaz had grown up healthy in a place where yearly checkups were not the norm.

But recently, while flipping television channels, he'd come across a program showing a doctor performing cardiovascular surgery. He'd watched the whole broadcast, fascinated. These thoughts propelled him up the steep, winding street and into the drab brick medical school building. In the hallway, a woman bustled past carrying a cage with white mice. He fought the urge to run back outside. *Let's move on,* he told himself. He found the admissions office and handed his high school records to the secretary.

"Young man," she said, "you're the 918th candidate to show up here. You'd better try somewhere else since we only accept 200 students."

Ilijaz had no time to try somewhere else. He had to meet his friends and return to Gladovići. In a couple of weeks, he would be leaving for his required year of army service.

"Just take these documents," he insisted, "and let's try."

On his way out, Ilijaz bought books to prepare himself for the entrance examination. He went home and closeted himself in his house to study. Days later, he achieved the highest possible score on the examination and was admitted to Sarajevo medical school. On July 5, 1983, he went to enroll, and the following day he left for the army.

He found military service a waste of time, though he proved himself a wit with Morse code and learned, battling seasickness in a ship's radiotelegraph room, that he could perform his job in the face of physical distress. After serving out his year, Ilijaz started medical school. He had a layman's distaste for the "ugly" things in medicine, and the goriness of anatomy, pathology, and forensic medicine classes allayed his initial enthusiasm for a career in surgery. By graduation in December 1989, he was ready to forsake blood and gore and enter a field like pediatrics—the nurses could give injections, not him!

Not long before, eastern Bosnia's villagers had buzzed with excitement when one of their own, Ejub Alić, finished medical school and went to work with the city folk in Srebrenica. It wasn't a common occurrence for a peasant to become a professional, and Ilijaz Pilav's parents had taken note. Now they, too, could boast as their son followed in Ejub's footsteps, beginning work as a general practitioner in the Srebrenica health clinic.

Ilijaz took a bachelor pad apartment in a town just north of Srebrenica called Bratunac. Each morning he drove south down a straight, paved road into Srebrenica. Just past the town's entrance he turned his car up the steep driveway of the hospital and health clinic. On the left the rectangular, three-story hospital building loomed over the road, its whitewashed and brown-tiled exterior framed by hills. Before it a pole-like evergreen stood a lonely guard, its branches blooming high on its trunk like petals atop a delicate stem.

To the right of the hospital sat the squat, orange brick-covered health clinic where Ilijaz worked. People frequently took breaks to smoke and talk on the steps of its verandah. Josip Broz "Tito" had died a decade previously, but no one had the heart to remove a giant poster of the adored leader from the lobby window. "Comrade Tito," read the front page of a Srebrenica newspaper, reporting his death, "we swear to you that we will not turn off your road." The eyes in his magnified head stared vaguely in the direction of Bratunac.

From the clinic's porch, Ilijaz had a view of Srebrenica's main street, the square PTT—post-telephone-telegraph—building and the town's only gas station. Noisy little cars drove by, and, when the weather was fair, men clad in blue jeans and women dressed in skirts and light summer blouses strolled past. Some older women wore kerchiefs on their heads and the patterned bloomers, called *dimije*, of Muslim villagers. They sauntered with the relaxed posture of people who could predict the contour of every inch of road in the small city and who recognized just about everyone who passed.

Once every hour, as cars zoomed by, hammers clanked, and buzz saws buzzed at the construction site of a new school, bells chimed from the white Orthodox church overlooking the town from a hill. The deep clanging "ding, dong-dong" set roosters crowing and dogs barking. Five times a day, praises of Allah spun out of the loudspeakers atop Srebrenica's five minarets to join the cacophony.

Organized health care in Srebrenica stretched at least as far back as the late nineteenth century when the area—then backward and unindustrialized—came under the governance of the Austro-Hungarian Empire. The Austrians mapped the area, developed its forestry industry, paved its main road, and, knowing that Srebrenica had been a mining town in medieval times (its current name means silver, its Latin name was "Argentaria," and in the Middle Ages it was the most prosperous inland town in all of the western Balkans), explored its mineral resources. They erected a one-story hospital to serve a large area of villages along the Drina River. Most of its physicians and nurses came from neighboring Serbia. During World War I, Srebrenica's reputed healing waters, known since Roman times and analyzed by the Austrians, were used to treat injured soldiers. The waters were bottled for export and a spa was built. After the war, health tourists thronged into Srebrenica for physician-administered bathing treatments in the waters of the medicinal springs on the far southern end of town.

During World War II, Srebrenica and the surrounding villages of Muslims and Serbs switched hands frequently between forces loyal to royalist Serb Chetniks, communist Partisans, fascist Croat Ustashe and their allies, Muslim Handžars. Acts of violence took place, even near the hospital, but locals also saved one another. In 1942, Ustashe authorities interned 3,000 Serbs from the district of Srebrenica in the hospital vicinity, but local Muslims intervened to prevent their execution. In 1943, as part of widespread massacres and killings by Ustashe in revenge for a Partisan attempt to take the area, two Muslim nurses were killed near the hospital. Srebrenica was liberated by the pan-Yugoslavist Partisans late in the war, on March 11, 1945, which came to be celebrated as liberation day. Srebrenica's health clinic was named after a Partisan leader, Dr. Asim Čemerlić, a Muslim physician who had helped protect local Serbs.

During the post-war years, the area remained backward and underdeveloped. Most of the hospital workers still came from Serbia. The area had more Muslims than Serbs, and only a few Croats. However, until the 1960s, aside from Čemerlić, one of the only other non-Serb hospital workers was a Croatian doctor who had served as a military physician for the fascist Croatian forces. After the war, he was sentenced to a long prison term, but a politician decided he would be more useful in a hospital than a jail, and his "punishment," instead, was being sent to work in the backwater of Srebrenica.

In the late 1960s a young doctor from the Srebrenica area, Sabit Begić, became one of the first locally born Muslim physicians in Srebrenica. He made a name for himself treating workers at a nearby lead-zinc mine in Sase, where roughly a third of workers were on sick leave every day due to lung ailments. In the early 1970s, Begić led a campaign to encourage local children to go into nursing and established small health clinics in the neighboring villages, including the one where he treated young Ilijaz's sore throat. At the time, the Yugoslav government targeted the area's mining and forestry industries for development and initiated new industrial activities. Battery and car-brake factories were built, a furniture factory, stone-cutting workshop, and textile factory were established, and the area enjoyed an upsurge in tourism at the medicinal spa and in nearby hunting grounds. To create a well-educated workforce, Yugoslavia invested in the education system, turning Srebrenica high school into one of the best in Bosnia.

Local companies, enjoying prosperous times, donated money for equipment, vehicles, and even apartments for physicians. Srebrenica's squat health clinic was built next to the old hospital building and used for general medicine, pediatrics, and women's health services. A separate building adjacent to the clinic served as doctors' quarters and later came to house an x-ray machine, ultrasound apparatus, and a small diagnostic laboratory. In 1981, the hospital was renovated and two new stories added for gynecology, obstetrics, and internal medicine. At the opposite end of Srebrenica, psychiatrists, rehabilitation specialists, and general practitioners worked at the now-famous Guber spa.

Doctors came from all over Yugoslavia and the world to spend a few years gaining the precious, hands-on experience obtainable only in such a top-notch small-town hospital. In the late 1980s, physicians of eleven nationalities worked at the health clinic, including one from Nepal and one from India.

One day in 1990, during Ilijaz's first summer working at the clinic, someone entered his examination room unannounced. With a start, Ilijaz turned from his patient to find a perplexed-looking young woman with long, black hair standing at the doorway.

"Oh!" she said. "Excuse me. I'm sorry to interrupt you. I was looking for my friend, Hamdija."

"He's in the next room. You can go through this door here."

She thanked him and left. When he finished examining his patient, Ilijaz didn't call for another. He went to Hamdija's room instead.

He was pleased to find the woman still there. She had beautiful, dark eyes. He watched as she read the name on his white coat and broke into a soft, high-pitched laugh.

"So you're Ilijaz Pilav," she said and offered her hand. "It's nice to meet the man I'm going to marry. I'm Doctor Fatima Dautbašić."

Ilijaz's friend, Hamdija, giggled.

In Bosnia, villagers have honed the art of future-telling over centuries. The woman explained that her great aunt had predicted she would soon find a husband. He would be a young doctor, and his name would be "Pilavović." That was close enough to Pilav.

"Then let's get started," Ilijaz told her. "Let's not waste any time." The two began to date.

Fatima was a serious yet loquacious young woman who, unlike Ilijaz, had grown up knowing that she wanted to be a doctor. She cultivated equally cherished dreams of world travel and of settling down in a nice house to raise a family in the traditional Bosnian way. For now, though, she was content to fall in love. The two took strolls every night along the pedestrian walkway in Bratunac. Trips to the River Jadar for picnics with lambs on a spit, games, line dancing, and singing framed their summer romance. At night, driving back from the dark hills above the valley of

Srebrenica, the lights of the town looked like a luminous strand of pearls spilled on black velvet.

THAT FALL OF 1990, a cultural festival took place in the building that housed Srebrenica's historical museum. At the time, such events held no interest for a young bachelor like Ilijaz. But if he had gone, he would have seen groups of dancers take turns performing in traditional costumes that represented every phase of Srebrenica's history—Roman, Serbian, Ottoman, Austrian, Yugoslav. The long vibrating tones that trilled from the tongues of the singers and moved the shuffling feet of the *kolo* dancers carried the distinct sound and the shared heritage of the Drina River valley where peace between neighbors had long outlasted periods of war.

They were simple songs, like the lullabies and love songs that echoed in homes high and low on both banks of the Drina—Bosnian and Serbian. From the coarse clucking falsettos of village women to the low-pitched croaks of tobacco-growing men, bowing the strings of their whiny, lute-like *gusle* or *shargija*, the songs and their sometimes-nonsensical words varied little.

> Nini, nini
> ninala te nana
> ninala te nana
> nini, nini
> Ninala te
> i uspavala te
> i uspavala te

There was little in Ilijaz Pilav's background to make him fear or dislike Serbs. He grew up hearing stories of World War II, when a multipartied civil war had ripped apart the region. But elderly villagers told Ilijaz that the occupying armies and local militias that passed through Gladovići conducted themselves with honor and left the civilians largely alone. Only one of Ilijaz's family members, a grandfather, had been killed, but by which side, nobody knew or said.

Ilijaz's first suspicions of Serbs traced back to medical school. In 1988 Serb students started to band together in the dormitory and post large photographs of Serbian Communist Party leader Slobodan Milošević in their rooms, replacing those of Tito. Ilijaz heard them say they felt threatened and needed Milošević to protect their interests. Some believed that Bosnian Muslim nationalists had plans to turn Bosnia into an "ethnically pure" state. They supported Milošević's campaign to increase Serbian control over Yugoslavia. To Ilijaz, they sounded like parrots mimicking one another.

When he came to work in Srebrenica, Ilijaz avoided forming friendships with Serbs and maintained only professional relationships with them. Some Serb doctors began to suspect Ilijaz was a Muslim nationalist.

The fall of 1990, strange news blew into Srebrenica with the chill air that came early to that part of Bosnia, heralding the long winter ahead. From the radios, television sets, and boys returning home from military service, it whispered of change and sent a small shiver up the backs of the town's Serbs, Muslims, and few Croats.

As Slovenia and Croatia headed toward independence, the leaders of Bosnia's mixed, multiethnic population were caught in a bind—not wanting to leave Yugoslavia, but made increasingly uncomfortable by Serbia's domination of the federal state. Bosnia's first multiparty elections took place in November. They brought nationalists to power from all three major ethnic groups. The new order sparked a scramble to claim resources and strategic positions at a time when the economy was faring poorly. In the 1970s, in an effort to decrease interethnic tensions through the fair sharing of resources, Communists had introduced a system of ethnic quotas for jobs, houses, business leadership positions, and scholarships. These were all up for grabs now.

In Srebrenica's local elections, the Muslim Party of Democratic Action (SDA) earned the majority, with the Serbian Democratic Party (SDS) in the minority. Srebrenica's Serbs accused the Muslim leadership of hegemony. Tensions heightened after the Croatian war broke out in 1991. Bosnia kept officially neutral, and Serbia's Milošević punished the republic with an economic blockade, which hit import-dependent Srebrenica particularly hard.

While Srebrenica and Bratunac were ethnically mixed towns, the villages outside, usually a few hundred inhabitants each, were a patchwork of purely Serb or purely Muslim—everyone knew which was which. Nationalist symbols began springing up in various areas, invoking memories of interethnic violence during World War II. The propaganda went all the way back to the Serbs' loss of their kingdom to the Turks in 1389 and the subsequent years of Ottoman rule during which many Slavs converted to Islam. Serbs started referring to the current Bosnian Muslims derogatorily as "Turks" or *Balijas.* Nonstop television propaganda inflamed the fears.

Serbs in Srebrenica complained of discrimination based on the fact that the proportion of Serbs to Muslims had declined dramatically in the area over the last fifty years. Serbs blamed this on pressure from Muslims and the lack of development of Serb villages. However, the demographic shift in Srebrenica paralleled the rest of Bosnia—after Muslims were recognized as one of Yugoslavia's constituent nations in 1968, well-educated Muslims increasingly joined the cadres—trained workers and leaders of various organizations, professions, and businesses—which had until then been dominated by Serbs. Serbs, losing political and economic power, increasingly sought opportunity in nearby Serbia. By the 1991 census, the town of Srebrenica was 64 percent Bosnian Muslim and 28 percent Serb.

In spite of the political fires raging about them in the early 1990s, though, most of Srebrenica's doctors would later say that there had been little heat within the medical community until the day Bosnia held its own independence referendum in 1992. If anything, small conflicts flared between village folk and city slickers or between people from different towns such as less-developed Bratunac, whose inhabitants were nicknamed "frog-catchers," and Srebrenicans, who were accused of snobbery and xenophobia and nicknamed "storks."

But change seeped into the health clinic building, too. Serb doctors in the clinic began to chill toward their non-Serb colleagues and complain of discrimination. Muslims pointed out that although Serbs constituted a minority in the city leadership, a Serb doctor had been allowed to keep his position as director of the health clinic. A few minor incidents ensued; workplace conflicts, allocation of medical specialization positions, and the assignment of free apartments were sometimes chalked up to "he got it because he's a Muslim." Serbs alleged that a cabal of "Muslim fundamentalist intellectuals" was active at the Srebrenica health clinic.

In early 1992, Ilijaz still lived in Bratunac and worked at the Srebrenica health center. Fatima also lived in Bratunac and worked at the health center there. She was more confident than ever that the two of them were meant to be together. Ilijaz, feeling stifled, was not as sure.

Before long, he had something much more serious to preoccupy him; his father was diagnosed with lung cancer. Ilijaz brought him to the capital, Sarajevo, to undergo chemotherapy and prepare for possible surgery. With the stresses of his father's illness, his job, and his changing relationship with Fatima, Ilijaz spent little time thinking about a potential war in Bosnia. He considered the few incidences of violence and increasing lawlessness a political problem that the Yugoslav army, the JNA, was going to solve. But when actual fighting broke out around Bosnia, and many people fled Srebrenica, he could ignore it no longer.

Doctors began failing to show up for work, and fewer and fewer patients came to his clinic. Some of Ilijaz's friends urged him to join them in leaving the area. As an unmarried man with a car and money, Ilijaz could go wherever he wanted. He knew that most of the clever people in town were leaving, but that was their idea, not his. He wasn't ready to make such a major decision.

Roadblocks flew up on country roads and city streets, manned by the tense citizens who lived on them. They checked cars and people for guns, raising more fear than security. Patients at Srebrenica's historic health spa were collected in a minivan, and a Muslim maintenance worker at the spa volunteered to drive them to their homes. Paramilitaries captured him at a roadblock on his way back, then tortured and killed him.

Ilijaz and Fatima started asking themselves what they should do. Should they go away together for a little while just until things calmed down again? But Fatima didn't want to leave her mother and younger brother alone. And her mother, a widow with strong memories of World War II, refused to leave their home.

"In that war, nobody touched old people and women," she'd say. "I can stay in my house. Nobody will harm me."

The days tumbled forward with a momentum that left little time to contemplate a course of action. For security, Ilijaz moved his year-old white Yugo car to all-Muslim Gladovići.

The health clinic ran with reduced staffing, and the few remaining doctors took long shifts. Ilijaz was assigned to work Friday, April 17. In the morning, before leaving Bratunac by bus, he stopped to see Fatima. They discussed their plans a little more, but made no decisions.

Ilijaz arrived at the clinic. Srebrenica was quiet. No patients came. About ten in the morning, Ilijaz called Fatima in Bratunac. She told him that the Serbian paramilitary leader Vojislav Šešelj and his soldiers had entered the town. The name Šešelj struck terror for the atrocities and mass killings he was accused of having committed during the previous year's war in Croatia.

"Fata, catch a bus," Ilijaz told her. "Go out. Anywhere. Tuzla."

She told him her mother wanted to remain in Bratunac. He begged her to reconsider, and she agreed to think about it. He planned to call her in the afternoon to check.

Not long after, Dr. Sabit Begić, Ilijaz's old pediatrician and the director of Srebrenica Hospital, burst into the clinic.

"There's nothing left. Everything's finished. It's war."

He'd come from a meeting with a Serb delegation at a hotel in Bratunac. For the past twenty days, Muslims and Serbs had tried to work out a power-sharing agreement that would have split the municipality of Srebrenica. Much of Srebrenica town, as well as the nearby villages of Potočari and Sućeska, was to have remained under Muslim control.

But this morning, the Srebrenica Muslim delegation had arrived in Bratunac to find camouflage-clad Serbs toting automatic rifles and surrounding the hotel. The Serb delegation made it clear there would be no power sharing and that there was room for just one armed group. For Srebrenica to be spared, Muslims, particularly armed reserve officers, had to surrender their weapons by eight the following morning.

Ilijaz picked up the phone to call Fatima again and plead for her to leave Bratunac. The line was dead.

4

EJUB

THAT SAME DAY, Ilijaz's colleague, Dr. Ejub Alić, left his home in Srebrenica and went to stay with his best friend in the neighboring, mainly Muslim village of Potočari. The house lay at the foot of a mountain called Budak near the main road between Srebrenica and Bratunac. A few hundred paces up the road stood a red Partisan star symbolizing *Bratstvo-Jedinstvo*—Brotherhood and Unity—the slogan of Yugoslavia.

The two men drank whiskey, smoked cigarettes, and talked for hours. They discussed their wives and families, whom they had sent out of the region for safety.

Like his younger colleague Ilijaz, Ejub also hailed from the eastern edge of Bosnia in the mountains that overlook the River Drina, from an even tinier, more backward village. The family Alić had settled there and multiplied, and one day the family grew as numerous as a village, and so people called the village Alići.

Ejub was born there in 1959, in the days when women still went to the wells to fetch water. His family subsisted on the vegetables they grew and the sheep they raised, plus income his father earned by constructing houses in neighboring Serbia. Although they lived in plain view of the giant Perućac hydroelectric power plant, which sat on the opposite bank of the Drina River in Serbia, electric wires had yet to stretch to Alići.

One year when autumn came, Ejub's mother took to her spinning wheel, spun wool from their sheep, knitted a book bag, and sent the boy to school. He walked the four and a half miles barefoot.

For a boy from a village with one clock and one battery-powered radio, the schoolhouse brimmed with treasures awaiting discovery. Books, and the joys of reading. The mysteries of science. Even the fact that teachers wore shoes and some children had colorful, plastic book bags impressed Ejub.

But to his illiterate mother and self-taught father, Ejub's schooling came second to his household chores. Ejub's father frequently kept him at home to work the land. On those days, Ejub cried and begged to be let go.

As he grew older, he found ways to earn money for the bus fare that bought him a bumpy ride up the winding dirt road to the library in Srebrenica. He brought home books to read at night under the light of an oil lamp, until his worried father restricted his dreamy son's reading time.

From books Ejub learned about science and space and the race to put a man on the moon. As a youngster, he visited the mosque with other village boys and memorized mysterious words of Muslim prayer. But as he grew, he realized that evolution, geology, and biology made sense to him in a way the prayers did not. He believed in science. The logic of science seemed to preclude the logic of religion, so at age twelve he forsook religion and declared himself an atheist.

He loved not only science, but also literature, and made up poems to fill the boring hours of field work. He recognized each member of his flock of sheep and noted their personalities as if they were characters in a book, hanging bells on the "unsheepish" ones so he could hear them if they tried to run away.

Once a year, Ejub received a pair of "Alpinaks," laced rubber foot coverings for working in the fields. Despite the fact they were his only purchased possession, he was as careless with them as a wealthy boy would be.

"Tie your Alpinaks!" his father admonished him repeatedly.

One morning Ejub brought the sheep out to graze after a big rain. He stuffed his feet into the rubbers, leaving their laces untied.

Each time he lifted a foot, the soggy earth held on to the rubber sole for a moment before letting go. A few times the mud held so tightly that the boy's foot lifted clear out of his Alpinak and he had hop back to scoop it onto his toes.

The heavy rains had made it an especially fine day for jumping across swollen streams. Ejub came to a swift one. He backed up a few steps to give himself a running start and then took a giant leap. One loose shoe slipped from his foot. He landed and spun around to see the stream carrying it away. He reached for it, but its black form disappeared in the current.

Ejub limped away wearing his one remaining rubber shoe, and wondered how he could return home to face his father. He cast about for answers to the question, "How could you be so careless?" But the excuses he conjured failed to convince even himself. As much as he feared being punished, he regretted even more the loss of something so valuable, something the family could barely afford.

The sun rose higher in the sky and other children joined Ejub and his flock. They came to another part of the river and pushed a tree trunk across to dam it so the sheep could wade without being carried away. Ejub lay on his stomach on the edge of the river and stuck his hand in deep to test the current. His fingers brushed something. He touched it— something rubber. His shoe! There it was, two miles or so from where he'd dropped it. He picked it up, spilled out the water, and tied it tightly to his foot.

It amazed him that something he had thought was lost forever had returned to him. Luck had saved him this time from his carelessness. He told no one of the incident, but remembered it.

Finishing primary school meant the prospect of a future spent, like his parents and several of his older sisters, working in the fields. The village had no high school. Ejub lobbied his parents to let him pursue higher education in the city of Bijeljina, more than sixty miles away. They agreed, and he went to live with his married sister there in the mid-1970s. Ejub studied hard, read widely, and planned to become a writer. A young romantic, he especially loved Bosnian author Meša Selimović, who wrote stories of souls, half-empty, who found one another and joined to form whole beings. Ejub found his spirituality in literature.

While Ejub was gone, his parents modernized along with the industrializing region. He returned home to find them enjoying electricity and a record player. Ejub's father, who had once gone to prison for refusing to send his four daughters to high school, now warmed to the idea of Ejub going to college. Even the village imam had daughters and sons at the university. Ejub's father decided he wanted Ejub to become the first local villager to earn the title of doctor.

What did Ejub know about medicine? He grew up watching women treat illnesses with plum brandy, honey, and jam. The village healer pulled teeth without anesthesia, many women gave birth at home, and people went to the hospital only to die.

But medicine would bring him a good income and a healthy dose of respect. His first love, writing, never would. Ejub applied to Tuzla medical school. He was admitted, performed well, and graduated in 1986, taking a job as a general practitioner in Srebrenica. He was so accustomed to being thought of as a hick that when the "city people" first called him doctor, he assumed they were mocking him.

Srebrenica, buried in a valley, oppressed him. In the mountain's shadows, rather than their heights, he felt as if he was living under siege, and he escaped to the hills whenever his schedule permitted. Years passed without the time to write poems. Medical training kept him too busy even to date. He found himself still single at age twenty-nine, an unusual status for a pleasant-looking, affable young man with a solid profession.

To earn some extra money over the New Year's holiday in 1988, Ejub worked duty shifts at the health clinic of a mine in the town of Sase, four miles northeast of Srebrenica along winding country roads. One afternoon, he took a coffee break with a friend, who brought along a woman named Mubina. She had manicured nails and a neat hairstyle and looked nothing like an uneducated village woman. She had plenty to say, too, and Ejub liked her instantly. Falling in love, he decided, was like seeing a pair of shoes on a shelf and knowing immediately they are the ones you want.

Mubina gave substance to the abstract ideas that drew Ejub to literature. He told her about Meša Selimović's ideas of half-empty souls searching to be filled. Poems poured from him again. And from these and the songs he wrote her, Mubina learned Ejub was not, as she had assumed, yet married. The two wed in six months. A year later they had a son, Denis.

Ejub's world settled into nearly perfect balance. Mubina and Denis inspired him and gave his life meaning. Medicine paid the bills and quenched his thirst for security.

A committee at the Srebrenica clinic determined that the town needed a children's specialist. They offered Ejub a stipend to study pediatrics in the city of Zvornik, a half-hour drive northwest from Srebrenica on a picturesque road that clung to the mountains rising over the Drina.

Ejub worked there for several months without trouble. But during the icy winter of 1992, he noticed that Serb physicians in Zvornik stopped talking when he entered the room. Things grew so uncomfortable that Ejub stopped traveling every day to the hospital, choosing instead to stay in Srebrenica with Mubina and two-year-old Denis. He watched the news and told Mubina that war was coming. She did not believe him.

Tension came up with the spring flowers that festooned Srebrenica's terraces. Back at the Srebrenica clinic, the Serb and Muslim medical staff remained respectful to one another, but Ejub noticed that Muslim physicians who had never been religious were greeting one another with the Islamic salutation, *sabahajrulah*. When fighting broke out in other parts of Bosnia, Ejub repeatedly told Mubina she should leave Srebrenica for a little while with Denis. If "something" started here, if war spread to Srebrenica, it would be even more difficult to survive with a young child. Besides, he assured her, it would only be for a little while.

"I don't want to go," Mubina said over and over again. "I don't want to leave you."

April 15, 1992, was a cold, sunny Wednesday. Ejub stayed inside while Mubina bundled up Denis and took him out for a walk. She returned in a panic. Two Muslims had been found dead on the road leading south out of Srebrenica the previous night. People were swarming out of town. It looked to Mubina as if everyone in their building was leaving, and she told Ejub she was ready to go. He realized he had never really believed she would act on his advice.

"Let's go together," Mubina begged him as they packed up her belongings.

"No," Ejub told her. He had recently bought some land in Potočari and was in debt. He could not afford to abandon their possessions and would stay to protect their apartment. He felt too proud to just give up his home. And he was also too curious. He wanted to see for himself what would happen.

"It won't be that long," he told her. "We'll be together again soon."

Like the short storms that come in April, he thought, *this soon will pass.*

Ejub took Mubina and Denis to the small, concrete Srebrenica bus station. Dozens of people scurried between the station and its curved driveway, adding to the air of chaos and panic. Mubina and Denis boarded a bus for Bosnia's second largest city, Tuzla, where Ejub had a few family members. Ejub counted out the expensive fare in Yugoslav dinars, handing it to the conductor.

He stood outside and looked at Mubina through the windows. Tears fell down her round cheeks. Little Denis did not cry. Perhaps he was too young to understand. Ejub stared into Mubina's eyes as the bus began to pull away. He started to wave. He waved and waved until the sight of the bus dangled at the edge of his vision and then slipped entirely away, untying their fates.

Ejub stayed at the bus station to smoke a few cigarettes with a friend whose wife had also left, and then he went home to sleep. Loneliness overcame him. Two days later, April 17, 1992, he went to spend the night at his best friend's house in Potočari.

Sometime in the night, the sound of explosions and his friend yelling, "Get up! Get up!" awakened him. He scrambled around the house, looking for a safe spot to hide. Artillery fire seemed to be coming from the mountain above. The two men created a kind of bunker inside the house by piling rocks left over from a construction project.

Hands trembling, they smoked cigarette after cigarette, not even finishing one before stubbing it out and lighting another. By the end of the morning, dozens of half-smoked butts lay wasted on the floor like dead bodies strewn across a battlefield.

5

WAR

THE AFTERNOON OF APRIL 17, Dr. Ilijaz Pilav, the skinny general practitioner whose father was ailing in his birth village of Gladovići, waited in vain at the empty health center for his replacement. With no patients to treat and no way to reach his girlfriend, Fatima, he'd had little to do but wander outside and scan Srebrenica for activity. He caught sight of two men in military uniforms as they disappeared between houses across the street. He watched buses packed with nervous faces rumble out of town, and this at last forced a question: "What am I still doing here?"

But what choices did he have? The rumors that Vojislav Šešelj's Serb paramilitary had entered Bratunac convinced him not to go back home, not even to find Fatima and warn her to escape. He heard about a bus leaving late in the afternoon and heading southeast on the main road that ran out of Srebrenica. Afraid this bus would be the last, he took it toward his family's village.

The next morning, April 18, he awoke to snow. He stood at the window of his parents' house and watched the flakes blanket the ground and build up a pillow that smothered the buds on the tree branches. It seemed as if all the snow that ever existed was falling on the village. He felt paralyzed—cut off from the world.

For days he rested quietly in Gladovići, believing "the stupidity" would last at most one month. Then he heard that other Serbian paramilitary forces led by Željko Ražnjatović, "Arkan," famous for his brutality in Croatia, had occupied Srebrenica. Ilijaz heard they were killing people and looting and burning houses. Maybe the stupidity would last much longer than one month. He grew impatient to organize some response.

But the old-timers in Gladovići urged calm.

We've seen war in these parts before, they said. Many an army passed through here during World War II, and only one village was burned. Keep quiet. They will leave us alone.

In the mornings, Ilijaz and a few friends hiked up the nearby hill, Kalina, to give themselves a view of the single paved road that wound southeast from Srebrenica toward the Bosnian border town of Skelani and ultimately across a bridge to Serbia. From the hilltop, they watched Serb military patrols pass back and forth and saw tendrils of smoke—first white, then dark—rise and bloom like flowers over the graves of Bosnian Muslim villages to the southeast. They witnessed lines of villagers stumbling into Gladovići, bent beneath hastily packed bundles of possessions, searching for refuge from the Serb nationalist soldiers they called Chetniks.

In the village, Ilijaz's profession gave him an inherent authority. People trusted him. They asked for his help and advice. Feeling he should make use of his influence, he began to organize a defense. To evade the scrutiny of the pacifist village elders, he recruited men with whispers and met with them by night.

If this was war, Ilijaz thought, that implied there were two armies—not just one. If a center of resistance existed nearby, Ilijaz guessed it would be in Osmače, population 1,000, the biggest village in the area with the most police reserve weapons and, according to rumor, the bravest men. The Muslim village had "resisted" both Serb nationalist Chetniks and Yugoslav Partisans during World War II and was said to have continued fighting after Berlin surrendered. Ilijaz sent runners to check if Osmače had organized a defensive force. They returned with disappointing news. The men of Osmače were no more organized than the men of Gladovići.

On May 6, Ilijaz climbed Kalina hill with several of his neighbors. They looked down and watched a military truck moving slowly along the Srebrenica-Skelani road. The idea of ambushing enemy vehicles had tantalized the men for days. Using the element of surprise to their advantage—that was a way the weak could fight the strong. Standing on the hilltop with Ilijaz, the sight of the truck so excited one of the men that he agitated for an immediate attack. That would be suicidal, Ilijaz told him.

But an ambush would indeed show the Chetniks that the villagers planned to stand their ground and resist attack. Perhaps the villagers could even manage to capture a few automatic weapons to add to their pitiful arsenal of old hunting rifles.

The men schemed and plotted and planned for an action the following day. Then Ilijaz returned to his family in Gladovići. He could have sworn his brother, Hamid, was eyeing him suspiciously. Never mind. Ilijaz would keep his military plans a secret. He wouldn't expose Hamid—ten years older, with a wife and family—to danger.

That night he lay in bed, unable to sleep. At 3 A.M. he rose as planned and stepped into a black jogging suit. To avoid waking his family, he crept down the hallway in the dark. But there, startling him at the doorway, stood his ill father.

"Good luck, son," was all he said.

Around fifteen young men from Gladovići gathered in a thin copse of trees near the main road. They included Ilijaz's cousin—a medical technician named Sulejman Pilav—and Ilijaz's good friend and neighbor Šefik Mandžic, a kind, confident man in his late twenties who specialized in constructing minarets.

Ilijaz might have been a doctor, but this morning the equipment he carried with him to work was a "Kragljevska" automatic gun given to him by a former policeman. He took a certain pride in that, what with most of the others carrying hunting rifles or, at best, the ubiquitous Eastern European warhorse, the Kalashnikov. Ilijaz's weapon had a longer range and was more likely, in the right hands, to hit its target.

Like so many military actions, this one was destined to enter history in many different versions. This much is clear: Ilijaz and his men set an ambush on the Srebrenica-Skelani road somewhere in the vicinity of Kalina. Others from neighboring villages, particularly Osmaće, organized attacks nearby.

The groups shot at trucks and they shot at cars, killing a number of Serbs. Ilijaz and his men insisted they killed only soldiers who returned fire—indeed two attackers from Osmaće also died. But Serbs in the area told a different story, that seven Serb civilians, including two women, were killed.

When gunfire erupted in that first military action, the sound surprised Ilijaz. It was like a roar. Thoughts raced through his brain:

This is war. We could be killed at any moment, could die in the fight. Just like that.

He returned to the village at day's end with a sense of shock, unable to meet the frightened eyes of neighbors who he imagined blamed him for stirring up trouble. Overwhelmed, he asked his cousin, Sulejman, to tell the family he was alive. Then he went back to the woods. He spent the night there alone doing nothing, not eating, not speaking, only thinking, surrounded, like the battle-shocked main character in Meša Selimović's *Fortress,* "by the only victor: the utter silence of the ancient earth, indifferent to human misery" and filled with "that deepest of all sadness, of defeat that follows victory."

War was not about fear, Ilijaz realized, it was about dying. It was about killing. It was about the ability of human beings to destroy others of their own species without feeling a thing. Ilijaz racked his brain to think of any other animals that killed their own so easily. He thought of none. Life, which he had dedicated himself to sustaining, was worthless in war. Taking a life came so easily. So quickly.

He felt sick to the depths of his soul, a sickness he was sure was here to stay. He had dedicated himself to saving lives, not taking them. What he had done today so contradicted his own being that he wanted to die himself.

"In that long, sleepless night," wrote Selimović," in the black fear that was not of the enemy, but of something within me, I was born as what I am, unsure of all that is me and of all that is human."

———

THREE DAYS PASSED before Ilijaz decided to emerge from the woods and live, not die. It took an extreme concentration of his will combined with the realization that the people he cared about needed him. From now on, he resolved, he would put aside all these tortured reflections. He would not think or feel, only act.

On May 17, 1992, exactly a month after Ilijaz fled to his village, a military runner arrived with a message from a young nurse Ilijaz knew from Srebrenica. She begged him to come quickly to Osmače to treat a man with a bullet wound to the leg. As a twenty-year-old fresh out of nursing school, she had no idea what to do. The day was clear and warm. Ilijaz hiked uphill to the main Srebrenica-Skelani road, followed it north for two miles, and then wound another two miles up a dirt road to Osmaće, reaching the village at nightfall. By the time he arrived, the patient, whose wounds were not serious after all, had gone.

Ilijaz decided to stay overnight rather than make the trip back in the dark. Without warning, the thunder of an explosion punctuated the air. Then several more. A grenade attack, someone said. Ilijaz could barely remember, from his days of military service, what a grenade was. A man came to tell him that injured people were lying behind the schoolhouse. Several of the small bombs had exploded there, showering the area with splinters of metal.

When Ilijaz arrived, the wounded had been moved inside the schoolhouse clinic. A teenage girl was moaning in pain, most of her knee blown away. Her mother lay dead. A pregnant woman was dead, too. Several others, including the girl's two younger brothers, had what appeared to be less severe injuries.

Ilijaz examined the girl's leg. He could tell from the damage that it probably required amputation, but he had only a scalpel with him. Everything was happening so quickly. He wasn't prepared to do something he had never done before, something that, for the moment, seemed so radical. Someone found some antibiotics and gauze, and Ilijaz cleaned the wound and pressed on it to stop the bleeding. He and the nurse stayed with the girl and her two brothers all night, wondering what to do.

The next morning, a man volunteered to row the children upstream along the River Drina to a small town, Žepa, where an organized hospital was rumored to exist. Their father agreed. After the injured left, Ilijaz and the nurse sat for a moment to process what had happened. In spite of Ilijaz's long history of squeamishness, the blood and torn flesh hadn't bothered him much. What disturbed him more was the terrible sense of helplessness he felt, and the realization that the girl would probably not be his last war-injured patient, or his worst. Without knowledge, without colleagues or books to consult, without supplies and equipment, what would he be able to do?

Over the next weeks, the group of armed men and women from Ilijaz's region grew to about a hundred. They established a base at a high point called Kragljivoda, where several village roads met the main road that stretched from Srebrenica down to the border town of Skelani and the bridge to Serbia. They dug trenches on either side of the road and constructed a real front line. Ilijaz's neighbor, the minaret builder Šefik Mandžic, came to lead the "troops." A large post office building and a smaller building that had housed a market sat at the forest crossroads. From the windows of the post office building, Ilijaz and the others looked across the Drina River to Serbia and saw tanks firing toward them from the road that zigzagged up Tara Mountain. During the war's quiet moments—and war has many of these—they sat on the balcony playing cards.

With supplies found in a nearby clinic and the assistance of two medical technicians—his cousin, Sulejman, and a dark-haired refugee named Naim—Ilijaz organized a medical station in a newly built house a couple of yards away from his family's home. He spent most of his time outside of it, visiting the ill and those injured by mines, shells and bullets. During military actions, he had to stay behind the lines in case one of the men was hurt. It frustrated him to sit back like a child watching his brothers and sisters at work. He wanted to take the same risk as the others and felt fully capable of fighting.

Keeping busy kept his mind off the most difficult subjects—his father's illness and the whereabouts of his girlfriend, Fatima. She was rumored to have been captured and killed in Bratunac, where paramilitaries had set up a detention center in the primary school and about 700 prominent Muslims were interned, subject to a "trial" presided over by a local Serb nationalist physician. Hundreds were tortured and executed.

One day soldiers from another region crossed Serb-controlled territory to attend a meeting in Ilijaz's village and brought with them good news. Fatima had left Bratunac in time and was staying with relatives in her deceased father's birth village. All these weeks, she'd been only eight miles north of him, but, with Chetniks holding much of the mountainous territory in between, she might as well have been on the moon.

Ilijaz wrote a letter on a tiny piece of paper to tell her he, too, was alive. Please send an answer, he wrote, so he could be sure that she was OK.

Some days later, another soldier came with a reply, a small note in Fatima's handwriting. It confirmed that she had escaped Bratunac unharmed and had gone to live with her mother and younger brother in the village. There, like Ilijaz, she was treating war wounded on an island of territory surrounded by a sea of Chetnik soldiers.

ON THE FIRST OF JUNE, Ilijaz and a few soldiers lay on their backs in a grassy ravine near Kragljivoda, propped on their elbows, taking advantage of the sunny day. Other soldiers manned front-line positions near a point called Vitez, about a half mile southeast along the Srebrenica-Skelani road.

The bright atmosphere belied the ominous situation. The Serbs had destroyed village after Muslim village, first bombarding them from afar, then, after their populations fled to the forests, arriving with infantry to burn the houses and kill anyone who remained. They had come within a mile of Ilijaz's village.

For weeks, the Serbs had controlled the local airwaves and broadcast repeated appeals for all Serbs, everywhere, to join the fight against the Muslims. The Muslims had started the war. The Muslims were the aggressors. Even Serb TV, though, was better than what Ilijaz had now, which was nothing. Electricity had just been cut off, and he assumed that the Serbs had interrupted the link to the power plant in Serbia.

To Ilijaz's surprise, a group of men whom he recognized from the southern part of Srebrenica, an area known as *Stari Grad,* or Old Town, approached unannounced. Behind them, riding bareback on a tiny horse with his feet nearly dragging on the ground, was their leader, a man in his forties whose name had grown synonymous with fearlessness: Akif Ustić.

"Where's the doctor?" thundered Akif, Srebrenica's fit former gym teacher. Ilijaz knew him from before the war, as everyone knew everyone in Srebrenica. Ilijaz stood up, and the commander flashed him a toothy smile framed by a thin mustache that ran along the sides of his mouth. He gave Ilijaz a bear hug and a hard pat on the back.

When the war started, Akif had organized this homegrown battalion with guns from the Srebrenica police station, and soon stories of his courage under fire spread throughout the region. He announced that he was here to help the Kragljivoda troops defend their shrinking territory.

His arrival failed to lift some of the men's pessimism, and one grumbled in a stage whisper, "People come here and they go away and nobody ever does anything."

Akif grabbed the man. "OK, we're going, you and I, for an action to Vitez."

"OK, fine!" said the other. "But I don't have a gun."

Akif gave him his rifle, took another from one of his soldiers, and the two of them trudged toward the front lines, quarreling as they went.

Ilijaz watched them go, sure that they would turn back around. This was no way for a small band of soldiers to start an action. A clear day made it impossible to reach enemy front lines without notice. Success depended on the element of surprise.

But the two kept walking, blind but for each other and their desire to prove themselves courageous. Ilijaz and some others picked themselves up from the grass and followed what Ilijaz considered the fools leading the way.

When the battle broke out, they had about thirty local soldiers assembled on their side. In the ensuing chaos, they began to advance and take the Serb position.

Ilijaz stayed back to help guard the original line. Eventually the clamor of shooting died away. Everyone wondered whether Chetniks had captured their men, and, at the sound of an approaching vehicle, they quickly drew their weapons. A Russian-built Lada Niva appeared. For a split second, they held their fire, just long enough for the driver to stick his hand out the window and scream at them by name not to shoot. They dropped their weapons.

Ilijaz peered through a car window and saw the cocksure leader, Akif, lying on his stomach, clearly in pain.

"What happened?"

"We destroyed them!" Akif grunted, "There's as many weapons as you like, and now we're moving on."

At Ilijaz's insistence, several men lifted Akif out of the car and Ilijaz surveyed his body for injury. A wounded Serb soldier had thrown a grenade at him when he entered the garage of the hunting lodge in Vitez. Fortunately, a piece of shrapnel appeared to have little more than glanced his right flank. Ilijaz bandaged his wound to stop it from bleeding and prepared to move him to the house that served as an improved clinic.

But Akif stubbornly insisted on returning home to Stari Grad in his captured car, in spite of the fact that Chetniks controlled part of the main road. The only other option was a treacherous journey over unpaved mountain paths—one that the Russian-built car, and the men, would likely not survive.

Akif asked for a man brave enough to drive him and very quickly more than one daredevil disciple offered. Ilijaz considered the trip senseless, but joined it out of duty. Someone had to look after Akif and reassure the soldiers, and Ilijaz wouldn't pass the risk to one of his two medical assistants.

His brother, Hamid, begged him through tears not to go. Ilijaz handed Hamid his beret and white bandanna to keep until he came back.

IF I come back, he thought to himself.

As he entered the car, a juicy thrill of fear-tinged excitement coursed through him. They took off for the main road with a rifle-toting soldier perched on the hood. A messenger galloped ahead on horseback to alert friendly soldiers to clear the route and repair a partially destroyed bridge that served as a barricade against Serb forces.

When the car reached the bridge, a soldier carrying an automatic weapon joined the other soldier on the hood. The car crossed and entered a zone controlled by Serbs. The men fell silent. Akif, lying on the back seat, quietly removed a pistol from his belt, checked it to see if it was loaded, and handed it to Ilijaz. "Doctor, if something happens, take me first and then do whatever you can."

Ilijaz looked out the windows, dazed. He had traveled this road hundreds of times before the war, knew its every curve, loved its shifting views of trees and hillsides. Nothing on the surface had changed, and yet the place felt foreign to him now, every seemingly innocent stretch of forest a potential hiding place for something sinister. Only yesterday, he would have described this area as his area, his region, his own. And now it belonged to someone else. How strange that the land that had always provided him sustenance now threatened to take his life away.

Ilijaz caught sight of three men sitting no more than thirty feet from the roadside beside a mound that appeared to be a bunker. Their hands and mouths were busy with food while their rifles lay beside them. As the car drew nearer, the men stood up. They followed the car with their eyes as it passed, but did not reach for their rifles. Nobody shot.

The Lada cruised through the rest of Serb-controlled territory, and it was Akif who realized they now faced a greater danger: friendly forces. Certainly none of the Muslim soldiers expected them to travel this road, especially not in a vehicle.

Akif slowed the driver to a crawl and the two men on the hood of the car began calling out to the local commander. They curved around a bend and came within clear sight of the Muslim gunners—who thankfully held their fire. "Are you guys crazy?" one came up to the car and shouted. "What if someone behind his machine gun had gotten scared and started shooting?"

Now they were firmly in friendly territory, and they continued downhill into the valley of Srebrenica, where houses began to dot, then line, the roadside. Ilijaz looked around himself. How different the old part of town appeared. It even smelled differently; acrid smoke and rot wafted through the open car windows. A few women with wan, scared faces hustled along the sides of the road, but Ilijaz didn't recognize them. They must have been refugees from outlying villages. Most of Srebrenica's original population, including its doctors, had fled at the start of the war. The car reached a vista offering a view of the center of town, and Ilijaz looked down through missing rooftops into the burnt, empty rooms of dozens of homes he'd known so well.

The car pulled up to the house of Dr. Nijaz Džanić, an experienced internist who had turned his home into a hospital and was treating patients with materials someone smuggled out of the hospital pharmacy. The forty-two-year-old doctor had never left Srebrenica, not even when Serbs held the town the first three weeks of the war. Nijaz stayed behind to care for his ailing parents. He had long commanded respect—perhaps that is why Serbs spared his house when they torched those of his neighbors. After a group of Muslim men set an ambush that killed the leader of the local Serb forces on May 7, nearly all Serbs, armed and civilian, abandoned Srebrenica the following day. Since then, some of the Muslims who had taken to the woods for safety ventured back to the southern parts of town.

Ilijaz greeted Nijaz and studied him. Before the war, the thin, dark-haired physician had suffered a heart attack and wasn't well enough to work full-time. It shocked Ilijaz to see him looking fresher than ever, apparently revitalized by the fact that people needed him.

Because Nijaz was more experienced and had better equipment, Ilijaz had sent several heavily injured patients to him over the mountain paths. One, just a few days ago, had a broken femur. Nijaz told Ilijaz the man was improving.

"It must be hard to work under fire every day," Nijaz said. For the first time in the six weeks since the war began, Ilijaz had a physician colleague with whom to commiserate. Together, they quickly cleaned up Akif's wounds and rebandaged him. Ilijaz and the volunteers from Gladovići had to return before nightfall.

Ilijaz was somewhat sorry to be leaving. How much more he could accomplish pooling his knowledge and resources with other physicians in a central location. Out of Srebrenica's original forty-five doctors, pharmacologists, and dentists, Ilijaz knew of at least three who remained in the area besides Nijaz and Fatima. But if they all left their villages for Srebrenica, who would care for injured patients who couldn't easily be transferred here? Besides, Srebrenica's hospital and clinic buildings remained closed and abandoned in the northern end of town, still too dangerous to visit.

Something needed to change, but for now, Ilijaz, Nijaz, Fatima, and the others could do nothing but work alone.

6

A BLUE FEAR

The same first week of June 1992, Eric Dachy, quite unaware of the goings-on in Srebrenica, was feeling pretty useless. With Bosnia engulfed in all-out war, distributing drugs and medical supplies to hospitals in peaceful Serbia seemed rather beside the point. Getting aid into Bosnia, though, would require navigating through a maze of multiple armed groups and rapidly shifting combat zones that were only now starting to stabilize into recognizable front lines. Serb nationalist military forces blocked access for humanitarian aid, and rumors abounded of widespread atrocities against civilians. It mattered little that two weeks ago the International Committee of the Red Cross convinced all warring parties to agree to respect the Geneva Conventions guaranteeing the protection of the wounded, sick, prisoners of war, and civilians.

The day of the agreement, Bosnia and Herzegovina, Croatia, and Slovenia became United Nations member states; their existence as independent countries was now recognized worldwide. This also gained them the right to self-defense under Article 51 of the U.N. charter. However, the arms embargo that had been placed on Yugoslavia the previous year was still in effect for the entire region, and Bosnian government forces remained at a significant disadvantage in heavy weaponry compared with the Yugoslav-backed Serb forces.

Just days after Bosnia's recognition as a U.N. member state, both the U.N. High Commissioner for Refugees and the International Red Cross announced the suspension of their Bosnia operations. Persistent violence and lethal attacks on aid workers and aid convoys led to the decision. To the great disappointment of the local population, the U.N. Protection Force, UNPROFOR, which had been based in peaceful Sarajevo for operations in war-torn Croatia, followed suit, pulling out all but a skeleton force from the Bosnian capital and transferring its headquarters to

Belgrade, Serbia. Its remaining 120 peacekeepers were practically the only internationals left in Sarajevo, and, without a clear mandate to work in Bosnia, were nearly powerless in their efforts to mediate ceasefires and deliver humanitarian aid.

The headquarters of Doctors Without Borders's semi-independent national sections split over how to respond to Bosnia's war. Leaders of the French section halted all aid activities. "This can't go on," the president of MSF France, Rony Brauman, told a reporter for Agence France-Presse, the leading French news agency. "We (the MSF) are stopping our work, because there is a failure and a cowardice among the European Community that borders on monstrosity."

The international community needed to stop the war and atrocities against civilians, he said. "The humanitarian and legal pretext has gone on long enough and what's needed now is a military intervention," Brauman said, shocking his colleagues in the aid community, "because we have all these dead and injured, and what we see among the international community is a complete void, indifference, people bashfully looking elsewhere."

The leaders of MSF Belgium had a different philosophy. Let the French give press conferences and write articles and books; the Belgians would act in the war zone. Eric, though he worked for the Belgian section, shared many of the French leader's opinions. Providing humanitarian aid was not the way to end this war. Still, he clung to the hope that humanitarians could accomplish something important in Bosnia, and not only with aid. He had another idea, an activist idea: to interpose between victims and aggressors.

The Doctors Without Borders headquarters in the Bosnian capital, Sarajevo, was burned and looted. The newly fledged Bosnian army, loyal to the Bosnian government, had managed to keep control of the city, but Serb nationalist forces ringed its heights, shooting and shelling at the city below. All MSF internationals had pulled out for safety reasons not long after the start of the war. What remained of the MSF mission was its local staff members, who'd relocated their office to the civilian hospital, the biggest and most advanced in all of Bosnia, and alerted Eric in Belgrade that it had a critical shortage of kidney dialysis fluid. Eric sent his translator combing through the chemical laboratories of Serbia looking for the exact type and concentration of fluid that would work in the hospital's machine. If the hospital had to stop providing dialysis, then those in the capital who had kidney failure and depended on the procedure to filter dangerous toxins from their bloodstreams would die.

Eric's translator found a local factory that produced the needed fluid, and Eric purchased more than 1,000 liters. He argued it, along with cases of external fixators, surgical kits, wound dressings, and some medications, onto a convoy of French peacekeeping forces headed to the Bosnian capital the first week of June. Then he set about seeking a way to get himself to Sarajevo to assess conditions in the city and the feasibility of supplying it regularly with medical aid from Belgrade.

He found his ticket a few days later with a bizarre lot of Bosnian Serb liaisons who'd congregated in a palatial, former Communist government villa in the nicest part of Belgrade. A large, scowling man, whom the aid workers jokingly referred to as Bluto, after Popeye's parrot-toting archrival, menaced Eric when he entered. Eric asked for permission to travel to Bosnia. Bluto and the other Serb officials grilled him. What did he want to do there? Why did he want to go? Eventually they relented, and the trip was set for the second week of June. Eric kept the date, despite suffering from a painful bout of tonsillitis. He loaded MSF's 4WD Toyota Land Cruiser with provisions for the local MSF team and boxes and boxes of the best surgical material in MSF's warehouse. He and three colleagues drove across the Drina River into Serb-held Bosnia. They didn't know exactly how they'd get across the front lines to reach the capital, but Eric knew that U.N. Protection Force soldiers had a base nearby in the hilly Sarajevo suburb of Lukavica. When he reached it, he was appalled to discover that the UNPROFOR soldiers were sharing a barracks with the separatist Serbs. They couldn't have avoided seeing Serb artillery emplacements slam shells into the hospital pavilions, historic landmarks, and high-rise apartment buildings of the Bosnian capital in the valley below.

The UNPROFOR soldiers referred to military activity in the matter-of-fact language meteorologists use to give weather reports. Eric's group was in luck. Today's weather was "calm." A small U.N. military convoy was about to leave for Sarajevo, and, rather than integrating MSF into the convoy, its leader grudgingly authorized Eric's car to follow at his own risk. They made it into the city with little incident, and the local MSF staff members greeted them in good spirits. Together, they sped to the hospital along streets crackling with sniper fire, ducking on reflex when the shooting sounded close. Eric sneaked glances at the proud former Olympic city he'd visited numerous times before the war. Its delicate Austro-Hungarian buildings were splattered with shell craters, its twin modern skyscrapers had been burnt in a rocket barrage.

After delivering supplies to the hospital and making their assessments, Eric's team returned to the dangerous streets, racing toward the apartment of an MSF worker to stay the night. The car ahead of them stalled for a terrifying moment at an exposed crossroads and Eric's own driver, a local hero for delivering drugs throughout the besieged city, took the risk of slowing down and nudging it to safety from behind. Inside the ugly high-rise block apartment, Eric listened as the shelling of the city intensified. He stepped out on the balcony and gazed at the city and the mountains that rose on its northern side. Before his very eyes, grenades slammed into houses, exploding with flashes of fire.

Maybe people are dying there. Maybe whole families.

He turned to his host.

"What if the Serbs start shelling this building?"

"We're all dead," the young man answered.

Eric's infected throat felt as raw as if live birds were pecking it. Exhausted, he lay down and, in spite of the continuous pain and the continual thunderclaps of shelling, he managed a fitful night's sleep. The morning of their departure, Eric and his colleagues reported to the sandbagged main Sarajevo post office, now headquarters to a small contingent of U.N. Protection Force soldiers, and prepared for the drive back to Belgrade. Eric strapped on a bulletproof vest offered by U.N. soldiers. The day was sunny and quiet, aside from remote bursts of gunfire. Eric sat down in the back seat of the Toyota Land Cruiser, and the MSF administrator started the engine. They joined a convoy of armored U.N. vehicles and rolled slowly out of the city along a deserted road bordered by dismembered buildings.

Everyone fell silent as the group began to cross the wide-open tarmac of an abandoned airport. The engine hummed. Then, with a metallic bang, a bullet hit the car. Sniper.

Eric hit the ground—as best he could. He folded his lanky body as tightly as possible behind the front seat of the car and squinted up at the windshield. He watched as the U.N. "Blue Helmet" at the machine-gun of the tank ahead of him withdrew into the turret and closed the hatch. Eric's vehicle was smack in the middle of a runway with a long way to go before reaching cover. He was sure that the sniper was adjusting his aim.

Then a second bullet hit, shattering both side windows. Eric ducked. He had to protect his head. *A bullet in the thigh, that would be OK, that would heal. But not the head.* Fear ran through him like a cold, metallic liquid. He felt pinpricks of pain from splinters of glass on his exposed skin.

The driver drove blindly, lying flat on the front seat holding on to the wheel. Eric peeked up between the seats, trying to guide him, trying to estimate the location of the sniper so he could direct the car beside one of the armored vehicles for protection. The Toyota drew dangerously close to the back of the armored vehicle in front of them.

"Slow down!" Eric shouted through his sore throat, and the driver hit the brakes. Then a third bullet cracked the dashboard. Eric contracted into a ball, muscles tetanized by fear. He awaited the next shot.

Somebody who doesn't know me, who never saw me, is trying to kill me, he thought. *He hates me without reason, without knowing me.*

Seconds passed. He felt the car inch forward, then turn. Eric opened his eyes. They were on a small road now, hidden behind trees. He straightened himself out and sat up.

"Everything OK, guys?" he asked. The people in the car took a moment to inspect one another. Except for a few bloody surface wounds, everyone was all right. They realized with relief that they'd more or less escaped the crisis and laughed nervously.

The U.N. soldiers had not returned fire. It was the first time Eric saw firsthand how wary they were of confrontation. The convoy continued back to Lukavica where Serb soldiers, possibly the ones who'd just shot at them, greeted them warmly.

Back at the MSF office in Belgrade, coworkers slapped Eric on the back and called him "cowboy." He didn't feel like one. He knew he'd been scared stiff. He'd had, as the Belgians call it, "a blue fear." The visceral experience only strengthened his opinion that humanitarian aid meant little in the face of deadly violence. Rather than providing aid, powerful countries should be pouring their efforts into stopping the war.

But that was exactly the opposite of what happened. Unwilling to go to war in Bosnia, but needing to convince their populations that something was being done to alleviate the suffering being shown on CNN, member states of the U.N. Security Council passed resolutions that punished Yugoslavia with sanctions and led the U.N. Protection Force, with great fanfare, to secure the Sarajevo airport for a massive airlift of humanitarian assistance. MSF co-founder Dr. Bernard Kouchner, serving as a French government minister, helped initiate the airlift. He favored stronger action against Serb forces, but conversations with French President François Mitterrand convinced him it wouldn't be forthcoming. Kouchner believed that multinational, state-supported humanitarian intervention, while not enough, represented major progress compared with the usual lack of interest of states in helping the victims of somebody else's war. The council called for a strengthening of the protection force and gave it an official mandate to work in Bosnia to protect humanitarian assistance delivered by the U.N. High Commissioner for Refugees and others.

The plan split the aid community. On the one hand, members of the International Committee of the Red Cross vehemently opposed what they considered a militarization of humanitarian aid, which could endanger humanitarian neutrality in the eyes of the combatants. Indeed, the May 22 agreement that had been initiated by the Red Cross and signed by the region's military leaders emphasized "that humanitarian activities have to be kept absolutely separate from military operations." In an article appearing the same month, a Red Cross leader wrote that the organization should not cooperate with efforts in which the military was involved in delivering aid. Aid delivery was protected by international law, he argued, and did not need protection from soldiers.

Even the U.N. High Commissioner for Refugees feared that large-scale international military intervention would be counterproductive, because any upsurge in fighting would interfere with humanitarian assistance efforts. So, while it had seemed, at first, that the United Nations would undertake a humanitarian enforcement operation similar to Operation Provide Comfort in Iraq, in the end, the U.N. Protection Force's authorization to use force was watered down. Countries were reluctant and slow to send additional troops.

Sure, it had made Eric Dachy slightly uncomfortable to travel with a military escort into Sarajevo, but there didn't seem to be another way. What bothered him much more was that the only thing the inaptly named U.N. Protection Force was mandated to protect was humanitarian aid and those who delivered it—not the actual victims of the war. An MSF France board member would later compare such a U.N. force to the colonial gunboats that "came to the rescue of worthy missionaries beset by natives."

The U.N. soldiers would fight to defend Eric's life, but not the lives of the children and civilians living in Sarajevo. This shocked him. It seemed surreal. He didn't want the force to protect aid deliveries. He wanted it to shoot back at the cowardly soldiers who were lobbing their shells at civilians.

7

INGRESS

CANCER WAS STEALING ILIJAZ'S FATHER. It stole his breath, his words. So weak he could barely stand, he seemed to have strength only for the terrible, unnatural cough that racked him.

Each day compounded Ilijaz's sense of helplessness as a doctor and a son. Before the war, the diagnosis had been devastating, the family's struggle intense, but at least they'd had hope. While lung cancer would kill him in a matter of months if left untreated, chemotherapy and surgery offered a shot at survival. The war had erased this chance. Front lines blocked access to a modern hospital. Ilijaz had only painkillers and asthma medicines to help ease some of his father's symptoms while he waited out the war, mainly in the basement.

The two-story home faced Serbia and the tanks on Tara Mountain. One late afternoon, the entire family was coughing and choking much as Ilijaz's father, trapped in the basement as smoke thickened the air in the wake of a strong explosion. The earth and the house above shook so violently that Ilijaz was afraid of being buried alive. Somehow, the structure held and all of them survived.

As the days passed, Ilijaz's father remained selfless, able to see beyond his own suffering and aware of the larger situation in the region. Even as he grew sicker, he encouraged Ilijaz to go out and help others rather than stay with him.

"It's more important for you to be on the field," he would say. "There are many people who need you."

It took more courage for Ilijaz to sit at home and watch his father suffer than to confront the Serb army with his band of lightly armed men. The risk of death for himself was abstract and random, but his father's illness made life seem too fragile. He was more afraid for his father than for himself.

Ilijaz's father died with Ilijaz beside him the morning of July 10, 1992, less than three months after the beginning of the war. Without treatment, the cancer had progressed so quickly. They buried him that afternoon on family property. News traveled fast and hundreds of men arrived to recite the Muslim *dženaza* prayers of mourning.

After the burial, Ilijaz refused to leave his father's grave. His two medical technicians, Sulejman and Naim, and other friends did their best to comfort him, and then respected his wishes and left him alone. The part of Ilijaz that was a doctor had known his father's cancer was progressing rapidly and that he might soon die. But as a son there was no way to accept or even conceive of a parent's death. It caught him unprepared. Ilijaz wasn't a crier, in fact he couldn't remember a single time he had cried in his youth. Now he sat at the graveside and sobbed for what seemed like hours. He felt completely helpless, like a child.

The next day he set out with twelve volunteers to join a risky offensive—a coordinated action of local militias for a high point in an area called Shpat from which Chetnik gunners and artillerists targeted Srebrenica and launched attacks on Muslim villages. Having heard about the death in Ilijaz's family, the others expected his unit to sit this one out. He felt he had to go, though he knew that an irrational, momentary zeal was driving him. *Inat.* The desire for revenge.

The battles were to be staged from the area where Fatima was living, and he was pretty sure he'd be able to meet her. For the first time since the war began, Ilijaz and nearly a dozen of his neighbors trod the dangerous paths to her village. When he arrived, he waited by a water well, chatting with two other men as an acquaintance went inside a house to summon her.

Fatima stepped through the doorway. For a long moment she just stood and stared, as if unable to identify him. He hadn't thought of how three months of war and the stress of his father's illness and death might have changed him. In fact, Ilijaz had turned from tall and slender to gaunt. He had let his dark hair grow long around his wide forehead, and he wore a long, scraggly beard that curved under his chin, leaving a dollop of hair below his lower lip. His small eyes gleamed, and above them a fuzz of hair sprouted between his thick, arched brows.

That day he carried his weapons and wore what had become his typical battle uniform—a white bandanna around his forehead and his old, black gym suit. Fatima knew that gym suit well, and at last a smile of recognition spread across her lips. Ilijaz smiled back and familiar creases formed under his cheeks. She embraced him, breathing in his strong, familiar smell.

That night Fatima listened to Ilijaz talk about his father. Ilijaz seemed sad to her, but she noticed he was able to smile. She figured that all the death he'd seen these last few months had toughened him.

She told him about her work in the field, similar to his, although she hadn't become a fighter. She didn't consider the young men who defended themselves, their villages, and her and her family as soldiers. They were protectors—civilians who'd been forced to take up whatever weapons they had and try to protect local Muslim villages from being overtaken by the Serbs and "ethnically cleansed" like so many others. The problem was, these men, in their youth, were fearless. She instructed them in first aid, trying to force them to understand that they faced real danger.

She went everywhere the fighters went, at first following a few feet behind them for safety. That changed the first time they came under fire. The man assigned to protect her froze in place shaking with fear.

"What are you doing?" she demanded. He told her, in a quavering voice, that he couldn't move his legs. That's when she'd asked for her own gun. They gave her a small Beretta 7.2 pistol, made in Italy. She kept it close at hand in case she needed to defend herself or her patients. It was a doctor's right, under international war law, but it earned her strange looks. The sight of a longhaired woman packing a gun in her back pants waist surprised the old-fashioned villagers.

Ilijaz and Fatima talked about wanting to be together again and how to find a way to do it. For now, while the inhabitants of their own areas needed them, they couldn't come up with any good options.

The fighting started early the next morning, July 12. This time Ilijaz refused to stand back. He pushed to the front of the lines and started shooting. He shot and he shot. For the first time, he felt pure hatred in his heart. The past weeks of the war he had insisted to the men from his village that they wouldn't commit atrocities like the Chetniks did, but at this moment he could have strangled every Serb in the world. Something in him had broken.

Ilijaz approached a clearing and lay down behind a stone. He saw what he thought was a Serb bunker about 250 yards away. Fury filled him with the urge to destroy it. His father had suffered and died. The men in the bunker were guilty. He stood up tall and strode toward them without a thought of what could happen or a plan in case something went wrong.

A string of bullets whizzed inches from his legs.

"Get back!" someone shouted.

Ilijaz turned around and several of his men grabbed him. They were furious at him for taking such a risk. They told him they needed him alive; they needed him as their doctor. But a doctor's role was to fix things, stop suffering, solve problems. How could Ilijaz fix the war using only the tools of medicine?

The locals took casualties, but their offensive succeeded. They pushed back the Chetniks and captured some Serb-held villages. At the end of the day, Serbs' houses were burning and several dozen had been killed, including some—perhaps many—civilians. The Muslims had chosen a Serb Orthodox holiday for their attack: *Petrovdan,* St. Peter's Day, the Patron Saint day of the church in the nearby mining town of Sase. They had also captured and destroyed a village called Zalazje, the loss of which was highly symbolic for the Serbs, who had suffered a massacre of forty persons there during World War II.

That evening, Ilijaz returned to Fatima, who had spent the day as a doctor with a diversion troop in Sase. Ilijaz and Fatima had little time alone to discuss what had happened over the day or to enjoy each other's comfort. Within hours Ilijaz left with others from his unit to retrieve the body of a friend killed near Osmaće. As the men walked away from Shpat, they tried to lighten the mood, teasing Ilijaz about Fatima, whose nickname was Fata. "I saw my Fata in Shpata," laughed Ilijaz's good friend Naim.

In battles over the following days, Muslim soldiers from the villages around Srebrenica linked their territories and the injured could finally be evacuated to a central location for treatment. Dr. Džanić reinaugurated Srebrenica Hospital. One by one, the handful of physicians who remained in the area returned to work there. Branka Stanić, a blond Croat general practitioner who lived in Switzerland, had been visiting her family here when the war broke out and trapped her. Avdo Hasanović was an older pediatrician who'd taken over as hospital director just before the war. Chubby Ejub Alić, whom Ilijaz had known since high school, moved back to Srebrenica from Potočari. His sixty-five-year-old father had also died recently. The month after the war started, the village beside Alići had been captured and set alight by Chetniks. Ejub's parents and sister had run from their house into the forest, as shells, which they judged to be coming from across the Drina in Serbia, exploded around them. Ejub's father fell to the ground in the wake of a powerful detonation—dead of unknown cause, perhaps a heart attack, with no signs of a mortal injury.

The family had buried him quickly as grenades fell. Then Ejub's mother and sister had journeyed to a safer village, finding shelter at the home of an aunt. The news had made its way to Ejub through former neighbors, also displaced from their homes, who'd managed to cross the front lines and reach Srebrenica. They also told Ejub that his beloved wife Mubina's mother had been shot dead by Chetniks in her home. Ejub had no idea if Mubina and their son were alive.

At first Ilijaz did not join the other doctors. His was the hottest front line, the closest to Serbia, and if it fell, the whole region would be endangered. For now, he believed the military needed him—not just medically, but in terms of morale. He would not leave his men.

But by the end of July the front lines stabilized, reason overcame emotion, and pleas for Ilijaz to come to Srebrenica and work as a doctor swayed him. He was a young general practitioner with very little experience. In the past months, he'd used a saw and scalpel to amputate a man's leg, only to watch him die. He'd walked four miles to tend to a woman who'd been in labor for two days, only to watch her hemorrhage and die. And a twenty-year-old who had come to him with a tiny abdominal shrapnel wound began to vomit blood and then died. He could do little for his patients without proper equipment and the ability to consult his colleagues and his books. As part of a medical team of doctors and nurses in a true health facility, he could do more and perhaps shake the sense of impotence that dogged him. He decided to join the war hospital.

PART TWO

THE BLOOD OF WARRIORS

The city lies ablaze like a rough lump of incense

Wherein the haze of our awareness twists.

The city implodes in latent emptiness.

A stone's crimson death

Bespeaks the house's blood-soaked tide. Plague!

—**Dr. Radovan Karadžić**
"Sarajevo," 1971

8

WAR OPERATIONS

ONLY FOUR MONTHS HAVE PASSED since the start of the war, but the hospital Ilijaz finds in Srebrenica is not the one he left. The only familiar features are four of the five doctors at work and the three-story, rectangular building itself, with its stone and mortar foundation, whitewashed exterior, and top floor covered in coffee-colored tiles. Inside, most of the nurses and technicians are different. Even the patients are different. The long, narrow hallways that used to echo with the cries of women in childbirth are now filled with the moans of the injured and dying.

The beds are full and most of the roughly seventy patients lying six or more to a room are young men, but some are women, children, the elderly, and even babies. Almost all suffer from injuries caused by shell fragments, mines, or bullets. There's simply no room for those with illnesses. Using what few supplies they have and what knowledge they can muster, Ilijaz, Fatima, and their four colleagues struggle to keep them alive in a town without any shops, electricity, or—because so many of its original residents fled and so many villagers were displaced here—many familiar faces.

The day Ilijaz arrives, authorities provide him and Fatima an apartment to share in the center of town, where they will live together as a couple for the first time. The place is more disaster zone than love nest. It looks, through its already open door, as if a bomb has exploded inside. They labor for two days to clean it, carefully packing away the clothing, documents, and photographs of the elderly Serb couple who left them behind. One day, they assume, the couple will return.

August 5, 1992, is a warm, sunny day a few days after their arrival. People are already out on the main street as Ilijaz and Fatima walk to the hospital in the early morning. A blond-haired, blue-eyed soldier peeks out from under a wide-brimmed hat to greet them. They stop to chat with the cheerful twenty-two-year-old, a drummer for a popular local band. He, along with other former musicians, schoolteachers, policemen, and truck drivers, is on his way to the front line.

Ilijaz and Fatima spend the day at the hospital. Around 5 P.M., unbelievable news arrives. A surgeon and his escorts are on their way to Srebrenica and have radioed from the edge of their territory, less than ten miles away. To Ilijaz it seems too good to be true.

The most elite of Srebrenica's ragtag bands of soldiers depart to fetch them in a truck powered with precious fuel. Soldiers have kept a few vehicles running on transformer oil and even cooking oil, on which they sputter along smelling like pancakes. Meanwhile, more than a thousand people gather outside the hospital in rapturous anticipation. The area has been sealed off from the rest of Bosnia for months now. Even the most powerful of Srebrenica's rival commanders, Naser Orić, feels like a "marble trapped inside a ball." If a surgeon succeeds in reaching them from Tuzla, Srebrenica will no longer feel so isolated.

Nobody can wait to meet the man who risked his life to help them, people who aren't his kin. He is to be lionized and welcomed as a dear guest in a culture that values hospitality. Whoever he is, he is already larger than life.

The truck rumbles back into town and people spill out of it, tanned and dirty young men in uniforms or civilian clothing and a few women. They jump down from the back of the truck, tired faces scanning the crowd for family members. The truck empties. People mill around, kissing cheeks, clapping hands on backs, and issuing hearty greetings. Others search the new arrivals for a gray-haired stranger, the expected surgeon.

"Which one is he?" they ask one another.

The commander calls the crowd to attention and introduces a tall, attractive man with a regal bearing dressed in a green camouflage military uniform. His name is Dr. Nedret Mujkanović. His hair is dark brown.

"This is a child!" someone snickers, loud enough for him to hear.

THE SURGEON'S ARRIVAL RELIEVES ILIJAZ. He sizes him up, assuming that anyone who would try to make it to Srebrenica without having some sort of family connection must be at least slightly insane. Nedret doesn't look crazy, though, just somewhat macho and adventuresome and, no doubt, courageous. He also seems hungry for the challenge of his new job. Although Nedret has walked for a week over hills and through forests, picked his way past minefields and run for cover from passing Serb patrols, he eagerly washes up, unpacks the equipment he brought— new surgical tools in plastic wrappers, bandages, gauze, and perfusions—and gets to work.

In the early evening a few dirt-covered soldiers rush into the hospital carrying an injured man. His left arm and hand hang from a cord of muscle.

With a shock, Ilijaz recognizes the wounded soldier, the cheerful drummer with the wide-brimmed hat whom he and Fatima had greeted in the morning. The young man recognizes him, too, and Ilijaz searches for a few words of encouragement.

They bustle into a large room just inside the hospital entrance and place him on a low cot with a black foam covering and white-painted metal legs that serves as an operating table. The medical staff leans over him.

A large bullet from an anti-aircraft gun known as a PAM or *protiv avionski metraljec* has caused his injury. The fellow soldiers who carried him six miles from the battlefield do not know first aid, and none thought to fashion a tourniquet out of a bandanna or piece of cloth to tie the upper arm and stanch the bleeding. The young man looks pale. Ilijaz supposes he is on the verge of shock, that his vital organs will soon fail from lack of blood and oxygen.

Nedret arrives. Ilijaz watches as he examines the patient and gently explains to him that the bullet has almost completely severed his lower arm. Not only that, it has shattered the humerus bone in his upper arm. Nedret has to amputate, but will try to save some of the limb below the shoulder. Perhaps four inches. To Ilijaz, watching, it seems the patient knows his fate and will be grateful for every one of those inches. *A typical Bosnian*, Ilijaz thinks, *he accepts whatever the surgeon tells him.*

Night approaches. Lice in the infested hospital begin to stir and bite, invisible creepy-crawlies scuttling their way over the skin of patients and doctors. With no electricity, the hospital, like the rest of Srebrenica, descends into darkness. Pieces of oil-soaked cotton smolder in coffee cups or medicine bottles, exhaling a smoky light. In the operating room, assistants scurry around the doctors, casting eerie shadows. The doctors feel rather than see their way around the cavernous hospital. Until morning, it will be too dark to remove the bodies of patients who die.

In the operating room, a single light bulb wavers and flickers, powered by a homemade hydroelectric contraption built on the stream that runs through town. Medical workers hook the patient to an infusion the surgeon brought with him and clean his skin with hydrogen peroxide. An arm is much more sensitive than a leg. The surgeon, expecting an anesthesiologist to follow him here soon, didn't bring any general anesthetics. They inject a couple of ampoules of local numbing medicine, but this has little effect on the patient's pain. Ilijaz guesses the medicine sat in the sun too long.

Nedret begins the amputation, and Ilijaz assists by holding instruments. Every time Nedret cuts, Ilijaz notices the patient wincing in pain. Ilijaz feels like fainting.

The young man moans but holds still. No nurses are required to restrain him. A few times he asks, "Could you please stop for a moment? I really feel bad."

He says please.

They save the worst part for the end. The surgeon has isolated the nerves and needs to shorten them. He touches one and the patient jumps as if jolted by an electric shock. A nurse and technician have to hold him down now. The doctors talk to him constantly as they work.

"Hold on. . . ." they tell him.

The young man requests a few moments to breathe and rest. The surgeon waits and then he cuts through the remaining nerves all at once. The patient lurches one more time and then falls silent, exhausted. Ilijaz imagines he has seen the limits of pain a human being can bear.

The man barely moves as they close his skin with sutures. Normally, contaminated war wounds are left open to drain to avoid infection, and they are closed several days later. Nedret makes the unorthodox choice to close the wound with sutures now and spare the patient another painful procedure.

Ilijaz returns home late in the evening. Fatima awaits him bursting with news. She has recognized the new surgeon as a former student leader at her medical school, just a few years her senior. The last she'd heard, he had gone on to specialize in pathology, not surgery. She has calculated the years since she lost track of him. Not enough have passed to make him a surgeon.

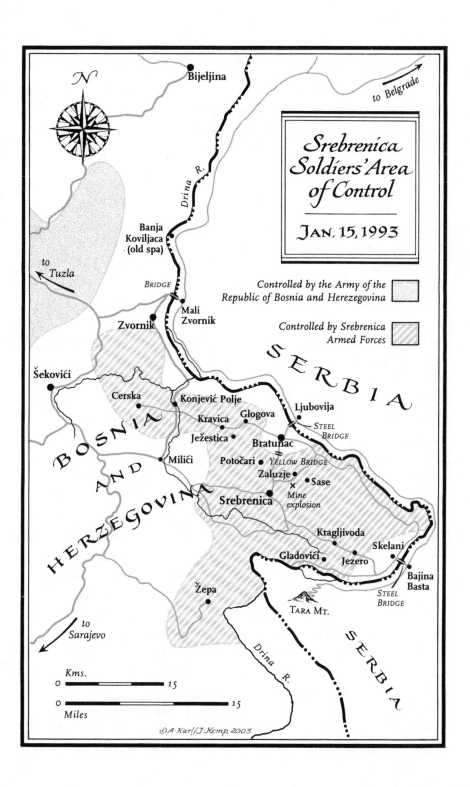

9

NEDRET

Evidence of the manual talents of Nedret Mujkanović and his taste for a challenge emerged early in his youth. Perhaps his drive to outshine others was a way to compensate for having had to grow up in Tuzla, Bosnia's *second*-largest city, in a metropolis filled with block apartments and not nearly as picturesque as its more notable sister, the 1984 Olympics host, Sarajevo.

At twelve, asked to depict the Partisan victory at the World War II Battle of the River Sutjeska on the occasion of its thirtieth anniversary, Nedret dipped his fingers in tempera and painted a dark forest. He smeared the center of the canvas with dark blue to form the river and added white caps of waves. Above the battlefield, shining through clouds of varying shades of red, the proud color of socialism, he sketched the ethereal face of Sava Kovačević. The hero, killed in battle, had led Yugoslavia's Serbians, Montenegrins, Bosnians, Croatians, and others in an effort to rebuff a major German offensive.

Nedret, a Muslim, gave not a thought to the fact that Kovačević was an Orthodox Christian. The five-pointed Partisan star shone from his hero's cap. He wrote the slogan *Bratstvo—Jedinstvo*, For Brotherhood and Unity, across the bottom of the canvas. Nedret's painting won the Yugoslav-wide contest of schoolchildren. His father boycotted the ceremony. He told his son not to pursue the arts, and later discouraged his passion for sports. Law and medicine were the only two "secure professions."

Tuzla had a medical school but not a law school. After high school graduation, Nedret enrolled and then departed for mandatory army service, where he spent a year tooling around in trucks as a military driver.

He returned home a footloose creature. Impatient with medical school's interminable lectures, he skipped class more often than he attended, traveling to the Adriatic Coast of Croatia, to the banks of the

Danube in Serbia, and to Ulm, Germany, where he had an aunt. There he wooed women and bought clothes to sell on the black market. Back home, he poured more energy into the medical school handball team than medical school itself.

"You need to study!" said his father. "You're just wandering around! I'll go after that army for ruining my son."

Nedret became a Socialist Youth Party leader, helping organize protests against government officials and earning the reputation of a stylish showoff who cultivated the look of a rock star. But he wore tinted eyeglasses, in part, to protect his blepharitic eyes from painful light, and his high-necked shirts and dramatic scarves covered an ugly childhood scar. An inexperienced surgeon had botched a tracheotomy when young Nedret choked on a dry bean.

In time Nedret returned to his studies with gusto, receiving top marks in a class taught by the very surgeon who had long ago extracted the bean from his throat. He took the exam in the professor's office surrounded by honeycombed wall displays filled with dozens of beans, beads, coins, and keys removed from the airways of other youngsters.

Nedret outscored his peers in the most difficult class, pathology, and gained the admiration of its professor, who invited him to be his assistant and protégé. Nedret agreed, and after graduating from medical school he channeled his artistic skills into careful dissections overseen by his gifted mentor, who had trained in Western Europe and the United States and over time became like a father to Nedret. The daily autopsies he performed as a pathology resident gave Nedret experience in anatomy that outstripped the training of many surgeons. He also learned from the surgeons' mistakes. "The best place to learn surgery is the autopsy room," his mentor would say.

In Yugoslavia's first post-Communist elections in 1990, Nedret's father won an opposition seat on the Tuzla city parliament as a member of the Muslim-dominated Party of Democratic Action. Nedret and other Socialist Youth Party leaders ran, too, and won, having reinvented themselves as members of the Liberal Party. Tuzla was the only city in Bosnia where a coalition of non-nationalist parties, including Nedret's, was elected to power.

The smelly, oft-maligned city was known for the kindness and solidarity of its people. While people in the capital, Sarajevo, relaxed in quaint coffee shops and browsed the old market quarter, practical Tuzlans mined salt, coal, and oil, extracting so much from the briny bowels of their city—200,000 tons a year—that they undermined its very foundation. One by one the most dignified buildings in the center of Tuzla sank into the earth. Newer Socialist-era shops and apartment buildings sprouted in their place, lining the streets in every rectangular incarnation of gray, beige, and white. In winter, the silos that loomed from Tuzla's coal-fueled power station turned the snow black. The wind pushed a chemical-tainted haze over the city that burned the lungs and smeared the horizon with a red-brown smudge.

As the months passed and war broke out in Yugoslavia's other republics, Tuzlans, too, began to feel the pressure. Nedret's father, suspicious of the Yugoslav National Army since it had "spoiled" his son, joined the underground Patriotic League, preparing the city for a potential attack by the country's own military. On March 22, 1992, soon after Bosnia's declaration of independence, he and Nedret's younger brother were forced into Tuzla's police station for questioning. He grabbed his chest and doubled over, dying of a heart attack before officers could rush him to the hospital. Nedret called his pathology chief, who lived in Serbia, for comfort.

By the following week, so many physicians had left Bosnia that Nedret was asked to lend a hand in the operating room of Tuzla hospital. The pathology chief called Nedret and told him that he was afraid to commute from his home in Serbia to the hospital in Bosnia, because Serb forces had barricaded the routes. He instructed Nedret on preparing students for their final exams, assuring him he would return the following week when all of this had blown over. It was the first week of April 1992. Nothing blew over. Nedret's mentor did not return to Tuzla. Nedret never left the surgery department.

The phone lines to Belgrade stopped working. Nedret packed his professor's belongings carefully in a brown cardboard box and sealed it with tape. A few weeks later, perhaps trying to outdo one another, Nedret and one of his former medical student classmates and political rivals jumped up at a meeting of Tuzla doctors and volunteered to work at a field hospital where Bosnian government loyalists of mixed ethnicities were battling Serb nationalist soldiers in the midst of civilians.

At first the skirmishes moved frequently and the field hospital followed. Eventually, the front lines stabilized and the medical team situated itself four miles behind in a quaint village restaurant, Two Lions. Nedret performed first aid and an occasional amputation in its kitchen, sharing surgical duties with his boastful colleague.

As spring stretched into summer, other villages near Tuzla needed mobile surgical units. Injured civilians and soldiers were dying before they could reach the city for medical procedures and operations. They required qualified doctors to stabilize and treat them in the field.

Leaders of the newly organized Bosnian Army Second Corps in Tuzla appointed a team of physicians and military experts to organize what had, until then, been spontaneous attempts to meet the health care needs of civilians and soldiers in northeast Bosnia. Its members were bewildered by the task. The Yugoslav Army Medical Academy's detailed plans for a wartime health service were of little use to them, designed as they were to provide medical and surgical care to Yugoslavia's citizens during an attack from abroad. The country had fractured instead. Hundreds of unanticipated front lines crisscrossed anticipated medical evacuation routes. Physicians often had no way to reach the towns where, according to the pocket Yugoslav Army Reserve cards they carried, they were supposed to report in case of war.

The team of physicians appointed to organize the army's health service in northeast Bosnia chucked the painstakingly handwritten organizational flow charts of the Yugoslav Army Health Service and began to reinvent their own health service from scratch. They scrutinized U.S. Army texts written about previous wars and settled on one basic principle: Get aid to the injured as quickly as possible. This meant locating surgical teams in highly populated areas and near front lines, even in several parts of northeast Bosnia that were difficult to reach because of fighting. They largely succeeded. Srebrenica was the one exception. The surrounded area was almost completely inaccessible.

When the ham radio operators in Srebrenica started calling for a surgeon, the responsibility for finding one fell to Tuzla's surgery department chairman, an Orthodox Christian in a still-mixed but increasingly Muslim city being attacked by separatist Orthodox Christian Serbs. He hadn't joined the army's medical service, and because of this he had lost much of the authority a chairman normally has over his apprentices. He knew he had little chance of convincing any surgeons to go to Srebrenica against their will, and, with 40 percent of the surgical faculty in Tuzla having fled at the start of the war, he didn't have much of a selection. After an unsuccessful search for volunteers among the better-trained surgeons, he landed on Nedret, one of his last hopes.

The chairman summoned Nedret from his field station to the hospital and made his request. Would Nedret go to Srebrenica? Nedret was flattered to be asked, but how could he get there given the intervening sixty miles of territory controlled by the nationalist Serb military? Over the summer, several groups had set out for the isolated enclave with supplies and military equipment but had turned back without even crossing the first set of front lines. He'd have to wait and see what happened.

"It can't wait. Are you willing to accept this assignment?" the chairman asked.

Nedret remained silent. A half minute or so ticked by.

"I accept."

The chairman's eyebrows shot up.

"Do you really accept?" he asked.

"Yes."

"You have until eight tomorrow morning to decide," the chairman responded, as if he couldn't trust his ears. "We'll meet here at eight to confirm."

That night Nedret went home to his rectangular government-appointed apartment. He really had no idea why he had agreed to the surgeon's request, and a nervous energy infected him. How could he possibly make it across all that enemy territory alive? He spent the evening with his three-year-old son and his wife, who also seemed to be on edge. He didn't want to talk with her about his decision. When they had met in the late 1980s as students, her boisterous and dramatic manner—shaking it up on the disco floor or speeding through books written by impressive-sounding British and American authors—had thrilled him. But Nedret found marriage hard; it was hard to be with the same person for many years. His wife worked, like women in the West and unlike his mother, whom he idealized. He regretted the loss of family closeness that resulted from not having a woman at home to cultivate it. To make matters worse, his exciting field work upset his wife. He often lost his temper with her.

Nedret turned on the radio and heard a man's panicked voice, transmitted over ham radio from Srebrenica. The man pleaded for help. Wounded people were dying from simple causes because Srebrenica lacked enough competent doctors and necessary medications.

Nedret later liked to say that it was the reporter's words that crystallized his decision to attempt the trip. Of course, there were a myriad other possible reasons, conscious and unconscious. Adventure. Escapism. Thirst for a new challenge. Going to Srebrenica offered Nedret a chance to one-up his medical school rival, earn glory, get away from his wife, and honor the memory of his dead father. But these weren't the motivations he'd later remember. He insisted that it was simple. He wanted to help, and like his old hero, Sava Kovačević, he would risk death for the opportunity.

10

PROFESSIONAL DUTY

IT ISN'T LONG AFTER NEDRET'S ARRIVAL in Srebrenica before his colleagues at the hospital begin asking him, casually, about his qualifications. How much surgical training has he done? Fatima tries to come across as curious, rather than suspicious.

"When did you pass your surgery exam?" she asks.

"You know . . . I haven't taken it yet." He will only say that he has worked at a war hospital on the front lines near Tuzla since April.

In fact, some of the doctors begin to suspect the truth, that Nedret has had almost no formal surgical training. At the moment, though, there doesn't seem to be a reason to prod him. Nedret's arrival has boosted the town's morale so much that, though the doctors whisper amongst themselves about his lack of surgical training, they don't broadcast it to the townspeople. Besides, from the instant he arrived, Nedret has taken charge of all the surgeries in Srebrenica. He is bold. He attempts operations, particularly abdominal repairs, that the rest of them never would have dared to try. Wounded and dying Bosnian peasants don't ask to see their surgeon's diploma.

Days after Nedret's arrival, the fighting around Srebrenica intensifies. Groups of local soldiers launch offensives and others fend off Chetnik advances. On August 8, with the hospital already full, the staff overwhelmed, and part of the enclave under fire, a group of soldiers plans a surprise raid on the Serb village of Ježestica, where Serb soldiers have directed cannon fire at a neighboring Muslim village for months. The action begins around noon. Some Srebrenicans stumble into a minefield and are carried back to the hospital. The remaining soldiers, many of them friends or family members of the dozens of Muslim men executed by Serbs in nearby Glogova at the start of the war, fire off a grenade and rush the village. Hand-to-hand fighting ensues and casualties mount.

Serb civilians flee. Eight Serbs are killed. The Srebrenica soldiers take livestock and other valuables and set fire to homes. The Serbs counterattack, injuring and killing many of the withdrawing Muslims.

By mid-afternoon wounded men—thin, dirty, and sunburned—are pouring into the hospital. The medical staff rushes about in a frenzy, unprepared for the influx. At 3:45 P.M., two white-coated men carrying one of the injured push through the hospital doors, brush past a man in green, and enter the makeshift operating room where they deposit the patient, moaning, on the operating cot. Ilijaz stands beside the cot wearing gloves and a short, dirty white coat. His hair is stringy with sweat and his beard is thin and unkempt. The patient moans as other white-coated doctors and nurses lean over his injured left leg. The room's shiny green floor reflects the light pouring in from two large windows.

Ilijaz steps back from the cot, shoulders hunched, holding his gloved hands slightly away from his sides. He looks as if he's not sure what to do. The patient moans again and Ilijaz looks away from him, bringing his glance to rest on the room's other cot. The man on top of it is completely naked except for a cloth placed over his genitals.

Ilijaz turns back to the man with the injured leg. Across from him on the other side of the cot stands Nedret, tall and authoritative, clad in a green surgeon's gown and cap. His mask dangles from his neck instead of covering his attractive, clean-shaven face. He moves to the patient's upper arm as nurses start an IV.

Ilijaz leans over to hold the patient's leg while someone else ties it with a tourniquet. He can hear Fatima's voice, strong and shrill, coming from the corridor. She sounds like a teacher trying to get a student's attention.

"Haso! Haso! Look at me! Keep your eyes open! Keep your eyes open! Haso, don't die! Listen to us! Listen to me, don't lose consciousness!"

She kneels beside a young man lying on the hallway floor, giving his chest a few hard pumps and then drawing her stethoscope to her ears. Her long black hair fans over the lapels of her white coat. Someone takes hold of the man's head and shakes it.

Outside, the sun shines on the upper hills, but in the narrow valley, the hospital driveway is already in shadow. More injured men move toward the hospital. Boys in tracksuits stand and watch the commotion.

In the operating room, leaning over his patient's partially amputated leg and holding a file-like knife, Nedret slashes at some bloody muscle. He needs to cut it so that it fits under the skin flap that will cover the patient's stump. The patient lows softly, like a cow. Then Nedret prepares to shorten the leg bone. He attaches two scissors-like hemostat clamps to the top edge of the skin flap and hands one of them to Ilijaz to hold steady. With his left hand, Nedret grips the protruding leg bone, the tibia, with a tool that looks like a giant pair of pliers. His right hand lifts a *zhaga*, a p-shaped saw. As he saws, the patient moans and bucks, and Ilijaz and the others holding him rock back and forth.

Nedret steps back from the table and erupts in anger.

"Hold it more steadily! I can't operate like this!"

The doctors and nurses reposition themselves. Nedret yells for more gauze rolls and sutures and a curly-haired instrument nurse, who's never worked in an operating room before this week, lets go of the patient's leg, ducks down, and scurries away to find them.

AT 4:05 P.M. FATIMA IS STILL KNEELING in the corridor trying to rouse her patient. Somewhere a woman screams. From somewhere else comes a terrible moan. The men leaning around Fatima's patient keep slapping his face and throwing water on him.

Some patients stop breathing as if paralyzed while their hearts continue beating and blue blood oozes from their wounds. The doctors suspect that the Serbs used chemical weapons in the counterattack. The Yugoslav Army is known to have weaponized several chemical agents, including the nerve agent sarin. Doctors try injecting some of the patients with atropine, a medicine that blocks nerve receptors overstimulated by the chemical agent. It helps some of the men, but not the one Fatima is trying to save, who dies.

IN THE OPERATING ROOM, Nedret makes a last-ditch effort to save the life of another man with a destroyed leg who has nearly bled out before getting here. What the patient needs most is impossible in Srebrenica: a blood transfusion to improve his circulation and deliver oxygen to important tissues. While blood transfusions were pioneered back in World War I to combat the second major cause of death for amputees—blood loss—Srebrenica still has no working laboratory, no reagents to check blood type, no bags for blood storage, and no stable sources of electricity to keep blood cold.

Nedret operates as quickly as possible in an attempt to stop the bleeding. Ilijaz assists. The man dies in their hands. There is no time to process feelings of guilt or responsibility. The hospital overflows with patients whose varying injuries require urgent treatment.

Ilijaz turns next to a thirty-five-year-old man who, like the man who just died, is hemorrhaging from a leg injury. He is awake, in pain, and asking quietly for help. Ilijaz believes he is verging on shock, and expects Nedret to amputate his leg immediately.

Multiple-casualty work has its rules. Every physician learns how to triage in medical school. Those with small, non-life-threatening injuries must wait. Those with devastating injuries are given comfort. And those in danger of dying, who might be saved with a quick operation like an amputation, take the highest priority.

Ilijaz finds Nedret cleaning the wounds of an elderly man whose skin is punctured by dozens of tiny shrapnel marks. Nedret carefully cuts away injured tissue. The work is slow and methodical; it seems to calm him. He doesn't want to rush to operate on the critically injured patient. Ilijaz wonders why. Is Nedret afraid to see another patient die beneath his knife? Is he recognizing his limitations, questioning his decision to pass himself off as a qualified surgeon, thinking about the medical tenet "first do no harm"?

Ilijaz does not know it, but what troubles Nedret are thoughts of Josef Mengele. Mengele, who "researched" human pain tolerance in Holocaust concentration camps, was convicted of crimes against humanity. And Nedret thinks—although his own motives are quite different, although he has no other choice and is working with his patients' consent—that when he cuts into a living person without anesthesia he is in fact doing what Mengele did, committing torture. What bothers him above all else is the thought that he is doing something unacceptable in the view of modern humanity.

Since Nedret's arrival three days ago, Ilijaz has tiptoed quietly around him. He has held clamps, listened to moans that made him want to faint, and remained impassive in the face of Nedret's eruptions. In the hierarchy of medicine, the surgeon is the boss, and Ilijaz knows his place. But watching a patient dying just feet away from the surgeon who might be able to save him lights a fuse inside of Ilijaz. He yells for Nedret to take care of the man with the injured leg.

"Just give him an infusion and we'll see," Nedret replies, continuing to dab at the old man's superficial wounds.

In vain, Ilijaz screams back at Nedret, and then he can't stop screaming. He spins around like a machine gunner firing at everyone in the room, yelling until he's hoarse, lashing out in a way he can't remember ever lashing out before. In the back of his mind he knows the situation is futile. The man will probably die no matter what Nedret does or doesn't do. But Ilijaz has seen one too many young men die. He roars with anger. Anger at Nedret, yes, but also anger at the war, anger at the injustice of so many young, promising lives taken away by war's stupidity. Anger that nobody is helping them in Srebrenica. Anger, perhaps most of all, at his own inability to stop the suffering.

Fatima, witnessing the conflagration, tries to rouse Nedret to action. "What are you doing?" she asks him. "That patient and others are waiting." She tells him she can take care of the old man while he does the surgery. He tells her that the old man's wounds are also important and he has to finish treating them. He can't do everything at once.

Meanwhile, the man with the leg injury waits. A technician places a temporary dressing on his wound, and this small gesture mollifies him. He dies before Nedret gets to him.

Ilijaz's anger rushes inward. He suddenly wonders why he didn't attempt the operation himself. Shame fills him, dampening his anger with despondency. It makes no difference that the patient had a good chance of dying on the operating table. Right now Ilijaz cannot bear to ponder the depths of his powerlessness. He would rather blame himself for passivity. He cannot forgive himself for not having tried to save a dying man.

NEDRET, STILL WEARING HIS GREEN, BLOOD-COVERED GOWN, strides out of the hospital to take a much-needed break. In all of his weeks on the front line near Tuzla, he has never experienced anything like this. There, he worked with trained surgical colleagues and had an advanced hospital close by. Here, the buck stops with him, but the commanders who chose to wage this all-out attack don't seem to have considered this. He catches sight of one of them, Hakija Meholjić, climbing the hospital driveway to check on his injured soldiers.

"You should have warned me about the offensive!" Nedret yells at him. He would have advised the commander to hold off until the medical team was prepared to receive casualties. "You're waging war like Indians!" he says. He insists that soldiers include him in all future military planning.

11

"DEAR DOCTOR"

In Bosnia as in Vukovar, Croatia, Eric Dachy frequently finds himself arriving too late, after the violence, after the massacres. He is nervous, unable to rest. The Balkans remind him of a conflict-ridden family. He plays the role of child. Upset by the fighting, impotent to make peace, he simply watches waves of violence break over and over again.

Sometimes he dreams of his dead father. On sleepless nights he tiptoes down the staircase and pads into the office. He sits in front of his computer and plays games for hours, racking up losses.

"What am I accomplishing?" he writes in a chronicle of his experiences. "Nothing. Or very little. It's all so inadequate. Civilians don't need humanitarian assistance; they need someone to protect them by force . . . Wouldn't it be better if we slammed the door and refused to participate in this scene?"

During this time of tortured self-questioning, Eric Dachy first learns of Srebrenica. Ham radio operators report that tens of thousands of displaced Muslims desperately need medical assistance and are in danger of being overrun by Serb forces. Representatives of the U.N. High Commissioner for Refugees have negotiated for access to Srebrenica and set out several times to reach the town, but were forced to turn around when Serb military and angry Serb civilians blocked their convoys. The head of the U.N. refugee mission in Belgrade concludes that, for whatever reasons, the Serbs are particularly determined that Srebrenica not receive aid. By November 1992 it is the last surrounded enclave not to have received any international assistance since the war began, more than seven months ago. To Eric, it sounds like a place where humanitarian action wouldn't just be a coverup for international indifference, but could actually help.

Late in the month, U.N. officials reach agreement with Serb forces to transport a twenty-truck convoy of food to Srebrenica. On the way, a human wall of angry Serbian women blocks it. The women brandish axes and wooden stakes and holler, "No food for Muslims." After a humiliating three-day delay, the convoy makes it into town, arriving to scenes of jubilation. The reception at the hospital is different. The U.N. has brought food but no medical supplies. Nedret is so furious that he refuses to be interviewed by journalists who've hitched a ride into Srebrenica with the convoy. One male nurse tells a writer for the *Christian Science Monitor* that medicine was more necessary than food. "It's a disaster," he says. "Seventy percent of the people we could have saved if we had medicines."

The next day's news stories describe doctors as shocked and aghast at the "unexplained oversight." Eric Dachy responds. He packs a truck with all the supplies he thinks an isolated group of doctors in a hot war zone need: a variety of surgical kits, a range of substances for anesthesia and painkilling, and plenty of dressings, syringes, infusions, and surgical instruments. Anything that might be useful in a difficult, precarious situation. He drives to a tiny town on the Drina River across the border with Bosnia and waits for the next U.N. convoy to assemble, confident that he can convince whomever it takes to let him go to Srebrenica.

ERIC AWAKENS IN AN UNFAMILIAR HOTEL BED to a cold December morning. He slips on his thick leather jacket and walks outside into darkness. No stuttering rifle fire or shell explosions interrupt the quiet. He sips coffee and smokes a few cigarettes in a small shop on the riverside where he threw back a few plum brandies last night. In time, his two colleagues amble inside, an administrator and the head of MSF Belgium, who has made a special trip to the Balkans to visit Srebrenica.

The shopkeepers eye them with suspicion. Perhaps, Eric figures, they're being taken for spies. Then again, the owners seem more than happy to accept their German marks, hard currency being much more valuable than the rapidly inflating Yugoslav dinar. One of the men hanging around the store asks where they are from and where they are going.

Srebrenica, they tell him. "You're going to our enemies," the man says. "Go and kill them."

Eric and his colleagues walk outside of the shop and wait for the arrival of the Bosnian Serbs who control access to Srebrenica. The sun rises, but the air remains cold. When they see a helicopter land, they jog to their car and drive to meet it.

A six-foot-tall man steps out of the helicopter and onto the grass. More than a half dozen bodyguards take their places around him, wagging automatic weapons at their hips.

Even if he had never met him, Eric would recognize Dr. Radovan Karadžić, the self-proclaimed president of the Bosnian Serbs, from his news photos and television appearances. The flabby-faced, forty-seven-year-old physician has hooded eyes and a conspicuous helmet of frizzy, graying hair that juts from his forehead and falls in waves over his ears. Journalists and human rights groups have linked him to the violence and torture being carried out in various Serb-run concentration camps, and some have compared him with Adolf Hitler. Until just a few months ago, he was a Sarajevo psychiatrist.

This leader of the Bosnian Serbs isn't even from Bosnia. He comes from a troubled family of Montenegrin peasants and moved to Bosnia's capital as a teenager. He attended Sarajevo Medical School and, like Eric, studied psychology, but he fancied himself a writer, wooing his wife with lyric poetry. Later employed to instill a winning attitude in a Sarajevo soccer team, he was jailed in 1985 for fraud and misuse of public funds, but released in less than a year. Not long after, as nationalism rose in the wake of communism's fall, Karadžić began to brag of the cleft chin and familial resemblance he shared with an earlier Karadžić named Vuk, a nineteenth-century Serb nationalist. As Serbia gained autonomy from the Ottomans, he standardized the Serb language, campaigned for a "greater Serbia" comprising all lands where it was spoken, and galvanized the illiterate rural population with epic folksongs about the Serbs' historical tragedies.

In 1990, the modern Karadžić became leader of the Serb nationalist Serbian Democratic Party (SDS), established on July 12, the holiday of *Petrovdan*, St. Peter's Day. He clung to the philosophy of SDS Croatia founder Jovan Rašković, also a Sarajevo psychiatrist, who analyzed and stereotyped the various Balkan ethnic groups in a book entitled *Luda*

Zemlja (The Crazy Country). The book explained why Serbs had to assert authority over the other Yugoslav nations. In the mid-1980s, Rašković helped draft a memorandum of the Serbian Academy of Arts and Sciences arguing that Serbia was being discriminated against economically and that Serbs were being subjected to genocide in parts of Yugoslavia. Just before dying in 1992, he took public responsibility for creating the emotional strain on the Serbian people that "lit the fuse of Serbian nationalism" and led to war.

Now Karadžić, who refers to Bosnian Muslims as the successors of the Ottoman occupiers so resented by the Serbs, is thought by analysts to be using psychiatric theories to create terror in civilian populations and to incite the Bosnian Serb public to violence. Fellow psychiatrists in the United States describe him as a "malignant narcissist" with dreams of messianic glory.

Eric has already met Karadžić. Over the summer, when rumors of concentration camps in Serb-controlled areas emerged, Eric wrote him a letter, threatening to cut off MSF support for Serb areas unless Karadžić met with visiting MSF France board members. Karadžić agreed, and during the meeting, he complimented MSF's work, denied the camps were anything more than prisons, and invited MSF to work in two of them.

Eric felt that there was nothing they could do to help people who were being locked up and tortured in concentration camps. He met some of the Red Cross and U.N. workers who visited the camps tossing back beers in the Belgrade bars and talking about the "interesting stories" they heard interviewing men who'd been beaten and tortured. It was easy to see horrible things—very easy. Meanwhile, their reports would be filed in cabinets and nothing would come of them. No, Eric would not run to see those horrors.

Still, the MSF board members brought the idea of working in the camps all the way back to France where Rony Brauman—the MSF leader who'd called for military action against the Serbs—rejected it out of hand as unthinkable. He would never allow his organization's staff members to become the medical auxiliaries of executioners and torturers. In a camp there would be no chance for independence, a fundamental principle of humanitarian work. There would be, in Doctors Without Borders lingo, no "humanitarian space."

Now, in front of the helicopter, Eric meets Karadžić again.

"Dear doctor," the Serb nationalist leader greets Eric, shaking hands and baring his lower row of teeth as he speaks. "I'm so happy to meet you. I'd like to be meeting you in some other circumstances. Isn't this all so sad?"

Eric is tempted to tell him to stop what he is doing to cause the situation, but the sight of Karadžić's armed bodyguards keeps him quiet. Karadžić strikes him as a paranoid Mafia chief who wouldn't shrink from having his men kill someone who embarrasses him. Eric bites back his anger and shakes the leader's hand, explaining that the MSF team wants to visit Srebrenica to assess the medical situation. He asks that MSF personnel be allowed to join the U.N. convoy, which is to depart in the morning for Srebrenica.

"Yes, of course, no problem," Karadžić agrees in a gravelly voice.

Having Darth Vader as an ally is useful. Eric and his colleagues join several U.N. Protection Force soldiers in an armored personnel carrier, an APC, a boxy, claustrophobic, armor-plated vehicle with tiny windows and Red Cross symbols on its sides. They set off in a column of trucks carrying medicines and other humanitarian supplies from MSF and the U.N.

At one of numerous Bosnian Serb checkpoints, Eric stands outside to smoke. He looks into the windows of a passenger bus that pulls up beside him and catches the gaze of a small boy, ten or eleven years old. The boy lifts his finger to his neck, sliding it silently across his throat.

The closer to Srebrenica the convoy draws, the angrier the people seem. At some checkpoints, soldiers snarl and swear at them.

"We Serbs just want to survive," one says. "The whole world is against us."

The two-mile journey down the road from Bratunac to the border of the Srebrenica enclave stretches on for hours. At last the trucks reach a short stretch of road that runs over an almost invisible creek. Looking out of the tiny windows of the personnel carrier, Eric can see small, flat fields that appear to have been cultivated. Beyond them are leafless forests of deciduous trees, a few clutches of evergreens, and mountains. The maps the drivers carry name these mountains—to the left, one called Chaus, and to the right, one called Zvijezda. The topographical lines beside the town are squeezed together, indicating that Srebrenica stretches along a deep valley.

At one point, yellow-painted guardrails, mounted on blocks of concrete, border the street as it crosses a small river. This "yellow bridge" no longer connects the municipalities of Srebrenica and Bratunac. For the past eight months, the unremarkable piece of asphalt has served as a dividing line between the Muslims and Serbs, as impassable as a gaping drawbridge.

The convoy crosses it at about 1:30 in the afternoon, and Srebrenica's soldiers quickly wave them past. The trucks trundle along the road for a mile and begin to pass burnt houses and abandoned factories of the former Potočari industrial zone. Then the people start coming. Wraith-like figures appear from every direction. By the time the houses lining the road give way to a soccer field, and the road curves hard to the left to reveal the first buildings of Srebrenica, thousands of folks have thronged the roadsides.

The convoy grinds to a stop before a building on a hill. Eric Dachy steps out of the APC, stretches his legs, and looks around. The people, gaunt and dirty, stare at him. Many women wear patterned handkerchiefs on their heads. Some hold babies. The adults flash smiles that contrast with their sallow, stricken faces. Most of the children look tired and expressionless. Eric can't believe he's here.

He hears a loud noise and senses something traveling overhead. A shell bursts nearby, its thunder echoing off the hills and making the ground tremble. Eric jumps, and the crowd around him snickers. They know that the explosions you hear are not the ones that kill you.

They've become experts, Eric thinks, noting their calm and wondering what will prevent the next shell from landing in the middle of the crowd.

As he reaches for a cigarette, a Bosnian man standing near him pantomimes that he wants one, too. Innocently, Eric draws another Marlboro from the pack and hands it to the man. A commotion of unintelligible, angry voices breaks out. Eric asks what has happened and someone tells him that a pack of cigarettes goes for 100 German marks, minimum—more than sixty dollars.

Eric thinks he might as well have stepped off a spaceship from Mars. Cigarettes for 100 marks? The place is shockingly isolated. He supposes the people jostling each other in the crowd are hungry and scared; he questions whether they understand what he has come to do. He becomes intensely aware of his freedom to leave.

Eric's attention turns to the purpose of his visit—to assess the medical situation in the town. He and his colleagues move toward the hospital, a rectangular building that resembles a schoolhouse on the hill above where the convoy has stopped.

A tall man approaches. He wears combat shoes and battle fatigues that sport a patch with the Bosnian fleur-de-lis. He has on a beret and, rather ridiculously on this late fall afternoon, a pair of shiny sunglasses.

Eric shakes his hand with discomfort. The man introduces himself as Dr. Nedret Mujkanović, Srebrenica Hospital war surgeon.

He looks more like an elite officer than a Good Samaritan.

They walk up the hospital's steep driveway and enter the building from behind, where it abuts a high hill. The moment Eric steps inside, foul air gags him. It reeks of dead tissue and everything that comes out of a human body—urine, feces, pus, and sweat.

They climb a stairway encased in thick-paneled glass windows, emerge on the second floor, and head down a high-ceilinged hallway with orange-painted walls. The Bosnian doctor unlocks a door, pressing down on its tapered silver handle. It opens into a private office, a small room with white tiled walls, green chairs, a bed, sink, and bookcase. Eric and the others seat themselves on the chairs, and the Bosnian doctor sits down on his bed, beneath the window.

Nedret removes his sunglasses. He has a broad face with high cheekbones, a cleft chin, sensual mouth, and elegant, well-shaped eyebrows. What strikes Eric the most are his soft, slightly crossed eyes. Eric sees in them exactly what most of Srebrenica's civilians—from the hundreds of patients Nedret has treated to the female nurse he comforted on their journey through the woods into Srebrenica—see whenever they look at Nedret: gentleness and kindness.

Eric and his colleagues explain who they are and what MSF is, and they tell Nedret that they've brought some medical supplies.

"Thank you for your help," the Bosnian doctor says. "We really need some."

Nedret looks askance at the U.N. translator, a Serb from Belgrade, apparently worried that what he is about to say will not be translated correctly.

"We're in a desperate situation," he begins.

He admits that he isn't a trained surgeon. He tells of his journey on foot to Srebrenica. Although he has done his best the past few months, now, in December 1992, he is tired and almost completely out of supplies, trapped in Srebrenica along with the rest of the population, ready to get out and go back home. He asks Eric for help.

"Everything is wrong here," he says. "I really need support."

Eric and his colleagues meet Dr. Ilijaz Pilav and follow him into the hallway, illuminated only by light from a window at its far end. Ilijaz takes them on a tour, ushering them into a room to have a look at some patients, and everyone's nose, just growing accustomed to the hospital's stench, is reminded of it again, more intensely than before. A row of beds separated by nightstands runs along both sides of the room. On each bed lies a patient. On each patient lies a dirty, stained bed sheet. That is all. No IV bags drip, no machines beep, no bottles of medicine sit on the nightstands.

On one of the beds, a small girl lies crying. Eric sees that she has a broken arm. Where there should be a cast supporting the arm and helping it heal, two tree branches are affixed with Scotch tape.

Eric has to control his impulse to demand, "How the hell can you leave patients in such a condition?" But he reminds himself that the whole place is a nightmare, the whole city.

"I want to show you what I brought," he tells the Bosnian doctors.

They walk into the room where volunteers have unloaded Eric's supplies—dozens of brown cardboard boxes, each the weight a healthy young person can heft, each labeled with a code. The boxes contain essential drugs, instruments, surgical supplies, and plenty of bandages. Eric explains to the doctors that the contents of each kit are written in their language and that they should open all the boxes, remove the supplies from the polystyrene chips, and sort like items for their convenience. Looking at their exhausted, passive faces, he fears they won't do it.

He leaves the hospital with his colleagues in the late afternoon. Tall hills block the waning sun. They descend the steep driveway and return to the convoy. On the hill above their vehicle, the hospital looms over them in the dying light.

Heartbroken by what he's just seen, Eric is tempted to stay and pitch in with the medical work. But with no communications equipment or supply lines and little ability to operate in Srebrenica with autonomy, he feels he doesn't have the conditions to do so. He ducks back into the

APC. After the convoy crosses over the front lines, it is again stopped in Bratunac. This time the policemen are eager for news of old friends and colleagues. One of them asks about a former classmate.

"Do you know, is he alive?"

Again, the war in eastern Bosnia reminds Eric of a passionate fight between brothers. On the way back to Belgrade, Eric questions whether the fact that they reached Srebrenica, even with their valuable medical kits, has meant anything. He thinks of the white-coated medical staff standing up in the hallways to shake hands. They seem to have had just enough strength to put on their dirty gowns. In the rooms behind them nobody has thought to separate children with burns—very susceptible to infection—from people with lung infections. A patient's broken femur wasn't even stretched into traction. And the most vivid image in his mind is of that crying little girl, with her pathetic homemade splint.

They could have devised something better for her, he thinks. All of it lends the impression of a medical team so overwhelmed by the situation that they are no longer able to see what they *can* achieve. They've all but given up. Eric thinks the burned-out, unmotivated doctors are finished. He doubts whether they will muster the strength to start treating their patients, even with the new supplies.

AFTER ERIC AND THE INTERNATIONALS LEAVE the hospital, Ilijaz, Fatima, and Srebrenica's other doctors and nurses bustle back up two sets of stairs and practically race to the small room where brown cardboard boxes filled with tons of medical supplies have been deposited. They pass around the packing lists.

"Penicillin." "Ampicillin." "Erythromycin."

Ilijaz cannot believe it! He rips open a box.

Sterile compresses. Bandages.

Ripppp.

Sutures. *Good* sutures.

Rippp.

It's all here. Every last item on the lists.

Each hospital room has a notebook. On each page, a nurse has made columns for the names of the patients in the room, their birth dates, daily temperature readings, blood pressure readings, and therapy. The spaces for therapy are uniformly blank. Patients have died for lack of basic drugs.

Now, the doctors and nurses stride through the hospital from end to end. They fill in the "therapy" column for each patient—antibiotics to fight infection, analgetics to fight pain, benzodiazepines to reduce anxiety. Ilijaz feels his heart growing bigger inside of his chest. It is a big day, he thinks, a big happening. He feels strong again. He feels that he can do something.

———————

WHEN ERIC RETURNS TO THE MSF OFFICE in Belgrade, he thinks of Vukovar and its hospital and the doctors killed there. He believes it will happen to Srebrenica, too. The city is a dying place, a place likely to be overrun, like most of the other non-Serb pockets in Bosnia, its population massacred, raped, deported. Unless . . .

He can think of one thing that might make a positive difference—install an MSF team in the town, at least one international surgeon, nurse, and assistant. Not only will they provide needed support at the hospital, but their presence could also play a protective role. They could stay until the war is over. They could interpose between victims and killers. This is where MSF has to be.

Eric plots his strategy. Then he begins writing. The first message goes by fax the next day to MSF headquarters in Brussels. Eric summarizes the trip to Srebrenica, lays out the need for an "urgent and important" MSF intervention, and outlines two obstacles to his plan: one is security and the other is the potential hostility of local Serb authorities to the presence of an international medical team.

Eric also drafts a proposal for collaboration to be sent to top UNHCR representatives, describing the devastating medical situation in the town and calling the placement of a permanent medical team in Srebrenica "crucial to aiding the population." He asks that the UNHCR help transport MSF volunteers on future aid convoys.

Another letter is for Dr. Nedret. Eric has it translated and sent along with a U.N. convoy of food and medical supplies that reaches Srebrenica a few days later. In typed Bosnian script on letterhead that says "MEDECINS SANS FRONTIERES," it reads:

"Dragi Dr. Mujkanović. . . ."
Dear Dr. Mujkanović.

During our visit I was very touched to see the hard conditions in which you work and live. I'm sorry that this time I won't be able to visit you, because I need to negotiate our next couple of trips into Srebrenica in Belgrade. . . .

I hope that you found the aid helpful and that you used it well. We sent you the specific aid that you requested in the amount that our finances allowed us, and I hope that you'll put this to good use, too. Our organization has decided to help you (for example, to send you the surgeon you asked for) but for now things are out of our hands. I hope that we'll find a solution by the beginning of January. While we're waiting for that we would like to keep in touch with you. We'll do that through our visits with the convoys, and we'll bring you as much as we can of the aid that you asked for. And don't hesitate to let our team know all your needs and all your problems.

I wish you much courage and hope that I'll see you soon.
Eric Dachy

Eric writes the final letter to Dr. Radovan Karadžić, the president of the Bosnian Serbs, convinced that access to Srebrenica hinges on his approval. He types a draft in French and shares it with his colleagues: "To the President of the Serb Republic, Dr. Radovan Karadžić."

Mr. President,

Thanks to a benevolent intervention on your part, a team from MSF was able to reach the town of Srebrenica. What we discovered there, among the civilian population, alarmed us greatly: There are no means of treating people; there are too few medical personnel; numerous children suffer and die there without the most simple modern medical materials available to save them.

Will that news horrify or please him? Eric does not know. He writes that he wishes to place a surgeon, nurse, and assistant in Srebrenica and appeals for the leader's approval of the plan.

As a doctor and as one responsible for the destiny of your people, we know you are sensitive to the weight of human suffering and we hope that you will look favorably on our suggestion. I hope equally that you are convinced of our impartiality and of our neutrality. Thanks to the excellent relations that we maintain with your representatives, we were already able to bring important help in the form of surgical equipment to the hospitals of the Serb Republic.

Eric writes that he plans to send an international surgeon to the hospital of a neighboring Serb-held town, demonstrating that MSF is eager to provide aid to all innocent victims, regardless of their origins, as long as the leader gives his agreement.

"We have confidence in your generosity," Eric concludes, "and we thank you in advance."

He sends the letter. Then, just days after the arrival of the three convoys, and perhaps emboldened by them, several hundred armed men from Srebrenica launch a surprise attack on a series of small villages near the Drina River east of Bratunac. The villages, previously mixed Serb and Muslim, were brutally emptied of Muslims in the war's early days and are now populated exclusively by Serbs.

Eric sends a team of MSF nurses to the area on an aid convoy from Belgrade three days later. The group arrives at the Bratunac health clinic on the Serb side of the front line, where doctors and nurses have treated 110 people injured in the attacks, performing first aid and overseeing transfer of the seriously injured to hospitals in Bosnia and Serbia. They've examined at least fifty-eight bodies; many are mutilated.

The team declines an offer to view the dead Serbs in the clinic's basement, wishing to avoid the appearance of voyeurism. However, they agree to see a videotape. Its graphic succession of naked bodies, which the doctors assert have not only been ripped apart by explosives, but also mutilated by the Srebrenica Muslims, horrifies them. They cannot discern whether the mutilations occurred before or after death.

"Castrated, breasts cut off, knee tendons severed, hands torn off, faces slashed," the MSF team writes in a report, adding that the Serb health clinic staff appears "beaten down, exhausted and very sad."

During the attack, Serb civilians had fled toward the Drina River. Some were captured, some killed, including, according to a doctor, two Serb medics. Srebrenica soldiers and civilians also raided homes, taking food, shoes, and other items—perhaps some of their own stolen belong-ings—and setting house after house ablaze before withdrawing.

In contrast to the medical workers across the front line in Srebrenica, those in Bratunac have ample supplies and can transfer the severely wounded to hospitals. However, they, too, labor under shellfire and treat wounded people daily. This is not the first time that butchered bod-ies have arrived after an offensive launched by the Srebrenicans.

The Serbs vent their fury not only at the Srebrenicans, but also at the U.N. Protection Force. Despite the fact that Serb soldiers had searched the aid convoys from tip to top, poking open the bags of flour with bayo-nets, the Bratunac daily paper insinuates that the convoys delivered arms to Srebrenica.

But arms are not the only weapons of war.

"The Muslims got their strength back from the convoy," a Serbian soldier tells a Reuters reporter.

Plans for another U.N. convoy to continue on its way to Srebrenica are scrapped. Over the coming days, Serb authorities refuse to approve further aid to Srebrenica. The UNHCR suspends convoys indefinitely.

12

SPECIAL K

NEDRET CHERISHES ERIC DACHY'S LETTER. The medical aid and the recent successful offensive have cheered him and restored his energy. They have brought him, finally, a medicine so powerful it makes patients on his operating table sing, and so mysterious that it challenges Nedret's highly intelligent mind.

The four months Nedret has spent here have been the most exciting and depressing of his life. He has relished his ability to participate in two major aspects of life in Srebrenica—performing all of its surgeries, and providing input on all of its military offensives. From the day he'd chastised Commander Hakija Meholjić for "waging war like Indians" and failing to inform the hospital of an attack, he'd been in on all the planning. The mix of his military and humanitarian roles would make ethicists at the Red Cross cringe.

A typical morning for Nedret begins with a walk to the hospital. On quiet days, he chats with people on the road. On other days, shelling forces him to stop and take cover. Once he heard something tumbling down the hill beside him. He froze, but when no explosion followed, went to investigate. Sticking out of the ground just feet away was the tail of a 2.24-inch rocket, miraculously unexploded.

At the hospital Nedret meets with doctors and nurses, finds out who has come in during the night, assesses the condition of his patients, and examines them if necessary. Then, using instruments the nurses have sterilized overnight by boiling, he starts with surgeries. They take place in the operating room, which he moved upstairs, away from the busy hospital entrance, to reduce his patients' risk of infection.

When he works all day, he takes breaks in the "green room," a lounge he set up next to the OR with green armchairs taken from the town's cultural center and a large shelf for medical books he's collected. People stop by to chat—friends he's cultivated, civilian and military leaders.

Nedret is perhaps the only man in Srebrenica always flush with cigarettes. Giving gifts to doctors, a tradition even before the war, has increased among patients and family members desperate for the hospital's limited supplies and the doctors' limited time.

In the late afternoon, on days he can leave the hospital, Nedret walks back through the town, socializing with the idle townspeople who spend the days standing around outside their dim, overcrowded, poorly ventilated apartments despite the freezing temperatures and daily risk of shelling. Nedret savors his contacts with those he calls "the regular people." Most of the other doctors wish they could avoid them. The one-and-a-quarter-mile walk takes Nedret past houses and apartment buildings with entryways bordered by giant piles of wood cut from Srebrenica's now denuded hills.

He ends his commute by climbing a small hill up the driveway of the Domavija Hotel, past the anti-aircraft gun stationed there. It has a seat, two pedals, two wheels for aiming, and three gun barrels. Once Nedret heard a Serb airplane overhead when nobody else was around and tried firing it himself, opening his mouth to equalize the pressure before the blasts. He missed, of course, but is proud of having tried.

Hotel Domavija, his home in Srebrenica, houses a gaggle of soldiers loyal to Nedret's friend, the commander Hakija Meholjić, whom they call "chief of the Hotel Fresh Air" because the hotel hardly has any intact windows. It faces a hill called Bojna, similar to a Bosnian word meaning battle. Nedret's room, marked "317" on top of the door, faces the other way, toward a hill called Kozaric, which means goat pen.

When he arrives from the hospital, workers bring him hot water to wash off the day's blood and grime. By the light from a small generator—a special luxury for the doctor—he types his day's medical notes.

A chef named Dule concocts remarkable delicacies from the available food stocks, and every day at 8 A.M. and 6 P.M., unless they are at the front, the soldiers eat on wooden chairs in a wood-paneled dining hall with stone floors, reminiscent of a hunting lodge. Nedret sometimes joins them.

At night his friends gather, using small torches to find their way through the dark halls of the hotel to his room. Nedret holds court, rolling tobacco, smoking and sometimes sipping a patient's gift of home-made *rakija,* plum brandy, surrounded by the soldiers who idolize him. They play cards, talk and joke, or listen to the radio—Belgrade news, Sarajevo news, Zagreb news, the Voice of America—while garrulously trading their own political analyses.

Some nights Nedret engages in other activities. Tall, beautiful Alma, ten years his junior, becomes a steady visitor after he cares for her injured sister. One of Srebrenica's few female soldiers, she sates what he considers his "human need" for companionship in the stressful war zone where he imagines he may die. He is far from the only married man to take a girlfriend.

One night the men conjure a worst-case scenario—what if Srebrenica is overtaken and they have to flee for their lives through the woods? What should they take? How could they make it?

"We shouldn't burden ourselves taking cans of food or flour," Nedret advises Commander Hakija. "If you have an ounce of salt or a pound of sugar, you can survive fifteen days in the wilderness without anything else."

Wouldn't they lose weight? Hakija asks.

Losing weight doesn't matter, Nedret says. What's important is to keep the brain functioning, to maintain the ability to make sound decisions, to keep from hallucinating. Salt and sugar, he insists, are the way to go.

Sometimes Nedret travels to the field to meet people living in the outlying areas. As a proud and curious member of the Srebrenica war council, eager to give confidence to the soldiers, he tours every yard of the front lines and visits distant medical stations.

He even witnesses some war actions, viewing the fighting from a distance and watching as thousands upon thousands of civilians pour in, like a lava flow, to pillage Serb villages. By their sheer numbers and the thunder of their voices, the howling, bag-carrying hordes help scare Serb inhabitants away. The rushing plunderers have earned a fake military designation, the "HPO division." The "H" stands for *hapsi,* a Bosnian word for petty thieves. If 1,000 soldiers take part in an action, the HPO division adds at least 3,000.

It is the rumbling of their empty stomachs that sets these *hapsi* on the heels of the soldiers. They come out of hunger and need and anger, many of them displaced from their own homes. Nedret sees them raging out of control, disobeying directives not to destroy things. Serb civilians lie dead in their wake.

Part of the reason the Serbs guard humanitarian access to Srebrenica so jealously is that it's one of the few areas of Bosnia where Muslims have fought back successfully, with such punishing and brutal effect. Nedret credits himself with some of this success, priding himself for having helped broker cooperation between some of Srebrenica's rival commanders, men who might have preferred to kill one another instead of killing Serb soldiers. Indeed, it has happened—the commander of a neighboring town, a man with whom Nedret walked part way to Srebrenica, was allegedly assassinated by those envious of his power.

Nedret packs his own pistol to and from work—a .25 caliber Beretta—although he makes other soldiers leave their weapons behind to enter the hospital. He likes war toys. His hotel room houses a small arsenal of guns that he's collected here, such as his Heckler, the fast-shooting special automatic useful for street fights that reminds him of terrorists in the movies, a Scorpion, and a homemade pipe gun. Even the soldiers refer to Nedret as "a little 'wild west.'"

Making friends with the soldiers has its downside, though, because soldiers tend to die. In October, Nedret's friend, the brave and wily Akif Ustić, the man who had visited Ilijaz's fighters at the start of the war and led an action, was caught in an ambush. Legend has it that as he lay wounded, he shot at the Chetniks with all the bullets he had. All save one, in fact, which he'd used on himself. He had been on his way to Sase to fetch hay for the livestock he cultivated for the army.

Perhaps Nedret's involvement in the military stemmed, in part, from the helplessness he felt in the hospital. Since the convoys, things have changed. The patients in his operating room sing, lost in psychedelic dreams, feeling no pain. The greatest gift the convoys have brought Nedret comes as a clear liquid in a misleadingly plain vial: ketamine. Even its pharmaceutical brand names seem to hint at this drug's mysterious effects—it's known as "Calypsol" in the Bahamas, "Soon-Soon" in Taiwan. Street users call it Special K or Vitamin K and take it alone or cut with Ecstasy.

Ketamine's history is enmeshed with the histories of both general anesthesia and drugs of abuse. As opposed to local anesthetics, which numb just the nerves or the region where they are injected, general anesthetics induce unconsciousness and a lack of response to painful stimuli. With patients anesthetized and their muscles relaxed, surgeons perform long, complicated operations that would never be possible on conscious, sentient patients.

General anesthetics, introduced in 1846, first auditioned for wartime during the Mexican and Crimean wars. Their widespread employment, however, came with the American Civil War. Roughly 80,000 times, in places such as Mission Ridge, Tennessee, under cover of pine forests, men whose legs and arms were injured by the famous Civil War rifle bullets, such as the heavy and deforming Minié, were laid out on crude operating tables. Just before the surgeon raised his blade to amputate, someone placed a funnel-shaped "bonnet" lined with raw, chloroform-saturated cotton over the patient's nose and mouth. He slipped into blissful unconsciousness. The race to make better and better anesthetics began.

In the late 1950s, more than 100 years after the birth of general anesthesia, a scientist named V. H. Maddox and colleagues produced a compound named phencyclidine. Surgeons started using it to put patients to sleep during surgery, but soon found it caused hallucinations and delirium as patients awoke. So PCP promptly left the operating room and migrated to the street where, as angel dust, zombie, whack, supergrass, killer weed, embalming fluid, peace pill, and rocket fuel, it gave its users feelings of strength, power, invulnerability, numbness, out-of-body experiences, and an inordinate quantity of bad trips.

In an effort to capitalize on the anesthetic properties of PCP while minimizing its psychological effects, scientists synthesized at least 200 derivatives of the chemical and found one—double ring-shaped $C_{13}H_{16}ClNO$—that worked best on laboratory animals. Named ketamine in the late 1960s, it soon became clear this PCP relative also caused dramatic psychic reactions on emergence from anesthesia. Patients experienced everything from vivid imagery and pleasant dreams to delirium and disturbing hallucinations. Again, the drug traveled to the street. This time it stayed in the operating room, too, for several specific uses— trauma victims with blood loss, patients suffering septic shock from infection, and those at poor risk for other forms of anesthesia.

In technically advanced operating rooms, anesthesiologists employ a complicated array of drugs—both injected and inhaled—and use sophisticated electronic monitoring devices to administer anesthesia. Mechanized ventilators breathe for patients whose own airway reflexes are dampened by anesthetics or thwarted by paralytic agents. But where trauma patients need urgent surgery in an environment without trained anesthetists or a stable source of electricity to deliver gases, monitor vital signs, and ventilate lungs, most of the typical anesthetics won't do. In conditions like the ones Nedret faces in Srebrenica, in spite of its bizarre psychological effects, ketamine is the drug of choice.

Tiny and easily dissolved in fat, it slips through the tight spaces and lipid-filled membranes of the blood-brain barrier. Within thirty seconds of a nurse injecting the drug, a patient is completely unconscious and ready to undergo surgery, airway reflexes intact, breathing spontaneously without need for a ventilator. Unlike many other anesthetics, ketamine does not depress the heart and respiratory systems. It wears off quickly, too. Within five to ten minutes, unless more drug is injected, it distributes to other, less perfused body areas. Within fifteen to thirty minutes, patients are awake and oriented to person, place, and time.

It's hard to kill someone with ketamine. Even if a doctor or nurse mistakenly administers ten times the therapeutic dose, the patient usually just has a good, long sleep.

A PATIENT SINGS DURING HIS OPERATION, and Nedret remembers that the instructions for ketamine warned of "psychomotor effects." He hadn't known what that meant. After the patient wakes up, Nedret asks him about his experiences. He says he didn't feel the operation and had a pleasant dream, although he can't remember it.

Each time he administers ketamine, Nedret monitors his patients' responses, fascinated. Some stay calm throughout surgery and others thrash and appear agitated. Nedret experiments with adding a relaxant, Valium, and finds that high doses in combination with ketamine help to keep his patients calm. But not always.

One day he performs a difficult double amputation. The patient, a muscular man in his late thirties, has sustained severe injuries to his right arm and leg in a mine explosion. Ketamine and Valium are administered and the nurses and doctors arrange the patient on the operating table, securing his left arm and leg to the table with bandages.

They anticipate a difficult operation, and tension pervades the operating room. Nedret knows he has to work quickly in order to minimize blood loss. Instruments fly from hand to hand. Voices rise. The patient grimaces and, with an aggressive expression, starts to lift himself from the table like Frankenstein's monster. The bandage holding his left arm snaps.

Nedret shouts, and immediately the patient's movements become more exaggerated, causing short-tempered Nedret to shout even louder. A handful of men have to hold the patient down. Nedret leans over, using his elbow to pin the man's right leg as he ties off bleeding blood vessels with lengths of suture.

After he finishes, Nedret theorizes that the agitation of the medical staff influenced the behavior of the patient. During the next operation, he tries an experiment. He speaks loudly. The patient becomes aggressive. When he hushes the staff for several minutes, the patient becomes calm.

These experiences intrigue Nedret. He is probably using too little drug, resulting in a partially awake patient. But some of the patients' movements are due to the so-called dissociative effects of the drug. Unlike other types of anesthesia that resemble normal sleep, ketamine produces a state similar to schizophrenic catalepsy, in which a rigid, insensate patient loses contact with the environment while keeping his eyes open and maintaining many reflexes. The patient often makes coordinated but purposeless movements.

Why does this happen? From what scientists have been able to gather, ketamine plays with the brain, turning off some areas and exciting others, wreaking disorganization. It also appears to block the transmission of pain information as it travels toward brain areas responsible for the emotional aspects of pain sensation and it affects the same brain-cell receptors as morphine does.

Unlike most agents used to induce anesthesia, ketamine has significant painkilling effects that outlast a patient's period of unconsciousness. That effect is welcomed in Srebrenica. For the first time in months, hope fills the hospital, as sweet, deceptive, and ephemeral as a good shot of ketamine.

13

HOLIDAYS IN HELL

ALL THE NEW MEDICINES and supplies in the world can't change the fact that there are only seven doctors to care for the perhaps 70,000 non-Serbs corralled into this part of eastern Bosnia. A ratio of one physician to 10,000 patients is more than fifteen times lower than the peacetime norm in Bosnia and twenty-five times lower than in the United States. For a population caught in a war zone, it is unthinkably low, particularly because none of Srebrenica's doctors are trained surgeons and only two have completed a residency in any sort of medical specialty. Nedret, Ilijaz, Fatima, Ejub, and Branka have become war doctors practically straight out of medical school.

Those who suffer from medical illnesses steer clear of the hospital, which is filled to capacity with injured soldiers and civilians. Dr. Nijaz Džanić, the dark-haired internist who had a heart attack before the war and stayed in Srebrenica to care for his ailing parents, treats the civilian sick on the other side of town, in a house attached to an old mosque with a wooden minaret. He established the clinic, on a hill near the Hotel Domavija, after the other doctors returned to reopen Srebrenica's hospital last July. The forty-two-year-old doctor works with one young, curly-haired nurse and manages to keep the clinic open twelve hours a day, seven days a week. Srebrenica's civilians keep him busy changing their wound dressings, measuring their blood pressure, and treating their sick children. Nijaz never turns them away. When supplies and medicines ran dry before last month's convoys, he sent locals to pick herbs such as *nana* (mint) for stomachaches and *zhara* for anemia and to collect pine tree resin for rheumatism. The compassionate and reassuring way he prescribed them seemed to make them work almost as well as modern medicines.

It's almost impossible to fathom what it would be like if one of the town's overworked doctors were lost. But moving back and forth between home and workplace exposes them to risk, and they all experience close calls. One night, as shells fell during his walk home from the hospital, Ilijaz clambered into the covered part of the dirty, stinking river that runs parallel to Srebrenica's main street, known as "the collector," because of its tendency to collect garbage. Once last summer, he heard the buzz of a plane and had just a moment to turn toward the entrance of his building before, with a sudden crescendo, the Russian MiG dove and rocket explosions blasted him into the corridor against the staircase. Nedret, lightly wounded several times, has removed pieces of shrapnel from himself.

There is an urgent need for more doctors, especially as Nedret, Ilijaz, and the others begin to burn out under the flame of constant responsibility. Ham radio operators continue to transmit requests to Tuzla for relief. Then, a few days after the last aid convoy and the offensive toward the Drina, thirty-six injured and frostbitten men stumble into town, some carrying others. They are remnants of a group of 102 who set out for Srebrenica from Tuzla, bent beneath American-made rucksacks filled with fifty to one hundred pounds of German medicines and munitions bought in Croatia by refugees from eastern Bosnia. Serb soldiers laid an ambush. Some of the Muslims managed to get away. Lost in the snowy hills, they trekked for twenty-one days in sub-zero weather, running out of food.

Most of those who embarked on the trip were soldiers, but not all. Two experienced internal medicine specialists and three nurses volunteered to return to Srebrenica and help ease the crushing load on the medical staff. They refused on humanitarian principle to carry guns and munitions, and the men who reach Srebrenica haven't seen or heard from the medical workers since the ambush.

The survivors are hospitalized, put on the intravenous drips they carried with themselves, fed, warmed by the heat of the hospital's wood stoves, and given pain medication. One dies. Others need their toes amputated. Meanwhile, everyone hopes against hope that the medical workers who set out on the trip are still alive and will make it to Srebrenica.

AS THE NEW YEAR OF 1993 DAWNS, the concerns of Ejub, the still-chubby pediatrics resident from the village near Ilijaz's parents' home, center on missing his wife and son and missing cigarettes. He pines in public for his beautiful Mubina and pens two poems for her, between gulps of plum brandy, on New Year's Eve.

"Others say they left their wives. I left my heart," he tells his colleagues again and again.

One cold, wintry day he trudges back to the house where he sheltered the first night of the war and rediscovers dozens of half-smoked cigarettes, the ones he thoughtlessly discarded during his first experience with shelling. Now, on his hands and knees, he gathers up every last one. Treasures.

Ilijaz also scrounges for something to smoke, puffing on whatever leaves he can find or his patients give him. First he wraps them in some blank, white paper left in his apartment by the previous tenants. When that's gone, he cuts around the edges of their personal documents for cigarette paper, and finally, when nothing else is left, he smokes the entire documents.

Ilijaz finds little time for romance with Fatima. He looks out for her, though, taking her place in the field when organized actions occur, trying to keep her out of danger. Their shared life ended in September when she moved out of his apartment to join her newly arrived mother and brother in a three-room flat granted by municipal authorities. As other displaced relatives moved into town, the occupancy of her wood-smoke-choked abode grew to ten people. Then forty.

New Year's Eve has always been Fatima's favorite holiday. The couple sits in Ilijaz's dark apartment with friends, trying to wrest some sort of New Year's cheer from the wartime gloom. This year they do not talk about the future.

WITH AID CONVOYS ON HOLD and Serb forces engaging in a strong counterattack, supplies peter out. The doctors hoard the remaining medicines. Almost a month after the last convoy, food is again in desperately short supply. Srebrenica's soldiers plan an offensive on Serb villages, calculating the expected weight and types of goods that might be captured in different places. They choose January 7, Serb Orthodox Christmas, the second time they have launched an attack on an Orthodox holiday. And they choose Kravica, a historic center for Serb nationalism whose inhabitants fought against the Ottoman Empire in the late nineteenth and early twentieth centuries and armed and trained local Serbs for this war.

Ilijaz slips out of Srebrenica by cover of night to set up a medical field station near the front. At 8 on the icy, snowy morning, patients begin to arrive at his station, their legs and stomachs heavily injured by mine explosions. Ilijaz cuts away dead tissue and dresses the wounds, administers painkillers, and organizes transport to the hospital.

Meanwhile, more than a thousand Muslim troops brave minefields, shoot, and shell their way past a thin line of defense and pour into the Serb-held village of Kravica. According to Serb sources, roughly four dozen Serbs are killed, most of them soldiers. The Muslim side counts about two dozen dead.

By late afternoon, some soldiers are stuffing their mouths full of cakes from the elaborate Christmas dinners left behind by the handful of village women who lived in Kravica. The air fills with the yodels and shouts of thousands of hungry Srebrenicans who follow the soldiers to gather sheep, cows, and oxen from the barns, potatoes and cabbage from the cellars, and anything else they can scrounge. Smoke billows toward the sky from dozens, perhaps hundreds, of houses set alight.

As much as Srebrenica's hungry civilians regard the attack as a desperate bid for food, Kravica is also a strategic military target linking Srebrenica with the two Muslim-held enclaves of Konjević Polje and Cerska to the northwest. With Kravica, Srebrenica's soldiers, under commander Naser Orić, now control about 350 square miles of territory, coming close to the front lines with Tuzla. Just five more miles and they will break the siege and link Srebrenica with the bulk of Bosnian government–controlled territory.

"Kravica is ours!!!" an ecstatic medical assistant in Konjević Polje writes in Bosnian in her diary. Since the war started, nurses there have performed amputations by themselves in houses, using plum brandy in place of any anesthetics. Now patients from the village, which has no medical doctors, can be transported by family members to Srebrenica Hospital. Unfortunately, this only adds to the burden on the already overworked Srebrenica doctors. The physicians from Tuzla who tried to join them last month and were ambushed have never arrived.

JUST AS EXCITING AS THE WIN IS TO THE SREBRENICANS, it is humiliating, tragic, and highly symbolic to the Serbs. Four days after the offensive, on January 11, at 11 A.M., after morning rounds, the loud buzz of a low-flying airplane shakes the hospital building. Ilijaz knows the sound. Upstairs in the operating room, a nurse cracks that they'd better prepare for casualties.

In his clinic on the other side of Srebrenica, Dr. Nijaz Džanić also hears the airplane. He asks his nurse to go see what kind of plane and how close it is. She goes out through the waiting room and runs back inside a few seconds later.

"It's very close."

"What kind of plane is it?" Nijaz asks her.

"God, I don't know."

Nijaz goes out to see for himself as the nurse sits back at her desk. Just then, an explosion rocks the room and the glass from the large window blows out and showers her with splinters. She sits for a moment, stunned, and then stands up.

"Nijaz?" she calls.

IT TAKES ABOUT A HALF HOUR for the injured patients and the bad news to hit the hospital: A bomb exploded on the old wooden minaret and rained shrapnel into the waiting room of Nijaz's clinic. Two people have been killed. One of them is the doctor.

Ilijaz and the other men attend Nijaz's *dženaza* burial prayers. They are gone just briefly; there is little time for ceremony. The supplies from the clinic are quickly transferred to the hospital and Ilijaz and the other five remaining doctors now share the burden of treating the ill in addition to the injured.

WHILE SERBIAN PRESIDENT Slobodan Milošević tells the world his country is not involved in the Bosnian war, Bosnians near Ilijaz's birth village have watched Serbian troops regularly cross a bridge from Serbia to the Bosnian town of Skelani. From the same high point, Kragljivoda, where Ilijaz first began treating war patients, they see fire spew from the muzzles of tanks on the asphalt road switchbacking up Tara Mountain in Serbia, six miles away. Sometimes, instead of merely watching missiles fly and awaiting their resounding boom, the villagers become their targets.

Three days after Nijaz's death, Ilijaz has to treat a dying family member. His thirty-one-year-old cousin, Sulejman Pilav, the medical technician who worked by his side during the war's early months in Kragljivoda, was eating lunch near the clinic when a shell exploded nearby. From the moment Ilijaz lays eyes on him at Srebrenica Hospital, he knows the injury is mortal. Sulejman's right hip is destroyed. Ilijaz wants to comfort him.

"You don't have to pretend," Sulejman says. "You don't have to lie. I know what's happening."

Somehow Ilijaz finds himself operating anyway, trying to help Nedret repair some of the damage. Futile.

Instead of staying in the hospital to watch his cousin die, Ilijaz packs some empty humanitarian aid boxes with emergency medical supplies—wound dressings, iodine, narcotics, IV fluids, chest tubes, an intubation kit, and a set of surgical instruments. He rides with soldiers south on the main road through the dark hills to Kragljivoda in a truck fueled by diesel from last month's humanitarian convoys. After visiting with former neighbors, he and several men carry the supplies about three miles east on small, hilly country roads to a designated position, a small Muslim village burned at the start of the war. There, Ilijaz establishes a medical station in a partially destroyed house in preparation for another offensive. Other medical technicians and physicians from the hospital situate themselves at satellite stations.

The Srebrenicans have two military choices: push further north in an effort to link with Tuzla, or attack south to take Skelani and cut off the bridge to Serbia. They've chosen the latter.

Ilijaz knows there is no way that the lightly armed Srebrenicans will be able to hold on to a strategic town that sits right on the border with Serbia. To him, the offensive has another purpose altogether—to show the Serbs who have taken over the region that the Muslims from the area are still alive and that they are coming back.

The action starts at 6 the next morning. The Srebrenica soldiers attack from multiple sides and meet stiff resistance. Ilijaz, working about a half mile behind the nearest lines of battle, stabilizes the injured and sends them to Srebrenica Hospital by cart, by foot, carried by comrades, or on couch cushions laid on the back of a tractor. By late in the day, the Srebrenica soldiers succeed in moving the battle lines further south near a village called Jezero. Ilijaz moves his station along with the battle to another destroyed village. In the evening, a group of eight of Srebrenica's most elite soldiers, injured while trying to take a munitions depot, reaches Ilijaz. Exhausted, he treats them. On this first day of battle alone, approximately thirty-five Srebrenica men and two women die and many more are injured. Serbs report forty-nine killed.

Srebrenica soldiers capture a great deal of territory and military hardware including another tank, their fourth, and their first mortar and howitzer. Thousands of civilian *hapsi* rush in to scrounge for food.

Ilijaz stays awake to speak with a captured Serbian special forces soldier, a volunteer from a wealthy family in Serbia who first fought in Vukovar. When Ilijaz asks why the soldier, whom he judges to be about twenty years old, has come to battle in Bosnia, the man answers, "To defend Serbianism." He believes that Serbs in Bosnia and Croatia are being slaughtered and it is every good Serb's duty to go to war.

For Ilijaz, the soldier's words provide a rare peek into the mentality of his enemies. He is reminded of the delusion of persecution and endangerment that he first detected when Serbs posted Milošević's picture in their dorm rooms back in medical school. The belief they are under attack and in danger gives them the mental justification to commit brutality. But fear and thirst for vengeance have infected the Srebrenicans, too, and Ilijaz knows it. The offensive to take Skelani is not without its atrocities. When the Muslims draw near to the town, Serb civilians take to the bridge, fleeing toward Serbia. A number of them, including at least one woman and one child, are shot.

Bosnian Serb Army General Ratko Mladić leads Bosnian Serb forces and Yugoslav army elements in a ferocious counterattack to wrest the strategic area, which pokes east like a sore thumb into neighboring Ser-

bia, from the Muslims. Within four days, they push the Srebrenica soldiers back. The Skelani offensive costs Srebrenica dearly. More than fifty
soldiers are killed and more than 150 wounded. The brother of one of
those killed takes revenge on two of the last few "loyal" Serbs who remain in Srebrenica, killing a debilitated, immobile woman and her well-
liked caretaker and son, "Zech" (Rabbit) with a rifle butt. The killer is
captured and jailed.

No victories are won after Skelani.

A squeeze in the northwest part of the enclave coincides with news of
a potential peace plan designed by negotiators for the European Community and the United Nations, Cyrus Vance and Lord David Owen.
American commentators deride the plan, which would divide Bosnia
into ethnic enclaves and appease those seeking "ethnically pure" territory, as "another Munich." Serbs try to wring the area free of Muslims,
perhaps to create a reality on the ground that will influence their area of
control in the peace plan. Thousands of Muslim inhabitants flee, either
undertaking a risky walk toward Tuzla or heading for Srebrenica.

Fighting rages. Displaced inhabitants tumble into the valley of Srebrenica along with the snow, filling its frozen streets with their blankets
and their wood fires and their desperation. The crush of patients forces
the doctors to send the wounded to recover in private homes that are
choked with wood smoke, crawling with lice, and packed with dozens of
displaced people.

Serb warplanes again blast Srebrenica, in violation of the no-fly zone
declared by the United Nations. With no new aid supplies, no new offensives for the *hapsi* to collect food, and thousands of new refugees, food
supplies vanish. People, especially those displaced from their homes in
the villages, turn to old war recipes, pounding flour out of corncobs, tree
buds, and the pulp of apples and pears. The diet constipates, but the doctors have no laxatives to offer.

More than one villager travels at night back to his burnt home, back
to the fields where he might have buried some food, and is killed or
injured by a mine as he crosses a front line or reaches into a corncrib.

Malnourished children die from common colds. An orphaned baby perishes of acute starvation.

The hospital does not have enough food for its patients and staff, despite the donations of generous villagers with land. The doctors lose weight. Ilijaz has one, sometimes two, small meals a day. He is six feet tall and weighs only 128 pounds now, roughly 45 pounds less than before the war. He suffers from chronic back pain as he bends over the low, makeshift operating table to bandage wounds or assist with surgery.

The non-injured begin coming to the hospital, desperate for food. A guard named Shevko sits inside the hospital entrance stroking his mustache and leering out the window when someone tries to enter. From time to time he stretches out a hand to "examine" someone who is being especially persistent. Despite his best efforts to scare patients off, the hospital overflows with the ill and injured. They fill the clinic next door, too, and course up the town's steep main street to occupy half of the health spa and the nearby Domavija Hotel.

To fight back against the Serb offensive, desperate means are considered. The army floats a pair of explosive-laden barges toward Serb-held areas—one explodes, but no one is hurt. A few days later, Commander Naser Orić and a small group of soldiers journey to Sase, the mining town where Ilijaz once worked in the health clinic and where Ejub met his wife, to investigate the possibility of releasing a pool of toxic chemicals into the Drina River. Accompanying them is a German photographer, Philipp von Recklinghausen, who recently walked into the enclave with Bosnian army soldiers, pulling his weight by carrying a rifle grenade and 300 rifle cartridges. He had bought a pair of hiking boots and come to Bosnia on holiday, on a young man's quest to learn what war is, to initiate himself into manhood.

Kicking machine gun casings out of the way as they walk, the group passes through a village, Zalazje, which the Srebrenica soldiers captured in their July 12 St. Peter's Day assault last summer. The Srebrenicans are proud of their victory here. Commander Naser encourages the photographer to take pictures, and a soldier begins to lead the photographer and his translator from the woods toward a high clearing, seeking a better view. The soldier triggers a mine. Shrapnel hammers the photographer's right forearm. Back at the hospital there is no ketamine left, or at least none that Nedret will use, not even for Srebrenica's guest, Philipp.

Nedret pokes his injured arm with a steel probe and pours disinfectant into his wound. The photographer winces with pain but stifles a cry because he has noticed that at this hospital even children rarely cry. He watches technicians sharpen an old scalpel the doctor will reuse.

Nedret finishes dressing the wound and tells the photographer he must come to the hospital every day to have it cleaned and covered. No antibiotics remain, and the ones the photographer brought for himself he has naïvely given away, thinking he wouldn't need them.

The injury starts a relationship between the two men. Every day the photographer walks into the hospital, dirty, stinking even to himself, and knocks on the door of the operating room. Nedret, who cannot bear most distractions or intrusions, always greets him warmly.

"Ahh, Philipp!" he laughs, "Let's have a smoke."

Sometimes Philipp joins Nedret in his room at the Hotel Fresh Air, watching him regale the soldiers. *These people are a tribe*, Philipp thinks. *Nedret is one of their kings.*

HOSPITAL SUPPLIES DWINDLE. Ketamine is gone or hoarded away. Again, the sound of screaming fills the operating room. In moments of extreme stress and anger, thrown instruments fly through the air and clatter on the floor. The doctors are exhausted and hungry.

The OR is such a stressful place that its chief instrument nurse comes to Nedret and asks to be relieved of her duties. She feels sick, she says, mentally sick. She cannot sleep and cannot even speak to her family about the daily horrors she witnesses. When Nedret tells her he can't spare her, she goes over his head. Nedret, for all his power and influence, is not the official director of the hospital. Dr. Avdo, the older pediatrician, still is, and he agrees to let her go.

Nedret is furious. His friends have noticed changes in him—emotional changes. He came into the enclave with a positive attitude, a friendly and gregarious manner, a sympathetic ear, and an inability to finish even one glass of plum brandy. Now he drinks, curses, and quickly loses his patience. He knows that patients are offering gifts in exchange for good service—some doctors refuse to take the gifts, but others seem to expect them. When Nedret hears that some patients are paying exorbitant fees for scarce, lifesaving treatments, it strikes him as morally wrong.

If a patient needs an infusion, Dr. Avdo, the hospital director, has to be convinced to let go of one of the remaining few. If a patient needs antibiotics, there is only one way to get them—pay 100 Deutschemarks per dose of penicillin on the black market. Desperate family members discover where to buy it. Some who have no money consider killing to get the drugs they or their family members need.

One day Nedret examines a patient with a groin injury who's been brought into the hospital after being stuck for days in the woods outside of Srebrenica. The patient has developed a dangerous infection and urgently needs antibiotics. Nedret tells him so, but says he has none to offer him. The next day, when Nedret stops by the patient's room, the man shows him a small bottle containing an injection of four million international units of penicillin. The vial looks suspiciously like the penicillin Nedret brought with him when he entered Srebrenica last summer. He demands to know where it came from, but the patient refuses to tell him. Nedret corners Avdo, the hospital director, and demands that he get to the bottom of it.

"You have to make this patient speak!" Nedret says and swears he won't come to work again until the source of the racket is discovered. He storms out of the hospital, the sound of his yelling echoing behind him.

The German photographer sits in Nedret's room at the Hotel Domavija, sipping plum brandy and admiring Nedret's "beautiful, stupid girlfriend" as he listens to the doctor vent. Nedret refuses to return to work. He is even willing to sacrifice patients, to let them die, to have this clarified. "I can't work. I can't work," Nedret tells the photographer. "I have to go when there's a chance to go." Day after day passes, and Nedret fails to reappear at the hospital. Other doctors and nurses have their own theory about Nedret's absence. They believe he has gone on strike over a dispute with the *opština*, the town authorities, because he wants to be granted a position of authority over Avdo.

A Serb attack near the Drina River leaves several wounded, and still Nedret will not return. A boy with a severe abdominal injury dies. Ilijaz believes he probably couldn't have survived, even with an operation. He is disappointed in Nedret for not coming to look at him, but he realizes that the problem of Nedret's strike may be more psychological than practical. Patients view Nedret as the surgeon and come to the hospital asking for him. Ilijaz and the other doctors defer to his authority. But in truth, although the other doctors expect so much of Nedret, he is not much more qualified than they are.

How far do the duties of a physician stretch? Is a doctor always required to be judged as a professional, or can he be seen as a human being, with extreme stress a factor in his decisionmaking? The intrepid photographer scribbles in the small, soft-cover notebook that he bought in East Germany and carried with him into Srebrenica. "The only surgeon of the self-described free area takes an apparent holiday," he writes. "Without medicine, without anesthesia, it all makes no sense."

14

ROAD TO SREBRENICA

THE VISION OF SREBRENICA HOSPITAL empty and cold, its patients lying dead and abandoned, haunts Eric Dachy. Nearly three months have passed since Bosnian Serb authorities allowed aid convoys to reach the town. As the Serb military closes in on the last remaining Bosnian Muslim villages in eastern Bosnia, frantic ham radio operators—the only sources of information from the besieged pockets—beg for help, telling of starvation, relentless shelling, and massacres.

Eric has found no way to deliver the MSF medical staff and supplies he promised in his letter to Nedret. His letter to Bosnian Serb leader Dr. Radovan Karadžić asking for approval to place an MSF team in Srebrenica was never answered. Eric wonders if the local staff members are even still there. Has Nedret attempted to flee back to Tuzla? Are Ilijaz and the others alive?

Evenings of food, drink and conversation at the homes of Yugoslav friends and their families temporarily distract Eric from these questions. When he climbs the stairs back to his room in the dark night, though, disturbing thoughts await him. He contemplates while drawing. He reads books by Yugoslav authors and poems by Bosnian sufi poets, trying to understand this place and these people. He takes in Balzac, Fernando Pessoa, Joyce's *Ulysees,* and texts of philosophy and psychology, too.

Mostly he thinks about the war, and the workings of international politics and aid. Eric concludes that the medicine, the food, and the blankets that MSF and the other aid organizations donate here are "bullshit" compared with what's really needed. Eric's success at his daily job—providing medical supplies and equipment to hospitals in Serbia and Serb-held areas of Bosnia—matters less and less to him. So when the U.N. High Commissioner for Refugees organizes a conference to introduce the humanitarian community to potential governmental donors and make a pitch for additional funding, Eric attends with a sense of duty, not purpose.

Dressed in an ill-fitting state-made Yugoslav suit jacket he bought and paired with his translator's dark red silk tie, he sits at a large table in an opulent ballroom at the Belgrade Hyatt Hotel, uncomfortable amid the fine china, the formality, and the diplomats in their conservative suits and dresses. Other representatives of humanitarian agencies play the money game, wringing their hands over the dire humanitarian situation, trumpeting their own efforts to relieve it, and lavishing thanks on the donor countries that the diplomats represent. Though Eric wants to be polite, he can't help plunking a sour chord into this symphony of praise, letting the diplomats know that by failing to address the root problem—the war—their humanitarian generosity is merely a show.

In fact, it's worse than a show. Saying, as the diplomats do, that humanitarian activity is "restoring peace" is a *lie*. World leaders are fully informed about the massacres and the "ethnic cleansing." The U.S. government regularly issues its own reports detailing the atrocities. It's clear that what's needed for restoring peace is, ironically, military action. Force must be met with force. It will take risking lives, killing people. That is a painful step. But that, Eric believes, is what it will take. And Eric suspects, though of course he cannot be sure, that Milošević is a paper tiger. If powerful nations use force against him, he will crumple.

The word "humanitarian" makes Eric want to throw up. When you enter a flooded room, you don't just start mopping up the water—first you turn off the tap. It's simple logic. Eric is so sure that humanitarianism is useless here that he again considers giving up and leaving the Balkans. There is one thing that stops him—his idea of "interposition," of aid workers stepping between victims and aggressors to break the pattern of ethnic cleansing, not as humanitarians, but as activists. He decides to stay and pursue a challenging ethical strategy: become a virtual "secret agent," acting for good from within the camp of the supposed do-gooders. His hope of achieving his goals in Srebrenica, however, dims by the day.

THE WINTER PASSES. At the start of March 1993, as another set of Bosnian peace talks are under way at the United Nations in New York, ham radio operators report the takeover of the eastern Bosnian town of Cerska and the massacre of at least 500 civilians. The U.N. High Commissioner for Refugees, Sadako Ogata, sends an urgent telegram to the United Nations, making reference to the barrage of desperate-sounding reports from eastern Bosnia and warning that villages around Srebrenica "are on the point of falling to the Serbs."

"Lots of civilians, women, children and old people, are being killed, usually by having their throats cut," she says. "If only 10 percent of the information is true, we are witnessing a massacre in the enclaves without being able to do anything about it."

In response, the United States and Bosnia convene an emergency session of the U.N. Security Council. The council demands unimpeded access for aid convoys and an immediate end to "killings and atrocities" by "Serbian paramilitary forces." It calls on the U.N. Secretary-General to increase the presence in eastern Bosnia of the only military force available, the U.N. Protection Force, UNPROFOR. The following day, the commander of U.N. forces in Bosnia, General Philippe Morillon of France, announces his intention to visit eastern Bosnia to assess the situation. Surely the Serbs won't deny him his freedom of movement.

Eric has a hunch, perhaps over-optimistic, that if Morillon can get himself and a convoy into Srebrenica, then he can get MSF in, too. He phones MSF headquarters in Belgium, his voice full of excitement.

"Georges," he says to the director of operations, Georges Dallemagne, "we have the opportunity to go to Srebrenica. Come!"

At thirty-five, several years Eric's senior, Georges is clean-cut with a round face and a receding head of straight, brown hair. His visits to the field have grown less frequent with his marriage and the birth of his two daughters, but he is as convinced of the importance of reaching the eastern Bosnian enclaves as Eric is. He wants to witness the situation firsthand so he can return to Europe and testify about it to governmental representatives and the media. Like Eric, Georges believes that distress, human rights abuses, and loss of human dignity—factors that don't fit as easily on a scale as health needs—are important indicators for MSF intervention.

Georges arrives quickly, and he and Eric set out for the border with two MSF nurses and a petite, sociable administrator, Muriel Cornelis, twenty-six, whose enthusiasm for her second MSF mission improves the group's general mood. Eric's strategy is again to drive directly to the

Drina River, the convoy's point of embarkation, rather than to stay in Belgrade and try to make official arrangements through Byzantine U.N. structures.

The MSF team joins hordes of agitated U.N. soldiers, journalists, and U.N. refugee workers awaiting approval to cross into Bosnia in a dilapidated old riverine spa. Every day a line of white trucks filled with food and medicine sets out for Zvornik Bridge. There, an irascible, mustachioed sergeant, who reminds Eric of Saddam Hussein, blocks their progress with barrages of insults in Serbian, acting as if he's the bridge's king.

Eric scurries back and forth to the bridge several times a day with the U.N. workers in a vain attempt to fulfill the latest demands issued by the Serbs for authorization papers, detailed manifests of humanitarian supplies, and a list of the weapons and ammunition of the accompanying U.N. soldiers, down to the last bullet. Getting through the days feels like wading through oatmeal.

At night, back at the Communist-era spa, the orange-brown cavern of a dining room fills with a bizarre collection of international characters. They lean around a large table holding cigarettes and brandy glasses and shouting over the manic din of a raucous folk band. One white-bearded U.N. aid official, Larry Hollingworth, looks like Santa Claus, and a giant British major with aristocratic bearing resembles his nickname, the Giraffe. The U.N. soldiers, especially the British who spoil for some real action, trade rumors and attempt to drown their impotence in gallons of plum brandy. Looking useless and humiliated, they bear little resemblance to the proud soldiers engaged in a "courageous" mission whom Eric reads about in glossy French magazines.

Serb soldiers share this hyperkinetic setting with the internationals. Aid officials and journalists, frustrated by day, spend their nights fawning over Major Vinko Pandurević, the massive, red-headed commander of what the Bosnian Serbs refer to as the 1st Zvornik Light Infantry Brigade. As best they can tell, the freckle-faced commander holds the key to their locked-up authorizations. The commander sits, smug, smiling, refusing to drink and looking, to Eric, as if he were observing flies repeatedly hitting the walls of a glass box. And as if the army unit he commands belongs to a state that really exists.

On a minor holiday, a troop of folk dancers joins the cacophony, weaving through the room in traditional dress. Eric turns thirty-one in this surreal environment, but he doesn't tell his colleagues. He never celebrates his birthday, anyway. This one marks the thirteenth anniversary of his father's death.

Meanwhile, General Morillon sets out to visit the besieged eastern Bosnian pockets of Cerska and Konjević Polje. On his return, he holds a press conference, surprising the journalists with his impression that conditions are not as serious as ham radio reports have suggested.

"What we have seen is a population that is overrun with refugees but . . . we consider no one is really endangered."

As for Ogata's reports of a massacre:

"*Je n'ai pas senti l'odeur de la mort*," he says. News outlets quote him worldwide: "I didn't smell the odor of death."

Eric, knowing what he knows about the conduct of war here, quips to Muriel that Morillon "doesn't have a very developed sense of smell."

Over the next days the general's blasé comments provoke public outcry from U.N. refugee officials, whose previous reports on eastern Bosnia—based on information from local ham radio operators—now appear hysterical. They, not the military, have the expertise to assess the humanitarian situation, and they point out that the general was not taken to see outlying areas where entire villages were said to have been scorched.

Indeed, even their most alarmist description of the situation turns out to be conservative. One of the members of the general's own traveling party, Simon Mardel, thirty-five, a brave, level-headed British doctor representing the World Health Organization, hikes into Srebrenica from Konjević Polje and sends back assessment reports that are as authoritative as they are horrifying. The first foreign physician to reach Srebrenica since Eric Dachy last December, he describes the medical care as more primitive than anything he has seen in war-ravaged Afghanistan or Liberia. Up to thirty people a day are dying of disease exacerbated by malnutrition. Roughly 200 people require immediate evacuation and 2,000 are sick and injured.

U.N. refugee officials hand his accounts to the media, who then report them widely. Now it is General Morillon's assessment that looks foolish and naïve. Serb officials, on the other hand, seem more than pleased with Morillon's statements. On the heels of Morillon's announcement, Serb authorities agree to allow an evacuation of the seventy wounded of Konjević Polje to the Bosnian government-held city of Tuzla. Eight Red

Cross buses outfitted as ambulances head toward the border, but a Serb mayor calls in soldiers to block their way, asserting that some of the purportedly injured Muslims must be "war criminals."

That night, General Morillon appears at the spa on the Drina River and convenes a press conference. Eric, Georges, and the frustrated lot of UNHCR officials, UNPROFOR soldiers, and journalists gather in the large dining room.

The French general, a former Legionnaire, is an athletic-appearing fifty-seven-year-old man with short gray hair, square metal glasses, and thin lips that curl around cigarette after cigarette. He tells the group that he has met with the Bosnian Serbs and is confident the evacuation of the wounded will go forward.

"I've also informed them," he adds, "of my intention to travel to Srebrenica in person with a group of military observers in order to work out a ceasefire and possibly to allow the entry of a humanitarian aid convoy."

Eric notices that the general is announcing his intentions rather than saying he will seek permission from the Serbs. He suspects that Morillon, bitter and embarrassed, needs to look as if he's doing something for Srebrenica, the largest enclave of non-Serbs remaining in eastern Bosnia, which now contains thousands of refugees fleeing Cerska and Konjević Polje.

"I will go to Srebrenica, if necessary even by foot," the general says.

Sensing opportunity, Eric stands up.

"*Mon général*, we're from MSF," he says. "We want to go there, too."

THE U.N. REFUGEE AGENCY REPRESENTATIVES also hope to send a fourteen-truck aid convoy to Srebrenica along with the general. But early the next morning, March 11, Bosnian Serb Commander Pandurević refuses to authorize the convoy. Morillon decides to proceed with a small party that includes Eric, Georges, and Muriel from Doctors Without Borders and just one truck of aid. Planning to return in the evening and warned that the Serbs will search everything, the three MSF workers carry no personal belongings, not even a change of underwear.

They travel south along the east bank of the River Drina, in a Toyota Land Cruiser marked "MSF," following a small line of vehicles carrying the general, two UNHCR officials, a small number of U.N. soldiers and military observers, some medical supplies and sugar, and, rather mysteriously it seems to Eric, two Americans in military uniform.

It's a clear, sunny day, and the rolling, snow-capped hills of Bosnia on the far side of the Drina River gleam in the sunlight, catching Eric's eye. The convoy bypasses Zvornik and its obstructionist "King of the Bridge," inching toward another bridge at the Serbian town of Ljubovija. Various groups of armed men stop them along the route to examine their papers and one, about halfway to the river crossing, tells them that they can't proceed. Morillon negotiates, responding to the harassment of low-ranking Serbian officers by threatening to call their leader, Serbian President Slobodan Milošević. One of the Americans attempts to mount the heavy tactical satellite communications equipment he is carrying, but is unable to find a signal. Morillon must ask local authorities for use of their Post Telephone and Telegraph, PTT. He finally reaches a high-level Yugoslav authority and then, after hours of waiting, escorted by a Yugoslav army general, they are allowed to cross the river.

They arrive in Bosnia and are stopped just north of Srebrenica in Bratunac. Morillon meets with a local commander and hears a litany of atrocities allegedly committed by Srebrenica Muslims against the Serbs. Then, the kicker. He is told that the "Muslims" blew up the yellow bridge on the main road between Bratunac and Srebrenica last night.

When Eric hears this, he suspects that the Serbs themselves destroyed the bridge to prevent the convoy from reaching Srebrenica. The day's many delays, he thinks, were coordinated to give them time to do it. The only way to reach Srebrenica now is via a road that winds through the snowy, wooded mountains, hasn't been used for months, and could be mined. Around 3 in the afternoon, the Bosnian Serbs escort them farther along the Drina River, show them a village they say was destroyed by the Bosnian army, and then turn them toward the hills. The Serbs bid farewell at the site of an abandoned mining complex, warning that they fear for the party's safety because of the risk of attack by the Muslims.

Eric is unsettled by the delays and warnings, but tries not to let it show. He goes only so far as to ask the U.N. military personnel, "Are the Bosnians aware that we're coming?"

Sure, they are, he will remember them saying. Of course, we told Sarajevo to tell them by radio.

BEFORE THE UNESCORTED PART of their journey begins, the U.N. military personnel take stock. It has recently snowed for nine days straight. According to the map, the all-weather road will change into a track meant for fair-weather use, and its path will climb. They decide the armored personnel carrier, painted white and marked "UN" on all sides, will take the lead with its crew of five Canadian U.N. soldiers. The boxy, mastaba-like Canbat M113 has, on both sides, five wheels covered with rolling tracks that help distribute its weight and facilitate its movement on difficult terrain. Because the area may be mined, the convoy's vehicles—the MSF Land Cruiser, the small Belgian transportation battalion truck filled with medical supplies and sugar, and a handful of jeeps carrying Morillon, the American soldiers, U.N. Military Observers (UNMOs), and refugee officials—will follow one at a time, fifty yards apart.

The road narrows and is soon covered with ice and snow, a blanket that thickens as the elevation climbs. The atmosphere is tense. The travelers roll down their windows to avoid shattered glass in case they are indeed targeted, a lesson from Eric's close call in Sarajevo. The air in the car turns cold. Above them the hills and pine tree boughs glow white.

The jeeps repeatedly get mired in snow. As daylight wanes, Morillon switches, with his aide and his translator-bodyguard, to the lead APC to try to reach the Bosnian lines before sunset. His vehicle progresses out of sight.

The UNHCR Nissan S.U.V. stops in front of Eric, and its occupants get out to put on chains. The MSF Land Cruiser has none. When the time comes to proceed, its tires spin. Eric remains at the wheel while Georges unloads from the car in his heavy flak jacket and walks behind it to push. He shoves the car forward, then stumbles through the one-and-a-half-foot-thick snow to catch up and push again. After Herculean efforts, he gets it rolling. Georges stops to catch his breath and, between huffs, shouts for Eric to keep going. Eric drives ahead and begins to navigate a bend in the trail.

An earth-shaking detonation rends the muffled silence. It rattles the vehicle and reverberates in the mountain air. Eric hits the brakes and closes his eyes. It sounds as if an anti-tank mine has exploded behind them. He trembles with the thought that his own vehicle passed over it. Then he thinks of Georges.

Someone shouts for the doctor. A U.N. refugee worker appears at Eric's window. "We have to go see," he says and Eric wonders, given the size of the explosion and the devastation it must have caused, whether he'll have any way of helping.

He grabs his emergency case from the back of the Land Cruiser, then carefully places his feet on the vehicle's tire tracks. Where there is one mine, there may be more. Walking on the path where the car has already passed should be safer. Or should it? He's heard of a kind of mine that detonates after several presses on its trigger.

Fuck! Eric is later unsure if he thinks it or says it aloud. *I could explode at any moment.*

Here he is, on a darkening mountainside in the middle of nowhere in a Bosnian no-man's-land full of mines. He isn't thinking about his sense of purpose, all the months he's waited to get to Srebrenica, all the suffering people he could help save. He wonders what the hell he is doing here. He shouldn't be here, shouldn't be taking these risks. He feels like an egoist for not having thought about the effect his death would have on his mother, brother, and sisters. If he loses his leg or his life, he'll have only himself to blame.

The others notice his hesitation.

Eric's eyes fix a laser-beam stare on the snowy path ahead, trying to figure out the best way to proceed. He would never forgive himself if he didn't try to reach the site of the explosion. He wants to walk gently, but he can't stop shaking. His mind reels with images of the amputees he's seen.

Where is Georges?

Eric braces for the shock of red blood on snow.

The site of the explosion comes into view just around the curve. The truck's cab is shattered and its front wheels blown away. Everything is stained black, including the snow. Smoke thickens the air with a suffocating smell.

Where is Georges?

The sight of him, upright, floods Eric with relief.

"It's incredible. It's incredible," Georges keeps repeating, and, with a far-off look: "I should have been on that running board."

The Belgian drivers had beckoned him up as they passed, but, exhausted by his efforts and weighted down by his flak jacket, Georges didn't attempt the leap. As the truck passed, he grabbed a cord hanging from its back and let himself be pulled along. After a tiring sixty feet or so, he let go. Within moments the truck detonated the mine.

"Did you think of your daughters?" Eric asks, as much as anything to assure himself that his colleague is oriented.

"Yes," he says. Instead of his life flashing before him at the moment of the explosion, he saw the faces of his little girls, ages four and two.

It seems miraculous that nobody is seriously injured. Aside from the APC, the truck is the only armored vehicle in the convoy. The Belgian government took the unusual trouble to line its cabs with expensive Kevlar mine-resistant plates. The plates absorbed both the impact of the blast and the slivers of metal, cocooning the drivers as their cab disintegrated. They are bruised and shaken, with eardrums shattered, but to Eric's examination, all right.

One Belgian even regains his sense of humor.

"There was this little noise in the engine anyway," he says. "It needed to go for service."

Eric, still nervous, tries to get the MSF car going, but it is firmly stuck now in the middle of the bend in the narrow road. Morillon and his armored personnel carrier are nowhere in sight. The remaining jeep doesn't have extra room. The aid workers and American soldiers have no choice but to walk. They spread out thirty feet apart, stepping carefully on the APC's tracks in case of more mines.

After a few hundred feet, Eric comes face to face with a Bosnian soldier dressed in white camouflage and bearing a gun. Georges sees him, too, and gives Eric a questioning look. The first thing the man does is pantomime a cigarette. A few of his companions emerge from the bushes. Eric musters some words of Bosnian to communicate and Muriel tries out her rusty Russian. The Bosnians are shocked that the convoy has come this way. Nobody warned them. They mined the route themselves. In fact, they say, a second mine is lying not far from the one that detonated.

They deny knowing of any problem on the main Bratunac-Srebrenica road. They're sure the Serbs have set them up to be blamed for a catastrophe. If, in fact, one happened, who would have been blamed? The

Bosnians for mining the route? The Serbs for blowing up the bridge, if indeed they did? Or General Morillon for leading civilians on a reckless journey and then leaving them behind?

The Bosnian soldiers let them pass. After about a half hour, they reach the spots where the other vehicles and General Morillon have stopped to await them. They are still far from Srebrenica. The sun has set and the countryside is dark and quiet, so different from the city. So seemingly peaceful. Eric borrows night-vision goggles from one of the soldiers and gazes at the snow-covered forest. The moment is magical.

They pack into the APC with the general and are jostled and bumped as it lists from side to side during their progress along the hilly path. At last the vehicle grinds to a halt. Eric pokes his head through the top hatch, behind a U.N. soldier at the machine gun, and sees rifles pointing back. They've been stopped by another group of soldiers outside the city. They quickly distribute cigarettes, repeating the words "United Nations" and "Morillon." After checking their identity cards, a few of the Bosnians climb onto the armored personnel carrier and lead them into town, heralding their evening arrival with bursts of gunfire.

ERIC EMERGES FROM THE APC, its motor still humming. In the beams of its headlights, he sees a crowd of people staring back at him, silent and unsmiling. He becomes acutely aware of his good shoes and pachydermatous jacket, his warmth and his comfort.

He half expects someone to demand, "Give me your jacket; I need it." This time he doesn't feel he has landed on Mars. The bitter eyes make him feel as if he has come from there. Eric has never known Bosnians to receive guests with anything other than exaggerated hospitality. The cold stares unnerve him. To try to get more comfortable, he ventures into the crowd and walks among the people for a few minutes. Morillon and the others discuss what to do next and decide to hold an impromptu evening meeting with town leaders. Everyone troops to a room on the top floor of the PTT building.

Morillon makes introductions and describes what each group of foreigners has come to do, and then a laconic Bosnian soldier provides a description of the situation in town. Soldiers hand around samples of what passes for bread in Srebrenica, the hard, terrible-tasting loafs made from corncobs, hazelnut tree catkins, beech tree buds, or dried apple and pear pulp milled on water-powered grinding stones. It is a skill remembered by World War II survivors and not a bad one considering that some residents of the area have stooped to eating cornhusks, tree bark, and animal feed.

The meeting ends with an agreement to gather again tomorrow morning for a more detailed discussion. Finally Eric is free to do what he has been waiting three months to do. He leads the MSF team out of the post office and into the night. The three-story hospital stands before them on its hill, miraculously intact. They cross the crowded street and make their way up its icy driveway. Armed guards control the hospital entrance.

The air inside is dark, thick with wood smoke, and permeated by a putrid stench, but the hospital is far from the empty and abandoned place Eric had feared. Wood-burning stoves keep rooms full of patients warm; the beds are in place, the staff at work. Eric notices these details with relief. He presents his metal emergency case to the staff as a token gesture, because ten tons of donated medical aid supplies will spend the night in the abandoned truck back on the mined forest track.

It is enough for one day. Just before leaving the hospital, Eric remembers he's stowed his personal flashlight in the emergency case. He asks to have it back and a young woman wearing a white coat flashes him a coquettish smile.

"You gave it to us," she says. "Now it's ours."

ERIC FINDS NEDRET AT THE DOMAVIJA HOTEL, freshly returned from the front line. He is shivering in a blanket before a fireplace, but stands up when he sees Eric. The two men share an emotional embrace.

In a few words the Bosnian doctor conjures the winter's stew of disaster—siege, hunger, cold, and now the fierce Serb attack. It has resulted in a hospital overflowing with casualties and a staff and population bereft of hope. Or nearly so.

He looks closely at his guests.

"Your arrival could change everything," he says.

The hospitable instinct of the Bosnians returns with a flourish. Nedret welcomes Eric and his team members as old friends, offering them dried meat, which they cannot refuse, and surrendering his bed so that two of them may sleep on it. Upstairs in the hotel room, Nedret's girlfriend insists Muriel use the meager store of soap and water to ready herself for bed.

"What's the outside world like?" she asks.

At last it's time to sleep. Eric stretches his long frame out on the bed with Muriel. He is exhausted, but the freezing cold air that breezes into the room through the shattered, uncovered window keeps him awake. Muriel arranges herself on the opposite side of the bed. Eric supposes the idea of having to sleep with him disturbs her. He has no intention of trying anything, but as he lies there shivering, unable to sleep, he wishes he could huddle against her for warmth. He doesn't dare suggest it.

He finally falls asleep, but a loud buzzing noise awakens him. Airplanes.

Nedret leads him down the staircase and out onto a terrace over the hotel's entrance. They look across the narrow valley at the snow-covered Bojna Mountain, rising 2,000 feet above sea level. Eric sees fires burning and, in the light of the waning gibbous moon, makes out an unreal sight—long, black snakes wriggling slowly across the snowy white mountainside. He is spellbound. The true meaning of the image sharpens under Nedret's narration.

The snakes are lines of hungry, exhausted Srebrenica residents who struggle up the mountain desperate for manna-like provisions falling from the sky. Awaiting supplies being airdropped by the U.S. air force, a small city's worth gather around burning car tires. Many, recently expelled from their villages by the Serb advance, have walked miles to Srebrenica only to find themselves stuck outdoors in the freezing cold with no food.

Airdrops such as these originated in World War II and have been used to replenish military supplies and deliver humanitarian aid in U.S. wars, military actions, and many humanitarian operations ever since. U.N. refugee officials, repeatedly failing to reach eastern Bosnia with overland supply convoys, appealed to NATO for airdrops in January. Days later, an internal U.S. State Department report, leaked to American newspapers, said the United Nations had "almost no success to date in reaching groups of people critically at risk" in eastern Bosnia and elsewhere and had given significant quantities of aid to Serb authorities to appease them. Ham radio reports from Srebrenica described people "surviving on the chaff from wheat and roots from trees."

Adding to the pressure, on February 12, Bosnian officials declared a "hunger strike," refusing to distribute aid in the capital while people in the eastern enclaves were starving. In frustration, the U.N. High Commissioner for Refugees, Sadako Ogata, astounded world leaders by suspending most of UNHCR's activities in Bosnia, curtailing an operation that brought 30,000 tons of aid a month to an estimated 1.6 million recipients.

During his campaign for president, Bill Clinton had slammed the Bush administration's handling of the war and had raised the possibility of undertaking military action against the Serbs. The news had made it to Srebrenica, where Ilijaz and the others had high hopes that it was true. Instead, aid took precedence, as usual, while Clinton's team reviewed the situation. Days after inauguration, the president announced emergency airdrops over eastern Bosnia. This effort, Operation Provide Promise, shared more than half a name with Operation Provide Comfort, which had supplied and protected the Kurds in northern Iraq, a last-ditch effort to aid a displaced population the United States had at first chosen to ignore. It was the operation where Eric Dachy cut his teeth on aid work in 1991.

Military leaders from UNPROFOR publicly disapproved of the Bosnian airdrop plan. Chief among them was General Philippe Morillon, who warned that the Serbs would think the U.S. planes were delivering arms. "If the Americans start dropping supplies by parachute, there will be an explosion here," he briefed reporters at U.N. headquarters in Sarajevo. "In the current climate of paranoia, everybody will shoot at everything in the air." Morillon called the airdrops "absolutely unnecessary" and assured reporters that the United Nations could deliver supplies by road to those who needed them.

Of course the United Nations could do nothing of the sort. Newspapers such as the *New York Times* opined that Morillon and other UNPROFOR brass hats opposed the airdrop idea "because it would require the United Nations to move beyond the posture it has adopted since arriving here of doing almost nothing that has not been approved by the Serbian forces."

Perhaps embarrassed, General Morillon quickly retracted his opposition and the airdrops began on February 28, a little over a week before Eric's arrival in Srebrenica. U.S. Air Force 435th Air Wing soldiers flew out of Rhein-Main Air Base in Germany and, at more than 10,000 feet over Srebrenica and the other eastern Bosnian enclaves, shoved 1,550-pound food crates and 760-pound medical supply crates out the open cargo ramps of their C-130 transport planes. The airdrop operation is one of the largest and most complex in history. At $2,800 a ton in U.S. dollars, the operation costs three to four times more than land aid convoys.

While the supplies are desperately needed, spreading the staff of life has spread suffering and death, too. The first attempts at airdrops fell into areas near Serb control, and Srebrenicans fetching the supplies came under sniper fire. The airdrops have also lured soldiers from their posts, leaving front lines vulnerable to Serb attack. Even worse, the huge pallets, although tied to parachutes, have crushed several people. The desperate have fought and killed one another over the contents. With no clear distribution system, gathering supplies is a fight of the fittest.

Eric watches, transfixed. When he finally returns to bed, the scene that burns behind his eyes is that of a Sisyphean struggle—people crawling on all fours, clawing their way up the mountain in a bid for survival. He dreams of apocalypse.

15

THE VELVET GLOVE

Day breaks, gray. The once-forested hillside above the hotel, snow-covered and stubbled with freshly cut tree stumps, looks like a man's thinning pate.

Eric and the MSF team walk back toward the post office building where the other internationals spent the night. They pass destroyed houses where snow has collected on jagged façades. It rims balconies that jut from nonexistent rooms, leaving a thick white layer on their bent railings. It frosts the long chimneys rising over the ghosts of rooftops and sits atop pocked stucco walls and the bottoms of empty window frames. Smoke stains accent the windowless, gray-faced buildings like eye shadow over empty eye sockets. Scavenged cars are banked on the snowy side streets. Mangy dogs weave back and forth between piles of trash. The streets are littered with empty brown plastic meal packages from the airdrops whose contents have been devoured on the spot. Groups of people camp out in the freezing cold. Last night saw them dotting the road, setting quick-burning plastic crates afire for some semblance of warmth. This morning, faces and palms stained black, they wander aimlessly while new arrivals—carrying bundles, pulling rough wooden sledges, leading horses, and pushing wheelbarrows and sleigh-bottomed carts—search for a place to stop and live.

Women wear layers of sweaters in lieu of coats, scarves around their heads and mud-covered baggy *dimije* on their legs. They walk in rubber boots, bent under immense bundles, holding babies in their arms. Children, some wearing socks but no shoes, carry their own, smaller bundles. A few lick orange drink powder directly from the air-dropped pouches. The observant British refugee worker, Larry Hollingworth, calls the sight of the thousands in the streets "Dickensian."

Inside the post office, the internationals again receive an icy reception from town authorities, cold enough to match the weather. The full-bearded locals sit on one side of a long table. Eric and the others seat themselves across from them, Morillon closest to the stove.

This time the chief commander, Naser Orić, is present, having arrived from Konjević Polje where the medical evacuation Morillon had promised him last week has still not materialized. Orić is well aware of the way Morillon publicly downplayed the situation after his departure and his failure to "smell the odor of death."

"How long do you intend to stay?" Orić asks coolly.

Morillon turns to his translator.

"How long do I intend to stay?" Morillon repeats in French. "As long as it takes." He breaks into the kind of sheepish grin that makes a man look as if he's trying to hide something, as if he might be lying. When he speaks he avoids the Bosnian commander's eyes.

Eric Dachy grows impatient. He wants to return to the hospital, where real priorities can be set, plans can be made, and where maybe they can actually do something. At last the meeting ends and he leads the aid workers up the hospital's two flights of stairs to Nedret's room. The Bosnian doctor greets them enthusiastically, but the daylight streaming through the broken, taped windows casts dark shadows beneath his eyes. His energy comes in fits of spastic motion, as when he discusses the assessment done by Simon Mardel, the World Health Organization doctor who hiked to Srebrenica last week. Mardel found that dozens of patients required urgent evacuation for specialized treatment: bone infections, large skin defects, and chronically discharging infected wounds. Several hundred patients need rehabilitation, chief among them amputees and paraplegics.

Dr. Ilijaz Pilav takes them on a tour of the fourteen patient rooms. He strikes Eric as quiet and passive. Foul smells, soiled bandages, and pained faces blur before them. Eric focuses on the medical side, cataloguing patients with his colleague, Georges, as the U.N. refugee team looks on, holding their breaths against the stench.

In a mixture of Bosnian, Russian, and broken English, Ilijaz tries to explain the injuries and operations the patients have had. Without asking her permission, he pulls back the blanket of a woman to reveal the stumps of her amputated legs. Muriel watches, touched, as Eric covers her back up and tucks her gently into bed. It is a cultural difference.

In the midst of the ugliness, Eric drinks in a pair of intoxicating eyes. The woman to whom they belong wears makeup and has a halo of red hair that reaches the shoulders of her white coat. She would stand out in any city in the world. It strikes Eric as strange, somehow, to find her here in Srebrenica.

The number of heavy injuries overwhelms Eric and convinces him of the need for an evacuation. He takes it as his mission to convince Morillon to make it happen. While the MSF doctors assess the situation, the armored M113 and the Belgian army jeep recover all the medicines and part of the sugar, and the U.N. military observers and Canadian battalion engineers try to unblock the road by pushing the truck off it. Eric's car is pushed out of the snow and driven into the pocket. He watches from the hospital as donkeys troop into town carrying rescued medical supplies and sugar on their backs.

———

THE SUN POKES THROUGH THE FOG. It throws shadows on the faces of dozens of purse-lipped women who stand on the sloping, snow-covered yard of the hospital, some of them holding babies. Their layered sweaters and baggy patterned pants make them a panorama of color. Their silent, unsmiling faces make them a wall with eyes. Around them, families scattered on the ground with their bundles of belongings look as if they've been dropped from the air. A man sits, leaning on a pair of crutches. Another, very thin, stands with a bag on his stomach stitched from a humanitarian parachute. A child's head peeks out from it.

Across the road, Morillon emerges from the PTT after a final meeting with town authorities. He has promised to organize land and air corridors to bring in aid and evacuate the wounded. He has also offered to leave a small contingent of U.N. military observers behind and to try to arrange for more to join them. He stands before the PTT ready to depart, wearing a light blue beret with a gleaming United Nations medallion. The French flag and the four gold stars of a French lieutenant general emblazon the front of his green, hooded jacket.

He begins to walk toward his vehicle, stopping to speak with a gray-haired woman whose face is stained with tears. His translator, also in military uniform, stands beside him. The woman's shoulders heave with sobs. She writes something in a notebook and then gives Morillon a beseeching look, the angle of her pitiful body giving her the look of a supplicant.

"We're coming back," Morillon says and extends his hand toward her like a priest giving a benediction. The woman shakes her head slowly. Morillon continues past her and enters the passenger seat of the white Nissan four-wheel-drive marked "UN," its tires readied with chains.

When the motor starts, a rumble erupts from the crowd, and hundreds of people press close to the vehicles, blocking them. Women and children raise their hands. At first they appear to be waving. But their fingers wag back and forth, back and forth—a silent, "No! No!"

"We want you, we want you!" they chant in Bosnian. The noise draws Eric to a hospital window.

A young woman wearing a blue-green cardigan over a white blouse knocks on the driver's side window of Morillon's car. It opens, and she unleashes a gush of words. "It's a shame for the entire world!" she cries hoarsely in Bosnian and tells him they won't let him leave for a year. "I've been kept from my home for over a year. . . . Thank you America for the food. . . . Everybody here knows about the little food packages, but that's not enough. A year!"

The wall of women is a dam. A sea of frustration presses at their backs. They have held it back for a year and now it flows from the mouth of this one woman, and the others clap and cheer her from the gap-toothed mouths of their lined village faces, long and drawn beneath their kerchiefs. The stream of words is so strong that it detaches Morillon from his vehicle. He pushes his way around the car and clambers backwards onto the hood, seeking high ground.

"He's going to escape!" the woman warns the crowd. "No, you won't run away," she tells him.

As he stands up on the hood of the car, those in the back of the crowd can now see him and the crowd erupts in applause, cheers, and jeers. A child shouts, "He wants to speak. Speak to us." A flutter of fingers continues to gesture, "No. No." There are shouts of "You're supporting Serbia." After a few moments, the crowd quiets.

"*Je vais vous dire ce que je vais faire!*" Morillon announces. "*Nous ne vous aban-donons pas.*"

"We don't understand anything," someone shouts in Bosnian. The translator gets up on the hood beside the general and begins to translate his words into Bosnian.

"We're not abandoning you," Morillon repeats. "Shhh. *Polako, polako. Polako.*" Relax. Relax. He extends his hands to the side and motions for the crowd to calm down.

"We're not abandoning you. The UNPROFOR soldiers will stay here."

"Hey, friend, what about the grenades?" one pinch-faced man yells in Bosnian. "Hey, what about the grenades, huh? Huh? What about the grenades? The grenades are killing us!"

Adults shout and babies cry.

"*Polako, polako. Polako, polako,*" Morillon tries to quiet them, to throw up a breakwater. "We are going now. I've seen your situation. I visited all the houses here. I've seen you. I know what you need."

A thousand voices drown out his words. "Grenades." "Serbs." "Killing us." "You are our only guarantee."

"*Polako. Polako.* Allow me to speak, please!" the general shouts. "Allow me to speak. You need peace."

"*Mir. Mir. Mir.*" Peace, peace, peace, echoes the wall of women.

"To bring back peace, I have to go to Tuzla immediately and ask for a ceasefire," he says, but his words are translated as, "I am here to ask, to try, that all attacks stop immediately."

"Immediately, immediately," the crowd repeats. The women throw up their hands and beat them together, making thunderous claps.

"If you please, tomorrow . . . ," Morillon yells, but to no avail. He is stranded on the hood of his vehicle. Morillon drops his gesticulating hand and turns to his translator with an embarrassed smile. He has no choice. He wades back into the sea, becoming one for a moment with the mingling, hollow-faced village people, and makes his way back toward the PTT.

"*Godina danu . . .*" the crowd hisses repeatedly. For a year . . . a year . . . a year we've suffered. A woman in a green jacket with long straight hair channels the desperation until her words peter out in a hoarse croak and then another takes up the mantle. Women tremble with sobs, wiping their eyes with the corners of their headscarves, then looking back up at the speaker, wet eyes beaming. With pride? With prayer? With relief and release? Babies wail. Young and old have the same weary look, the same lined faces and teary eyes; even the men are crying.

"He came here and he said that he is going to help us," shrieks a woman. "We don't have any more strength . . . We won't disperse until this is solved. The question of peace is not to be solved in New York or Geneva; it's to be solved here. This is where it's been questioned for the past year. They don't trust us. Let them just come here and be here for a week and then let them do whatever they want. Let them live my life. Nothing else. I won't ask that from the ones who had a worse life than mine, though. We won't disperse. We want bread. We want peace. And we want UNPROFOR here."

The crowd claps and cheers. "That's right," the people shout. "Long live the speaker!"

———————

MORILLON STANDS NEAR THE ENTRANCE to the post office. With his translator, he tries to communicate with the people around him, trying still, it seems, to convince them that he must leave Srebrenica. Then he throws up his hands. "OK, OK, OK," he says, clearly frustrated, and turns toward the doorway. The crowd parts for him, some people pushing others back to clear his path. Before he disappears inside, several women push pieces of their ersatz bread toward his face.

"*Znam!*" he says in Bosnian, gesturing back. "I *know!*"

———————

ERIC IS THRILLED, having witnessed the scene from the hospital window. The Serbs haven't shelled the center of town since their arrival. The people are right, he thinks, Morillon's presence is their best hope for of survival. He remembers a colleague's comment on their last visit, "They should kidnap us." Eric suspects that if he were Bosnian, he would have put Morillon in a corner, trained a gun on him, and kept him hostage until the end of the war. Eric isn't scared at the thought of having to stay here with the people of Srebrenica.

Eric suspects that careful planning lies behind this "spontaneous" appeal of women and children. He figures Nedret must have played a part. The Srebrenicans' tactics remind him of the old saying: "The iron fist is in the velvet glove."

IN THE AFTERNOON, Eric, Georges, and Muriel join Nedret, who has long since ended his strike against drug-selling, in the operating room. Bandages, scrubbed but still stained, hang drying, and bubbling pots boil the instruments into some semblance of sterility. Throughout the day, the air has rumbled with the sound of distant shellfire. The injured, embodiments of that sound, arrive.

One of the first patients to lie on the operating table has a gunshot wound of the buttock. Nedret probes for the bullet with a metal rod, causing the patient to thrash and groan with pain. It takes five or ten minutes before he notices, by turning the man, the exit wound. None of them, not even Eric, thought to check for it.

After several other patients, Nedret examines a man who has a very tiny shrapnel hole in his abdomen. The wound looks so small that it surprises Eric when Nedret says, "We have to open." A male nurse anesthetizes the patient with an injection of newly arrived ketamine, and Nedret cuts a long incision across the man's abdomen. The bowels are full of blood. He finds a perforation in the intestines. Nedret was right. An innocent-appearing wound masked a devastating injury.

Eric supposes they can do nothing. The location of the injury indicates a difficult bowel resection and colostomy, neither of which seems possible here. In these conditions, he believes, the patient has a negligible chance of survival. He keeps his skepticism to himself, though, deferring to Nedret's experience, and soon he, too, is silently rooting for the patient to stay alive.

Nedret carries out the operation in disorderly fashion. Each time he finds another injury he seems exasperated, but then painstakingly works to fix it. Without muscle relaxants, the belly is tense and difficult for Nedret to maneuver. The patient regularly emerges from anesthesia, and his movements awaken an inattentive nurse, who quickly injects another bolus of ketamine into his IV.

Hours pass. It grows dark and Eric takes turns with other aid workers shining a flashlight onto the operating field. At one point, a shell falls close enough to dislodge a piece of plaster from the ceiling, which falls into the patient's open abdomen. Eric begins to despair—it would take an artist, he thinks, to fix these wounds. Then a heavyset man appears in the operating room like a character in a bizarre dream. He stops before the doctors and lifts his shirt. The fleshy belly that protrudes over his pants has a long, vertical scar.

"I operated on him without *any* anesthetics," Nedret boasts.

The man smiles broadly.

"Nedret good," he says.

Eric pictures him on the table like the current patient, losing blood, being exposed to infection, and somehow surviving. So, there is a chance—maybe it's one in a hundred or one in a thousand—but he is convinced that Nedret performs some miracles. He learns what Nedret has already learned, that the human body is so well designed, with so many compensatory systems, that it's actually quite hard to kill a man. Real war is not like the movies, where one bullet makes a man fall down dead.

As the hours pass, Eric and the others, gazes constricted to the narrow operating field, are transfixed by its mélange of red blood, yellow fat, pink skin, and silver instruments. Unraveling the intestines, Nedret finds seemingly endless injuries. The doctors and nurses keep working with dogged determination through their exhaustion, cracking silly jokes, but inside themselves they will the patient, as they will Srebrenica itself, to survive against all odds.

Contrary to Eric's expectations, the patient lives. Nedret patches the last of his injuries and offers a liberal libation of iodine. The man's anatomy has reemerged like a puzzle pieced together.

A nurse is instructed to administer high doses of antibiotics throughout the night via the patient's IV to help prevent a severe infection from feces contaminating his abdomen. His bowel tissue could still die, insufficiently nourished by damaged blood vessels. The patient needs a modern intensive care unit—with monitors recording his vital signs and dripping lifesaving potions—but in Srebrenica, of course, there is no such thing. Eric feels he has just witnessed the most prehistoric, ridiculous, yet noble practice of medicine that exists.

THE SKY IS DARK when Eric crosses the street to the post office to join the rest of the internationals. On the way, he notices refugees still flooding into town, children falling asleep in the snow when their families stop to rest. People are gathered outside the post office to ensure that Morillon doesn't escape; many—the new refugees—have nowhere else to go. The street is dotted with campfires. Someone throws a green plastic milkcrate into one fire and flames roar to the height of the tallest heads. The displaced villagers face the fire, hands raised, with scarves or blankets wrapped around their heads. The temperature is far below freezing.

The expatriates meet together in the post office to discuss whether they are hostages. The U.N. soldiers make a contingency plan for a breakout by force. The idea sickens Eric, but he doesn't believe they'll do it. Morillon announces, as he did at the spa in Serbia, that nobody will deprive him of his freedom of movement. He makes plans to sneak out of the enclave on foot, instructing the soldiers to rendezvous with him on the road to Bratunac in the U.N. vehicle.

Morillon disappears. As the night progresses, the crowd of Bosnians around the post office swells instead of diminishes, preventing the Canadian soldiers from moving the vehicle. Eric decides to sleep, lying down on the freezing, concrete floor, fully clothed. He reminds himself that such discomfort is a daily occurrence for the people around him in this hellish town. Still, he awakens feeling pummeled.

In the morning, Morillon is nowhere to be found, and his aide-de-camp takes charge of the small roomful of soldiers and aid workers, mounting a table to address them. "It's a putsch!" Georges whispers, sotto voce, to Eric and Muriel. The only ones able to giggle about the situation, they take care to hide their whimsy. The soldiers gripe amongst themselves that they are hostages: "Next thing you know, we'll have guns at our heads." In a grave voice, the officer announces that they must pool and ration their food, eating only once every other day. The MSF team members neither object to the idea nor tell the others that the Bosnian medical staff insisted they eat at the hospital.

The frightened young soldiers, seemingly insensitive to the plight of the tens of thousands of endangered people around them, evoke little sympathy from Eric. Still, he reassures them that the MSF team hasn't detected any hostility in town. He tells his own team that the only thing to fear is a Serb takeover of the town, and it isn't worth discussing or worrying about something over which they have no control.

He returns to the hospital and finds the patient they operated on last evening still alive. But now an infusion is dripping imperceptibly through a tiny butterfly needle in the patient's vein rather than flowing through an IV catheter. The patient looks as if he's in pain and, upon further investigation, it seems as if he hasn't received the heavy doses of antibiotics and painkillers the doctors instructed the nurse to provide. The internationals can't understand it. From what they can gather, the IV came out and the nurses didn't see the point in replacing it, spending precious resources and time on a patient they believed would soon die.

Eric suspects that the medical workers' blasé attitude is a result of the fact that they are so battered and worn, malnourished, stressed, and exhausted that they can no longer organize themselves to work effectively. They aren't used to having resources and have lost practice with simple procedures such as starting an IV. Yesterday, the nurses hadn't even seemed to know whether they had any infusions in stock. It makes Eric even more committed to supporting them with a full team of MSF medical workers. Here in Srebrenica, doctors and nurses have been practicing "virtual reality" medicine.

One of the first tasks that needs to be done is to organize the medical supplies. Yesterday Eric dug around the so-called pharmacy, a room overflowing with boxes and dirty bags brought straight from where they were airdropped in the mountains. He found a box of infusions that he could have sworn were delivered with the first aid convoy, four months ago. While a severely anemic woman was lying in the hospital in need of a blood transfusion, eight unmarked, instructionless boxes filled with plastic blood-collection bags were sitting in the storeroom.

Eric decides that it will be much more useful for the MSF team to organize the pharmacy than to watch Nedret operate again. Eric, Georges, and Muriel get busy sorting goods. Then the crackle of a loudspeaker brings them to the windows of the room, which sits on the top floor of the hospital facing the post office.

The sun is in Eric's eyes, but he can make out General Morillon standing at an open window above the building's entrance, framed by a projecting concrete canopy. A large crowd is assembled outside. Eric assumes that Morillon is about to demand the immediate release of the U.N. soldiers, something he fears will destroy all credibility with the Bosnians.

The general begins to speak slowly, in English, through a white megaphone. His voice is deep and robotic as he enunciates every syllable. "I del-i-ber-ate-ly came here," he says, looking down at a black notebook. "And I have now de-ci-ded to stay here in Sre-bre-niche-a." Below him, parked beside the post office, five Canadian soldiers sitting atop their white U.N. armored personnel carrier look up with surprised expressions. Morillon continues.

"You are now under the pro-tec-tion of the U.N. forces."

The jaw of one of the Canadian soldiers literally drops. Watching from the hospital, Eric cracks, "Now we're in real shit." White-bearded Larry Hollingworth pushes a U.N. flag out the window beside the general. It ripples in the breeze as Morillon waves.

As the announcement is translated, the people in the crowd on the sun-drenched hill break into huge smiles. Happiness beautifies them. They begin to clap and whistle and shriek with joy. Some clasp hands to their ears against the deafening ruckus. The noise of their jubilation echoes across the narrow valley.

Eric is stunned. He looks at Georges and Muriel.

"I think we're living a moment of history," he says.

Is the general sincere? If so, then finally! Finally! Finally! Finally a U.N. commander has clearly declared that he will stand between the Serbs and their victims. It's fabulous! If only Morillon will spread his statement to the world and then stick to his guns, no matter how the Serbs respond.

This is exactly what Eric has been hoping for. He watches Morillon descend into the crowd. Tony Birtley, an ABC news correspondent who sneaked into Srebrenica several weeks ago, pushes his way through the people and trains his video camera on the general's face.

"If this doesn't work, General, what do you think it will do to the people?"

"It wi-i-i-i-ll work, it will work," Morillon says, raising the pitch of his voice like a parent soothing a silly child. He grins and dismisses the reporter with a wave of his hand, then turns his back and walks away.

Morillon's statement that his headquarters is now in Srebrenica is underlined with ceremony. The Canadian soldiers form a color guard in front of the APC. Morillon faces them, and on his order they lift their guns and fire. Morillon salutes, and a soldier slowly raises the blue U.N. flag, hand over hand, up the flagpole of the Srebrenica post office.

Eric moves away from the windows and sits down on one of the cardboard boxes of medical aid. Georges and Muriel seat themselves, too. What does it all mean? Impossible to know. Reality dampens their joy. Practically, what has changed? The city is still encircled and besieged. At least 200 patients need to be evacuated. The medical and humanitarian needs are still unmet, and the local medical staff is exhausted and leaderless. All of MSF's work lies ahead of them, and nearly everything they need to do it must come from outside the pocket. Trucks and helicopters. Medical supplies. Hygiene kits. Most importantly, a surgeon. Eric and Muriel will make arrangements in Belgrade, while Georges plays the role of advocate at MSF headquarters in Belgium. He'll tell the world what he witnessed and demand international action to protect the city.

Eric would like to stay longer, but, becoming acutely aware of his lack of a change of underwear and uncomfortable about relying on the Bosnians for everything, he prepares to leave the enclave with the team. The following day, Sunday, the town authorities permit a U.N. military observer to leave with one refugee official and the three MSF workers in exchange for the promise that more military observers and a relief convoy will be delivered within three days. On Eric's way out, he bids General Morillon farewell, congratulating him on his decision and inquiring whether his statement is being publicized outside of Srebrenica.

Yes, the general tells him. Little does Eric know, but Morillon's unscripted actions and unapproved media statements have circled the globe. Over ham radio, the general spoke directly to the Serbs, telling them that his presence in Srebrenica served not only the interests of the thousands suffering in the town, but also the interests of peace and therefore the Serb nation. "Understand that it is also for you, Serbs, that I am present and that I will stay in Srebrenica," he told them. However, it is Morillon's demands to Serb leaders, read over HF radio to U.N. headquarters in his car, that are sending U.N. leaders scrambling.

Fully conscious that a major tragedy was about to take place in Srebrenica I deliberately came here and I have now decided to stay here in

Srebrenica in order to calm the population's anguish in order to try to save them.

I demand:

1. An immediate halt to the Serb offensive as it was promised to me in Pale.
2. The immediate and complete implementation of all ceasefire agreements.
3. The immediate and permanent installation of the necessary U.N. military observers.
4. The opening of a route corridor from Srebrenica to Bratunac to Konjević Polje to Zvornik. UNPROFOR engineers will repair the small bridge and the road between Srebrenica and Bratunac.
5. The opening of an air corridor to Srebrenica to evacuate the hundreds of seriously injured by helicopter.
6. The immediate release of the convoy destined for Srebrenica, which is at present stuck in Zvornik.

Signed Morillon, Srebrenica 1993

Eric has a long ride back to the border. It takes time and effort to convince the Serbs to allow the U.N. military jeep to cross over the front line without Morillon. Eric looks out the windows at the radiant, snow-covered countryside, and smiles.

16

"THE TIME FOR TALKING IS NOW FINISHED"

IN THE FEW MOMENTS it takes for General Morillon to read his speech, Dr. Ilijaz Pilav, also peering through a hospital window, feels the course of the war change. For weeks, everything has been going one way—toward catastrophe. They have lost strength, lost lives, and they are in danger of losing the entire Srebrenica area.

But General Morillon puts his lips to his megaphone like a trumpeter heralding the arrival of hope. Ilijaz smiles with relief at the other doctors, nurses, and hospital technicians gathered in the room with him. He believes in Morillon's promises. He believes they've been saved.

In the afternoon, Srebrenica authorities offer to escort a team of newly arrived U.N. military observers south along the Srebrenica-Skelani road to Kragljivoda. The hill, where Ilijaz's men established their first base at the start of the war, provides a view of Serbia's Tara Mountain and of the Skelani Bridge over the Drina River between Bosnia and Serbia. The goal of the trip is for the U.N. observers to see that some of the attacks are coming from Serbia proper, contradicting Serbian President Slobodan Milošević's denial that his country is involved in the Bosnian war. In fact, more and more often Ilijaz's family has had to take shelter in the underground bunker that his brother, Hamid, built for safety against tank fire, artillery rounds, and aircraft bombs from Serbia.

Upon reaching Kragljivoda, the military observers hear the rumble of airplanes and soon three single-engine propeller planes—one biplane and two monoplanes—are heading toward their position. The military observers take note of the location, Universal Transverse Mercator Grid point 730740, and the local military time, 1640. The aircraft draw dangerously close, but instead of attacking the observers, they drop six bombs on Ilijaz's village, Gladovići, and three on the neighboring village of Osatica. Then they disappear in the direction of Serbia.

This tidbit of eyewitness information, like a firework missile climbing the sky, races silently and almost imperceptibly up the layers of U.N. bureaucracy, slipping stealthily from the U.N. observers to the head of U.N. forces in the Balkans, General Lars-Eric Wahlgren of Sweden, to the head of the U.N.'s Department of Peacekeeping Operations, Kofi Annan, to United Nations Secretary-General Boutros Boutros-Ghali, who buries it in a regular reporting of flight ban violations to the president of the United Nations Security Council.

Then the information explodes. Four days after the incident, at a meeting of the Security Council, someone realizes that Gladovići is the first place where U.N. military observers have reported witnessing air-to-ground bombing activity in Bosnia. It doesn't seem to matter that air attacks, such as the one that killed Dr. Nijaz Džanić, have taken place for months, widely reported by local media and detailed in memos sent by local American officials to the U.S. State Department. Suddenly the name of Ilijaz's tiny village is being invoked to justify a U.N. resolution that brings the United States and NATO the closest they have come to taking military action against the Serbs.

The previous October, all sides in the war agreed to a ban on military flights over Bosnia. The U.N. Security Council codified the ban in a resolution and requested that UNPROFOR monitor compliance. Since then, U.N. military observers have documented almost 500 unauthorized flights, but the attacks on Gladovići are the first to involve combat activity. Now, the United States, along with France, Morocco, Pakistan, Spain, and the United Kingdom, puts forward a draft resolution that would authorize NATO to shoot down warplanes in Bosnia-Herzegovina.

Serbia's traditional ally, Russia, opposes the proposal. So, too, does the U.N. Protection Force commander, General Wahlgren, who is General Morillon's only superior. Wahlgren cables his "grave concerns" over the proposed resolution to Secretary-General Boutros Boutros-Ghali, who sums them up in a letter to the Security Council president:

> "In brief [General Wahlgren's] view is that the activity that has so far occurred from the air has had no significant impact on the military situation. His apprehension is that the proposed enforcement action will have

negative consequences for the viability of UNPROFOR within its existing mandate. In particular, he is concerned that the delivery of humanitarian aid, the protection of which constitutes the predominant part of UN-PROFOR's work in Bosnia and Herzegovina, would be seriously jeopardized. The Force Commander is also deeply worried about the safety and security of the most vulnerable elements of UNPROFOR, viz., military observers and civilian personnel in locations in the region where they would become vulnerable, notably, the air fields."

A vote on the resolution is delayed. The front line at Kragljivoda begins to buckle under the pressure of the Serb offense. For the moment, at least, the United Nations holds off NATO military involvement that could save Gladovići. Ironically, it does so, in part, to avoid endangering humanitarian aid.

———

IT IS EXACTLY THIS ATTITUDE—that humanitarianism is the U.N.'s primary concern in the Bosnian war—that has long infuriated Eric Dachy. What Srebrenica needs, first and foremost, is an end to the Serb offensive. To shy from enforcing a military flight ban in order to keep UN-PROFOR viable and protect aid workers on the ground strikes him as hypocritical, criminal, and disgusting. Nobody needs anything more than he needs physical protection against the violence.

On the other hand, Eric knows that NATO *is* avoiding military action. And the stated policy of the Western world toward Bosnia *is* humanitarian intervention. All he can do is to seize the long-awaited opportunity that Morillon's announcement has given him to get medical aid and personnel into Srebrenica.

He is about to confront yet another irony.

On the one hand, the major country sections of Doctors Without Borders sit squarely behind him. Srebrenica has mended the split in the movement between those who argued for and against MSF intervention in Bosnia. Everyone now recognizes that Srebrenica needs an international presence for medical aid, witnessing, and advocacy. Even the French section is willing to participate in a mission to Srebrenica. The day after Eric returns to Belgrade from Srebrenica, MSF leaders in Brussels submit a revised funding proposal to the Soros Humanitarian Fund stating that the Belgrade team will "concentrate all possible intervention on SREBRENICA, given the fact that the afflux of people is enormous and the needs of the people are increasing every day and despite of the huge risks these interventions might bring for our team-members. A determination that is highly sustained by the rather Holocaustic visions they were confronted with."

However, Eric finds the attitude of U.N. refugee officials markedly different. When the U.N. officials invite Eric to the Belgrade UNHCR office for a debriefing meeting, they argue that Srebrenica is virtually in the hands of the Serbs. The frantic reports they've received from their man on the ground, who's been spooked by some close calls with Serb shelling, have led them to believe in the town's imminent fall. The head of office is advocating for safe passage of the civilian population out of the city toward Tuzla. She's seeing "holocaustic visions," too, and if this is the Holocaust and the world is again standing idly by, then isn't it best to get the victims out? She and the other five U.N. workers in the meeting with Eric want to evacuate Srebrenica. It's so cynical, it makes Eric laugh. They want to do the "ethnic cleansing" themselves!

Eric urges them to try anything to get in crucial aid convoys. They argue they can't risk spoiling the agency's relationship with the Serbs, with whom they must negotiate in order to get aid into many areas of Bosnia. "It's time to use your credit with the Serbs," Eric insists, nearly in tears. What situation could be more critical than tens of thousands of people trapped without food supply, without adequate shelter, and on the verge of being overtaken by enemy forces?

Again, Eric feels utterly alone. Is nobody willing or able to take the risks and make the compromises necessary to get aid into the town? Even his girlfriend, a Serbian woman who works for the ICRC, fails to see Srebrenica the way that he does. She understands the region's strategic importance for the Serbs as well as for the Muslims living there, and she feels that Eric has lost his objectivity.

There is still one true believer left. Eric notices that, in spite of the criticism heaped on Morillon by U.N. superiors and inferiors for his actions in Srebrenica, the general still seems convinced, like Eric, that something can be done. Morillon is still living in the enclave, traveling in and out to negotiate with the Serbs, and he personally escorted the first major aid convoy to reach Srebrenica since last December. So a few days later, Eric drives like a maniac to catch up with the general when he is stopped at a Serb roadblock on his way back to Srebrenica and convinces him to take along four MSF workers. Serb soldiers stop the internationals at a checkpoint in Bratunac and send one car back to Serbia. Of the MSF workers, only a surgeon, riding in Morillon's personal car, remains. At every checkpoint, he shrinks his portly body against the seat in an effort to make himself inconspicuous. They reach a stretch of road marked by signs reading *Achtung Minen!* The driver hesitates and the general, declaring, "Life is a poker game!" shouts for him to "Go! Go! Go!" The surgeon grabs his hard hat and shoves it under his buttocks.

———

THOUGH IT TAKES ILIJAZ and the other doctors and nurses a while to accept Dr. Thierry Pontus as anything more than Nedret's assistant, or to get used to his idea of operating on a schedule, rather than whenever Nedret shows up, they view the arrival of the MSF surgeon as another turning point in the war. The presence of the short, ebullient Belgian, who spouts a constant stream of banter and carries a trademark bottle of iodine with him wherever he goes, singing the praises of the red-brown disinfectant while squirting it on everyone and everything as he operates, makes them feel safer. He makes them smile, too, as he cracks jokes and hands out Rothman cigarettes left and right, spreading encouragement and acting as if he is unafraid to be here. Best of all, the forty-four-year-old surgeon is brilliant in the operating room. The first time they watch him perform an amputation, Ilijaz and Fatima marvel to each other that the patient didn't even lose as much blood as would fit in a *fildjan*—a small Turkish coffee cup.

Thierry, like most surgeon volunteers with MSF, doesn't work for the organization full time; he pitches in when needed, using his vacation time. MSF's call came on a Sunday. By Tuesday, he was on his way to the airport, having gained permission from his colleagues and hospital administrators in Belgium to take an urgent "vacation." He frittered away the first week on the Serbia-Bosnia border, awaiting a chance to cross. Because his most dangerous foreign assignment to date, he likes to say, was opening an MSF office in Los Angeles, he is, in truth, mortified by the situation he finds here. At first, he simply cannot believe his eyes. *How is this possible?* he wonders, looking around himself at the shattered town. *We are in Europe. We are at the end of the twentieth century; it's not possible what I see here.* The first time he hears a triple boom in the distance, Fatima has to explain to him what a grenade is.

A seasoned urologist with a steady stomach for foul smells, he is nonetheless overwhelmed by the stench of Srebrenica Hospital. Every time he cracks open the hospital door, it takes him several minutes to catch his breath and habituate to the odors of death and gangrene before he can force himself to walk inside.

So many injured people have arrived in the days since Eric's departure that Thierry finds the hospital filled beyond capacity with 124 patients, and two additional buildings—a hotel wing and the town's former spa—are being used to house nearly 400 additional patients. Thierry quickly judges that by European emergency criteria some 80 patients need to be taken to the operating room immediately. This impossible task is further complicated by the dearth of supplies, the continuing influx of newly wounded, and, perhaps most of all, by the lack of motivated personnel.

"Why should we work?" the apathetic and impassive staff members ask him. "We will all die anyway."

Although it has seemingly taken the Serbs a year to find a way to shell the hospital, which clings tightly to a hill that provides some protection, they have finally done it. Days before Thierry's arrival, a shell exploded just before the hospital entrance, killing an injured man being carried into the building, and reinjuring a patient recuperating next to a window that shattered. Now the medical workers are even more afraid.

Whether from this incident or the cumulative effects of a year of war, loss of hope, or pure physical degradation from exhaustion, extreme stress, and lack of food, the workers' approach to performing medicine is hands-off at best. The structured and formal trappings of medical practice have disappeared. The regular schedule of morning and evening rounds, the hierarchy of experience and responsibility, has, to Thierry's eyes, drifted into chaos and disorganization. The only remaining principle is authority—the director behaves like a communist functionary and curries favor with the military. He chastises Thierry for distributing sanitary napkins to the female hospital staff, insisting that the first priority belongs to the wives of military leaders. Furious, Thierry grabs a box of napkins and dumps them out the window.

It is not unusual for Thierry to walk into the hospital in the morning, identify several patients who need operations, and then arrive in the operating room only to hear that the instruments haven't been cleaned from last night or, perhaps most commonly, to be told: "Nedret isn't here. If Nedret isn't here, we can't do it."

Nedret rules the operating room, his authority unchallenged, but his appearances are erratic. When he does show up, he seems eager to operate with Thierry, an older and more experienced colleague, and to learn new techniques. But as operations draw to an end, Nedret often takes off his gloves and gown and says, like a senior surgeon speaking to an intern, "OK, you can close. I have a job to do."

That job, from what Thierry can tell, involves matters at the front lines. Nedret offers to take Thierry along with him, but Thierry refuses.

"I'm not here to make war, I'm here to work at the hospital," Thierry says and explains that as a representative of Doctors Without Borders, he has to be neutral. What if the Serbs captured him on the front line and accused him of taking part in the Muslims' war efforts? It could put all of MSF's other programs at risk.

"Why are *you* going there?" Thierry asks Nedret in return. "We have a lot of work here in the hospital. Stay with me."

"Oh, no," Nedret says, "I have to go."

And when Thierry presses him with, "Why?" Nedret only answers: "I have to go because I have to go!"

Nedret leaves and then Thierry must await his return before he can operate on another new patient. Given this situation, Thierry's first priority is to evacuate the severely wounded, a goal toward which General Morillon has been expending most of his energy. One possibility would be to wait for a second convoy to get through and then, after aid has been unloaded, to fill the empty UNHCR trucks with the wounded and take them out via overland convoy. There are two problems. One is that when the first convoy attempted this maneuver a few days ago, hundreds of women and children desperate to leave the city flooded into the trucks, crushing the injured.

Even if the crowd could be controlled, another, more chilling, problem exists. Roughly 75 percent of the injured are men. They are clearly, under international law, *hors de combat*, out of combat, and entitled to protection under the Geneva Conventions. But local Serb commanders have repeatedly said that any male between the ages of approximately sixteen and sixty traveling through Serb areas will be regarded as a combatant and a war criminal.

This leaves only one possibility, more complicated and expensive: evacuation by U.N. helicopter. In negotiations with General Morillon, Serb leaders insist that any evacuation of Srebrenicans be contingent upon the "evacuation" of Serbs from the Bosnian government–controlled city of Tuzla, a move seen by many to be abetting ethnic cleansing, as many of the Serbs are thought to want to stay there. Morillon goes to Tuzla with a list of Serbs to try to convince the Bosnian government officials there to let them go.

This action infuriates UNHCR leaders, who see a potential exodus of Serbs from Tuzla as a form of U.N.-backed ethnic cleansing of one of Bosnia's last multiethnic cities. On March 22, Jose-Maria Mendiluce, special envoy of the U.N. High Commissioner, sends a memorandum of protest to Morillon's UNPROFOR superior, General Lars-Eric Wahlgren:

> The common objective to save the Srebrenica population could, on the basis of this type of negotiation, become the beginning of the end of our capacity to negotiate on the basis of the most basic humanitarian principles and is further jeopardizing our already limited capacity to maintain, in the most hostile environment, the humanitarian character of UNHCR involvement.

The next day, the head of the U.N.'s Department of Peacekeeping Operations, Kofi Annan, also chastises Wahlgren in a cable: "I trust you will have advised Morillon that he must coordinate his negotiations closely with UNHCR. I need hardly remind you that UNPROFOR's role in B&H is to support UNHCR's humanitarian efforts, and not the other way around."

Nevertheless, the Bosnian government agrees that forty-seven Serbs—all of whom it says require medical attention or are verified as citizens of Yugoslavia, not Bosnia—will be allowed to leave Tuzla. Serbian nationalist political leader Dr. Radovan Karadžić, in New York for peace talks, then endorses the Srebrenica helicopter evacuation.

When the approval comes, Thierry prepares quickly for the evacuation. He inspects the soccer pitch where the helicopters will land, taking note of a shell crater in its midst. He receives information on the layout of the helicopters, which have room for several patients to lie, several to sit, and several to stand. Back at the hospital, with no experience or training for such a vast undertaking, he invents a system of evacuation triage, assigning each patient a priority level from one to four. He first identifies the patients by bed, only to discover later in the day that stronger patients, in a bid to be evacuated, are pushing the weaker, higher-priority patients out of their beds. He then takes to marking evacuation priority in indelible ink on the backs of hands.

U.S. ARMY MAJOR REX DUDLEY, a thirty-six-year-old intelligence officer and one of the two mysterious Americans who entered Srebrenica with Eric, awakens at 4:30 the next morning, March 24, 1993, to coordinate the evacuation. United States European Command sent the attractive, square-jawed officer into Bosnia nearly a month ago on the first day of U.S. airdrops, tasking him with identifying the key Bosnian military players and learning about the military situation. The mobile, secure satellite communications device he could provide then bought him a ride into Srebrenica with General Morillon.

During his time here, Dudley has labored to improve the effectiveness and safety of the airdrops. Coordinating with the local military, he picked drop zones throughout the besieged area where local soldiers could guard supplies, varying the locations from night to night so that people, not knowing where to wait, wouldn't get killed by falling pallets. Dudley also worked with the hospital to discover what medical supplies were most needed and was deeply disappointed when told one night that thousands of doses of typhoid vaccine he worked hard to have airdropped were found by villagers who, not knowing what they were, tossed them into a fire.

Constantly shadowed by two Bosnian minders, he has also mapped the perimeter of the enclave and attempted to understand what the Muslims and Serbs in this part of Bosnia are fighting about. He has concluded that the valley of Srebrenica is eminently defendable, and identified positions from which it can be protected. He explained to some key Bosnian soldiers that they should dig up the roads and block the trails leading into the town and set up defense in depth—forward positions with multiple fallback positions. This way the light infantry could fight off an armored Serb attack. When the Bosnians argued they couldn't pull it off, he advised them to get out. *The place is the Alamo*, he thinks. *It isn't going to last.*

As the senior international officer remaining in the enclave after Morillon left yesterday for negotiations, Dudley is taking charge of the medical evacuation. Early in the morning, he dispatches Bosnian police to the soccer field to secure a helicopter landing zone. Two artillery shells impact beside the field as the police arrive, killing one and injuring another. For the first time in his military career, Major Dudley has sent a man to his death.

The evacuation is allowed to proceed as planned. Around noon, dozens of wounded men are carried out of the hospital on stretchers and driven in two ancient, hobbling flatbed trucks to the soccer pitch, where short green grass has sprouted just days after the last snow. Three white helicopters marked "UN" await them, rotors churning. U.N. and Bosnian soldiers load the gaunt, bandaged patients onto the helicopters.

Srebrenicans gather along the graffiti-covered walls surrounding the soccer field, watching the events behind a military cordon. A French pilot wearing dark sunglasses smiles behind the mouthpiece of his helmet and waves from the helicopter window.

The soldiers fit about thirty of the wounded into the unarmed helicopters and then pull the doors shut and the crafts lift off. On the middle of the soccer pitch, three air controllers stay behind to coordinate the next evacuation from the ground. One wears a set of headphones connected to a radio and antenna held in a knapsack on his back.

Moments later, an explosion startles them.

"Turn on the radio, we're being shelled," one soldier shouts, pulling on his blue-covered helmet, then taking it off. "Tell him to get on to the liaison officer."

The men crouch and talk into their radios. At the sound of a second blast, they flatten to the ground. A dozen Bosnians run for the exit nearby, clinging to the wall of the soccer field like drops of water sliding along a glass. The air controllers are left alone, lying flat on the ground in the middle of the pitch.

"I think the best is to go on the APC," one says.

Before they can move, a ferocious explosion hits the field. The air blackens with smoke and debris. Several soldiers—U.N. and Bosnian—are blown to the ground nearby. A woman screams. Everyone heads toward a low metal fence. Some stop to pick up the wounded. Others jump the fence and make it across the street behind a house, and they huddle against a wall with dozens of children, men, women holding babies, and several of the intended evacuees.

Major Dudley was with his tactical satellite device beside a concrete wall, partly protected, when one of the shells landed about sixty feet away. The huge craters in the soggy ground suggest to him large-caliber shells shot by a Serb artillery battery. The great accuracy of the strikes makes him think they've been called in by a forward observer with a clear view of the evacuation from the hills above.

After the blasts subside, Dudley returns to the communications equipment and crouches beside the pockmarked wall. Wearing a camouflage military jacket, large dark sunglasses, and a powder-blue helmet, he speaks into the tactical satellite receiver with studied calm.

"Alleycat, Alleycat, this is Washington, Washington," he calls in a military drawl to a U.N. Protection Force node outside the enclave. "Clear all nets, I have important communication."

He pauses.

"This is Washington, roger. I have more incoming, more incoming, over."

"This is Washington. . . . I am ordering an evacuation of this area so we don't have any more hurt or injured personnel. Alleycat, Alleycat, this is Washington. . . . I believe they are registering on our communication signal. Over."

Fresh brown gashes have rent the green field. Smoke billows from the brown hillside above the soccer pitch. A thunder-like boom sounds in the distance. The soldiers light cigarettes and smoke them with nervous expressions.

AT THE HOSPITAL, the MSF surgeon takes care of one of two injured Canadian soldiers, soothing him in broken English while squirting iodine onto the skin of his head.

"What are you doing to me?" the disoriented soldier whines.

"I'm cleaning your . . . what are they called? *Oreilles*."

"Ear," someone offers.

"I'm cleaning your hear, because they are so dirty," he jokes. "Relax, guard! What's the name of the guard?"

"John."

"Relax, John."

Thierry doesn't say it then, but the blood in the soldier's ears makes him fear that shrapnel has fractured his skull.

It has been an overwhelming hour in the life of Dr. Thierry Pontus. As the soccer field was shelled, so, too, was the area around the hospital. Roughly two dozen casualties arrived simultaneously at his doorstep. Voices from every corner beg him to please come, please come. Still, he works calmly and deliberately, communicating with his Bosnian colleagues in fractured German.

Just beyond the soldier on an adjacent cot, face turned toward the doctor, lies a small five-year-old boy with a grave abdominal wound. Overwhelmed by the number of wounded and fairly certain the boy has no chance to survive, Thierry has decided to evacuate the child on the next helicopter rather than attempt to operate, as Nedret wants to do. The boy's exposed intestines are covered; he is wrapped in an aluminum blanket for warmth. Thierry tries to start an IV to give the boy fluids, but he is in shock, his veins collapsed because of all the blood he's lost. Thierry has to expose the large saphenous vein on his leg in order to insert an IV catheter. Now the child lies quietly—clearly under the effect of painkillers—but with saucer-like open eyes, face an almost luminescent white, only occasionally furrowing his brow and whimpering. He stretches his hand out to one of the men in the room, who stops what he's doing to hold it.

The Bosnian hospital workers stir stiffly around the room, staring at the injured U.N. soldiers and chattering about them in Bosnian. One complains that a Canadian refused to let her touch him. Next to the cot where Thierry works, a local nurse sutures the wounds of a local man.

Dr. Ejub Alić stands beside the man, looking tired and uncharacteristically thin, with dark circles under his eyes. Everyone is afraid because General Morillon, their protector, left Srebrenica yesterday to negotiate and hasn't returned. The Serbs in Bratunac are essentially holding him hostage. Now, with Srebrenica being shelled, the front lines outside of the city under heavy fire and reportedly about to collapse, and two U.N. soldiers injured, the townspeople fear that the U.N. troops will pull out. Many Srebrenicans are considering fleeing for their lives.

Fatima enters the makeshift emergency room where the injured Canadian soldiers lie surrounded by their colleagues.

"Fatima, look at this," a woman says. "What are we going to do?"

"We won't leave yet," Fatima says. "Let Morillon leave; we won't leave."

U.N. LEADERS IMMEDIATELY EXPRESS THEIR OUTRAGE at the attacks. Serb authorities agree to stop shelling and allow the evacuation to recommence, but each time the U.N. soldiers attempt to move toward the landing zone with patients, artillery from the northeast open fire.

The soldiers make a last-ditch effort to evacuate at least their own injured men. At 2:25 P.M., Thierry joins a handful of U.N. soldiers on a hill outside the hospital. One of the wounded soldiers holds the aluminum-wrapped boy in his arms as the child's father stands nearby.

A U.N. helicopter, this time a British Sea King, swoops down and hovers overhead. Its rotor whips the air into a storm of wind and debris. People gathered on the hillside turn away, hunching their shoulders against the gale and covering their mouths and eyes. The soldier holding the boy tells Thierry that the child has a strange look on his face.

Thierry examines him.

"The baby's dead," he says, and closes the child's eyes. The soldier faints. The bearded father takes back his son in tears. His cries are drowned by the helicopter's roar.

Two injured Canadian soldiers and three air controllers are winched up, and then the aircraft glides away. As it disappears, people on the ground yell and jeer.

"Aren't there any more?" a woman shouts.

Minutes later someone in Srebrenica, communicating via UNHCR radio, reports that at least twenty-five shells have landed in town. The evacuation is officially called off pending a ceasefire.

FEAR ENGULFS SREBRENICA. Rumors zip from mouth to mouth. The word on the street is that the helicopters landed in neighboring Bratunac and the wounded were taken to jail instead of the hospital! Men from Kragljivoda, near Ilijaz's village, appear in the hospital to warn him that the front line there is falling and to expect many casualties. At any moment, Ilijaz expects his family to float into Srebrenica on the stream of refugees. And now news spreads that the Serbs are about to enter Srebrenica. Ilijaz walks into the operating room while Thierry is operating on one of the day's wounded and announces the news in Bosnian. The expressions on the locals' faces drop. They quickly finish the operation and leave the hospital to make preparations for an exodus on foot through the hills to Tuzla.

Thierry has no idea what has happened—none of the locals will tell him. He returns to the PTT and a U.N. soldier fills him in, warning that a bad night lies ahead. The U.N. soldiers have made a breakout plan in case they need to evacuate. To Thierry's horror, it involves "neutralizing" several Bosnian guards. Thierry spends a sleepless night pondering the possible abandonment of his patients. If he stays and the Serbs take over Srebrenica, the locals have warned him, the incoming Serbs will seize him as a spy.

A UNHCR situation report is sent by radio and distributed overnight in English translation to UNHCR headquarters in Geneva and offices throughout the former Yugoslavia:

THE TIME FOR TALKING IS NOW FINISHED, IMMEDIATE I REPEAT IMMEDIATE ACTION IS NOW REQUIRED TO AVOID A MASSIVE NUMBER OF VICTIMS OF THE CIVILIANS IN THE NEXT 24 TO 48 HOURS. ALL I REPEAT ALL MEASURES SHOULD BE TAKEN TO GUARANTEE A SAFE EVACUATION OF THE CIVILIAN POPULATION OF SREBRENICA. WE REQUIRE CONVOYS TO EVACUATE A POPULATION OF AT LEAST 30,000 PEOPLE. THE WORSE SCENARIO IS NOW

PLAYING IN FRONT OF OUR EYES. OUR QUESTION IS, WHAT IS THE DESTINY OF THE CIVILIAN POPULATION OF SREBRENICA?? WITH OR WITSOUT [sic] OUR HELP PART OF THE POPULATION WILL LEAVE SREBRENICA TOMORROW. IF WE DO NOT EVACUATE, A MASSACRE COULD TAKE PLACE.

———————

THE NEXT DAY, General Morillon and the UNHCR Belgrade team meet with Serbian President Milošević in Belgrade, Serbia. Morillon demands an end to the offensive, telling Milošević that the Americans were ready to intervene, but that he had held them off. Only hours remain before the international community will commence military action, Morillon warns.

Srebrenica does not fall this day, but Gladovići does. In the evening, Ilijaz finds on his doorstep his mother, two brothers, their wives, five children, several bundles filled with food and clothing, and a horse. It relieves him to see his family alive.

They recount the past days' events. The family took shelter in their underground bunker as more than 100 shells an hour hammered the area around Gladovići. On the plateau of the mountain Tara, right across the Drina, tanks fired relentlessly at the local villages. Planes flew over, dropping bombs. Every day, Serb ground troops could be seen crossing the bridge at Skelani into Bosnia. They took more and more territory; the local Muslim soldiers could not resist such a force. Everyone believed that the entire region was going to fall.

This morning Bosnian soldiers ran into Gladovići to warn the villagers that the line at Kragljivoda had been lost and the Chetniks were coming. Ilijaz's family quickly gathered some necessities and took to the road. They looked back to see pillars of smoke rising from the villages behind them.

17

INTERLUDE

Snow comes again, freezing the offensive. A late-winter storm blankets the region with more than three feet of whiteness, silencing the guns. A Bosnia-wide ceasefire negotiated by Generals Philippe Morillon and Lars-Eric Wahlgren takes hold, and the injured trickle rather than flood into Srebrenica Hospital.

"Srebrenica is safe," Morillon declares. Colleagues toast him with champagne at his headquarters in Sarajevo.

Because the mass exodus of Srebrenicans that U.N. refugee officials predicted hasn't taken place, they send a second aid convoy into Srebrenica: twenty trucks filled with 200 tons of food, medicine, mattresses, blankets, and plastic sheeting to repair broken windows and use for shelter. After the supplies are off-loaded, more than 2,000 people—clearly lacking Morillon's optimism that Srebrenica is saved—storm past guards and U.N. drivers onto the flatbed trucks in a desperate bid to reach Tuzla. Soon there is no space left for the wounded and vulnerable whom Thierry has selected for evacuation. Srebrenica soldiers, called in by authorities overnight, succeed in clearing only three of the trucks for the injured before losing control to the ever-increasing crowds. As the morning hour of the convoy's departure nears, hundreds more struggle onto the trucks, screaming and trampling the weak, heedless of the soldiers firing warning shots into the air. Young women heave out old women; mothers throw their babies aboard and try to clamber up behind them.

Meanwhile, Thierry Pontus is busy wrapping up his work in the hospital. Having reached the end of his MSF assignment, he bids a tearful farewell to the colleagues he's grown close with over the past week and climbs into a UNHCR jeep at the head of the departing convoy. At the front line, Thierry watches Serb soldiers force all the women and children off the trucks. The soldiers lead away a fifty-nine-year-old man hiding among them. Thierry wants to protest, but others warn him to keep silent, and in Bratunac they take up the man's case with the head of the Bosnian Serb army, Ratko Mladić, who appears to meet them. Playing good cop, and looking to Thierry like nothing so much as a kind grandfather, Mladić releases the man and promises free movement of the convoy to Tuzla.

As they proceed through Serb-held territory, villagers pelt the trucks with stones, and armed men subject them to hours of searches, accusing Thierry, who doesn't have official permission to travel on the convoy, of being a spy. The people on the overcrowded trucks are for the most part eerily silent, but during one long wait, hundreds begin begging for water. Some of the internationals standing on the roadside scoop up snow and pass it to them. The convoy gets rolling again, but the tailgate of a truck breaks open in a tunnel minutes before reaching Tuzla. Twenty-five people spill onto the concrete; some are severely injured and are rushed away in the back of a British army Scimitar tank. When the convoy of trucks finally reaches Tuzla, five bodies are unloaded along with the living.

U.S. ARMY MAJOR REX DUDLEY DEPARTS the same day and reports back to high-ranking individuals. His conclusions about Srebrenica are clear; the Serbs want to achieve free reign over the whole of eastern Bosnia. The besieged Muslim enclave, straddling a key line of communication, stands right in their way. The Serbs desperately want to take it out, and they have a proven modus operandi: Take no prisoners. If the Serbs are allowed to capture Srebrenica, Major Dudley warns, the result will be genocide.

THE NEXT DAY, six days after Ilijaz's birth village went up in flames, Resolution 816, authorizing the use of military action to enforce the flight ban over Bosnia, is adopted by a vote of 14–0–1, with China abstaining. Security Council representatives make much of their newfound determination to back up their own demands. "It is the first real step toward addressing the actions of the aggressors in this conflict and draws a firm line beyond which further disregard of our efforts and positions will not go unanswered," declares the representative from rotating council member Djibouti. The resolution is referred to as a "landmark." It will go into effect after a brief delay.

Bosnian Serb General Mladić announces the following day that no further aid convoys will be allowed into Srebrenica. U.N. trucks will be permitted to enter Srebrenica empty, only to evacuate civilians. The head of UNHCR, Sadako Ogata, writes to the U.N. secretary-general that only two options remain to save those trapped in Srebrenica: Either inject internationals and turn the enclave into a U.N.-protected area or organize a large-scale evacuation.

"As time is running out," she writes, "more drastic action needs to be taken urgently to ensure the survival of the population in Srebrenica."

The Security Council responds by issuing a toothless demand for the Serbs to immediately "cease and desist forthwith from all violations of international humanitarian law," stating it is "shocked by and extremely alarmed at the dire and worsening humanitarian situation" and commending, for good measure, the "brave people" of the UNHCR and UNPROFOR. No further military threat is made.

The ceasefire around Srebrenica begins to break down in spite of the presence of the small contingent of U.N. soldiers. Under Serb attack, front lines in the south dissolve, leaving the main Srebrenica-Skelani road into Srebrenica wide open for Serb tanks. The local commander of the area must force his fleeing men back to the front lines to fight.

Around 10:30 A.M. on April 3, a Canadian captain ventures into the dangerous front-line area near Osmaće, ostensibly on "humanitarian patrol." He looks out across the valley through his binoculars and sees the Serbs. They see him, too. One after another, mortar bombs rain down on his position, exploding with a deafening boom. He tries to flee, but is injured on a snowy hillside along with a Bosnian machine gunner and ABC reporter Tony Birtley, who initiated the dangerous trip in an effort to assess the military situation.

Nedret, working alone since Thierry's departure, takes Tony to the operating room first, over the protests of U.N. soldiers who want their fellow soldier to receive priority. Nedret doesn't bend to their pressure, but neither does he base his triage system on medical criteria. "Even if his body was hanging in threads," Nedret tells the journalist, who's become a close friend, "you would be first."

A few weeks ago Tony watched Nedret treat the injuries of Philipp, the German photographer, whose bumbling ways and repeated injuries led Tony to nickname him "grenade magnet." The photographer awoke from ketamine anesthesia and described a beautiful dream. He was flying away, and the earth below looked like a beautiful ball.

"Did you see the earth very clearly?" Tony had asked him.

"Yes," said the photographer.

"Was Bosnia on that earth?"

———

The next day Srebrenica authorities, shooting guns in the air and shouting through megaphones, prevent civilians from climbing onto sixteen U.N. trucks leaving the enclave. More than 5,000 people have scrambled aboard the three outgoing convoys of the previous two weeks. About nineteen of them, mostly children, died from overcrowding or exposure to the elements.

"We don't even transport livestock that way," a Bosnian army commander says in a statement.

Upon each convoy's arrival, soldiers abandon the front lines and rush to Srebrenica to help their family members get aboard. Military leaders, as desperate to hold on to the town as many civilians are to leave it, fear that an exodus of women and children will sap the men's motivation to fight, devastating Srebrenica's defenses. Every thousand civilians removed by U.N. trucks brings the Serbs that much closer to emptying of Muslims the town they covet for themselves.

The Bosnians accuse the United Nations of collaborating with the Serbs in the ethnic cleansing of the town. Eric Dachy, disgusted by the way the evacuations are being carried out, and fully aware that men of fighting age won't be allowed to leave, can't help agreeing with this view. The massive evacuation being proposed by the United Nations seems like a capitulation, a predetermination that Srebrenica will fall. He believes they should try to prevent ethnic cleansing, not carry it out.

The UNHCR special representative for the former Yugoslavia, criticized from many corners, fires back angrily that his organization is only trying to save lives, and that Srebrenica is filled with refugees from other areas who have no place to live. "When we are trapped, as we are in Srebrenica, by all sorts of complications, the only thing we can do is to save the people who are asking us to save them," he says in an interview quoted in the *New York Times*.

In Srebrenica, Thierry is replaced by another Belgian MSF surgeon, Piet Willems. The fifty-three-year-old is an older, stiffer, and more formal man from a peaceful neighborhood outside of Brussels where he has a large, neatly kept house, a neat, manicured lawn, and a neat, well-kept wife. He has decided to use three weeks of vacation volunteering with MSF, inspired by the Christian belief that he must do something to help those in trouble. Deemed too inexperienced in international work to be sent to Cambodia when he applied to work at MSF, he has somehow been dispatched in a pinch to Srebrenica. He nearly turned himself around at the border after Thierry, on his way out of the enclave, described the situation. What stopped Piet from returning home was imagining what it would feel like to face his family without having done what he'd set out to do.

MSF headquarters in Belgium has been recruiting a team for Srebrenica with the goal of keeping at least one surgeon, anesthetist, general practitioner, and logistician in the enclave at all times. Some of the doctors, particularly the surgeons, will come for short assignments.

The day they arrive, Piet and an MSF anesthesiologist begin work in the operating room on the top floor of the hospital. Like Thierry, they find the local medical staff unmotivated and listless. Even artillery fire doesn't shake them. During one nighttime kidney operation, the locals barely flinch at a sound—close shellfire—that terrifies the new surgeon. The local nurses make fun of his trembling and make light of the intensifying artillery attack until one explosion rocks the hospital and sends part of a shattered windowpane flying narrowly past the MSF anesthesiologist's head. The team quickly finishes operating and heads for the cellar. More than thirty mortar bombs and other artillery rounds land in the town overnight.

The Belgian surgeon leaves Srebrenica with the next convoy, too anxious to work in these conditions, at least for now. A U.N. report of the attacks motivates General Morillon to announce he is returning to Srebrenica and that he is negotiating with the Serbs for a contingent of 150 Canadian peacekeepers, already on the ground in Bosnia, to enter. He leaves the capital, Sarajevo, the following day. But when Morillon nears Srebrenica, hundreds of Serb civilians surround his armored vehicles, pounding steel spikes into bulletproof windows, pulling off antennas and flags, scrawling graffiti, including "Morillon—Hitler," and preventing them from advancing.

In spite of Morillon's failure to re-enter the town, a relative calm descends on Srebrenica over the coming days. A recently arrived MSF general practitioner takes advantage of the quiet to try to improve the situation in the Srebrenica schoolhouse. Hundreds of displaced persons live inside, packed fifty to sixty to a classroom, sleeping on pushed-together desks under the gaze of the old leader, Tito, whose framed photographs still adorn the high walls above green chalkboards. Almost all have the characteristic itchy rash of skin infested with scabies, and about half look anemic. The school lacks showers or baths, its toilets are stopped up, and people defecate in the open. When Chetnik soldiers capture Srebrenica's water treatment plant and cut off the meager supply of running water, diarrhea spreads in the schoolhouse. The doctor installs a water bladder, organizes cleaning of the schoolrooms, and begins to treat patients with the now-ample supply of drugs. In fact so many boxes of medicines sit in the hospital in such disarray that MSF's new logistician, Hans Ulens, has to request, by radio, that the Americans stop airdropping them.

Serb authorities allow another aid convoy to pass through to Srebrenica on the Saturday before Easter, warning that it must be filled with women and children on its way out. But Srebrenica soldiers again shoo away the hundreds of desperate people trying to mount the trucks, firing into the crowd and injuring several. The convoy crosses back into Serb territory empty.

18

THE HOTTEST PART
OF HELL

THE NEXT DAY, APRIL 12, 1993, dawns in bright sunshine and the long-awaited freshness of spring. It provides the perfect backdrop for what has been nearly a week without shelling. The MSF team awakens refreshed after having enjoyed Easter dinner and a rare bath at the Hotel Domavija the previous evening.

What's more, today is the "landmark" day when U.N. Resolution 816, authorizing NATO to shoot down unauthorized aircraft over Bosnia, will go into effect after many delays. Srebrenica residents, the majority of whom have precious little with which to occupy their days, spill out of their cramped quarters and take to the streets. Refugee children from the schoolhouse run to play in the open air, their mothers strolling outside to watch them. Dozens crowd the amphitheater-like steps that wrap around the schoolyard to watch soccer matches played with balls air-dropped at the suggestion of a UNHCR official. In a far corner of the stands, a knot of young fans surrounds three teens who strum folk songs on a guitar-like *shargija*.

The exhilaration of the day contrasts with Ilijaz's depressed mood. He has lost too many friends and family members to this war—among them his cousin, Sulejman; his colleague, Dr. Džanić; and several weeks ago the good friend who'd introduced him to Fatima, Dr. Hamdija Halilović, who was killed by a tank shell near the front lines in Sarajevo while trying to pull an injured fighter to safety. Ilijaz, given the news by a ham radio operator, was the one who had to break it to Hamdija's parents.

Last night brought yet another loss, his niece's husband—a good friend—mortally wounded on the front line south of Srebrenica. By the time the man was carried into a room on the hospital's ground floor, he was dead. Ilijaz sat alone beside his body and cried. Hours passed, and someone gently led Ilijaz upstairs to the doctor's room to lie down. He was too upset. For the first time in his life, he took a Valium to calm his nerves.

Now, on this beautiful Monday afternoon, family members arrive to take the man's body away, planning to bury it in a tiny wooded cemetery not far from the hospital. Ilijaz, exhausted and disoriented, stays behind to finish some work and will join them later for the *dzenaza* ceremony.

———————

AROUND 2 P.M., at the airport in Sarajevo, Serbian nationalist commander General Ratko Mladić concludes a meeting with U.N. General Lars-Eric Wahlgren. Mladić promises to respect the ceasefire and work toward peace. About the same time, U.S., French, and Dutch warplanes take flight from bases in Italy and roar off the aircraft carrier *Theodore Roosevelt* in the Adriatic Sea to begin patrolling Bosnian airspace.

It is fifteen minutes later that the shells and rockets begin to hit Srebrenica's schoolyard.

Many people will later attempt to describe this day that turns in a minute from bright to dark. The internationals who experience it will use words such as "infernal" and "catastrophic." A displaced person from Konjević Polje, perhaps more desensitized by all she has seen and experienced, will remember it in her diary as "one of the most horrible days of the war."

Stories will turn to legend—that one *shargija* player survived beneath the bodies of his two friends; that blood ran like a river down the street from the schoolhouse to the hospital; that Canadian soldiers patrolling the town in an APC when the shelling began couldn't make it back to their headquarters in the post office because the roads were blocked by bodies. A U.N. refugee official will describe seeing body parts caught in the schoolyard fence.

"I will never be able to convey the sheer horror of the atrocity I witnessed on April 12," he will write. "Suffice it to say that I did not look forward to closing my eyes at night for fear that I would relive the images of a nightmare that was not a dream."

The tragedy coalesces at the Srebrenica Hospital, where within the span of minutes, more than 100 dead and wounded are pushed by hundreds more relatives and friends on oxcarts, carried in arms, and wheelbarrowed up to a building already so full of patients that some are lying in the corridors and in the spaces between beds.

The scene inside is confusion incarnate—the sight of blood, the sound of tears, the smell of vomit, and a maze of bodies strewn in doorways, topping stairs, and lying on the ground filling every patch of floor space. There is no water. No light. The doctors have to climb over patients, sometimes stepping on them, to reach other patients, shining flashlights in a useless effort to triage people whose wounds are buried under thick layers of winter clothes. The already beaten-down hospital staff cannot bear it.

"I was in the corridor when everyone arrived," the MSF logistician, Hans Ulens, will remember later. "There was no organization, like 'How are we going to attack that situation?' . . . They were not prepared at all for that. You would expect another reaction. . . . I would suspect that every nurse or doctor would run in, but it was like . . . 'Awww, what can we do? We can do nothing.' . . . Piet came in and shouted, 'You give morphine! Morphine. Morphine. Morphine.' Then the whole thing started to work." Piet Willems, the MSF surgeon, returned from Belgrade a few days ago to combat the senses of shame, failure, and cowardice that nagged at him after leaving.

He and the others spend the next five hours stabilizing patients. With the help of an assistant, the MSF anesthesiologist roves the corridors injecting morphine and, with a flashlight in his mouth, placing IVs. Just weeks ago, before the arrival of MSF and their battery-powered flashlights, it would have been nearly impossible to see and work in the darkening corridors of the hospital, the only light dim and smoky from improvised wicks burning in cups of oil. The staff begin to operate at around 7:30 P.M. The first few patients have more complicated injuries than expected and die soon after surgery.

In the corridor outside of the operating theater, people wait, arms out, begging for operations.

"There was also a lot of pressure from the family members, including people with weapons," one of the MSF doctors will remember. "We were never threatened, but it's always a bit impressive if you see people with guns insisting that *their* family members will have to be treated first. So, that also influenced a bit the selection for surgery."

The MSF anesthesiologist records the injuries. "Gastric perforation"; "spleen, liver, stomach"; "shrapnel in the eye with brain coming out—dead, the fourth son of five in the same family"; "five-year-old child with large injury of an arm and fractured femur." The selection, or triage, system—if not well implemented at first—is at least clear in the mind of the MSF surgeon, Piet Willems. He divides the injured into three categories: "they shall wait," "they shall die," or "we shall give salvation." That second category is the most excruciating. Those injured in the head or chest will die without immediate intervention, but for each one, surgery would require three to five hours in the operating room. That is too much precious time. In another place, at another time, they might have been saved.

But Piet doesn't make these decisions. After each operation, he barely has time to clear away an amputated arm or leg before the next patient is brought in. He just takes them as they come. Though he has never been trained for a situation like this, he gives the biggest effort of his life. He has no time to insulate himself from his patients with new pairs of gloves and clean gowns; he works elbow-deep in blood, performing surgery after surgery, seemingly unconcerned by the nearby explosion of shells. Something has changed in him. His fear has given way to a stronger emotion.

"Then I was not afraid," he will later remember. "There was something like . . . you became angry, eh? You became angry about people who would do something like this."

Somehow Ilijaz Pilav manages to push away the memory of his friend's death last night and tend to the pain of others. The day will stick to his memory in fragments, like shattered glass. Darkness. Crying. Every ten minutes someone else dying. He stops for a moment and considers what life will be like for the severely injured children they are treating and whether it would be better to leave them alone and let them die.

Nedret Mujkanović is seen in the corridor outside the operating room, holding his head in his hands, looking utterly defeated.

The doctors operate well into the night in the single, makeshift operating room, using its improvised operating table—a low-standing bed—

and a small, steady light powered by a generator. It arrived, providentially, two days ago. They stop for a brief break, then begin again in the morning. By 8 P.M., they still have eighteen cases to go. They call over U.N. radio for the urgent delivery of helmets, an operating table and lamp, and fluids to help expand blood volume.

They will remember it always—the single operating room and the impossible choices. How they stood in their flak jackets for hours performing surgery; how they ran to the corridor each time there was shelling. How in the end their fear gave way to anger. How they saved perhaps twenty lives, while sixteen others died that first night. In the end, the story will be told in numbers. At least fifty-six dead. More than 100 injured. Most of them were displaced persons. Fifteen of them were children.

EVER PRACTICAL, those Srebrenicans not immediately affected by the tragedy turn to their radios for news of how the incident is playing and what the international reaction will be. At a press conference in Sarajevo, Larry Hollingworth, the white-bearded UNHCR worker who recently departed from Srebrenica, sheds his characteristic diplomacy:

My first thought was of the army commander who had ordered the shelling. I hope that he burns in the hottest part of hell.

I then thought of the soldiers who had loaded the guns and fired them. I hope that they suffer from nightmares. I hope that their sleep is broken by the screams of the children and the cries of their mothers.

I then thought about Doctor of Medicine Karadžić, Professor of Literature Koljević, Biologist Mrs. Plavšić, Geologist Dr. Lukić and I wondered if today they will condemn this atrocity and punish the perpetrators or will they deny their education and condone it?

I then thought about my Serb friends whom I have met on my travels. Do they wish to read in future history books that their army has chased innocent women and children from village to village, until finally they are cornered in Srebrenica, a place from which there is no escape, and where their fate is to be transported like cattle or slaughtered like lambs?

Fierce condemnation rings from many corners. Former British Prime Minister Margaret Thatcher warns that Bosnia may become "another Holocaust" and upbraids Western nations for standing idly by.

Bosnian Serb leaders fire back, reviving the now-familiar canards that the Muslims shelled themselves or that the dead were really Serbs. The people of Srebrenica get more bad news. The media report that the French government plans to withdraw Srebrenica's outspoken ally General Morillon from his job as commander of U.N. troops in Bosnia.

On the streets of Srebrenica in the days after the massacre, the doctors see wagons piled with cadavers pulled by family members. Another aid convoy arrives and the empty trucks fill with about 800 evacuees, including some of the wounded women, children, and elderly. Again the unbearable scenes unroll of shouting, crying, and violence, of mothers and fathers separated from their sons and daughters, of desperate family members yanking children into trucks by their sweaters.

The shelling of Srebrenica resumes and turns relentless. The number of people requiring all types of medical assistance is far beyond what the small medical staff, even with MSF, can handle. "The selection is terrible, but indispensable," the MSF anesthesiologist writes in French in a diary he will later submit as a report to MSF. "I think of Auschwitz."

Nedret is ill and unable to work. Naser Orić, Srebrenica's chief commander, is lightly wounded, and many of his soldiers withdraw from the front lines. The Srebrenica authorities—Naser, the mayor, and the president of the war council—meet with the Canadian commander to discuss capitulation. The mayor's only condition is a helicopter evacuation for the wounded men, who he is sure will otherwise be slaughtered by the Serbs.

Another U.N. convoy arrives. The authorities again prevent desperate civilians from scrambling aboard the trucks to be evacuated. The four MSF workers in the enclave, fearing a Serb "reprisal" the likes of the Easter massacre or worse, decide to evacuate themselves from Srebrenica on what they believe will be the last convoy to reach the enclave, along with representatives of the UNHCR and the International Committee of the Red Cross.

One MSF doctor assuages his own conscience by assessing that, at this point and under these conditions, he can do "nothing important" for the people. The MSF surgeon, Piet Willems, has mixed emotions but a clear conscience—after all, he will later say, I needn't have come in the first place. He is glad to have saved at least a few people's lives and showed the population by his presence that they were not forgotten. The anesthesiologist wants to stay, but the U.N. commander finds him in the hospital and says he will no longer take responsibility for MSF staff-member security. Furthermore, with only a few armored personnel carriers in the enclave, the officer cannot guarantee the anesthesiologist a ride out if the worst occurs. He, too, decides to go.

MSF's local translator, who celebrated his fourteenth birthday last night, cries and pleads with them in his broken German. "Please stay," he begs, in tears. He tells them that they are needed, that if they go, nobody will stay. At the last moment, the pleas sway MSF's logistician, a short, energetic Belgian named Hans Ulens who, owing Doctors Without Borders a year of service for supporting his studies, had asked to be sent anywhere but Bosnia.

With no reinforcements in sight, but no orders to evacuate either, the U.N. military observers and soldiers also decide to remain with the people. On Thursday, April 15, diminutive Hans, four military observers, and nine Canadian UNPROFOR soldiers are the last internationals to stand physically between the Serbs and the residents of Srebrenica. They are the last, as Eric Dachy termed it, to interpose.

FRIDAY, APRIL 16, 1993. NEW YORK, NEW YORK, USA.

United Nations Security Council Resolution 819:

". . . Demands that all parties and others concerned treat Srebrenica and its surroundings as a safe area which should be free from any armed attack or any other hostile act . . . "

ILIJAZ PILAV FEELS CLOSE TO ROCK BOTTOM. The days will fuzz together in his memory when he tries to describe them later. He will remember feeling that the world is falling apart, wondering "what it's all for," finding "no meaning in anything," and knowing that Srebrenica's fall and the end of his suffering are just a question of time.

Mostly, though, he will remember being numbed and indifferent to his fate as he works mechanically, doing whatever needs to be done in the hospital. He will remember the sense of being surrounded by thousands of other suffering people, a part of "one of those masses that are meant to suffer." So much remains to be done at the hospital. He has eaten and slept very little for days. It has become physically difficult to go on.

On Saturday, April 17, he stands across the operating room table from Nedret, performing surgery. The nearby explosions of grenades and mortar bombs are relentless and by 4 P.M., thirty-two new wounded have been brought to the hospital, most of them civilians. Every fifteen minutes or so, a messenger runs into the hospital warning that the Chetniks are coming closer and closer.

Ilijaz looks up from the operating field and notices that Nedret's face appears pale. He realizes his own face must appear the same way.

Nedret looks up, too, and for a moment their eyes lock while their hands continue working. Ilijaz feels as if knives have already been put to their throats. There are no defense plans, no disaster plans, and no evacuation plans for the population, who will undoubtedly flee to the woods as the Serbs arrive. He is sure they will all die, and for the first time he pities Nedret for having chosen to come here.

IN THE UNITED STATES, Bosnia has become the number one subject of television news, with nearly twice as many stories in the first three months of 1993 as the inauguration of Bill Clinton or the February 1993 World Trade Center bombing. In the past weeks graphic footage of Srebrenica refugees has heightened the pressure on the new administration to respond. The Srebrenica saga makes top news in other Western countries, too, such as Canada and Great Britain. The local ham radio operator issues a final cry to the world, which headlines the April 17, 1993, London *Guardian*: "We beg you to do something, whatever you can. In the name of God, do something!" Exactly one year has passed since war broke out in Srebrenica.

AT DAWN ON APRIL 18, the clamor of artillery and mortar-fire suddenly ceases. An eerie silence envelops Srebrenica. At the hospital, Ilijaz, who hasn't slept in days, has a strange feeling that the world is teetering "just on the edge of real catastrophe." A few hours later the ominous rumble of tanks draws him to a hospital window. He can hardly believe what he sees. The company vehicles rolling into Srebrenica are painted U.N. white, not military green. The maple leaf of Canada, not the Serb tricolor, marks them.

SARAJEVO AIRPORT TARMAC, sixteenth hour of negotiation, "Agreement for the demilitarization of Srebrenica":

At a meeting held at Sarajevo on 17 April 1993, Lt.-Gen. Mladic and Gen. Halilović, in the presence of Lt.-Gen. Wahlgren, representing UNPRO-FOR, acting as a mediator, agreed the following:

1. A total cease-fire in the Srebrenica area effective from 0159 on 18 April 1993. Freezing all combat actions on the achieved lines of confrontation including supporting artillery and rocket fire.
2. The deployment of a company group of UNPROFOR into Srebrenica by 1100 18 April 1993. . . .
3. The opening of an air corridor between Tuzla and Srebrenica via Zvornik for evacuation of the seriously wounded and seriously ill . . . The seriously wounded and seriously ill will be evacuated after identification by UNPROFOR in the presence of two doctors from each side and the ICRC . . .
4. The demilitarization of Srebrenica . . .

PART THREE

A SAFE AREA

Let people's memory of all that's ugly die,

so children may not sing songs of vengeance.

—**Meša Selimović**, *The Fortress*

19

THROUGH THE
LOOKING GLASS

JUST AN HOUR AFTER twenty-eight-year-old Dr. Boro Lazić finally closes his strained eyes after a night of operating and falls asleep, the unrelenting trill of his telephone badgers him awake. As a Serb physician working in the surgical department of Zvornik Hospital, he's already invested more than his share of time treating casualties of the Srebrenica offensive. Why are the nurses disturbing him? It's only 9 in the morning. He asked them to leave him alone for as long as possible!

He grabs the phone receiver.

"*Ha*-lo!" The nurse who answers him is not calling about a patient. She puts him through to his Bosnian Serb army commander, Lieutenant Colonel Vinko Pandurević.

"Do you want to go to Srebrenica?" the commander asks, as if it was something they'd been discussing. Boro thinks he's making a bad joke. The commander's an arrogant, impudent, incompetent jerk.

"Why not?" Boro plays along.

"All right, be ready," says Pandurević. "I'm sending a car."

So fifteen minutes out of a deep sleep on April 18, 1993, Boro is whisked to the commander's office. Then the lean, sandy-haired doctor is sitting before the massive, red-headed commander. Pandurević explains that last night's ceasefire agreement calls for two Serb physicians to oversee the helicopter evacuation of Srebrenica's wounded to the Bosnian government–held city of Tuzla. The commander wants Boro to go and make certain that all those evacuated are truly wounded and not healthy "war criminals" trying to slip out of Srebrenica. Boro agrees to go, yes, but knowing that Serb forces spent last night pounding Srebrenica, he fears he will be a convenient target for vengeful Srebrenicans.

He suggests that a Serb soldier accompany him for protection. Not possible, the commander tells him. Boro must choose whether to take the risk. But he won't be alone; traveling with him will be some U.N. soldiers, another Serb doctor, two International Committee of the Red Cross doctors, and two Muslim doctors from Tuzla.

Tuzla is where Boro's parents, his wife's mother, and at least fifteen members of his extended family still reside. It's where he grew up, went to medical school, and lived before the war. All year he has wondered what life is like there and longed to find a way to help his parents, but aside from one brief ham radio conversation and one Red Cross message, he has had no contact. At times he has come close to various front lines and thought of stepping over them. Never before has he had the chance to visit the other side.

When war started to tear Yugoslavia apart, Boro Lazić and his wife—a smart, petite psychology student—were staying at a Holiday Inn near Disneyland in Los Angeles, California. It was 1991 and they were on their first visit to the United States. Boro had saved up money back in medical school, skipping class to travel to Turkey and buy blue jeans to sell back home, returning just in time to cram for and then ace his final exams. With his boyish face and blue-green eyes, Boro charmed the bookish girls into lending him notes for missed classes and the teaching assistants into postponing his exams. For his enterprising antics and his razor-sharp intelligence, his schoolmates and even his future wife referred to him fondly as a "vagabond," "entrepreneur," and "Mafioso."

After medical school, when jobs and money were scarce in Bosnia, he'd trotted off to Switzerland, seeking fortune. For a year he worked as a medical technician and studied alternative medicine, but the Swiss had no use for his Yugoslav medical diploma. He grew impatient with the idea of working several more years before he could secure a visa for his family to live there. His wife and young daughter came for a visit and they bought tickets for a trip to New Zealand, planning secretly to stay there and exploit financial opportunities far greater than those in Bosnia. They landed, instead, in a pickle. When the plane made a stop in Los Angeles, their lack of visas for New Zealand was discovered. Officials confiscated their passports, but allowed them to stay in the United States for several weeks while their applications were being processed.

They took advantage of the time to shuttle back and forth to Disneyland and other sights. Once an Angeleno taxi driver asked them where they came from. Boro's wife was fluent in English. "Yugoslavia," she'd told him.

The driver turned around in his seat. "There's a war in Yugoslavia," he said. At that point, just some low-level fighting had broken out in Croatia. She was surprised he knew about it.

"There's not a war in all of Yugoslavia," she said, "just a part of Yugoslavia." The driver had visited the ancient city of Dubrovnik on the Croatian coast, which was now under fire. "Are you Serbs or Croats?" he persisted. Impressed that he knew enough to ask, she explained that she was a Croat and Boro, a Serb. They came from Bosnia, not Croatia, far from the fighting.

"It's a bad thing," the driver pronounced. The way he said it chilled them, as if he had some foreknowledge that war would spread to Bosnia, too. The couple could not imagine it.

Boro's visa application for New Zealand was eventually denied. His wife and daughter went back to Bosnia, and he returned to Switzerland. He tried his luck in Austria, but could not secure a visa for the family to stay. Defeated, he rejoined them, taking a job as a general practitioner at a health clinic in his eastern Bosnian birth town, Šekovići, population 4,323. Many of the non-cosmopolitan areas of Bosnia had a predominance of one ethnicity, and Šekovići—at 97 percent Serb, 2 percent "Yugoslav," and 1 percent "other" in the 1991 census—was no exception. His wife became one of a handful of ethnic Croats in the entire municipality of roughly 10,000 citizens. However, Šekovići, nestled beneath hills on the Drinjaca River, had been a pivotal backdrop in the fight for Yugoslav "Brotherhood and Unity" and against fascism and nationalism—it was the most important Partisan stronghold in eastern Bosnia during World War II. Until recently, one of the area's frescoed sixteenth-century Serb Orthodox monasteries housed a museum that commemorated the war and Šekovići's part in it. But when Communists lost the 1991 elections, the museum was shuttered and the building returned to the church.

By the start of the new year, 1992, the war drums were beating. Serb leaders, refusing to recognize the authority of the Bosnian government, established a "Serbian Autonomous Region" of Yugoslavia centered in Šekovići. As tensions continued to rise, and Bosnia moved toward a declaration of independence from Yugoslavia, the Serbian department of state security established a "Serbian voluntary guard" in Šekovići. Boro joined it. All the local men he knew did, too. It seemed as if everyone in

Bosnia was splitting into sports teams. Boro's Muslim friends back in Tuzla booed Serbian leader Milošević and told Boro they were joining the Muslim "Green Berets." The Šekovići voluntary guard was Boro's team, and, with his friends and cousins in the game, he couldn't just sit on the sidelines and watch.

His joining the Serb military infuriated his Croat wife. He argued that he had to do it; otherwise people in Šekovići would see him as a traitor. Besides, being in the army would give him the strength to protect her. Other non-Serbs, threatened by the growing Serb nationalism, were leaving Šekovići. One Muslim, the wife of a friend, converted to Christianity and took a Serb name for security.

Boro never would have predicted that he'd end up in a nationalist militia. His family had no historical ax to grind—his only relative killed in World War II, a grandfather, had been murdered by fellow Serbs in Šekovići. His parents' best friends were Muslims and Croats. He and his sister had been raised to differentiate people on the basis of relative goodness, not nationality. In fact, nationality was never even mentioned. Until the war, he wasn't aware that people could be divided that way.

Slowly, the barrage of media stories about atrocities against Serbs, which first appeared implausible to him, gained credence. Boro's team began looking to him like the underdogs. In March, more than a dozen Serb civilians were reported to have been killed by Croats and Muslims in the strategic northern Bosnian border town of Bosanski Brod. Boro, shaken, feared for the entire Serb nation. A steady television-viewing diet of World War II movies expanded his apprehension. The films, shown continuously on state-run TV, depicted thousands of Serbs in eastern Bosnia dying at the hands of local Muslims and Croats allied with the fascists—including many in Šekovići. The memories revived on television stretched back to the defeat of Serbs at the hands of the Ottoman conquerors in 1489, convincing Boro that the Serbs had a "too long" history of tragedy. Although he didn't feel personally threatened, he believed that the "Serbian national being" was endangered and that he had to do his utmost to protect it.

The stories defined his enemy. They gave him a reason for hating his former neighbors, friends, and colleagues, and sometimes these past months, particularly when the other side seemed stronger, he did. It took time for the transformation to occur. For a long while he didn't believe that war would come. But the stories were like recruiters. They turned him into a player.

His Šekovići voluntary guard, at first loosely attached to the Yugoslav National Army, was aimed at neutralizing paramilitary formations—basically Muslims arming themselves in preparation for Bosnia's independence. As the group's only physician, Boro readied his fellow soldiers for the types of injuries they might suffer in the field and taught them how to treat themselves before help came. The volunteer Serbs set up guard posts on the road between Tuzla and Zvornik, searching car trunks for weapons. Once, they rambled through a village where Muslims were rumored to be organizing weapons, but the men in question slipped into the woods and Boro's troops could not find them.

The group saw its first real action around 3 one morning in April 1992. Along with forces from other areas in Bosnia and troops from Serbia, the troops took Vlasenica, a Muslim-majority town of about 8,000 inhabitants with a sizable Serb minority. It surprised Boro to meet almost no resistance.

"In the morning, Muslims were called to give up their arms," Boro later recalled. "People came and brought pistols, rifles, hunting rifles, whatever anybody had. And we stayed there until 11 in the morning. . . . We went back to the base, and Vlasenica was taken over by [other] units . . . and the local [Serb] population."

During the time Boro was there, he said, he did not hear a single gunshot. The same pattern was repeated next in the town of Kamenica. "The assignment was the same: to go into the village and call people to give up their arms. And then the officers [of] the unit usually gave lectures to the people, the inhabitants of the place, how there is no need to be afraid and organize any kind of [resistance]; that basically the cause of coming into this village or city is to prevent anything worse. Then the army would go back, take the arms and go back. And the people who were living there stayed to live there."

It didn't remain this way for long. One morning in June, Boro's sister came to take his wife, Sanja, away to their parents' cottage in the hills.

"It's going to be a bad day," she told her.

Buses arrived near Šekovići to remove the 150 or so remaining Muslims. Their belongings were confiscated. The only Muslims allowed to stay were two women married to Serb husbands.

When Boro appeared at the cottage hours later, his sister and wife rushed to him. "What happened?" they asked.

"Nothing," he answered.

Did he feel bad about it? Boro wasn't one to talk about his feelings. Long after the events, when pressed, he'd look back and wryly remind the questioner that times when people were *asked* to leave and left were the best times in the war—then nobody was killed. In other places the "ethnic cleansing" turned far crueler. Boro's first military action in Vlasenica helped consolidate Serb authority. Soon after, Muslims were removed from their posts in the police and army. Then came the harsh treatment. Muslims were "arrested, beaten and interrogated, and some arbitrarily killed," according to the report of a U.N. commission of experts investigating violations of humanitarian law. Conditions worsened over the following months, after 80,000 troops from Serbia along with a significant amount of weaponry were transferred to local control. Muslims' homes were looted and set on fire. "Then, in the beginning of June, the systematic eviction and execution of Muslims began," the U.N. commission found. Muslims were detained in at least eight camps where beatings, rapes, individual killings, and mass executions occurred. Those considered politically influential were taken to fields and murdered. The commander of one of the camps was later accused of crimes against humanity in the first indictment issued by the International Criminal Tribunal for the Former Yugoslavia.

But by that time, Boro was long gone from Vlasenica. Every once in a while, he heard that one or another of the soldiers he was treating had participated in some atrocities. As a doctor, he felt ethically bound to care for whoever needed him. Still, Boro began to pity the people on the other side of the front line as it became clear how much stronger his side was than theirs. Practically the only wounds he treated at the start of the war were the self-inflicted injuries of inexperienced soldiers, reflecting the imbalance of power. His voluntary guard became an army brigade. For the first several months of war, he worked out of a car in the field, moving along with the mostly offensive actions. He gathered the medicines and materials he needed from the donations that Doctors Without Borders, among other organizations, made to civilian health clinics. For the seriously injured, he had at his disposal several nearby hospitals. Those who needed a higher level of care were flown by helicopter to major hospitals in Belgrade, Serbia.

Over the year of war, the Army of the Republic of Bosnia and Herzegovina gained strength, and its forces, particularly those from Srebrenica,
conducted some punishing actions, including a blitz offensive in fall 1992
against a strategic village, Podravanje, from which Serbs fired tank cannons and mortars into Srebrenica. After Srebrenica forces retreated,
Boro saw the bodies of ten men who appeared to have been burned and
driven over by tanks the Srebrenicans captured. The sight gave him "the
creeps." Many Serbs were killed in the same village during World War II.
Now it had again been completely plundered—from its livestock to the
windows and roof tiles on its homes—and its haystacks burned by the
civilian *hapsi* who rushed in with the estimated 2,000 to 2,500 Srebrenica
troops who took part. Boro and everyone else on the Serb side heard terrible rumors of what happened to Serbs living in Muslim-controlled areas, and he worried about the welfare of his parents in Tuzla.

Boro tired of the grueling front-line work. Never partial to a life of all
labor and no play, one day he asked his commander, Pandurević, if he
could spend more time doing regular hospital work. The commander
agreed. Boro took a job at a nearby hospital in the wealthy bauxite-
mining town of Milići, learning surgery on the job with its strong-headed
neurosurgeon director. When it became clear that the director would not
grant Boro and his family an apartment in town, Boro left, making an enemy of the director, and hustled his way into his current job in Zvornik.

These days hospital work is nearly as grueling as field work. This week
the Srebrenica forces managed to do some damage when counterattack-
ing with all the usable weapons they had left, a ZIS cannon and small
arms. While a ceasefire for Srebrenica was being hammered out on the
tarmac of Sarajevo airport last night, Zvornik Hospital received about
twenty wounded Serbs. Their injuries were what kept Boro busy all
night. He is tired of the constant work here. Going to Srebrenica sounds
like a good chance to break up his routine.

Boro and a Serb medical colleague arrive at the Zvornik soccer
field, where helicopters await them. The two Muslim doctors picked up
in Tuzla look frightened to be here in Serb territory. One of them was
threatened with jail if he refused to come. Soon, the tables will turn and
the Serb doctors will be among enemies. Boro's colleague asks a French

U.N. officer whether his and Boro's safety will be guaranteed in Srebrenica. The officer points out that dozens of U.N. Protection Force soldiers are now stationed there.

"I can't guarantee their safety, let alone yours," he says.

Boro tries not to dwell on his fear. On the helicopter journey, he schemes up a way to avoid being identified as a Serb by those waiting on the ground. Nobody would expect a Serb to be the first to walk, with confidence, off the helicopter into his enemy's territory, so this is exactly what he decides to do.

As the helicopter descends, Boro peeks out the window and sees a crowd of thousands of people gathered around a soccer field. *This is terrible. All those people probably think I'm the enemy. But now there's no way back.* He disembarks first, as planned. Then it hits him. He has stepped through the looking glass. It is an unforgettable moment. His hopes and wishes have come true. He has crossed the border line. He is on the other side.

AT FIRST, never mind the fact the U.N. soldiers can't "guarantee" him anything, Boro sticks close to them on the soccer field. He gets to work with the other doctors checking the wounded, who are being ferried to the field.

After about half an hour, a jeep pulls up. It astonishes Boro to see Dr. Nedret Mujkanović get out. They recognize one another immediately even though three or four years have passed since the two tall, attractive men shared the black market for imported clothing at Tuzla medical school. In addition to living in the same Tuzla apartment block, Nedret was Boro's pathology teaching assistant, and Nedret's younger brother was one of Boro's close friends.

They greet one another with a Balkan-style hug and kiss on both cheeks.

"How is it in Tuzla?" Nedret asks.

"I didn't come from Tuzla . . ." Boro begins to explain.

"Ah, you're the Chetnik coming from Zvornik!" Nedret backs away from him in mock horror. "Fuck! My people will kill me!" He says it with a smile, and then invites Boro for a tour of the hospital.

It's a relief to find a friendly face in a potentially hostile environment, but Boro's been warned by the French U.N. officer not to set foot outside of the U.N.-protected soccer pitch. He glances at the U.N. soldiers, loading patients onto helicopters as if they were pieces of wood. His mind performs a quick calculation. One, he's known Nedret a long time, which means Nedret probably won't do anything to harm him. Two, Nedret probably has a lot more stature in town than these insensitive U.N. soldiers do. Boro accepts the offer and informs the U.N. officer that he's going with Nedret to the hospital. The soldier looks surprised.

"Is anyone forcing you to go there?" he asks.

"No, he's my friend," Boro explains. "I went to school with him in Tuzla, and I feel safer with him than with you."

As they get ready to go, Boro sees yet another familiar face. Sadik Ahmetović was a student nurse in a hospital where Boro worked before the war.

"No one will harm you here," Sadik says. Still, Boro can't wait to disappear into the relative safety of the hospital. They travel there in the jeep and arrive at a crowd scene, hundreds of people drawn to the hospital by the prospect of evacuation.

"Here's my buddy," Nedret announces to some colleagues outside the hospital, "Boro." Boro is a Serb name. Everyone within earshot turns to stare. Boro feels even more nervous and uncomfortable, but Nedret just keeps standing there chatting. Then a woman shrieks with delight.

"What's up, Boro? Oh, Boro, it's you!" People in the crowd turn their heads as Fatima approaches, smiling deliriously. Boro recognizes her from medical school, a kind and studious girl who used to lend him notes when he skipped class.

"What's up, Fata?"

From Fatima's perspective, sweet, funny, carefree Boro is about the only Serb in the world she'd still be happy to see land in Srebrenica. He reminds her of their youth in the days when nobody knew or cared who came from what ethnic group. She peppers him with so many questions and with such loud enthusiasm that Boro must accept that his cover is blown. By now, everyone around him knows he's a Serb.

For the next couple of hours, Nedret hosts Boro at the hospital, introducing him to staff members and showing him patients. Boro couldn't have imagined conditions this poor. It shocks him to see how much harder the doctors here have to work compared with those on his side. When he sits down for coffee in Nedret's office, Boro brims with questions. How do you perform surgery without electricity, with no x-rays, with no anesthesiologist? It occurs to him that he might help.

"What do you need?" he asks Nedret.

"I need everything."

They catch up, discovering that their early days of war were spent as combat doctors on opposite sides of an active front line near Tuzla. Nedret describes his overland journey to Srebrenica. Boro tells of his field actions and, comparing stories, the two realize that Boro was probably with a patrol of soldiers that Nedret and his fellow travelers had slipped past. They'd narrowly avoided detection and with it the possibility of a deadly firefight between old friends.

The two have nearly forgotten about the evacuation, which is proceeding without their assistance. They return to the soccer field hours later to find throngs of Nedret's former patients awaiting examination and certification to be loaded, about twenty apiece, onto helicopters. Dozens of amputees have led a procession through town on their homemade crutches, demanding to be evacuated too. An International Committee of the Red Cross physician, Louisa Chan-Boegli, and the U.N. refugee worker Larry Hollingworth lock horns over procedures. Louisa wants to give each patient a thorough check and gather the required one signature each from Srebrenican, Serb, and international doctors to avoid violating promises given to the Serbs. Larry, still convinced that Srebrenica will fall, wants to shove as many Muslim men as possible onto the helicopters while there's a chance to get them the hell out.

OVER THE AFTERNOON, French Puma and British Royal Navy Sea King transport helicopters shuttle 133 men out of Srebrenica before the operation draws to a close for the day. Boro declines Nedret's offer to stay the night and returns to Zvornik. His fellow Serbs look at him as if he's a ghost, as if they expected the Srebrenica Muslims to kill him. In the evening, he crosses Zvornik Bridge from Serb-held Bosnia to Serbia and buys loads of fresh fruits and vegetables, coffee, chocolate, cigarettes, beer, and a liter of cognac for Nedret. Back at Zvornik Hospital, he swipes some special suture meant for the delicate work of sewing friable, damaged liver. He obtains permission to bring goods back with him to Srebrenica, slyly avoiding mention of how much and what he has.

THE SIGHT OF THE HUNDREDS OF INJURED MEN gathered on the soccer pitch has renewed Boro's awareness of the tragedy the war has brought on all of Bosnia's people. For three days he travels to Srebrenica and works with Muslim colleagues. On the last day of the evacuation, unbeknownst to the internationals, he and the local doctors conspire to billet a few special cases onto the helicopters. The non-injured people they want to evacuate have compelling reasons to leave the town, but can't travel by overland convoy either because they are men or because they have links to the military. Nedret secures evacuation spots for the ailing father of deceased Dr. Nijaz Džanić and for the widow and children of the war hero Akif Ustić. Ilijaz and Fatima help some others. Even Boro signs a doctored medical certificate when beseeched by a former school friend. The Serbs and Muslims find they have much more of a connection to each other than to the internationals. The way some of the U.N. soldiers act makes Boro think they care much more about themselves than the people they've come to help. When an UNPROFOR soldier twists his ankle and a swarm of internationals descend on him, Boro and the other Bosnian doctors chuckle amongst themselves.

"He has to go to Paris, emergency case," they laugh.

NEDRET WANTS MORE THAN ANYTHING TO LEAVE Srebrenica on one of the helicopters. He pleads with the Red Cross physician, Louisa, to grant him a space, but she asks him who will do surgery if he goes. The Bosnian surgeon from Tuzla who was drafted and sent, under threat of prison, to help oversee the evacuation doesn't have permission from the Serbs to remain here and won't take the risk of defying them. And Eric Dachy hasn't yet secured agreement from Serb authorities for MSF doctors to return.

In fact, Nedret's departure is long overdue. The commander of the Bosnian Army Second Corps in Tuzla ordered him to withdraw last month, mainly because Nedret's wife was making repeated, dramatic appearances at army headquarters begging officers for his return. The officers at the corps considered her to be on the brink of a psychological breakdown. At the time, Nedret announced that he was refusing to leave until a replacement arrived. Now, with a realistic and relatively safe way out of Srebrenica dangling before him, he is more than ready to grab it.

The Red Cross doctor, seeing that Nedret is too exhausted and demotivated to work anyway, takes pity on him and grants him permission to travel. Boro and the other Serb doctor have no objections. Now only one obstacle remains—Srebrenica's local warlords. Some of them argue that Nedret, who traveled to the field with the soldiers, watching their actions and participating in their military meetings, just plain knows too much. Nedret's powerful allies insist he is trustworthy. After some remonstration over whether he might squeak about the crime, black marketeering, and other indelicacies he has witnessed over the past eight months, the Srebrenica authorities decide to let him go.

Nedret gathers his belongings, takes off his military uniform, and dresses up to leave in fancy clothes given to him in Srebrenica by friends and patients. He arranges a farewell meeting with his longhaired best friend, Commander Hakija Meholjić, king of the Hotel Fresh Air, whose beard now reaches to his stomach. Nedret shows up on the terrace of the hotel at the agreed-upon time, but Hakija isn't there. Nedret waits a while, staring at the back of a short-haired man until the man turns around and Nedret sees, from the missing tooth and the characteristic smile, that it is Hakija himself, Hakija who had long ago said to him, "Doctor, when I feel the war is going to end I'll cut my hair and shave my beard."

The men embrace. Hakija hands him 100 Deutschemarks.

"Go to the Hotel Tuzla," he says. "Order two dinners and two beers. Sit alone. One dinner and beer are for me, and one dinner and beer are for you. Then raise your glass."

The two men cry as they say farewell. Nedret promises that he will return. He goes to the hospital one last time and makes the same promise to his colleagues.

"I will find a way back."

He leaves his girlfriend behind. Over the past difficult weeks, he always made sure her family had food and firewood. He helped some of her kin escape to Tuzla on U.N. convoys, but at the time she hadn't wanted to go. Now she cries and begs him to take her, too. He refuses, saying that he can't put another healthy person on a helicopter meant to evacuate injured men.

Nedret gets into the jeep with Louisa, the Red Cross doctor. He weeps as they drive along the main road toward the soccer field where the last helicopter of the evacuation awaits them. Louisa tells Nedret she can't understand why he's crying after having begged to leave. "You should be happy," she tells him. "You're going back to your family, your wife and son."

OVER THREE DAYS, nearly 500 wounded soldiers have been airlifted from Srebrenica to Tuzla. A swarm of journalists awaits the helicopters. Millions of folks back home are eager to know what it was like to live in the city described by a ham radio operator as being "on the verge of madness."

Nedret steps out of the final helicopter. In sharp contrast to the bedraggled, wounded soldiers being unloaded around him, the tall, attractive doctor makes his entrance upright, in a brown Borselino fedora, dark sunglasses, swanky red silk shirt with matching Italian suit jacket, and fine leather shoes.

He sticks out in the dusty jumble of aid workers and patients, looking, in one reporter's opinion, like a "black market kingpin." Journalists close around him on the landing tarmac, shouting questions above the whir of the helicopter rotors.

A day later, Nedret sits in an outdoor café, sipping coffee, chain-smoking, greeting old acquaintances, and holding court for hours with international journalists. He tells the story of his weeklong overland journey sneaking through a patchwork of enemy territory to reach Srebrenica last August. He describes how he arrived to find the town cut off with no surgeons and practically no medical supplies. He estimates that he has performed 1,390 operations, 100 amputations without anesthesia, and four Caesarean sections over his eight-month stay. He rounds out the story with an emotional description of his grudging departure from the city yesterday and how his grateful patients dressed him in flashy clothes so he wouldn't have to appear in Tuzla in dirty combat fatigues.

In their stories, the reporters liken Nedret to a medieval surgeon, cutting into howling patients without anesthesia and unable to save lives with such basics as blood transfusions and antibiotics. They turn him into a hero, an archetypal doctor/angel, a fighter against the devil of death in a place, Srebrenica, that everyone calls "hell."

THAT EVENING, those with working televisions can watch images of events taking place thousands of miles away in overcast Washington, D.C. President Clinton lights a flame to inaugurate the United States Holocaust Memorial Museum, with Auschwitz survivor Elie Wiesel at his side. Wiesel takes the podium, the collar of his coat turned up against a wind that riffles his hair and whips the line of flags behind him. He has a surprise for the president.

"I have been in the former Yugoslavia," he says, shaking his fist and staring straight at Clinton, "and, Mr. President, I cannot *not* tell you something. We *must* do something to stop the bloodshed in that country."

The crowd cheers. Clinton's face remains impassive. The harrowing tales pouring out of places like Srebrenica show that the war has only intensified since he took office three months ago. The pressure is mounting for him, as the leader of the world's last remaining superpower, to do more than just airdrop supplies.

NEDRET, WHO LEFT TUZLA an ambitious medical resident, rapidly becomes a national hero and an international sensation. The evening of his first day back in Tuzla, he attends a reception hosted by Tuzla's mayor and meets Bianca Jagger, the Nicaraguan-born activist and celebrity ex-wife of the Rolling Stones' Mick Jagger, without a clue as to who she is. Days later he is trundling over bumpy back roads with her in a four-wheel-drive jeep toward the Croatian port city of Split in a dramatic bid to save the lives of two dying Bosnian children denied an air evacuation by the United Nations. They deliver the children to an awaiting American specialist Bianca has called to Croatia, and then together, Nedret and Bianca continue on to France as guests of Dr. Bernard Kouchner, the founder and former president of Doctors Without Borders.

Days later, a fax arrives to notify them that one of the two children has died. They fly back to Split, Croatia, and go to the pathology department to view the girl's body. She looks serene, as if she is sleeping. Nedret touches her hair. Bianca is afraid at first, but then touches her, too. In spite of all he's seen the past year in Srebrenica, Nedret breaks down in the corridor and cries in Bianca's presence.

BORO LAZIĆ RETURNS HOME from his stint in Srebrenica gushing about Nedret and the hundreds of surgeries he performed without anesthesia and electricity. Boro's wife is surprised to hear her laconic husband tell story after story about "Nedret, Nedret, Nedret." Boro typically doesn't speak about what he sees and does in wartime. More than once his wife has answered a knock at the door to find grateful family members of Boro's patients standing outside bearing gifts of dried pork and bottles of plum brandy and bursting with stories she's never heard. They speak not only of his medical work, but also of his heroics—how he once pulled a man from a burning tank that nobody else would enter, which then exploded; how at another time he vaulted across the front lines to carry out a wounded Serb soldier.

When she asks him about these stories, Boro answers with a question: "Who told you that?" If she presses him further, he will only say, in a tired, mildly sarcastic tone, "What else could I do? I had to help."

At home there is no war and no talking about war. Boro refuses to watch the evening news. When he comes home from field actions, he wants to play with his daughter and new baby. Then he asks his wife to make some coffee for the two of them, and they sit together and talk, remembering funny stories and good times past, or dreaming and scheming about their future.

Srebrenica changes Boro. His wife senses this, even though he does not tell her, at first, about the plan he is hatching. One morning some weeks after his return, he travels to the stadium in Zvornik to meet a

U.N. helicopter coming from Tuzla, stopping to pick up Serb authorities on its way to Srebrenica with a delegation to help set the safe area's boundaries. He's heard that Nedret might be aboard, making good on his promise to return to Srebrenica.

Indeed, Nedret is, and in the afternoon, Boro returns to meet the helicopter on its way back, handing Nedret cookies for his son and cigarettes to give to Boro's parents in Tuzla. A few weeks later, the commission passes through Zvornik again. Boro meets Nedret at the helicopters and they chat a while about Boro's parents. Then Boro asks Nedret what he thinks of organizing negotiations and possibly "mutually beneficial exchanges" between their two sides.

"It's a good idea," Nedret replies. He has to check with his superiors.

Boro does, too. He goes home and convinces the local authorities in Šekovići that negotiations offer them a chance for personal gain, a way to help relatives stuck on the other side—to help get them out or at least channel food or money to them. A municipal authority then travels with him to Pale, a Serb-held area near Sarajevo that serves as the headquarters of the self-declared "Serb Republic." There, he meets with the president of the republic, Dr. Radovan Karadžić, and others who govern the 70 percent of "ethnically clean" Bosnian territory the Bosnian Serb army now controls.

"OK, try to do it," Karadžić says in his deep, gravelly voice. Boro takes away a good impression of his fellow physician. He honestly believes that Karadžić wants peace.

A local commission on the Serb side organizes the first meeting. The location and time are passed through military radio and then telephoned to Nedret, who has received permission to conduct negotiations from his own authorities in Tuzla.

ONE CLEAR, SUNNY DAY a few months after his first meeting with Nedret in Srebrenica, Boro waits in a car at the farthest point of Serbian-held territory just east of Tuzla, wearing blue jeans and a white vest, a Motorola radio in his hand. Soldiers man the Serb front line with automatic rifles and mortars.

Less than a third of a mile away, Bosnian soldiers with M-72 light machine guns sit hidden on a riverbank. At the agreed-upon time on this agreed-upon date, Boro speaks into his walkie-talkie and then it crackles back to life with the sound of Nedret's voice coming from the opposite side of the front line. They have trouble hearing one another on the chosen frequency and get out of their cars to shout across the lines. After reconfirming that the meeting is on and that both sides are holding fire, they move toward one another by car, crossing into a no-man's-land.

Entering a zone where guns are trained at him from both sides gives Boro a strange thrill. He is unafraid. Ever crafty, he inaugurates the negotiations by presenting a package of cigarettes to the Muslim soldiers accompanying Nedret to improve their mood. The meeting is short. Like a first date, they stand around and spend most of their time making small talk. The second meeting is more comfortable. Someone pulls a wooden table from one of the nearby abandoned houses, and they spread maps on top of it, gathering around with soft drinks, coffee, and cigarettes.

In the substance of the discussion, each side presents the names of soldiers who've been killed on territory that the other side has come to control. They ask that bodies be dug up and returned. Neither Boro nor Nedret talks about an exchange of military prisoners. There aren't thought to be any.

They also talk about exchanging goods. The Serbs can use Tuzla's salt and coal. The Bosnian government side needs flour, coffee, and cigarettes. They need more sensitive items, too—oil; gasoline; grenades and other munitions for cannons, guns, and rifles—and these might come in exchange for money or for ethnic Serbs living in Tuzla, perhaps some spies, whom the Bosnian Serb military wants to get out.

Nedret asks Boro to send greetings to his old pathology professor, his mentor living in Belgrade. Boro does, and the professor, perhaps remembering how his two former students were in medical school, assumes that they are meeting to make money.

Boro and Nedret view their motives for these negotiations as pure as contributing to peace, helping both sides achieve positive goals, and of course, for Boro, helping his parents in Tuzla. If they succeed in negotiating sales, they will take a percentage, but so far, nothing has materialized.

Boro does engage in some "business," though, just not with Nedret. He helps a man smuggle cigarettes from Serbia, a far more lucrative and easier job than working as a doctor. In fact, he skips his duty shifts at the hospital more and more often to attend to this work and to the negotiations he conducts with Nedret every few weeks. One day his boss, a hardworking surgeon barely sleeping under the stressful conditions, chastises him for his absenteeism.

"How can you just not show up for duty?" he rails.

Boro just smiles. Then he resigns. He's fed up with the overwork, attracted by the adventure of his new activities, and sees now his chance to help his parents. Besides, he isn't one of those people who always wanted to be a doctor. When Boro was growing up, he planned to study law, not medicine. His father considered him incapable of finishing law school and instead enrolled Boro, without his knowledge, in a high school for medical technicians. There, Boro took an unexpected liking to medical subjects. He ended up being the best in his class, and his teachers insisted he study medicine at the university. He always did extremely well; his intelligence and winning personality allowed him to play and only study at the last minute for exams. But this wartime medical work is different; it requires constant presence and can't be divided into bursts of hard work and then rest.

By quitting the hospital job, Boro loses his work-provided apartment in Zvornik to another doctor. He moves his family back to his birth town of Šekovići. Ultimately, nothing concrete comes of his negotiations with Nedret. They meet and make agreements, but those with the power to carry them out fail to act. The two begin to feel as if they are united on one side of the war against their higher-ups on the other.

Local authorities lose interest when Boro's efforts fail to bring them their anticipated personal gain. Some locals even turn hostile when they discover that Boro is fraternizing with the enemy. A woman who lost her son in the war runs down the street in Šekovići, screaming that she'll kill Boro for negotiating with the Muslims—at least that is the story a friend tells Boro's wife.

Boro understands the opposition. Before he'd stepped across the front lines and met his "enemies" face to face, he hadn't realized that the attitudes and ideas on the other side are identical to those of his own. Even his opinions about the genesis of the war are changing. He suspects it was planned, step by step, by power-hungry politicians who planted emotional seeds in the minds of the people to grow their will to fight. He and everyone else involved in carrying out the war has been fooled and manipulated. They are the losers, the ones who suffer.

Boro and Nedret continue to plan meetings, even as support dissipates on both of their sides. Nedret is convinced that a military security detail is tailing him, trying to catch him in the act of negotiating. Boro worries, too. As their next meeting is about to begin, the commander on Boro's side pretends he doesn't know about the plan and refuses to tell his soldiers to hold their fire. Boro watches as Nedret's car begins to roll into the no-man's-land. He wangles a Motorola from a policeman and shouts, "Go back! Go back!" Nedret retreats in time. Days later, the Bosnian Serb army launches operation "hammer and anvil" west toward Tuzla. Rifle and tank fire eradicates the silent space between the two front lines and brings a permanent end to negotiations between doctor-friends.

Eastern Bosnia after Mladić's Offensive

SPRING 1993

U.N. Safe Areas

Gradačac

Bijeljina

Tuzla

TERRITORY CONTROLLED BY THE ARMY OF THE REPUBLIC OF BOSNIA AND HERZEGOVINA

Memići

Mali Zvornik

Drina R.

SERBIA

Zvornik

Kamenica

Šekovići

Drinjaca R.

Konjević Polje

Kravica

SREBRENICA SAFE AREA

Kladanj

Bratunac

Potočari

Vlasenica

Milići

Jadar R.

Srebrenica

Višnjica

Zeleni Jadar

Han Pijesak

SUŠICA MT.

Gladovići

Skelani

ZLOVRH MT.

Žepa

TARA MT.

BOSNIA

AND

SARAJEVO SAFE AREA

Sokolac

ŽEPA SAFE AREA

Drina R.

Sarajevo

Pale

HERZEGOVINA

GORAŽDE SAFE AREA

Goražde

Kms.

0

15

0

Miles

© A. Karl/J. Kemp, 2003

20

TO INTERPOSE

THAT LATE APRIL DAY, that last day, when the Serb military had pushed ever closer to Srebrenica, shelling and shooting and sowing destruction, Eric Dachy lost the most dear of his heart's possessions, his hope. He lost it only briefly, and he had kept it almost right up to the end, right up until the moment that nobody in his right mind could possibly have kept it anymore. Even that morning, when the sun rose and the roosters crowed in Mali Mokri Lug, the little wet garden patch where Eric lived in the huge, stagnating metropolis of Belgrade, he stood firm in his conviction that international pressure could save Srebrenica.

It wasn't an entirely unreasonable hope. After all, just the previous day the U.N. Security Council had demanded "that all parties and others concerned treat Srebrenica and its surroundings as a safe area," which seemed like a step toward creating a protected zone for civilians.

The "safe area" concept was first raised eight months previously by the president of the International Committee of the Red Cross and shot down by the U.N. Security Council as a bad idea. Where were all the international military forces capable of peace enforcement going to come from? Wouldn't the Serbs attack any areas of Bosnia not deemed "safe"?

But as Srebrenica was about to fall, and pressure on international governments increased, a version of the idea was revived as a compromise. Calling Srebrenica a "safe area," without specifying a mechanism for enforcing its protection, became a position on which most Security Council member nations could agree.

On April 16, 1993, the day the resolution passed, Eric busied about readying another surgical team to enter and replace the physicians who had left Srebrenica. But the day went on and the news came in, hour after hour. Bad news. Fighting inside of Srebrenica. The post office hit, the post office where the MSF logistician, the lone MSF outpost in the town, had been staying. Fortunately, he escaped injury.

"This time it's the end," Eric announced to his colleagues in Belgium. "The town will be taken. It's done for."

What to do now? He switched courses, setting his mind, his voice, and his phone-dialing, letter-typing fingers to the new task of aiding the manifold thousands who would undoubtedly flee.

But somehow—and who knew exactly why it happened, out there in the middle of the night on the darkened tarmac of a gutted, pitted airport that lay between two front lines in a former Olympic City—somehow three hands representing the Bosnian government, the irredentist Bosnian Serbs, and a witnessing international had scribbled signatures on an agreement that stopped the offensive. The Srebrenica soldiers would give up their arms in return for a ceasefire, the deployment of a company of U.N. soldiers, and an evacuation of the wounded, among other provisions. Pieces of paper were transformed into a city's reprieve.

Hours later the evacuation helicopters lifted off, rotors whirring noisily over the skies of Srebrenica, bellies full of the wounded and sick. It took just a few short days to empty the hospital. The Red Cross physician Louisa Chan-Boegli presided, but Eric's MSF doctors were not there.

Eric is furious. The ceasefire agreement calls for the free passage of humanitarian aid, but the Serbs are turning his doctors and nurses back, not letting them into Srebrenica. Eric wastes hours in border towns facing off with slouching, square-headed boys in camouflage, their sidearms slung casually over their shoulders as they drag on cigarettes between pinched thumbs and forefingers and gaze at him with bored eyes. The U.N. convoys can roll and the Red Cross doctors can fly, but the MSF team hears only: No, no, no.

Why? Eric has taken care to maintain a sterling reputation with the Serbs. If anything he has even tried too hard, being obsequious at times when he should have spit on someone's shoes, giving aid to Serb hospitals to foster good relations. Unlike U.N. leaders, Eric doesn't mind referring to Radovan Karadžić, the self-declared president of a self-declared state carved in blood, as "Mr. President," if that will help get aid to places that need it. Eric can only speculate that Doctors Without Borders has been confused with another medical organization, one with a similar-sounding name that hasn't taken so much care: Doctors of the World.

The group, which MSF leader Dr. Bernard Kouchner founded in 1980 after parting ways with MSF, has taken a much more confrontational approach with the Serbs, going so far as to compare them and their leaders with the World War II fascists they purport to despise.

Eric's storm cloud of anger needs a release. He pours out a letter that the heads of the U.N. refugee agency, its targets, call a "critique," sending a draft first to his bosses in Brussels. In it, Eric notes, "sadly," that members of Doctors Without Borders "were the only ones to attempt to ameliorate the conditions of life on the ground" in Srebrenica. While calling the medical evacuations "totally necessary and recommended by us," he criticizes the fact that "all energy" is going toward them, "which we don't consider ethically acceptable unless an important effort is made to ameliorate, even temporarily, the lot of the local population."

The refugee agency's leaders promise to help Eric get his doctors inside Srebrenica, but even these efforts fail to break the ban. Meanwhile, the need for the doctors is increasing. The military offensive has brought Serb soldiers and heavy equipment right to the tops of the hills that ring Srebrenica. The ceasefire agreement keeps them there, but they use their strategic position to violate the agreement in smaller ways, harassing the population by sniping and sporadically shelling the town with heavy artillery and tanks. The United Nations reports "clashes" along a front line.

As for the "demilitarization of Srebrenica," practically everyone but the Serbs agrees that it would be absurd to go house to house, forcing the Muslims to give up all their weapons, what with only a few hundred U.N. soldiers in town to protect them. Eric has to laugh at their show of demilitarizing the Muslims. The U.N. Protection Force interprets "Srebrenica" to mean the city of Srebrenica itself, rather than the entire enclave, so the Srebrenica forces take advantage of this loophole and move some of their light weaponry to areas outside of the town.

U.N. representatives use the Doctors Without Borders satellite telex inside the enclave to transmit a report of the weapons the Muslims have voluntarily deposited in the U.N. collections depot. The machine's computer saves the information, and later someone sends it to Eric, saying, "Have a look at it. It's too much fun." The list of approximately 300 weapons comprises mostly unserviceable arms, hunting rifles, and a few heavy weapons for which, as the United Nations later discovers, there is no significant amount of ammunition.

"Children's toys," Eric calls them, chuckling. He hangs on to the list for when he needs a smile. "Demilitarization of Srebrenica a success," reads the title of the U.N. press release on April 21, the demilitarization deadline.

The next week, ceasefire violations send more wounded into the hospital, where—without Nedret or MSF—there are now no local or international surgeons to treat them. The U.N. refugee agency representative inside the enclave radios, "We urgently require Médecins Sans Frontières doctors to come to Srebrenica."

But even the dramatic outrage of a high-level United Nations Security Council delegation visiting Srebrenica, who accuse the Serbs of "a crime of genocide" for impeding medical assistance and instruct the Security Council to "consider urgent measures" to respond, fails to break the ban on Doctors Without Borders. In fact, the diplomats themselves are forced to undergo—and this seems to shock them—disrespectful treatment by the Serbs. The U.N. representatives and deputy representatives of countries including Venezuela, Russia, France, New Zealand, Hungary, and Pakistan are subjected to a one-and-a-half-hour delay at submachine gunpoint for having brought along a camera. The team comments on the incident in a report of its mission:

> The fact that five Serbian soldiers were able to defy a large group of soldiers and officers who were with the Mission should be noted by the [U.N. Security] Council in order to understand the actual conditions that UNPROFOR faces. The attitude of defiance of the Serbs towards the United Nations in general is a matter that should concern the Council. The Serbs obviously have little respect for UNPROFOR authority.

This comes as no surprise to Eric, but after the delegation issues its strong media statements, he thanks the head of the delegation in writing for being "publicly indignant of the ban" on MSF. In his letter, Eric refers to the generally unrecognized "Serb Republic" in quotation marks. But as the days pass sitting at his desk, running back and forth to the border, Eric realizes what he has always suspected: The key to MSF's operations in Srebrenica lies not with the United Nations, but with the Serbs. He writes another kowtowing letter to Dr. Radovan Karadžić.

"Hello, Mr. President . . . ," he begins and immediately cuts to the chase: Despite three requests to Karadžić's government, MSF has still not received authorization to enter Srebrenica.

"It seems to me that you no longer consider MSF a friendly organization. I'm saddened without understanding why. Above all I hope to be able to maintain the excellent relations that I've kept up with the representatives of the Serb Republic." Eric writes it as a proper name this time, without putting quotation marks around it. "I hope that all confusion between Doctors Without Borders and Doctors of the World is now resolved. . . . I would draw your attention to the important aid (more than a million [German] marks) that we have brought these last months to hospitals of the Serb Republic, as we know that they function under difficult conditions."

The letter ends with offers and a request. Doctors Without Borders will open an office in Pale, the "capital" of the Serb Republic, and more aid might be on its way to help hospitals in difficulty. What Eric wants is an immediate meeting with Karadžić . . . at his convenience, of course.

Unless Eric is going to hop a plane, though, that immediacy is not going to be possible. The day Eric drafts his letter, Bosnian Serb President Karadžić is wearing a suit and sweating under pressure from his patron saint, Serbian President Slobodan Milošević, at a peace conference in Athens, Greece. Milošević, under threat of a further set of crippling international sanctions and possible international military intervention, demands that the Bosnian Serb leader add his signature to the peace plan designed by Cyrus Vance and Lord David Owen—the decentralization plan creating ethnic cantons, which American commentators dubbed "another Munich." Although the United States has some strong objections, the mounting public pressure over Srebrenica has led many world leaders to want to be perceived as "doing something," and pushing through the Vance-Owen peace plan is another compromise.

The Serbs have their own reasons for opposing the peace plan, and one of the biggest is Srebrenica. The plan calls for Srebrenica town and much of Serb-held eastern Bosnia to be included in a Bosnian Muslim majority province. This, the Serb leaders have said, they cannot abide. However, on May 2, Karadžić sits at a small table before news cameras and signs the agreement. He does it with a crafty catch. Seeming to know just how to appear to do what international leaders are demanding, while not really doing it, he approves the plan pending the nod of the "National

Assembly of the Serb Republic." The diplomats brush off the significance of this qualification, pat themselves on their backs, and go home.

The pressure is off. The most serious threat ever to take military action against the Serbs, a threat that opened a divide between the United States, which supported it, and its allies, which didn't, has been lifted. When the Bosnian Serbs not surprisingly renege on the plan, refusing to give up territory they took by force, the momentum to launch military action has been lost.

Peace in Bosnia is officially off, but the ceasefire in Srebrenica more or less holds. The U.N.'s plan for Srebrenica's "safe area" status is still a confused mess, though. Are the 150 Canadian soldiers there to monitor the ceasefire? To deter any future Serb assault? To defend against one? It isn't clear.

The leader of the Canadian House tells the *Gazette* of Montreal that his country's forces will, in any case, escalate "the price that would be paid by any aggressor to attack the town itself, making it an attack on the entire world."

SERB AUTHORITIES PERMIT an additional fifty-six Canadian peacekeepers to augment the 150-strong U.N. force inside the enclave. A series of least-common-denominator U.N. Security Council resolutions concerning the safe area are passed over the spring of 1993.

After all is said and done, what the United Nations agrees to do is create six "safe areas" in Bosnia—among them Srebrenica, Tuzla, Sarajevo, and Srebrenica's neighbor to the south, Žepa. The big question is how far the U.N. Protection Force should go to ensure that the safe areas are safe. To foster agreement among Security Council members, the force is mandated to "deter attacks against the safe areas" rather than the original plan, which was to "defend" against them. UNPROFOR's authorization to use force to respond to bombardment, armed incursion, or obstruction of the free movement of humanitarian aid convoys is qualified in the final version by the addition of the phrase "acting in self defence."

U.N. member states are authorized to use air power to support U.N. forces, but the exact triggers for NATO air strikes are left unspecified. The safe areas are referred to as a temporary measure. General Wahlgren suggests that 34,000 additional U.N. troops will be needed to effectively deter attacks against the six safe areas. The Security Council authorizes the deployment of only 7,600. Analysts refer to the option as "safe area lite."

"While this option cannot, in itself, completely guarantee the defence of the safe areas," the U.N. secretary-general writes, "it relies on the threat of air action against any belligerents."

———

WITH THE FAILURE of the Vance-Owen peace plan, U.N. member nations again split on an approach to ending the war. A trans-Atlantic rift opens between the United States, which, along with "nonaligned" countries, endorses a policy of "lift and strike" (lifting the arms embargo on the Bosnian government and supporting Bosnian forces with air strikes), and its European allies, which oppose it. A U.N. resolution to lift the embargo is put forward for a vote on June 29, 1993, but rejected. In the end, President Clinton, unwilling to act unilaterally, backs down.

Eric Dachy supports lift and strike. The option dies because countries that contribute to the U.N. Protection Force argue that increased military activity will make conditions more difficult for U.N. troops and aid workers on the ground. This is the same old irony that Eric has long railed against; the internationals seem to forget that providing aid shouldn't be their primary objective.

But to Eric, the mere fact that the Serbs have allowed armed U.N. troops into Srebrenica indicates that at least they've accepted the safe-area idea. Almost immediately after the ceasefire, his attention is drawn to an even-graver threat than military action in Srebrenica—lack of water.

During the recent offensive, Serb forces captured the site of the water treatment plant supplying Srebrenica, in a place south of the city called Zeleni Jadar. The plant ceased to work, the intake pipe clogged, piped water supply was cut off, and the Serbs refused to allow internationals in to inspect and maintain it. Hans Ulens, the MSF logistician who stayed inside Srebrenica when the other international aid workers left, is also a trained sanitation engineer. Short, energetic, and nicknamed by locals *atomski mrav,* "the atomic ant," he has been working single-mindedly to supply Srebrenica with water by constructing reservoirs in the hills to collect spring water and organizing its distribution via the fire brigade water truck to three collapsible water reservoirs in town. As the Serbs will not approve gasoline deliveries, the truck is fueled by diesel extracted—by Hans's team of eight diesel suckers, each with his own pipe and jerry can—from the tanks of the trucks that come in with U.N. convoys. The system provides two liters of potable water per person per day whereas the minimum required, Hans tells Eric at headquarters, is five.

People have been making up the difference by hiking into the hills to collect water from springs, but as these begin to dry in the heat of the approaching summer, Hans panics. He needs to fix the water treatment plant. Already scabies and lice are at epidemic proportions and doctors fear that outbreaks of other diseases will follow.

"If there is no access to Zeleni Jadar this city will fall soon without water," Hans telexes Eric in Belgrade. "I have the impression that nobody outside of Srebrenica takes this seriously. . . . The whole world needs to realize that this town will be strangled in several days if they do nothing. At the meeting tonight the authorities said clearly that they'll restart the war if there isn't access to Zeleni Jadar."

Before Eric can jump into action, Serb authorities relent and escort Hans and a team of internationals to the pumping station, only to announce at its door that no one has brought the key. Hans is able to clean the intake so that water, although untreated and not of drinking quality, flows by gravity to the town and can be used for washing.

After several days, the water stops flowing again, and Hans asks for permission to visit the plant and fix whatever problem has occurred. He arrives to find the plant blown up.

That is when the real battle for water begins. Hans deems the water treatment plant beyond repair and focuses his attention on a small, disused plant inside the enclave that provided Srebrenica with water long ago and is now being used to shelter war refugees. To get there, Hans has to walk up a winding dirt road to a hilltop where an old concrete dam forms the intake. The lined concrete pipeline between the intake and the treatment plant is broken in many places and needs extensive repairs or replacement. The problem is getting supplies. The Serbs have imposed "sanctions" on Srebrenica, and will not approve any kind of construction material.

As summer approaches, bored women wait hours in water lines holding large plastic jugs, restless children at their sides. Men and boys hike farther and farther toward the edges of the enclave in search of springs. The emergency reservoirs lose water, and the stench of human sewage fills the city.

It takes teamwork to rehabilitate the old plant. Hans finds an expert pipe layer in Srebrenica and makes detailed plans for the repairs, scrounging as many supplies—cement from an old concrete factory in Potočari, wheelbarrows, shovels—as possible. In Belgrade, Eric takes down the specifications for water pipes and the amounts of chlorine and aluminum sulfate coagulant needed to purify the water, and passes them on to Muriel, who is running the new MSF office in the fairly isolated Bosnian Serb capital, Pale. Opposed to any aid projects that will rehabilitate structures in Srebrenica, Serb authorities refuse to give MSF permission to bring in pipes. Muriel begins buying their wives knickknacks, getting their glasses fixed, and performing other favors on her weekends off in Belgrade. At last the Serbs relent and allow the pipes to go through. Eric starts calling Muriel "Mata Hari."

Now Hans, back in Srebrenica, must find workers to do the job, but most men aren't used to working anymore and won't volunteer without some sort of payment. Only one thing seems to animate the exhausted, demotivated Srebrenicans: cigarettes. And not just any cigarettes—real Marlboros. Eric has to figure out where to get them. Because of the trade embargo, there shouldn't technically be any real Marlboros in Serbia. But someone has to be getting rich in wartime. Eric finds a bar advertising black market cigarettes. After smoking them himself to guarantee their authenticity, he sends them into Srebrenica to be used as payment—one per day of work—for the local staff. The internationals start referring to Srebrenica as "Cigarica."

AFTER SOME FITS AND STARTS AND DIFFICULTIES, the rehabilitation of the water plant gets under way and the predicted catastrophe is averted. With continued effort, Eric succeeds in getting Doctors Without Borders physicians and surgeons back into the enclave in early May, and throughout the spring, their rotations go fairly smoothly. The last big battles for Srebrenica, it seems to Eric, have been won. Now it's on to other challenges. But does he have the energy for them?

In June, a tiff arises over which MSF section will supply Goražde, another surrounded Muslim "safe area" that has initially been designated as a site for MSF Holland, not MSF Belgium. When the first opportunity to reach the town on a U.N. convoy is offered to Eric in Belgrade, and he insists on sending a Belgian surgeon who's already in the region, an MSF Holland representative sends an angry letter informing him that a Dutch surgeon will arrive in Belgrade and make his own way to Goražde. Eric sends a letter back reminding him that, for security reasons, all MSF staff members in Serbia have to be under his authority. When the MSF Holland representative fails to relent, Eric snaps.

"Look," he threatens, "if you send any MSF here without my authorization, I'll get him sent to jail."

Eric knows he is fed up with this place, knows that he will have to fight to reach and supply this other new enclave—not just fight with MSF Holland but with the Serbs. The mere thought of spending hours arguing his way across front lines exhausts him, and he has no interest in speeding through shellfire or plying roads that are potential minefields.

In June, a reporter catches up with Eric as he performs a needs assessment in an isolated Serb village with a local name that translates into English as "Lower Little Hell." She describes Eric as "frustrated, bored, burnt out and leaving."

He tells her the war is an endless problem that's getting worse and worse, and that success in channeling humanitarian supplies into Muslim villages hasn't stopped some of them from being "ethnically cleansed" afterwards. He also complains about the difficulty of getting humanitarian supplies, let alone anything else, into Serbia.

"The sanctions are a scandal," Eric tells the reporter. "It's collective punishment. It's very cruel and it's ineffective. It simply kills and enslaves sick people and poor people, the lowest layers of the people, and it reinforces their leaders. It's not even an effective political weapon. It only slowly and deeply destroys the structure of the society."

One summer day, Eric performs a needs assessment at a Serbian mental institution that doubles as a chicken farm. On the way back to Belgrade, neither the bucolic scenes rolling past the windows nor the

ABOVE: The town
of Srebrenica
lies in a valley.

FROM LEFT TO RIGHT:
The Srebrenica
hospital, the clinic,
and the building
used by Doctors
Without Borders
during the war.

The main road leading north from Srebrenica toward Potočari and Bratunac.

General Philippe Morillon atop armored personnel carrier in front of Srebrenica Hospital, March 1993.

Dr. Eric Dachy of Doctors Without Borders on a visit to Vukovar, December 1991.

In the pharmacy, filled with new donations. From left to right: hospital director Dr. Avdo Hasanović, Belgian MSF surgeon Dr. Thierry Pontus, Dr. Ilijaz Pilav, Dr. Fatima Dautbašić, and head nurse Zilha Abdurahmanović.

First attempted helicopter medical evacuation
from Srebrenica, March 24, 1993.

A young child mortally injured in the shelling of the helicopter landing
ground on March 24, 1993, wrapped in gold foil for warmth and held in
the arms of a nurse, awaiting an evacuation helicopter.

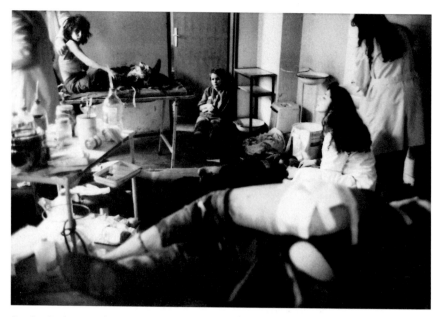

In the Srebrenica hospital "emergency room," an exhausted Dr. Fatima Dautbašić (in profile, right) and other medical workers treat five girls injured in a grenade attack while playing outside, April 2, 1993.

Srebrenica was flooded with displaced villagers who camped outdoors in early April 1993.

Srebrenica's amputees march through town, demanding to be included in evacuations of the wounded, April 1993.

Local soldiers shoot into the air to prevent thousands of civilians from filling empty UN trucks and leaving Srebrenica with a departing aid convoy, April 1993.

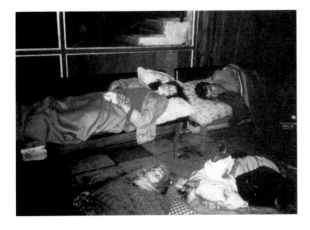

Injured patients lie on the floor and benches of the Srebrenica Hospital lobby in the wake of the Easter Monday shelling attack, April 12, 1993.

Dr. Nedret Mujkanović after returning to Tuzla from Srebrenica, April 1993.

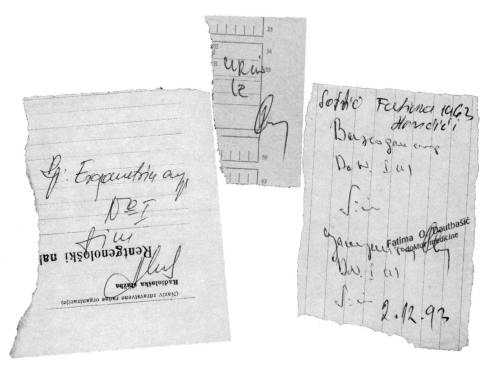

Because of a severe paper shortage, doctors wrote prescriptions on old medical records and other scraps of paper that could be found around the hospital.

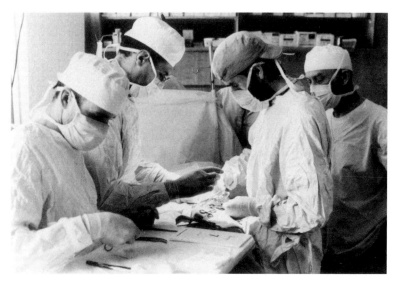

In the Srebrenica hospital operating theater, Dr. Ilijaz Pilav (right foreground) learns to perform surgery under the tutelage of Russian MSF surgeon Dr. Sergei Zotikov (far right), with assistance from instrument nurse Jusuf Sulejmanović (far left) and Lithuanian MSF anesthesiologist Dr. Andrei Slavuckij, September 1993.

MSF party with hospital staff at the hotel Domavija in the summer of 1994. Front row, from left to right: Dr. Ejub Alić, Dr. Ilijaz Pilav, Naim Salkić (leaning forward), Dr. Fatima Dautbašić, Aida Hasanovic, Samira Hodžić. Back row, from left to right: Eldina Selimovic, unidentified MSF worker, Jusuf Sulejmanović, Abaz Tabaković, Besima Sulejmanović, unidentified MSF worker, Ajka Avdić, Nijaz Salkić (the "Professor").

The "Ljiljanijade" sports competition at the Srebrenica school playground, organized in 1994. Dr. Ilijaz Pilav (center, in uniform) marches between Srebrenica military leaders Smajo Mandžić and Safet Omerović to raise the flag over the opening day ceremony.

Bosnian Serb army physician Boro Lazić greets his daughter, Dunja, as he arrives home from offensives on Srebrenica and Žepa, late July 1995.

beautiful Serbian psychiatrist sitting next to him can lift Eric's mind from the never-ending war.

"What am I doing here in all this violence?" he asks the psychiatrist. He has asked himself the question since Vukovar.

"When people are in violent situations," she answers, "it's usually because they've been there before."

Something in that simple statement rings true to him. As time goes on and the psychiatrist's observation percolates through him, he begins to realize that the fight between brothers in Yugoslavia is serving as a metaphor for the conflict-ridden family of his youth. His struggle to mend the twisted, broken frame of the Yugoslav family portrait is so emotional because it is also so personal. Yugoslavia has given him a second chance in his aborted attempt to fix a family. He's been staying here, in part, as a form of "life therapy," attempting to find himself, heal himself, reorganize himself. Why didn't he see this before?

Now that he realizes what he is doing, he knows that any changes he is going to make as a man must come from the inside, not the outside. His past does not condemn him to a violence-saturated future. He doesn't need a war zone to catalyze his personal growth—he can resolve his emotional issues in other ways.

He originally joined MSF with the desire to help people who really needed help, and he can put these good intentions to use in other, equally important situations. Nonviolent situations. He begins to envision engaging in "nice and positive" international work, such as immunizing and nourishing children in need.

These thoughts grow more insistent as the war in the former Yugoslavia intensifies. The summer of 1993 brings with it the first test of the "safe area" concept. In late July, Bosnian Serb forces advance on a strategic mountain above Sarajevo, shelling the capital and pulling the trigger for NATO air strikes. But instead of firing off an air campaign, NATO leaders spend weeks in discussion with U.N. officials over the procedures and circumstances whereby NATO air strikes can take place. This time, the mere threat of force makes the Serb military back down, and eventually the United Nations and NATO settle on a "dual key" approach. It requires that both the U.N. force commander for the former Yugoslavia and NATO's commander-in-chief of Allied Forces South agree before air strikes commence. The U.N. secretariat interprets the safe area resolutions as allowing for the use of air power in three cases: self-defense, bombardments of or incursions into the safe areas, and obstruction of the free movement of the U.N. Protection Force or humanitarian convoys.

Fighting breaks out between the formerly allied Croats and Muslims in central Bosnia, complicating the war. With international diplomacy at an apogee, Eric realizes any settlement is a long way off. He has reached the limits of what he can feel for this place, these countries. He's had it with war, violence, hatred; had it with long waits at borders; had it with kowtowing to bored, evil men. He's especially had it with fear, with danger, with sucked-in breath as shells arc overhead.

For a while longer he battles within himself. To abandon this place and these people would leave him with a terrible guilt. In his mind, the "right" thing to do is to stay here and see his work through to the end. But what will that end be? Death is all he can see anymore. He is close to believing that his choice is either to stay here and die with the people of the former Yugoslavia or leave and save himself.

One day in his office he notices himself reading the same line over and over again. The phone feels like it weighs a ton. He manages to lift it to call his desk officer in Brussels, telling him he's had enough of Yugoslavia.

"I'm finished," he says. "Send me someone else."

Within days his replacement arrives, an optimistic young woman who Eric senses has all the energy that he now lacks. He tosses her the reins of power right away. The realization that MSF's work will continue and the world will still revolve without him here relieves him.

In late summer, he leaves Serbia. Looking back on twenty-one months of work, Srebrenica stands out as his one success. He was able to intervene there, to interpose his medical team between the Muslims and their enemies. A small international presence has saved the town— seemingly against all odds—from the grisly destiny that awaited it. This allows Eric to escape the former Yugoslavia with an important piece of his idealism intact. He still believes that individuals, dedicated to doing good, can protect vulnerable groups. Srebrenica is his sole consolation.

He returns to Belgium and visits Belgrade a few times over the coming months for brief consultancies. Then he goes on to take MSF positions in other countries, including Haiti and the United States. He does not plan to look back.

21

LIFE IN THE TOMB

FROM THE MOMENT THAT MSF brings in a large, twelve-kVA generator to replace the small one that has powered just the operating room lamp, life for Ilijaz Pilav and the other doctors in Srebrenica Hospital changes. For the first time since the war started, they can flip a light switch and see rather than feel their way blindly around the hospital, can sew up a wound or an episiotomy without a smoky makeshift candle or, at best, a flashlight. Bathed in what seems like the strongest light he's ever seen, Ilijaz wants to stay in the hospital forever rather than go home to rooms haunted by stuttering candlelight shadows.

The hospital staff's first impulse is to find a television and, because the signal repeaters on the hills around Srebrenica have been destroyed, a VCR. The days take on a new rhythm, with after-dinner movies almost every night in the doctor's lounge, the "green room." Starved for entertainment, they watch again and again the only films available—*Rambo 1, Rambo 2, Rambo 3, Rocky,* Vietnam War movies, and porn, varying the menu only on the rare occasions when the owner of the ad hoc movie theater in town lends them cassettes. Fatima lives next door to the hospital and spends almost every night in the green room. Joining her often are her cousin and a thin young lawyer named Smail whom she came to know and admire when he spent months caring for his injured, paralyzed brother in the hospital.

Ilijaz plays cards in the green room with his best friends and sometimes even drinks the plum brandy he usually abhors. Over the summer of 1993, he and Fatima enjoy more leisure time together, exploring the limits of the enclave by taking walks on Srebrenica's nature trails, making picnics daringly close to Chetnik lines (where Chetniks come to picnic, too), or spending time with friends in Fatima's aunt's weekend house in the heights of Srebrenica.

On the other hand, Ilijaz doesn't like the fact that his relationship with Fatima is a public secret. It bugs him when others make their relationship out to be some kind of war romance. Since everybody knows about it, everybody feels they can comment on it, and both the positive and the negative remarks grate on him. At times he feels that the relationship is more real for others than for him.

"When are you going to get married?" people ask.

"When the war's over," Ilijaz always answers.

"Oh, how long will it last?" they ask rhetorically. "Maybe a long time. Maybe we'll get old here."

"I'll probably stay a bachelor then," he tells them. Ilijaz can't imagine getting married to anyone in Srebrenica. He is constantly aware that his own life is in peril, so how could he possibly take care of a family or create a new life? It seems crazy to him make plans for the future in this jail.

He convinces himself that he's been honest and open with Fatima about all this, that she should know by now where he stands. After all, even before the war he told her that he thought their relationship would end one day. He has his reasons for feeling this way, and he doesn't want to share them with other people, or with her. Perhaps he isn't a very good communicator, though, or perhaps he's sending mixed messages; he can tell that she has never stopped hoping that they have a future together.

More than the marriage issue divides them. Ilijaz doesn't have the same feelings for Fatima as he once had. He finds it easier to pretend than to provoke a scandal or to try to explain the intimate details of their lives to their many friends and acquaintances. They are a famous couple in Srebrenica. He can't figure a way out from under the "couple thousand pairs of eyes" that he feels watching him, surrounding him, imprisoning him in his relationship.

The sense of being trapped permeates his life. The ceasefire made him believe for a moment that internationals were powerful enough to flick a switch and change destiny, put an end to many, many human tragedies just by one simple move. But the ceasefire and safe-area declaration haven't changed the fact that the Bosnian Serb advance reduced eastern Bosnia's remaining 50,000 to 60,000 mostly displaced, non-Serb inhabitants from living on roughly 350 square miles to fifty-five here and forty-two in Žepa, maintained under siege by 1,000 to 2,000 Bosnian Serb soldiers armed with tanks, tracked armored vehicles, artillery, and mortars, paid in part by the Yugoslav government, well-organized, well-supplied, and in control of the most strategic positions around the enclave. The Demilitarization Commission, with which Nedret has traveled a few times to Srebrenica, has frozen the situation in place, decreasing the chance of Srebrenica's annihilation while at the same time erasing any hope of breaking its encirclement. The Chetniks drew so close to town in the days before the ceasefire that Ilijaz can now see them on the hills above Srebrenica, and seeing means being seen.

"They know when we're going to the toilet," Fatima jokes.

Entire swathes of countryside, including the one where Ilijaz grew up, remain in the hands of the Serbs. Living in the tight cincture is almost unbearable to Ilijaz, who has despised enclosures and savored freedom since his childhood days roaming the hillsides around Gladovići. With his daily survival no longer in question, his struggles shift inward.

That's when the prospect of learning surgery presents itself. Since June, a Bosnian surgeon from Tuzla, who'd been dragooned—under threat of imprisonment by Bosnian military authorities—into replacing Nedret, has repeatedly expressed his desire to return home. In early August, after he's been in Srebrenica three months, representatives of Doctors Without Borders, UNHCR, and the International Red Cross write an appeal for his evacuation by helicopter on "humanitarian" grounds.

The surgeon, who was appalled on arrival by the lackadaisical attitude he found at the hospital and the fact that nurses accepted death to the point of failing to call a doctor when patients developed complications (reporting later that they had "died off," using the Bosnian word *izumro*, which also means "go extinct"), has gone crazy lighting fires beneath the buttocks of the hospital workers. He's earned the nickname "Mad Max," but whereas the violent avenger in the movies loses his mind trying to restore order to a decaying, anarchic, post-apocalyptic civilization, the Bosnian surgeon instead succeeds; he has instituted medical rounds, morning meetings for doctors, a blood bank, and separate departments for internal medicine, pediatrics, obstetrics/gynecology, and surgery.

A raucous outdoor party is held to mark his departure and the summer's first distillation of plum brandy. Aid workers and Canadian soldiers attend with the local hospital staff. The next day Mad Max flies away.

That leaves Srebrenica with one surgeon from Doctors Without Borders, Dr. Sergei Zotikov, an encyclopedic urologist from Archangel, a White Sea port city in northwest Russia not far below the Arctic Circle. A slender, cheerful man, he's brought into Srebrenica his dentist wife and—to the bemusement of everyone, particularly Ejub, who notes its freedom of movement in comparison with his own—his big shaggy black and white dog. Sergei has the rare ability to perform almost every type of surgery, from abdominal to urological, gynecological to vascular, orthopedic to plastic. He is one of the first few Russian doctors to work with MSF since the fall of the Berlin Wall.

Two mornings after Mad Max's departure, Sergei needs an assistant to help with a hernia repair. Ilijaz, who once upon a time balked at so much as giving an injection, steps forward. A couple of hours later, he helps Sergei stabilize a broken femur. Then, in the afternoon, he assists with a Caesarian section. The following days bring Sergei and Ilijaz another hernia to repair, a birth defect that requires plastic surgery, an abdominal lipoma that needs to be removed, an anal fistula to be closed, another hernia repair, a right foot amputation, another C-section, another right-foot amputation, a fistula, more hernias, and a number of circumcisions.

Suddenly, Ilijaz is being groomed as the local surgeon, a backup in case Doctors Without Borders, for whatever reason, can't provide an international. At first, he doesn't believe he has the capability, nor can he imagine how he'll quickly develop skills that surgical trainees normally spend at least four years learning.

Fatima tells him he can do it. This is a tremendous chance for him, she says. Without ever complaining about the extra hours, she adds his clinic shifts to her already crushing schedule of clinic, hospital, and emergency room work so that he has more time and energy to devote to the operating theater.

Who knows how long I'm going to be in Srebrenica? Ilijaz wonders. *Who knows how long they'll come and help us? So, I should sit down and start studying.*

He requests books from the internationals, reads voraciously, takes initiative in the operating room, and learns more every day. Surgery is a galaxy for his mind to explore while his body is stuck in microscopic Srebrenica. His trepidation, his tendency to believe himself capable of less than what he can actually do, makes him a careful surgeon; he tries to envision each small step of the operation he is about to do before he even begins.

A few weeks later, he can perform simple circumcisions alone. In October, he repairs his first hernia without supervision. Dr. Sergei Zotikov leaves Srebrenica at the end of 1993. In his final report to headquarters, he predicts that an MSF surgeon will be needed for the foreseeable future. Although Ilijaz can perform a hernia operation independently, he needs about four more months of tutelage to complete his basic surgical training. Even then, he will not be ready to take full responsibility for all surgeries in Srebrenica.

But, just a few weeks later, that is exactly what Ilijaz must somehow do. The surgeon who follows Sergei departs in mid-January and his replacement, a Frenchman waiting for a "visa" from Bosnian Serb authorities, fails to arrive. Ilijaz isn't a typical surgical trainee hotshot who relishes the challenge of being in over his head. The thought of having 50,000 people depend on him frightens him.

On the other hand, he doesn't shrink from his responsibilities. The morning after the surgeon departs, Ilijaz performs a regularly scheduled hernia repair on a fifty-seven-year-old man. In the afternoon, he faces his first urgent case, a patient with an infected appendix that he removes successfully in an hour. Over the next eight days, Ilijaz performs a dozen surgeries, nine of them operations under general anesthesia, including hernia repairs, appendectomies, the setting of a femoral fracture, and the removal of an ovarian cyst. He is also constantly on call, visits all of the recovering surgical patients, sees patients in the clinic, and handles all emergencies. With each successful operation he surprises himself and grows more confident. The entire operating room staff, from the newly trained anesthetists to the instrument technicians, seem sure of him, trust his judgment and respect his authority. It isn't Ilijaz's style to yell at them or, as a surgeon, to set himself apart; in the operating room, he treats them as colleagues, outside, as friends. They coalesce into a close-knit team. Naim Salkić, the dark-haired medical technician Ilijaz worked with in the field at the start of the war, has moved to Srebrenica with the fall of Gladovići, and is rapidly becoming Ilijaz's best friend.

On the afternoon of Ilijaz's ninth day without a surgeon supervisor, a man rushes into the hospital holding his right index finger—all of it— in his left hand. The man, in his late twenties, has been chopping wood nearby with an ax. Ilijaz has seen plenty of limbs amputated, but never reattached. Nevertheless, knowing the simple anatomy of the finger, he does what makes sense to him, pinning bone to bone, stitching together the ends of a tiny artery, and joining what look like nerves and tendons. He is fairly certain the finger won't take, and when he finishes his work, he writes the man's name on tomorrow's operating schedule for an amputation.

Meanwhile, Fatima has an emergency in the obstetrics department. Several months ago, a pregnant woman in her mid-thirties came to the hospital with cramps, spotty bleeding, and a history of three previous miscarriages. It looked as if she was about to have another. With a lack of birth control methods such as condoms or IUDs in Srebrenica, Fatima is used to seeing women desperate to terminate their pregnancies. This woman was desperate to keep hers.

Fatima used a common asthma medication to stop the woman's labor and has kept her convalescing in the hospital for the better part of the last four months, rather than sending her back to the dark basement where she and the rest of her displaced family live. Now, two months shy of her due date, the woman is starting to hemorrhage.

Fatima took charge of obstetrics and gynecology much as Ilijaz came to run surgery—because somebody had to do it. Although one of her most memorable experiences in medical school was observing a delivery (she can still remember watching the live baby girl emerge from her mother; it made her cry), she never considered becoming an obstetrician. Before the war, cutting an umbilical cord was the sum of her practical experience. When the war started, she didn't know when, during a difficult labor, to refer a woman for a C-section, and some women didn't reach the operating room in time to avoid the catastrophic rupture of their uteruses and the distress or death of their babies.

She studied diligently to improve her knowledge, using an American textbook from 1961 as one of her guides. Now Fatima oversees a delivery department with five trained nurses and a midwife and treats outpatients for gynecological problems in the clinic twice a week. Obstetrics does a booming business—seventy to eighty deliveries per month, of which seven to eight are referred to the surgery department for C-sections. Fatima thinks that perhaps an equal number of women have their babies at home. The gynecological and obstetrics ward, a single room down the hall from the operating suite, has only nine beds for patients in various stages of labor, gynecological illness, or recovery from surgery or delivery. Because space is so tight, healthy women are checked and discharged two hours after delivery, instead of the pre-war standard of a weeklong hospital maternity stay.

At 6:20 in the evening, Ilijaz and Fatima take the bleeding woman to the operating room to deliver her premature baby by Caesarian section. The surgery lasts just over an hour, and the tiny baby they retrieve weighs only three pounds, four ounces, the smallest baby to be born alive since the war began. They wrap her in cotton wool, show her quickly to her mother, and then take her away to warm her by a stove. Ilijaz, exhausted, thinks it would take a miracle to keep her alive. He walks out of the operating room and heads to the doctors' lounge to collapse, only to be shocked at the sight of a slight Asian man of indeterminate age waiting there to meet him. The man introduces himself by his first name, Dr. Neak, the long-awaited MSF surgeon from France. He wears large, wire-rimmed glasses on his small, animated face, which winces and jerks, brows jumping, as he speaks. Absently, he strokes a long, stringy goatee. Ilijaz, who has only twice before in his life seen an Asian person face to face, thinks of Ho Chi Minh.

"I'm very tired," is practically the first thing Ilijaz tells Neak.

"Yes, I'm here to replace you," Neak says. "You can take a few days off."

But the next day, with nowhere better to go, Ilijaz is right back at the hospital. He finds that the finger he reattached is a healthy pink, not blue, and scratches that patient's name off the operating list. The premature baby, under the constant care of nurses, who sit with her next to a stove for warmth and feed her through a tiny tube with a syringe, survives and thrives, becoming the hospital mascot.

A few days after Neak's arrival, a twenty-nine-year-old woman is brought to the hospital complaining of abdominal pain. The tall, raven-haired woman gives a poor history, saying only that she's felt ill for two days. When Ilijaz presses on the left side of her abdomen, she says it hurts. He palpates something hard that Neak thinks might be an abscess.

"Are you vomiting or having diarrhea?" Ilijaz asks. The woman giggles and answers strangely.

"I vomited when I was sick."

Ilijaz assumes she is slightly retarded—Neak assumes psychotic. In either case, her description of her symptoms is vague and inconsistent, so they admit her to the internal medicine department for observation. The woman maintains her disturbing sense of good cheer, but she complains that her pains are growing stronger. Without the benefit of x-rays or other imaging techniques to aid in diagnosis, Ilijaz and Neak take her to the operating room for a laparotomy—a surgery to open her abdomen to see what is happening inside.

Her stomach appears unusual, enlarged. When Ilijaz tries to lift it, he finds it adhered to her intestines. Carefully, he palpates its contours and feels some strange protrusions. He asks the anesthetist to pull back the naso-gastric tube to see if that is the cause. Ilijaz feels again. Nothing has changed. The anesthetist pulls the tube out completely, but the bumps remain.

Ilijaz opens the stomach and finds a steel factory. Nails. Dozens of them. Ilijaz nearly collapses in shock at the sight. Most, forty-two to be exact, are of the small, two-inch variety, but a handful are three times as long. Just when he thinks he's found all of them, he spots another slipping its way out of the stomach through the muscular sphincter toward the intestines. Ilijaz removes and examines the nails. Their points are dulled, presumably by stomach acid, so Ilijaz guesses they have lain there a long time. It surprises and relieves him to see that the delicate inner lining of the stomach is intact.

When the woman awakens after the operation she smiles and laughs and asks Ilijaz, "Doctor, when am I going to get some food?" Five days later, when she has recovered enough to eat and walk again, Ilijaz gathers the nails and takes them into her room to ask why she swallowed them. The woman looks at him as if he is the one who's retarded, then smiles and changes the subject. Ilijaz never does find out. Someone tacks a bagful of the nails to the wall of the operating theater as a souvenir.

Nobody knows the extent of psychiatric problems in Srebrenica. An MSF medical coordinator suspects that families are hiding mentally ill relatives to avoid stigma and that the psychiatric knowledge of the local doctors is "minimal." When MSF established an institution in an old store building, the town authorities opposed it, arguing that there were no psychiatric problems in Srebrenica until "the refugees" arrived from the villages.

As the weeks pass, the hospital atmosphere improves under Neak's care. He maintains the supply of Turkish coffee and biscuits in the break room, nabbing the treats from MSF stock when necessary. He returns from weekends off in Belgrade, luggage laden with gifts of jeans, English instruction books, nylon stockings, and shoes for those who, unlike Ilijaz, are not shy to ask him for the things they want. His most popular gift is weekly cigarette paper for the operating room staff, allowing them to smoke their locally grown tobacco leaves without scavenging for paper from, among other things, the *Guardian* newspapers he brings back with him from Belgrade or the wrappers from the hospital's sterile tongue depressors (when someone first discovered how suitable the paper was, the staff rampaged through the hospital, opening every single one). Whenever the convoys are blocked and there is little to eat at the hospital, Ilijaz notices Neak slip away at lunchtime to return minutes later with food for the medical staff from the MSF reserves. Neak never smokes a cigarette without sharing it. He finds ways to sneak Ilijaz into the U.N. soldiers' canteen to buy cigarettes and beer.

All this Neak does in silence, rarely speaking a word. He seems to enjoy just being in their presence, sitting quietly in the break room as the young doctors and nurses laugh and tease one another like brothers and sisters, choosing a daily "victim" as the butt of jokes.

Once he walked into the green room while they were watching, for the umpteenth time, one of their Vietnam War movies.

"Shit," he said, and walked back out.

Ilijaz has heard that Neak was born in Vietnam. He wonders what the doctor went through there and whether it explains why he seems to understand the Srebrenicans so well.

THE NEXT MONTHS ARE QUIET, and Neak and Ilijaz focus mainly on the so-called cold surgeries of peacetime—appendectomies, hernia repairs, gall bladder removals, and ulcer operations. Neak even has a chance to try acupuncture on some patients, and the hospital staff starts calling him "the needle guy." But people in Srebrenica fear that the Serbs, though not attacking overtly, are plotting their undoing in other, more insidious ways. The Bosnian government leaks a copy of "Bio-131-S"—

allegedly a secret Yugoslav military strategy for harming Srebrenica's population through its food supply, which comes, for the most part, on aid trucks from Belgrade.

The plot revolves around salt. Before the advent of iodized salt, Srebrenica used to be the only region in Bosnia with endemic goiter—thyroid disease caused by lack of dietary iodine. Srebrenicans were nicknamed "goiters," and the famous seventeenth-century travel writer Evlije Celebije noted that city residents were disfigured by goiter and plagued by diseases caused by having drunk water from the "cursed" creek that ran through town. According to the leaked document, Yugoslav military researchers tested the creek and the water supply around Srebrenica before the war and confirmed its dearth of iodine.

"Thus," the report says, "the deprivation of salt from the diet will lead to a number of malfunctions in the so-called endocrine organs and, in the psychological area, will lead persons to experience confusion, instability, and aggressiveness; an inclination toward anarchy and panic; and a susceptibility to psychological manipulation."

The locals believe that the Serbs are preventing the U.N. refugee agency from bringing iodized salt into Srebrenica, something the agency denies. Humanitarians suspect foul play within Srebrenica and report that enterprising businessmen are making extremely risky journeys through the mountains to Tuzla or Žepa, or raiding Serb farmhouses across the front lines, to bring back salt to sell on the black market. Their fellow Bosnians, famous oversalters who love sodium chloride almost as much as they love nicotine, plunk down the price in Deutschemarks—thirty to forty per kilogram in August 1993; sixty in December; and a whopping eighty by January 1994, roughly what it cost before aid convoys began supplying Srebrenica.

The fears might not be entirely unsubstantiated, though. In his two years of practice before the war, Ilijaz never saw a case of goiter, but in 1994, he begins to diagnose it in some patients. He also diagnoses thyroid cancer and what he thinks are a disproportionately high number of stomach, uterine, and liver cancers, particularly in the young. Although scientists believe cancer takes years to develop, Ilijaz, Fatima, and others of the local doctors wonder whether the Serbs might be contaminating or irradiating their food supply.

The cancer patients need treatment outside of Srebrenica, but by the spring of 1994, U.N.-organized medical evacuations have been stalled for nearly eight months. The Red Cross, whose physician oversaw the large helicopter evacuation a year ago, now refuses to participate, in large part on principle. Red Cross officials are unwilling to compromise their "humanitarian neutrality" by working with the armed forces of the United Nations.

Doctors Without Borders officially ceases participation, too, also on a matter of principle: MSF opposes the Serb demand that patients flown out of Srebrenica be exchanged for Serbs living in Bosnian government-controlled areas. Still, during his six months in the enclave, Neak sends list after list of patients to a U.N. evacuation commission in Sarajevo. He never receives so much as a response, and he wonders whether they are even seeking approval from the Serbs for evacuations. Meanwhile, the patients waste away, trapped in Srebrenica.

Spring 1994 comes, and so, too, the second anniversary of the war. The weather warms and the military situation remains quiet, so the medical staff relaxes, accepting invitations from former patients and their families living in various parts of the enclave. Ilijaz uses these visits with the "common people" to escape from the reality of his everyday life. He brings a walkie-talkie with him and usually doesn't permit himself to drink, in case of a hospital emergency. Still, he relishes the chance to spend time with his team outside of the hospital.

After a particular MSF nurse with long black hair, clear white skin, and a natural sort of beauty begins working in Srebrenica, Naser Orić, the Srebrenica commander, starts showing up at parties thrown by Doctors Without Borders. He takes the MSF team on horseback to the countryside for picnics, riding the enclave's single white horse. Rumor has it that the two are having an affair, which seems to violate MSF's principle of independence from the military, not to mention the commander's marriage. On the other hand, this nurse works so hard and is so sympathetic and respectful to the local staff—even going so far as to dress for a party in traditional Bosnian Muslim *dimije* trousers—that she endears herself to almost every local staff member at the hospital. Then she helps solve one of Srebrenica's biggest problems.

In Bosnia, having a baby out of wedlock is considered trouble. There is a special word for it, *belaj*. But as of the spring of 1994, none of the humanitarian agencies have brought a single means of birth control into the enclave. Women are so desperate to avoid having unwanted children that several infant killings are rumored to have taken place. The police once brought a woman and her newborn to the hospital after catching her trying to drown it in the river. The baby died a few days later.

In the early months of the war, Dr. Avdo Hasanović, the bulbous-nosed pediatrician who serves as hospital director, watched a woman die of infection after someone tried to terminate her pregnancy with a piece of metal. Avdo had never before performed an abortion and had no books to guide him, but, with some theoretical knowledge, a gynecological table, and a set of instruments he found in the hospital, he began offering the procedure. He "trained" several of the other doctors to do it, too. A few girls in the enclave had been charged with prostitution, rumored to be "seeing" the Canadian soldiers the previous year, and doctors performed three or four abortions for them, free.

It wasn't long after beginning to perform abortions that Avdo, in his incompetence, ruptured a woman's uterus and nearly caused her to hemorrhage to death. Ilijaz helped save her in the operating room, and then he took Avdo aside.

"This has finished happening," he told him. "Don't risk it again. Maybe I won't be able to fix something more complicated the next time. You're not competent."

"No problem," Avdo said. "I'll stop."

Since then, Ilijaz has found himself rushing to save the lives of several more women whose abortions Avdo has botched. Avdo's practice has grown to roughly two abortions a day. The women bring him offerings of cigarettes, coffee, and plum brandy. He calls their "grateful" gestures "good will." Everyone else—from MSF to the local medical staff—calls it payment. They start referring to him as "Dr. Abortus."

In June 1994, the MSF nurse manages to bring 15,000 condoms into the enclave. She wants to distribute them widely and offer them at a popular reopened discotheque, but in Bosnia, condoms are considered odd. They're things to giggle about, items to wear with prostitutes rather than to use for birth control. Town leaders insist they must be prescribed at the clinic.

The MSF nurse's randomized survey of more than 1,000 families shows that well over half of the population wants another means of contraception besides abortion. But while they seem to want the condoms, the Srebrenicans don't always use them or their packaging as prescribed.

Long, thin balloons begin popping up all over town in the hands of children. Patients walking out of the doctor's office, where paper is in short supply, look down to find their prescriptions written on condom instruction sheets. And MSF staff members still complain of being awoken every Sunday morning by the howls of girls undergoing abortions without anesthesia in a clinic room near their bedrooms. It takes MSF bringing in birth control pills to begin to solve the problem. The demand for the pills is so overwhelming at Fatima's twice-weekly gynecology clinic that she must delegate the job of dispensing them to nurses.

JULY 6, 1994, IS A SUNNY SUMMER MORNING in Srebrenica. Beneath baby-blue skies and green hills, the scent of linden blossoms wafts through the valley as it did two years previously when Srebrenica's war hospital first opened. Conditions have changed dramatically since that time, when amputations were done with a crude saw and no anesthesia. Now, the eighty-five-bed hospital has departments for emergency, surgery, anesthesia, general medicine, pediatrics, and obstetrics and gynecology. There is a sometimes-functional x-ray machine, a laboratory staff capable of performing urinalysis, hematocrit, blood cell counts and blood typing, and a transfusion service. The hospital's outpatient clinics average 300 consultations per day, and twelve nurse-staffed dispensaries provide basic services throughout the safe area.

The operating room has acquired the same sterile, generic look as any operating room in late-twentieth-century U.S. or Europe. There are neat shelves of surgical supplies, a small oxygen concentrating machine, and a wooden box filled with glass ampoules of anesthetics, painkillers, and other operating room drugs in small, neatly labeled bins. The room has a real, adjustable operating table, operating lights, a generator, and the antiseptic smell of a normal medical facility. Medical workers dressed in bright, clean scrubs glide back and forth, laying instruments in place and chatting with one another while preparing for an operation.

Two local male nurses, trained by MSF anesthesiologists for over a year, now function independently as anesthetists. This morning's patient lies calmly on the operating table while one of the two anesthetists holds open a shiny metal drum. A male instrument nurse, wearing sterile gloves, selects a hemostat and a shiny silver bowl from among the ample stock of equipment, laying them on a cart atop a sterile, creased green cloth.

All at once the double doors of the operating room swing open and Dr. Ilijaz Pilav breezes in from the scrub sink, his hands held out in front of his body, dripping wet.

"Come in, chief!" the men in the room greet him in Bosnian.

Ilijaz takes a sterile towel from the instrument nurse, dries his hands, and then waits with mock impatience to be helped into a pair of sterile gloves.

"I have to put my gloves on, but he's not serving me well," Ilijaz teases. His playful eyes are framed from above by his unorthodox surgical cap, a green cloth creation someone made for him in the style of a baseball hat. Ilijaz wears it with its bill pointed backwards. A fringe of dark hair peeks out from the sides of his cap and his sideburns merge into a beard that grows well behind his white paper mask. With his head and most of his face covered, his most notable features are his small, intense eyes and the tuft of hair growing across the bridge of his nose.

The low cut of Ilijaz's v-necked scrub shirt reveals the bony prominences of his collarbone and upper ribs. He has not regained many of the forty-five pounds he lost during the worst days of war. His scarecrow appearance is evidence that stress, hard work, and an inadequate diet have continued to wear on him throughout his year in the "safe area." There are days he can't stand up due to his back problems, which ibuprofen and even acupuncture with Dr. Neak haven't touched.

"Are you afraid?" someone asks the patient.

"He's quaking like Armenia."

"Who, the professor?" Ilijaz teases the twenty-two-year-old anesthetist who has earned this moniker for being more thorough than his MSF instructors.

"No, this one." The professor indicates the patient.

"I understand why *he* is shaking," Ilijaz points to the patient, "but why is the professor shaking? Here, move your legs here."

Daylight from the top story windows illuminates the patient. The operating room faces west, away from Serbia, toward the rest of Bosnia, toward the city of Tuzla.

With practiced hands, a nurse snaps open a glass ampoule and the professor draws its contents into a syringe.

Suddenly the routine is broken. Someone rushes into the operating room to tell them that a man's been injured in a landmine explosion. The current patient is swept off the operating table, and the nurses wait with Ilijaz for the new patient to arrive.

Less than fifteen minutes later, just after 11 in the morning, a group pushes through the glass double doors carrying the injured patient on a stretcher. A tiny woman in a white coat holds up a bag of IV solution and a short man in a sweatsuit holds aloft what remains of the patient's right leg, which ends in a gauze-wrapped stump where his ankle should be.

The patient, naked except for his blue briefs, winces. Dried blood stains his chest, his arms, and his other leg. The group maneuvers to the side of the operating table and the man wriggles onto it. Then stretcher-bearers duck out of the way and the nurses and the man cupping the patient's calf step up to the table.

The "professor" quickly runs through the checklist on the anesthesia record form.

"When did you last drink something?" he asks.

The patient mumbles a reply.

"On the stretcher? Your wife brought something?" This will make anesthesia riskier. The patient could regurgitate and choke while they're trying to place the breathing tube.

"Move your head over here."

The professor turns the patient's head toward the large bank of windows, exposing his left neck. He rubs it with disinfectant-soaked gauze and holds a needle above the skin while pulling the patient's necklace out of the way. The patient squeezes his eyes shut and grits his teeth. The professor pokes into the external jugular vein on his first try. The other anesthetist tapes the catheter into place while the professor screws an intravenous fluid line into its end.

"Muha, give me one big compress," the professor directs a nurse. "How much do you weigh?" he asks the patient.

"Eighty-two."

"Eighty-two, good."

The other anesthetist, who's just taken the pulse, normal at eighty-four, marks down eighty-two kilograms—180 pounds.

"OK. Do you smoke? . . . You don't smoke."

The professor inspects the man's neck, putting his fingers beneath the chin to estimate its length, which roughly correlates with the ease of intubation.

The injured man is thirty-two years old and hails from a neighboring village. He's been in good health until today, with kidney stones his only medical problem. He's only gone under the knife once in his life—for a tonsillectomy. He hasn't had a tetanus shot. He is the first patient in nearly half a year to arrive in the hospital with a serious mine injury.

When all is ready, at 11:30 A.M., the anesthetists hold an oxygen mask over the patient's face and put him under with a rapid sequence of painkillers, ketamine anesthetic, tranquilizers, and muscle-paralyzing agents. They give his lungs some pumps of oxygen. The drugs have rendered the patient unconscious and paralyzed—he can no longer breathe on his own nor protect his airway if he regurgitates. The anesthetists can only pump oxygen through a mask temporarily, as the air will just as easily go into his stomach. They lift the mask. They have a precious few minutes to insert a plastic breathing tube into his mouth, position it correctly in his windpipe—his trachea—with the guidance of a lighted metal tongue blade, and re-start the flow of oxygen before brain cells begin to die. Some patients are easy to intubate. Others—especially those who are heavy-set, have short necks or have experienced trauma to the face—can be difficult, even impossible.

This patient is easy, and the number eight endotracheal tube slips right into his airway. The anesthetists remain behind the head of the bed to monitor the patient throughout surgery, while the rest of the operating room staff turn their attention to the patient's injury. A tourniquet has been tied around his leg to reduce bleeding, the timing of its placement noted to avoid leaving it on too long and damaging healthy tissue.

Ilijaz stands at the foot of the bed as a nurse cuts the gauze off and holds the leg up for him to see. The foot has been blown off completely. The stump looks clean, with healthy red muscle, white bone and pink skin. It contrasts with the putrid, worm-filled wounds Ilijaz used to see early in the war, when it took men days to travel from the field to the hospital and their legs had taken on the bluish, mottled, swollen look of gangrene. Even so, the ragged end of this wound will necessitate further amputation for control of bleeding and so that the stump will close nicely and the patient can eventually be fitted with a prosthesis.

It's one of the last days of Dr. Neak's MSF rotation in Srebrenica, and he joins Ilijaz by the operating table, pointing to the leg with a gloved finger. He, too, wears a creased white sterile paper gown over his scrubs, but his white mask nearly covers the entirety of his small face, and his large, wire-rimmed glasses hang over it. The two doctors take their places across from one another at the operating table. The stump is now wrapped neatly in blue sterile towels, the leg has been shaved and cleaned between the knee and the ankle, and the rest of the patient's body is covered with a blue sterile sheet clipped to two poles on either side of his head.

Ilijaz points to the place where he plans to cut, drawing his forefinger across the top of the shin, asking a silent question of Neak, standing across the table.

"A little to the right," Neak says.

"What?" Ilijaz asks, and someone translates the surgeon's words into Bosnian.

Neak spreads his hands wide on the leg—one on either side of Ilijaz's. A beam of light from the adjustable silver operating lamp is focused on the patient's shin. The instrument nurse hands Ilijaz the scalpel, which he takes in his right hand like a pencil. The thumb and forefinger of Neak's left hand form an L that frames the area where Ilijaz should cut.

At 11:38 A.M., Ilijaz incises the skin with a firm, confident stroke of the blade. Neak lifts his hand and dabs at the incision. Then, using a second scalpel, he extends the incision toward his side of the table.

Ilijaz slowly deepens his incision, cutting with the scalpel and daubing with gauze to keep the operating field visible. With a facile hand, he clips hemostats to the edges of the skin incision when he encounters a tiny blood vessel, a "bleeder." Neak plugs a plastic, pencil-shaped "bovie"—an electric device for cauterizing blood vessels—into a humming generator. Ilijaz holds up the scissors-like handle of a hemostat and Neak touches its lower portion with the metal tip of the bovie. Then, with a hiss, crackle, and puff of smoke, Ilijaz lifts off the hemostat. The bleeding has stopped.

With feather-like strokes, Ilijaz extends his incision longer and deeper. A large vessel comes into view: the anterior tibial artery. Neak threads bent-tipped scissors beneath it to isolate it. Each man clips one side of the vessel with a hemostat, cutting off the blood flow. Only then do they cut it.

The rest of the surgery goes smoothly. By its end, in the summer heat, Ilijaz's white mask is wet and clinging to his nose, and the hair below his cap on the back of his neck is stringy and dripping with sweat. He looks intently at the operating field, his hands working slowly, like a novice's, but with the delicate touch of a natural.

———

GOING-AWAY PARTIES for MSF staff are fancy affairs, often held at the Domavija Hotel. Long tables are covered with white cloths and laced with silver platters heavy with food brought from Belgrade by MSF and whipped into delicacies by the local chef. Late in the night, white plates with partly eaten salads and cake are scattered between half-drunk glasses of wine, clear vases filled with colorful flowers, and open cartons of cigarettes.

Dr. Ejub Alić holds a cigarette between two thick fingers and leans toward Ilijaz. Ilijaz leans in, too, and the two lift their glasses, giving glassy-eyed grins to a camera as its flash bulb goes off. The two—thin Ilijaz in a white shirt with blue stripes, neatly buttoned up high; round Ejub in a white shirt open lower, showing chest and a snatch of undershirt—are inseparable at parties. Ejub loves to eat and drink and relies on Ilijaz as his "inhibitor."

Ilijaz knows that it can take two hours of nagging to get Ejub out the door of a party. He marvels at the fact that Ejub can still walk after imbibing a liter or two of plum brandy. Ilijaz is sure that he would die if he drank half that much. Ilijaz, Neak, and many others of the hospital staff marvel, too, at the fact that no matter how drunk Ejub becomes, he still talks only about his wife.

"I miss my wife," he says over and over again.

Neak likes to tease him. There's a war going on, he says, and your wife is far away—why are you thinking about her? But even in his most besotted state, nobody can get Ejub to so much as talk about cheating on his wife. How unusual he is. In Srebrenica, married men who sent their families away before the war remarry. As Fatima—a keen observer of the phenomenon—explains it, men don't want to die alone. To *not* cheat on an absent wife is the deviant behavior.

Fatima loves the Doctors Without Borders parties and enjoys dressing up for them. When she arrived in Srebrenica she had nothing much to wear besides second-hand donations from an aunt with daughters around her age. None of it felt like hers, and none of it would do for parties. Fortunately, a shopkeeper relative who departed Srebrenica before the war left some silky cloth behind. Fatima cut the cloth by hand to flatter her figure and stitched it, using a sewing machine that she cranked for power and any color thread she could find, into blouses and flaring, knee-length skirts. Her hems were straight, and she affixed tiny gold buttons for decoration.

To this party, she wears a shimmery turquoise top with a plunging v-neck. Part of her dark-brown hair is pulled up in a white band at the top of her head, showing off her long earrings, and the rest of her hair cascades over her shoulders. Her face is radiant, nose and cheeks pink as if she's recently had some sun, and the eyebrows above her made-up eyes are thin and carefully shaped.

The photographer gathers the medical staff for another picture. Fatima comes up beside Ilijaz and cranes her body toward him with a big smile. Ilijaz sits stiffly, lips pursed and arms crossed, leaning slightly away from her. A dozen other hospital and MSF staff gather around them, all smiling. One raises his glass. The flash goes off.

FOR A WHILE NOW, Ilijaz has been romantically involved with someone else. Ironically, it was Fatima who first drew his attention to her, a surgical nurse from the operating room team named Hajra. One day, Fatima jealously insisted that the woman had a crush on him. The next time Ilijaz saw Hajra, he took a better look at the slender, dark-haired woman, who cast youthful smiles in his direction. She reminded him of an old girlfriend. He started to like her. She liked him, too.

Since the day that Fatima discovered and confronted him about the "affair" that is refreshing him, their relationship has been fraught with conflict. They argue every day. Fatima talks about Ilijaz with others, galling him. He accuses her of having a "long tongue."

"Leave him to do what he wants, and he'll come back," Ilijaz's brother-in-law tells Fatima. "Keep your tongue in your mouth. We could stretch it from Srebrenica to Tuzla and walk right across it."

Fatima tries to move the nurse out of the surgery department, and Ilijaz snaps at Fatima in the green room, telling her that while she is in charge of gynecology and obstetrics, he is in charge of the operating room. He feels her eyes following him in the hospital, checking to see where he's spending his time.

Despite their arguments, Fatima is still a good friend and a support to Ilijaz. They are both prepared to help one another at any time, even late at night when an emergency comes into the hospital. Sometimes Ilijaz is even romantic with Fatima. He doesn't see why this might confuse her.

As Ilijaz draws away from Fatima, he grows closer to a group of male friends. They meet every late afternoon beneath the heart-shaped, sawtoothed leaves of the linden trees in the center of town. When Ilijaz cannot be found at the hospital, everyone knows to look for him here among the small circle of about ten men whom Ilijaz likes to think of as the town's "intellectuals." While those in charge of the town are not well educated, Ilijaz's group boasts lawyers, engineers, and former professors. He didn't know them before, but the war has forged close friendships between the similarly aged men.

Now, in the early summer, the broad linden branches are laden with stalks of small spicy flowers.

> Lindens are blooming
> Everything is as it was before
> Only your heart and my heart
> Are not in love anymore. . . .

So goes a popular Yugoslav song from the 1980s. The men talk and laugh and sing and, for a time every evening, they nearly forget where they are.

The klatch develops rituals. Whoever is last to arrive under the linden tree is the butt of jokes for the evening. Everyone tries to avoid being the last, but someone has to be, and often, when the hospital is busy, it's Ilijaz. No excuses! When he walks up and sees their smiles, he knows it's him.

The group gathers for parties, singing *sevdalinke*, traditional Bosnian love songs, until late at night, long past curfew. Whoever is the most drunk is named the *zmaj*, or dragon, the main character in Ilijaz's favorite song, *Vjerna Ljuba*, "Loyal Love," a sad rhyme about a nineteenth-century military captain, nicknamed "the Dragon of Bosnia," who fought for Bosnian autonomy during the days of the Ottoman Empire. The captain rides away to his last battle. His wife prays and waits for the "the lord of her heart" to return. A messenger arrives to give her the news that her husband has died: "Go wed, white princess, your captain is not coming back." Her heart breaks and she, too, dies, for she will not marry another. The *mujezin* chants from the minaret, hawks screech, and sad music can be heard all the way to Istanbul, emanating from the walls of the deserted white fortress. The war has made Ilijaz identify with the song and its themes of true love, youth, and the fight for Bosnia.

Anyone who misses "linden tree" parties has to have a good reason or he is sure to be chastised the next day. Ilijaz always has a good reason— his work. On the nights when he fails to appear, the linden tree members pour out of whatever apartment they've gathered in and stumble down the street arm in arm, singing all the way to the hospital. Then they stand under its windows and belt out Ilijaz's favorite, "Loyal Love."

The group talks of serious things, too, such as the fact that the main occupation in town is "do-nothingness." They decide to restart the high school, using the former professionals as volunteer teachers. They also establish a club in Srebrenica's cultural center, which dozens of men and women join, including many hospital staff members.

That's when the local authorities—Srebrenica's former military heroes—get nervous. The new club represents a challenge to their uncontested power. Most Srebrenicans shrink from criticizing the authorities, but Ilijaz, Fatima, and a few other club members are growing more vocal in their condemnation of the crime and unsavory black market activities sanctioned by some local leaders.

One day an authority comes to the hospital and warns Fatima to be careful or she could end up dead or in jail. Armed men sometimes burst into the hospital, yelling and cursing at the hospital staff. But Ilijaz, aware that he has become irreplaceable, feels fairly secure in expressing his mind. He charges the authorities with selling donated humanitarian aid on the black market at the same time they regularly deny requests for a portion of the donated food, shoes, and clothing to be distributed to the hospital workers.

"Nobody is above the law," he tells some military officers. "Just because you did some great things during the war and were great soldiers and fighters doesn't mean you can do whatever you want to do now. . . . Even commanders have to obey the law."

Ilijaz begins flexing his muscles. His attitude toward authority has typically been friendly and deferential, with little or no conscious desire for power himself. One morning on rounds, he discharges three soldiers who have been convalescing after being injured by mines. There is no longer any medical reason for them to stay in the hospital, but one of the soldiers refuses to go home. An hour or so later, Srebrenica's commander, Naser Orić, barrels into the hospital, striding upstairs with his weapons strung across his broad shoulders. He confronts Ilijaz in the operating suite, where he is preparing for surgery.

"Why are you expelling my guys from the hospital?" he demands and orders Ilijaz to keep them.

"You're commander when you leave this building, but not here," Ilijaz explodes. "As long as you're under this roof, I'm the commander! . . . Now one of us has to leave this building, you or me," he continues, mustering all of the authority that his position as Srebrenica's sole local surgeon lends him. "If I leave, I'll never come back and you'll have to answer for the consequences."

Silence. Everyone in the room has stopped moving, paralyzed by fear, Ilijaz imagines, or shocked to hear these words issuing from his usually polite mouth.

The commander stands still for a moment, too, looking at Ilijaz with wide-eyed surprise. Then he gathers his men and leaves. After this, whenever Ilijaz meets Naser on the street, he feels the commander greets him with a little bit more respect. After a while the two men even laugh about the incident.

Ilijaz's ability to improve life for his fellow Srebrenicans—as a doctor and moral leader—has grown enormously in the past year, but he barely realizes his own influence. Through bizarre twists of fate, an unassuming villager with no great career ambitions has become, though it surprises even him, one of the most powerful and respected men in Srebrenica.

22

ANOTHER WORLD

AT THE END OF THE NIGHTLY LINDEN TREE MEETINGS, after the jokes and songs and conversations, at least one man usually pats the man beside him on the back and sighs.

"Hey, we'll all grow old in Srebrenica," he says. And for a while they talk about the impossible situation each one of them is in and what might be done to help. Sometimes, often, they speak of leaving.

As the summer of 1994 edges toward fall, it looks as if another winter of war awaits them in the prison of Srebrenica. The Serbs reject the latest peace plan, unveiled July 4, again objecting to the stipulation that Srebrenica and the Muslim-held "safe area" to its south, Žepa, be left as a Bosnian Muslim-majority area. The Serbs propose an exchange of territories—Srebrenica and Žepa for parts of Serb-controlled areas around Sarajevo. Bosnian government and Bosnian Serb leaders even go so far as to meet and discuss the idea. Then the peace plan—proposed by a "Contact Group" representing the United States, United Kingdom, France, Germany, and Russia—is scrapped for a variety of other reasons.

With the latest diplomatic failure, military operations around Bosnia recommence. Bosnian Serb attacks on several other safe areas make Srebrenicans feel vulnerable. The countries that have committed soldiers to the U.N. Protection Force, including Britain and France, continue to oppose any Security Council initiatives that threaten bringing them into conflict with the Serbs. They deploy and equip their forces for peace-keeping rather than peace enforcement. Meanwhile, other countries without forces on the ground, such as the United States, argue weakly for a more robust mandate that will allow U.N. forces to confront the Serbs.

International tension over Bosnia is high. No other issue has ever engendered so many U.N. Security Council resolutions in a similar period—forty-seven in the first year and a half of war alone. But, as an outgoing commander of U.N. Protection Forces in Bosnia points out, there is a "fantastic gap between the resolutions of the Security Council, the will to execute these resolutions, and the means available to commanders in the field."

The U.N. Secretary-General has been reanalyzing the very concept of the safe areas after Serb forces attacked several of them. In mid-April, 1994, in response to "pinprick" NATO air strikes (against a Bosnian Serb artillery command facility, a tank, and two armored personnel carriers attacking the safe area of Goražde), Bosnian Serb soldiers seized 150 U.N. soldiers and held them hostage at heavy weapons collection depots in Serb-controlled territory near Sarajevo. They continued to press their offensive toward Goražde and succeeded in shooting down a NATO aircraft. The Serb advance finally halted after intense diplomacy and another NATO air strike ultimatum. The U.N. hostages were eventually released.

The events have led the secretary-general to express, in a report, his concern about the implementability of safe areas in Bosnia, emphasizing that civilian populations, rather than territory, should be protected through the presence of U.N. troops and the application of air power. So far, the U.N. Security Council has not responded to the idea.

When the Serbs again violate the weapons exclusion zone around Sarajevo, the U.N. commander in Bosnia opposes NATO air strikes, arguing that they will jeopardize humanitarian aid work, expose U.N. personnel to retaliation by the Serbs, and cross the "Mogadishu line" between neutral peacekeeping and fighting a war. Another U.N. officer terms this "a policy of endless appeasement."

Sometimes Ilijaz feels he is in a waiting room. Sometimes he feels he is in a concentration camp. Neither he nor anyone else in the linden tree group has any idea how long the war will last or how long they can stand it.

"In Srebrenica, there is no time," Ilijaz says.

Doctors Without Borders surgeons report back to headquarters that Ilijaz seems depressed and exhausted, that he needs support, that he needs a holiday. Srebrenicans say he works like a slave and lives modestly, rather than taking advantage of his position as he could for perks like a larger apartment. Grueling night shifts every fourth night compound

Ilijaz's surgical duties and heavy clinical responsibilities. He feels his adrenaline level leap each time he leaves home for a duty shift. Overnight in the hospital, sleep comes in fits and starts. He catches a nap in the doctors' room and is startled awake by the sound of a nurse knocking to rouse him. Sometimes the sound is imaginary, only the product of his anxious mind. But more than once after such a phantasmagoria, a serious casualty arrives at the hospital. It's like a premonition before something bad happens. Back at his apartment, the same thing occurs. At some time during the night, he'll bolt awake, certain the nurse is knocking at his door. Such "hypervigilance" is a clear sign of post-traumatic stress disorder—the problem is, Ilijaz's traumas are still happening.

Ilijaz struggles. Sometimes just knowing that people need him helps him fight with the "last bits" of his "logical, rational thinking" the depression that he feels hovering above him, about to take him over. Other times, he turns to God and his religion for strength, and he feels his faith growing quietly. He doesn't want to lose his fight against despair like three men he knew who hung themselves in Srebrenica. He wants, instead, to get out of here.

"I want to be everywhere except in this enclave," Ilijaz tells his friends, but there is almost no way out. Trying to leave is something like plotting an escape from Alcatraz. Many of those who attempt the reverse of the journey that Nedret took in August 1992—through the woods back to Tuzla—never make it. But still, people keep trying, undaunted by others' failures. The groups, which begin as small parties of ten or fifteen, grow to fifty, even 100 people.

Ilijaz begins to think seriously of trying to leave. At first he tells only people he trusts, like Ejub, who himself talks of attempting to reunite with his wife and son in Tuzla.

As Ilijaz grows more serious about the idea, he stops hiding the fact that he's considering it. One day the military commander, Naser Orić, confronts him about rumors of his impending departure. Ilijaz admits that they're true. He wants his action to draw the attention of national authorities as a protest against the situation in the enclave. He also wants the local authorities, including Naser, to take his exit as a protest against the way they tolerate criminal activity and fail to provide the hospital and its workers with a proper share of humanitarian assistance.

Naser advises Ilijaz not to leave, warning that his departure might have "great negative consequences." Rumors spread and a panic arises in town. Many will follow Ilijaz if he goes. Ilijaz still can't decide. He weighs his options until the day that a soldier he treated long ago warns him of a plan for his assassination should he decide to go. Life in Srebrenica looks a little more bearable compared with near-certain death. Ilijaz gives up his plan.

IT TAKES MONTHS before Ilijaz finally has the chance to travel outside the enclave. The fall and winter of 1994 pass into the spring of 1995, and then Naser Orić shows he hasn't forgotten Ilijaz. The military will reward him for his work by clearing a corridor through Serb territory to the safe area of Žepa so that Ilijaz can take a several-day holiday with his best friend Naim Salkić and one of the anesthetists. Žepa, a similarly sized enclave as Srebrenica, but less densely populated, is roughly fifteen miles away. The path between the enclaves is a popular, but dangerous, smuggling route. Srebrenicans go there to buy cigarettes from Žepans, who supposedly get them from Serbs, paying Ukrainian U.N. Protection Force troops as intermediaries.

Snowstorms in April 1995 force Ilijaz to delay his holiday five times. In the meantime, Orić and a dozen other top Srebrenica commanders fly to Tuzla on a Bosnian military helicopter for consultations and training. With Orić gone, others in the military keep his promise to Ilijaz. At last, on the night of April 28, Ilijaz sets out for Žepa. More than 100 local soldiers wait in the woods at various points along the route, creating a path that Ilijaz moves through with roughly twenty other soldiers around him. The rocky, mountainous terrain and the dark night make it impossible for Ilijaz to ride the horse they brought for him, so he walks instead.

Ilijaz isn't scared. He just feels incredibly lucky and happy to experience a brief change in routine. It isn't fair that for the better part of three years of war, he, Fatima, Ejub, Avdo, and Branka have been the only Bosnian physicians to care for the entire enclave of Srebrenica, with just a few MSF internationals to help them. Ever since "Mad Max" took his leave of them in the summer of 1993, nearly two years ago, they have appealed repeatedly to Tuzla's Second Corps for reinforcements or replacements. Some candidate doctors were identified, but Serb authorities would not grant them the right to travel through Serb territory to Srebrenica.

Ilijaz is elated to arrive in the tiny, backward village of Žepa, somewhere he never would have imagined wanting to visit before the war. He feels he's entered another world. After these past three years of nonstop work, Ilijaz doesn't know what to do with himself. Incapable of merely relaxing, he and the others vacationing in Žepa decide to do something for the village. Sparsely populated, Žepa has no foreign aid workers, and until one of its two doctors, Benjamin "Benjo" Kulovac, spent six months in Srebrenica learning surgery, those requiring operations had to be carried over the dangerous, forested mountains to Srebrenica. The town has never had so many experienced surgical staff in its midst, and so Ilijaz decides to make history. Someone wedges wood under the legs of Žepa's makeshift operating table to raise it to his height, and he repairs two hernias. Several days later he performs an emergency Caesarian section. Someone even videotapes the event.

Benjo's father throws a party for Ilijaz the day before his planned departure. By early afternoon, a group has gathered in the house, eating and drinking, laughing and singing along with a talented accordionist. Ilijaz, who usually can do without plum brandy, finds the batch they offer him divine. Everything seems perfect—the food, the music, the spirits, and the company. The war folds up and slips away.

At 1 A.M., he is overwhelmed by a sudden desire to leave. Letting loose like this makes him nervous. Something bad could happen and he'd be needed. He jumps to his feet. At almost the same moment, Benjo does, too, announcing that he is going to sleep.

"You can't go yet!" people argue.

They both insist.

ON THE SAME NIGHT, in a heliodrome in Tuzla, a Russian-built M-18 transport helicopter owned by the Bosnian army, painted white with a red cross, lifts off into the night. Inside it, Dr. Dževad Džananović, a thirty-one-year-old general practitioner from a village near Srebrenica who has spent the war working in Tuzla, bites back a sense of foreboding. Dževad, a handsome, dark-haired physician and an old friend of Ejub

Alić, looks around the cargo hold at his three nervous medical colleagues, a pulmonologist, a gynecologist, and a pediatrician, who lean against large boxes and bags full of medical supplies, military equipment, and ammunition being smuggled into Srebenica to help bolster its defenses. An elderly woman heading for a family reunion bounces her young grandchild on her knee. Several soldiers and top Srebrenica military officers sit, solemn-faced.

Dževad didn't volunteer for this trip. The other three doctors didn't, either. The Bosnian Army Second Corps conscripted them, its medical officers having received an order from higher command in Sarajevo to choose doctors for Srebrenica. The order came not long after Dr. Avdo sent yet another official request for medical personnel. This time, Srebrenica's Commander Orić was in Tuzla to push it through. All four doctors chosen for the trip practiced in Srebrenica or Bratunac before the war.

Dževad was frightened when his mobilization orders came. He has been separated from his family members in Srebrenica since the start of the war and has long wanted to reunite with them, but now he senses something bad in the air. With the spring thaw, a cessation-of-hostilities agreement, signed in December 1994, has broken down, and warfare is re-erupting all over Bosnia. Dževad has been in recent radio contact with his father in Srebrenica, who warned him not to come. Not now. Srebrenicans are uneasy in the absence of Orić and their other top military authorities. Dževad has a strange feeling that the town won't be around much longer.

The other three doctors are scared, too. They've been described in public as volunteers, but in fact they've been compelled to go to Srebrenica. One considered hiding to avoid the trip, but was threatened at army headquarters and gave up the idea. He handed his wedding ring to someone to keep for his son in case he didn't return. Another went to the hospital just before the planned trip complaining of chest pains—nothing was wrong and he is here, too. There is supposed to be a fifth doctor traveling with them, a female psychiatrist originally from Srebrenica. She went into hiding and couldn't be found when they came for her today.

The helicopter lifted off once already tonight, but a Bosnian army base received intelligence that Serbs discovered the flight, and it radioed for the pilot to turn back. Army officers figure that the Serbs won't expect them to attempt to fly again the same night.

Their forty-five-mile journey should last only twenty to twenty-five minutes. The pilot has made this flight many times before. The helicopter has little in the way of navigation systems and will travel most of the way with its lights off to avoid detection, maintaining radio contact with a Bosnian army base that does not have radar.

Nobody attempts to talk over the noise of the helicopter's engine. Dževad keeps a nervous watch out of a small window. Bright flashes of anti-aircraft fire fill him with fear, but the engine noise prevents him from hearing anything. In his mind, he predicts they will not reach Srebrenica. Then he hears a terrible clatter that fills his head and seems to emanate from every direction.

What's happening? he wonders.

THE FLIGHT CREW RADIOES the Bosnian army base to say that they've been hit. They estimate their location and report that they are having trouble turning. They ask whether they should try, somehow, to come back. The soldiers on the ground advise the pilots to continue the final half mile to their goal.

ON THE PLATEAU OF A SNOW-COVERED MOUNTAINTOP between Srebrenica and Žepa, keeping warm inside a small house, are several people who plan to return with the helicopter to Tuzla. When they hear its low rumble, at about 1 A.M., they go outside and watch the helicopter appear from behind the mountains. They twist on American-army-style flashlights, using colored lenses to signal the pilot.

The helicopter seems to be losing height and listing from side to side. It doesn't put on its lights as it usually does when it descends for landing. They watch the aircraft regain some height and clear the mountain. But instead of landing gently, it starts spinning as it angles toward the awaiting crowd. People scream and scatter. After four or five rotations, the helicopter catches itself on a huge beech tree and crashes to the ground on its side.

INSIDE, BOXES FLY. The elderly woman leans over her grandchild to protect him. Dževad feels he is on some sort of slope. Then everything goes blank.

AROUND 4 A.M. SOMEONE COMES to awaken Ilijaz with the news: There's been a helicopter crash in the mountains between Žepa and Srebrenica. Ilijaz knew nothing about the helicopter. He and Benjo rush to the clinic building to pick up some medical supplies and then travel by car and on foot to the crash site in the rain. They arrive to find half of the helicopter's two dozen passengers dead and most of its survivors injured, a few severely. Ilijaz is shocked to learn of the doctors' presence. Three of them are dead. The sole survivor is Dževad, whom Ilijaz knows from before the war as a delicate, tender man.

With their paltry supplies, there is not much more they can do than apply first aid. The grandmother is dead, but the grandson she protected has lived. Ilijaz makes an assessment of the injuries and draws up a list of supplies he needs, giving it to a soldier and asking him to radio the request to Srebrenica. Some soldiers have already started to walk there to retrieve supplies.

Žepa is closer than Srebrenica, so the injured are transferred to its clinic, coming under shelling as they're carried down the mountain. Within about six hours, an incredibly short time for the journey, twenty to thirty men show up from Srebrenica with more than 200 pounds of medical supplies on their backs, far outstripping Ilijaz's request.

Perhaps the most seriously injured is a black-haired man of about twenty-four years, who is alive but unresponsive. He has a small wound on the side of his head and when Ilijaz palpates his scalp, he thinks, but isn't sure, that he feels bone moving beneath it.

At the clinic in Žepa, the man's pulse begins to slow, an indication that pressure inside his head is reaching a critical level. Family members of the patient live in Žepa and come to ask what can be done. Ilijaz prefers to be brutally honest. He describes the man's condition and poor prognosis.

"He needs neurosurgical treatment," he tells the family, "but I've never done it. I've never even seen neurosurgery."

The patient's father begs Ilijaz to do something, anything. "My son's life is in your hands," he says. "I forgive you, even if he dies, but just do something. Just relieve us from the feeling that we didn't do everything we could."

Ilijaz feels trapped. As if by fate, the equipment the runners have brought includes a neurosurgical set with a drill and a large-bore metal bit. When cranked by hand, the drill can grind a hole through skull bone. A chill goes through him. Ilijaz knows the man will probably die no matter what he does. He reaches back, far back, to the books he studied in medical school and the theory he learned.

In order to see what is happening in the patient's brain and how he might fix it, Ilijaz has to remove a piece of skull bone, a procedure known as trepanation. The skull is fractured, which gives him a head start, but he still has some work to do. The first step is to drill several holes in the skull and then "connect the dots," using a wire saw to file away the bone between them.

Because skull bone is a thick, hard mantle that protects the fragile gel-like brain within, drilling through it by hand will take elbow grease. The first time is scary. It is hard to know how far to go and when to lighten the pressure in order to avoid a novice's worst nightmare, cracking through the last bit of bone and puncturing the brain. It takes Ilijaz a whole hour to drill the first hole. By the fifth, he has the hang of it.

He finally lifts the window of bone he has freed and finds a large collection of blood beneath it. The fractured bone has damaged an artery running along the membranes that cover the brain. The vessel is small, as arteries go, but whenever blood collects in the closed cavity of the skull, it puts pressure on the brain, slowly pushing it the only way it can go—downward into the narrow opening at the base of the skull. If there's too much pressure, the brainstem begins to herniate through, strangling the centers for breathing, heartbeat, and consciousness and killing the patient.

Opening the skull has relieved the pressure, but now Ilijaz has to remove the clot of blood and ligate the small artery. He does so, following principles of vascular surgery that he learned in Srebrenica. Then he closes the membranes that cover the brain, puts some antibiotic on top, replaces the piece of bone he removed, inserts a drain, and stitches the scalp closed around it.

The operation takes about five and a half hours. It is nighttime again. Ilijaz, exhausted, leaves the clinic immediately, afraid to stick around and watch his patient die. He is sure the surgery has come too late to save the patient from serious brain damage.

In the middle of the night, his host, a medical technician, awakens him in a panic.

"We don't know what to do with the black-haired guy," he says breathlessly. "He's yelling, jumping, wants to get up."

Ilijaz looks back at the flustered technician.

"You should sing, Shaban," he says. "The guy survived!"

The next morning at the clinic, the black-haired man glowers at Ilijaz.

"Are you the doctor who treated me?" he asks.

"Yes."

"I'll kill you when I get back on my feet!" he says. "I have a headache. I can't stand it!" Ilijaz finds his recovery nothing short of a miracle.

———

TWO DAYS LATER, the bodies of the dead are transferred to Srebrenica. A funeral is held for the three doctors, and a great sadness settles over the town, particularly the hospital. The injured doctor, Dževad, is transferred to Srebrenica, where he undergoes treatment for a hip fracture and kidney contusions. Traumatized by his experiences, it will take weeks before he is able to begin work in the hospital.

Later a group of local residents investigates the crash site. They find the remains of the helicopter lying on its right side on a grassy hillside, its front crumpled like a Coke can from its impact with the nearby beech tree. They inspect the back propeller and conclude that it was hit by a .50-caliber anti-aircraft missile.

———

THE DAY OF THE HELICOPTER CRASH proves a fateful day for all of Bosnia. A Serb mortar round kills eleven people in a district of Sarajevo. Twice, the Bosnian UNPROFOR commander, Rupert Smith, calls for air strikes to protect the safe area, but Bernard Janvier, the Theater Force Commander for all U.N. troops in former Yugoslavia, opposes them. The command structure of UNPROFOR has recently been reorganized, and not only do air strikes depend on the turning of a "dual key," held by the United Nations and NATO, but the U.N. Secretary-General's decision to call in air strikes now has to be based on the agreement of three levels of U.N. command: Smith, Janvier, and the Special Representative of the Secretary-General, Yasushi Akashi, who has overall command and control.

Two weeks later, fighting intensifies around Sarajevo. Smith issues an ultimatum to both Serb and Bosnian government sides, and after the Serbs fail to meet two deadlines to remove heavy weapons from an exclusion zone, Special Representative Akashi authorizes air strikes.

On the afternoon of May 25, NATO aircraft, most of them American, attack two Serb ammunition bunkers near the capital. A thick plume of smoke billows from the direction of Pale, the Bosnian Serb headquarters.

The same evening, in Srebrenica, Fatima strolls through town with her cousin and her increasingly close friend, the lawyer Smail. Around 7:30, a loud explosion sends them into a panicked search for cover. Smail grabs Fatima's arm and they run into the open door of a small house on the roadside. As they huddle inside catching their breath, she notices that her hand feels heavy. She realizes something is wrong, but Smail is gripping her arm.

"Let me see!" she screams. "Let me see! Move your hand!"

"I can't move my hand while yours is on top of it!" he says. They lift their hands to find blood welling from a hole in her forearm. They bandage it quickly and inspect themselves for other injuries. Her cousin's shirtsleeve, which has a hole where the shrapnel that hit Fatima passed through, appears to be the only other casualty. When the shelling subsides, they head for the hospital, leaving what they realize, only then, is an ancient, rickety structure that has provided them little more than psychological protection.

It has been a light day in the operating room for Ilijaz, who performed just one surgery, a circumcision, early in the morning. He is in his apartment during the attacks, and someone comes to fetch him with MSF's car. Several casualties are brought to the hospital at once. The MSF surgeon currently rotating in Srebrenica takes a thirteen-year-old girl to the operating room to reposition her fractured arm bone.

Ilijaz takes care of Fatima, his face tight, probing at the gashes on either side of her forearm where a piece of shrapnel has sliced clean through. Her hand is swelling up, suggesting that a bone is broken. At least nothing appears to be displaced. He cleans the wound, cuts away some damaged tissue, and wraps plaster-coated strips around her arm to make a cast. In the morning, he'll x-ray her arm with Srebrenica's sometimes-functional machine and then decide whether there is more to do. He gives her painkillers and antibiotics and tells her to rest tonight in the hospital.

Fatima's cousin and her friend Smail stay in her room.

"You can go," she tells them. "I'm OK." Smail refuses to leave her. He remains by her side all night, his presence comforting her.

An x-ray is taken the next day. The shrapnel glanced one arm bone, the ulna, and fractured it, but avoided, by what seems to have been a hair's breadth, the bundle of nerves and vessels that run between it and the other arm bone, the radius. Fatima has to keep the cast on, take antibiotics, and eventually do exercises to get her strength back.

What is harder is the emotional impact. The helicopter crash and now this. More than two years after the death of Dr. Nijaz Džanić, it again comes as a shock to think that something could happen to the tight hospital clan. Fatima is alive, she'll be OK, but she and everyone else are shaken.

The same day as Fatima's injury and the NATO air strikes, the Serbs vent their wrath at four of the other five "safe areas." An artillery and mortar attack on the center of relatively peaceful Tuzla exacts the highest death toll. It kills roughly seventy people, mostly teenagers gathered at a café.

As Fatima recuperates at Srebrenica Hospital the day after her injury, Serb forces continue to fire on the capital, Sarajevo. NATO launches further air strikes against six Serb ammunitions bunkers. Then the Serbs strike back against the internationals, taking several hundred U.N. personnel hostage around the country and chaining them to strategically important engineering structures as human shields against NATO targets. NATO halts the air strikes. The hostages remain captive. Over the following days, Bosnian Serb forces with shoulder-launched missiles and anti-aircraft batteries fire at NATO surveillance aircraft monitoring the no-fly zone, shooting down an American F-16 with a radar-guided surface-to-air missile. Although its pilot, Captain Scott O'Grady, successfully ejects and is ultimately rescued from Serb-held territory by American marines, the incident shows that the Bosnian Serbs can see NATO aircraft on the radar screens of the integrated Air Defense System they inherited from the former Yugoslavia. They are willing to put their anti-aircraft batteries to use against NATO. NATO requests permission to take out the Bosnian Serb air defense systems, and when the United Nations says no, NATO halts monitoring flights over Bosnia.

The next weeks of recovery give Fatima time to think hard about her life. She realizes that she has spent so much time obsessing about her on-again, off-again relationship with Ilijaz—who still hasn't ended his affair with the operating room nurse—that she has neglected her own needs. While she encouraged Ilijaz and helped him to become a surgeon, she forgot to think about her own career. She wants to make changes. She wants to take advantage of the presence of the MSF and Dutch surgeons and develop her own skills in surgery, particularly gynecologic surgery, rather than leaving all the operating room experience to Ilijaz. She also wants to develop her personal life. Over the next days and weeks, she begins to walk with friends more often on her own, without Ilijaz. She also notices, though she doesn't say a word and neither does he, that she is beginning to feel something more for Smail than friendship.

THE FIRST OF JUNE 1995, less than a week after Fatima's injury, a Serb raiding party ambushes and kills several civilians in the southwest corner of the enclave. The same day, the Bosnian Serb army instructs the U.N. Protection Forces in Srebrenica to move one of their observation posts, Echo, north in order to provide the Serbs with better access to a road just south of the enclave. The U.N. commander refuses. Two days later the Serbs surround the post and fire at it with rifles, mortars, and anti-tank weapons. The U.N. commander calls for NATO close air support, but higher authorities deny the request, presumably because it might jeopardize the lives of the hundreds of U.N. personnel still being held hostage by the Serbs. The U.N. soldiers abandon the position, regroup, and establish new observation posts nearby. Their backing down infuriates the Srebrenicans.

The current contingent of U.N. soldiers in Srebrenica is Dutch. U.N. leaders had to scramble to find troops to replace the 140-odd Canadian soldiers who came into the enclave when the safe area was declared back in the spring of 1993. Most countries that voted in favor of resolutions creating the safe areas, such as the United States, refused to allow their troops to be deployed in them. Offers from Muslim countries were rejected. The U.N. force commander directed elements of a Nordic battalion to replace the Canadian battalion in Srebrenica, but the government of Sweden instructed it to refuse.

The Dutch were asked next and they accepted the assignment, eager to contribute to the international humanitarian effort in Bosnia and failing to put much consideration into the feasibility of the mission. They dispatched a Dutch Air Mobile Battalion to the enclave around the time of Dr. Neak's arrival, in the early winter months of 1994. The soldiers were met with a less than enthusiastic welcome in Srebrenica. A frenzied crowd of women and children blocked the exits of the Canadians' compound and tried, as if their lives depended upon it, to prevent them from leaving. Neak, who was inside visiting, watched a Dutch officer grow furious at the reception his troops were receiving.

Despite their inauspicious arrival, the Dutch U.N. Protection Force, Dutchbat, quickly became a boon to the hospital, particularly the surgical ward. The size of the Dutch medical team and the quantity of equipment in their complete surgical hospital suggested they were expecting all-out war here. Although their duty was to treat the Dutch troops, one day, about a week or two after the troops' arrival, Dutch military doctors showed up at Srebrenica Hospital. They had nothing to do, they said, and wanted to volunteer their assistance.

That was just the beginning. Soon providing health care to the local population became the Dutch medical officers' major activity. At first, the work violated a U.N. directive that specified a strict division between military and humanitarian tasks, the latter being left to the U.N. refugee agency. A year later, the military doctors laughed when a Dutch army medical officer in the Netherlands called them on the satellite phone to announce that the directive had changed. They were now officially allowed to engage in the humanitarian activities they had performed for so long.

The first Dutch surgeon to rotate in Srebrenica saw patients once a week in clinic and then operated on them either in Srebrenica or at the U.N. headquarters compound, a converted battery factory in the nearby village of Potočari. To Ilijaz it seems that with each successive Dutch force rotation, which occurs every few months, the cooperation between the Dutch army surgeons, MSF, and the local doctors grows greater. He relies on the Dutch surgeons for many things, from technical advice to material assistance, and the population, particularly those who live close to Potočari, go freely to the Dutchbat medical hospital in case of emergency.

The fifth rotation of Dutch soldiers, beginning in February 1995 for what was supposed to be a three-month period, has had it tough. Upon their arrival, while their attention was occupied with the handover, Serb forces to the west of Srebrenica established new positions that encroached on the enclave. Naser Orić instructed the new Dutch commander to keep off the Srebrenicans' turf. When he failed to comply, a local Srebrenica commander held about 100 soldiers of the new Dutchbat rotation hostage for four days. This could not have endeared the Srebrenicans to the new Dutch commander. Beginning in February, Serb forces increased restrictions on humanitarian and UNPROFOR supply convoys, denying the soldiers their supply of diesel. They have had to borrow fuel from the U.N. refugee agency, resort to foot patrols of the enclave's borders, and hire locals to carry their supplies on horseback. Since late April, the Serbs have refused to allow Dutchbat personnel to enter or leave the enclave, effectively shrinking their forces from 600 to 400, after those who went on leave were prevented from returning. In the town, rumors abound that the Dutch want their soldiers to be replaced after the current battalion's rotation ends. In fact, since May there have been debates among U.N. Security Council members and U.N. commanders about whether to withdraw UNPROFOR from the entire country, leaving the Bosnians to fend for themselves. This is exactly what some Bosnians pray for. If UNPROFOR was gone, and with it the threat of hostage-taking by the Serbs, one of the main excuses against lifting Bosnia's arms embargo and using NATO air power would be moot. But the United States—unwilling to contribute the 20,000 troops it is bound to commit in a NATO plan to support the U.N. pullout, and loath to threaten the NATO military alliance by refusing to deploy its troops—opposes the withdrawal.

In the spring of 1995, a woman from Srebrenica is treated at the Dutch military hospital for a severe blood infection after a self-induced abortion. She ends up in the ICU with multi-organ failure. A ventilator fills her lungs with oxygen, a tangle of intravenous lines drips antibiotics, diuretics, and heart regulators into her blood, and a pharmacologist crushes vitamins into a homemade milkshake to feed her through a tube that runs from her nose to her stomach. Serb authorities refuse to permit her evacuation, and as the weeks go by, in the process of her treatment, supplies and medicines such as nasogastric tubes, the cardiac drug dopamine, stomach acid blockers, and certain IV antibiotics run low. Every week, Dutch soldiers and medical personnel meet to discuss her care and decide whether to continue it. Some oppose it, arguing, among other things, that supplies that might be needed for the soldiers are being used up on a comatose woman. Others insist that now that they've provided her care, it would be unethical to terminate it. After seven weeks of twenty-four-hour treatment, she begins to emerge from her coma and speak and move again. Then she contracts a severe gastrointestinal infection and dies within forty-eight hours.

The normal elective operating program at the Dutchbat hospital was stopped because of the comatose woman and now it cannot be restarted. There is not enough gasoline to fuel the generator that lights the windowless room and runs the anesthesia and monitoring equipment. The Dutch surgeon has stopped seeing patients in Srebrenica's surgical clinic, too, in sympathy with MSF, which went on strike after municipal authorities conscripted their local driver. Srebrenica authorities have long insisted that MSF, whose local staffers are practically the only workers in Srebrenica to receive salaries, rotate their local staff members. MSF expatriates, believing that municipal meddling violated their organization's fundamental principle of independence, stayed in the enclave, but halted all non-lifesaving activities.

The strike makes more work for Srebrenica's local doctors and reduces the number of elective surgeries that Ilijaz can offer. Over the past few months, the Bosnian Serbs have not only cut off U.N. military supplies, but also severely restricted humanitarian aid for the Srebrenica population. By spring 1995, the food warehouses are reportedly almost empty, and normal smuggling routes and front-line bartering have become too dangerous for most to attempt. People living on the outskirts of town move closer to the city. After the Serbs' attempts to encroach on the enclave, Dutch soldiers begin allowing Srebrenica soldiers to carry weapons openly, in violation of the demilitarization agreement, and to take shadow positions near U.N. observation posts.

People in Srebrenica are painfully aware of a growing rumor that control of Srebrenica and Žepa might be ceded to the Serbs in a new peace plan. The Serbs have objected to multiple peace plans in part because Srebrenica and Žepa would remain Muslim-controlled areas. The two enclaves are a perceived obstacle to the larger goal of peace in Bosnia. Every day, Srebrenicans flock to the center of town where news pours out of a loudspeaker rigged up to a radio. They listen for hours, trying desperately to discern whether rumors of Srebrenica's impending demise could be true.

23

EGRESS

DR. EJUB ALIĆ HAS COME TO BELIEVE that the groups in Bosnia are mired in a state of conflict as sticky and intransigent as any in the world. He still views war as something comparable to an out-of-control marital spat. In some ways, the fighting has gone too far—there is no easy way back to the halcyon days of Brotherhood and Unity. In other ways the fight has not gone far enough. Nobody is yet willing to compromise.

Now that his friend Dževad has recovered enough from his injuries to replace him, Ejub is on the verge of deciding to take his chances and try to make it through the woods to Bosnian government–held territory. He aches to see his family and longs to reunite with them.

Back in April 1992, soon after he put his wife, Mubina, and son, Denis, on the bus to Tuzla, Ejub lost track of them in the current of war, much as the precious, store-bought shoe of his childhood had swirled out of sight in a rain-swollen river. Almost as soon as they were gone he realized that what was important in life was not the experience of roaming careless and free on his land, nor the desire for financial security represented by the deed to his apartment, nor the curiosity to see what would happen—none of those things that kept him here in Srebrenica when he sent his family away were truly important. Mubina and Denis were.

He heard rumors his wife had died in Tuzla, but he knew in his heart they couldn't be true. Months after the war started, he reached a relative there who told him, via ham radio, that his wife and son had boarded a bus bound for the city of Bijeljina soon after the start of the war, seeking a place to stay with relatives. Within days of their departure, Chetniks took control of Bijeljina, and nobody had seen or heard from them since.

For a year, Ejub didn't know for sure whether his wife and son were dead or alive. One day in the spring of 1993, right around the time of Srebrenica's ceasefire and demilitarization, his best friend handed him a note on the street. When he saw his wife's handwriting, a shock ripped through Ejub, then disbelief. It was a measure of his resignation that he first assumed that somebody had copied his wife's handwriting as a prank.

On one side of the paper were numbered lines with his wife's and his own vital information: name, sex, address, father's name, and birth date. The other side had twenty-two dotted lines filled with the news that she and Denis—nicknamed "Deno"—were all right in Bijeljina, that he shouldn't worry, that she wanted to know, how was he? Facing the other way, and separated by a perforation, was a nearly identical form entitled, "Response to Message," left blank for his reply.

The note was made of exquisitely thin paper. Ejub soon discovered that Red Cross messages were excellent for rolling tobacco. He didn't smoke his wife's letter, of course. Instead, he wrote back, and then over the following weeks and months and years of war wrote and wrote again, cramming the lines of each half sheet with more than 400 words in tiny cursive.

The first letter convinced him that Mubina was alive, but he wondered how she was being treated as a Muslim in Serb-held Bijeljina. Was she a hostage? He wanted to hear her voice. With the address he had, he was able to reach her by ham radio, disguising himself as "radio amateur Kemo" to hide his identity, which he thought could endanger her. The conversation was confusing; she hadn't figured out who he was.

"How is Ejub?" she had asked, not recognizing his voice.

"Ejub is doing fine," he'd answered.

When the surgeon Mad Max, Ejub's old friend from medical school, left Srebrenica to return to Tuzla in the summer of 1993, Ejub asked him to help get his wife out of Serb-held Bijeljina. He also gave him some poems written on pages of a datebook in the dark days of 1992 and sent along a "real" letter, dated July 26, 1993, that wouldn't have to pass through Red Cross censors.

"Please know that I'm yours and I'm only yours," he wrote. "I say that to everyone. Here, morale is zero. So many horrible things are going on. That's why I'm happy that I have you. Please stay the same as you always were. Morally pure and physically strong. No matter what. Because life without moral purity is no life at all. Take care of Deno. I will try to send you some money. Spend it all. Don't save it. You can ask for help from Dr. Dževad . . . Write to me what you need. And if helicopters are still flying over there, I will send it to you. I cannot go over there. Here, it's like we're in a big concentration camp . . . Write to me about Deno. He probably forgot me already. Is he talking? Is he good? Does he listen to you? . . . "

Mad Max managed to help Ejub's wife get to Tuzla. Ejub still worried, though, and used his connections to send more messages than his allotted two per twice-weekly Red Cross pickup, stuffing them full of fatherly wisdom, medical advice, anxious admonitions that she remain "pure," and overwrought pledges of his fidelity.

"I'm sending you a photograph taken in November," he wrote last January. "I'm not happy, even if I'm smiling, and we were fooling around, and they suggested that one foreign girl stand beside me. I said, 'No, get away,' and that's how my posture was. Please don't ever doubt me."

"My dear," he wrote a few months later, "here love has become very cheap, almost worth nothing, and people who I never would have expected are doing the most stupid things . . . I love you with the same devotion and warmth as two years ago."

It was as if what he'd seen in these times—not only the active fighting, but the way that people trapped in Srebrenica behaved toward one another—had nearly destroyed Ejub's faith in humanity. Only his belief in his and his wife's love and faithfulness sustained him and saved him from utter despair. As an atheist, he had no God to rely on. The ugliness he saw led him to read his favorite author, Meša Selimović, with a new understanding of one of the main characters, wise Mula Ibrahim, who became convinced that war is human fate, a way to "let out the evil blood of the masses and divert the accumulated discontent from itself . . . If there weren't wars, we'd massacre each other."

"People are evil children," said the wise Mula, "evil in action, children in mind. And it'll never be any different."

Ejub came up with his own version of the quote and sent it to Mubina.

"*Ljudi su zli, ljudi su dobrad.*" "People are evil, people are scum," he wrote, days after witnessing a particularly evil event occur in Srebrenica. A Serb man was captured and taken to the hospital after wandering drunk into Srebrenica territory. Ejub, on duty, stitched a large gash in his forehead, congratulating himself on an unexpectedly fine result. He put the man in a private room and removed the door handle to prevent anyone from disturbing him, giving it to the nurse on duty.

The man, it turned out, was the father of the police chief in Bratunac, the Serb-held town on the northern side of the enclave's border where Ilijaz and Fatima lived before the war. Red Cross representatives jumped into action, mediating negotiations to exchange the man for a Muslim being held in Bratunac.

The patient was still in the hospital the next time Ejub had overnight duty. Ejub worked until the wee hours of the morning and finally made it to the bed in the second-story doctors' room. As he drifted off to sleep at about 2 A.M., he heard a gunshot. By the time he made it downstairs, the Serb was dead.

A young local man had pushed his way past the hospital guard, Ejub was told, and threatened to shoot the nurse on duty unless she gave him the doorknob. Then he went into the Serb patient's hospital room and killed him. Ejub was sure that if he'd been present, he would have stood up to the gunman and probably been killed in the process.

Yes, people were evil, the people shooting on Srebrenica and then, after being victimized, even the victims themselves. In some ways this was even more disheartening. He's heard that the people inside this strange, closed society, this sadistic sociology experiment called Srebrenica, have turned on Serbs who chose to stay here, killing an old nurse named Rada whom he liked and tried to protect. But mostly he's watched them turn on one another. In their fight for power, they seem to have forgotten that they are all in the enclave, that the enclave is enclosed, that on the heights of the enclave the guns and mortars perch, and, close by, are their enemies, waiting.

ONCE, USING A VIDEOTAPE brought in by an American and a camera attached to a car battery, Ejub made a brief recording for Mubina. He showed her the homemade generator he had patched together using a motor, wire, and an old spinning wheel, unused for a decade or two, that his mother had somehow seen fit to bury in the yard in Alići for safekeeping and then unearth and carry all the way to Srebrenica.

His mother especially liked to use this generator to run the radio. At news time she would turn the crank just as she had done years before to spin wool for his clothing and schoolbook satchels. The generator reminded Ejub of a respirator—at fifteen to twenty cranks a minute, it kept a radio alive, just as a respirator, at fifteen to twenty breaths a minute, kept a person alive. Ejub's silly observations about wartime conditions always brought a smile to the people around him.

He turned the camera on his apartment, too, which had belonged to a Serb doctor who'd left at the start of the war. It was larger than his and Mubina's small, one-room apartment. He moved here when his mother and sister joined him in Srebrenica after the Chetniks took Alići, not long after the shelling attack during which his father died. The house where Ejub grew up was burnt to the ground. The tiny village built by generations of the family Alić was destroyed.

How ironic it was for him to have given up the very apartment that was one of his major reasons for staying in Srebrenica at the start of the war. Now he had something even bigger. The problem was—it was in Srebrenica, and Mubina and Denis weren't here! That showed exactly how much possessions were worth fighting for.

Ejub walked outside and filmed Srebrenica, showing its raw woodpiles, the smoke drifting out of its windows and tomatoes and corn growing on its balconies, and its people, idle or walking aimlessly along the main street. His wife's sister, who worked in the kitchen of the U.N. battalion in Srebrenica, found a soldier willing to carry the tape out of the enclave. Mubina wrote to tell him that she had received it. She cried for days, watching it again and again.

Ejub awaited each Red Cross message delivery with great anticipation and not infrequently great disappointment. He felt that he lived from message to message that he received from Mubina. Sometimes the letters came in a great batch after weeks or months of delay.

"Yesterday I received three letters from July 25, four from August 9 . . . two letters from August 16, one letter from August 10, and one each from the 19th, 20th and 21st," he wrote in September 1994. "All together 13 . . . My dear, in May I sent you six letters. In June, the same, in July, eight, and in August, none. I was waiting for your reply. My soul could not take it. Oh, my dear, how I miss you. To see you in a dress, soft and thin, and to hug you and to hold you like before while you make coffee for the two of us. My dear, I feel so much better since I received your messages yesterday. I wish you were here. In these difficult and gray days, just for a moment. Just for a day. Alone, but with your messages, through memories, I live with you. Memories of you, of your soft dress, our apartment, give me strength to endure all of this and to put an end to this most difficult time in my life."

Ejub has anticipated that end for some time now. "I'm very hopeful about these new political agreements," he wrote her nearly a year ago, around the time that Dr. Neak left and yet another peace plan was introduced. "If they don't come true, and if this prolongs, I will come to you even if it costs me my life."

A few months later the peace effort failed. A former patient offered to guide him to Tuzla. Ejub struggled with whether to accept. He hoped that physician replacements would come from Tuzla and at least make the decision to leave his patients and colleagues easier. Before he managed to make up his mind, winter arrived and the snow on the mountains, which lasted well into this spring of 1995, rendered the trip impossible. After Dževad and Fatima were injured, Ejub found himself staying into summer, too.

———

HIS LONGING TO REUNITE with his wife and son is his main reason to leave Srebrenica, but there is one other. Ejub is on the verge of feeling that he can no longer function as a doctor. The demands of the long lines of patients who push their way into his office outstrip his ability to deal with them. Sometimes 150 patients a day wait to see him. He has always taken pride in doing what he considers a thorough job, performing focused physical exams, rather than just prescribing medication based on symptoms. For years he dealt easily with knots of clamorous, illiterate villagers jostling each other in the clinic hallways, barging through the doors of his consultation room without permission, pulling on his arm whenever he passed demanding, "Doctor, what should I do?" Even when his patients became too unruly, he couldn't bring himself to shout. He would simply leave the clinic, telling them gently, "When you make some order, please call me back." Things would be perfectly calm when he returned.

Here in Srebrenica, the townspeople, ill and well, swarm around him everywhere he goes, and he begins to mind the demands they make, inches from his face, for prescriptions of aid—blankets, juice, food, and sleeping bags. One of Ejub's standard jokes is about his desire to jump into the "collector," the small, polluted stream that runs, partly covered, through town, and swim home underground to escape those he refers to as "the illiterate people." Still, he never blows up at his patients. He just feels alternately tired, numb, nervous, and annoyed. Mostly tired.

———

So FOR EJUB, the decision to leave becomes not if, but when. He hatches a plan with a former patient who has offered to guide him, and tells few about it.

Ejub spends the night before his planned departure with a few friends, drinking to dissipate the anxiety over whether he'll survive, whether he'll see his family again, whether he'll lose a leg to a mine in the mountains. On June 8, his day off, he strolls around town as if nothing unusual is afoot, bumping into Ilijaz outside the old police station, and telling him he is going to go drinking with friends.

Instead, he returns to the apartment and fills a backpack with a variety of high-calorie foods—marmalade, sweets acquired from the Dutch battalion, and some MREs, meals-ready-to-eat, left over from the American airdrops. He packs some important documents, his driver's license, and, because they'll be crossing minefields, medical materials suitable in quantity and type to perform an amputation should one be necessary—a scalpel, suture thread, a needle, antibiotics, painkillers, and gauze bandages. He carries a water bottle and a deliberate attitude; what he is doing is risky and dangerous, but he will proceed, come what may.

In the late evening he leaves Srebrenica with a cousin and a friend, wearing a sweatshirt and tennis shoes and carrying a pair of rubber boots. They head southwest toward Žepa, where Ejub will meet his guides. The first leg of their journey has three dangers—mines, Serb forces, and Srebrenica soldiers pursuing them as traitors.

Doubts and questions reel through Ejub's mind as he crosses the front lines.

What if I stay? Maybe I'll survive. Maybe I should go back. I can't go back. Will I see my family again?

The group takes a break on a hillside and talks about "what if"—What if they meet up with Serb forces? How will they react? What will they do? Ejub says he'd rather kill himself than be captured. His cousin teaches him how to trigger a hand grenade.

Overnight they climb Sušica Mountain. Thirsty, tired, sweating, and nauseated by the cloying smell of wild garlic, they stop for a spot of brandy that Ejub's cousin thought to bring. Ejub stands on the hilltop amid the trees. The air is garlicky and the Chetniks are all around, but suddenly he feels fantastic. Surrounded by Chetniks, yes, but no longer by patients! No more pleading voices to ambush him with their problems and their "What do I do now, doctor?"

I'd rather face Serb forces tonight than a horde of patients in the halls of the clinic tomorrow.

They reach Žepa, and in the evening, Ejub sets out west toward the main body of Bosnian government territory with a group of thirteen men, a mixture of civilians in T-shirts and sportswear, trying, like Ejub, to rejoin their families, and guides—hunters who know the paths through the forested mountains—who wear military uniforms. The guides and some of the men carry pistols or hunting rifles. Ejub is unarmed. At night they travel through a tall forest on wide timber-hauling paths. Nocturnal birds call with strange warbles, and after a while in his exhaustion, Ejub can almost imagine they are calling for him . . . *Ey-yoob* . . . *Ey-yoob*. . . . He wonders if he is hallucinating.

About 1 or 2 in the morning as they walk, a terrifying shriek fills the air.

"What's that?" someone asks.

Another howl follows, and then another. Ejub has never heard such anguished cries before, not even in the days when he cut into men and women without anesthesia. He has the prickly sensation of being in a horror movie.

"That's deer," one of the guides reassures them, and the other former hunters agree that deer make these sounds when they detect the presence of men.

Overnight they travel about twenty-five miles, and in the morning they find cover in a forest high in the mountains where they lie down and rest. Around noon they hear rifle fire—then the low rumble of old men's voices interspersed by the barking of dogs. Ejub and his fellow travelers haven't expected to confront military patrols this far from the front line. Deep in the forest on the weekend, the likelier culprits are hunters. Still, whoever they are, they are certainly Serbs with guns. The voices draw closer, perhaps only 100 yards away. Ejub's men lie still. Then, with a rustling of underbrush, a large hunting dog appears. He stops and stares at them.

One man feels for a small stone. He lobs it at the dog, which sprints away.

Later, in the shadowy half-light of waxing night, they come to the edge of a major road that stretches between two Serb-held cities: Han Pijesak—the headquarters of the Bosnian Serb military leader, General Mladić—and Sokolac. A guide offers to cross the road first, and he instructs the group that if he makes it, they should follow one by one. When he arrives without incident, most of the other men jet across the road in a nervous pack. Ejub, who abhors selfishness and who has long prided himself for being the kind of man to step aside and let everyone on the bus before him, is left standing alone. He then crosses calmly, secure in the knowledge that at night, any cars will be heralded by headlights.

His first casualty awaits him on the other side of the road. Ejub's frenzied cousin has run into a wire fence and dislocated his ankle. Ejub wraps it, teasing him that God is punishing him for having failed to give his horse a proper rest the first night of their journey.

They continue through the night, walking in a line through the forest, single-file in each other's footsteps to minimize the chance of detonating a mine. In the quiet darkness, even the cracking of twigs beneath their shoes sounds loud to them. A fox slides past. They communicate in whispers only when necessary. But as the lonely night wears on, the forest seems to belong only to them, and the men, forgetting their carefully observed silence, begin to chatter. Ejub refuses to go farther while people talk. For a while quiet reigns again, but after a time the men forget themselves. Even though they are only a small group, Ejub has to stop them twice to restore quiet order.

By the fourth night of walking, the men are exhausted and shivering from the cold. Toward morning, just as it begins to rain, they reach the set of front lines they plan to cross near a Bosnian government–held town called Kladanj, about thirty-five miles from Tuzla on a main road.

Over the next several hours, they tiptoe past empty Serbian trenches, ford two rivers, climb down and up two canyons, and finally, at midday, descend a steep hill to an asphalt road that marks the Bosnian government side of the front line. Ejub stands with his arms out in the rain and turns his face up to the sky. An intense happiness and a sense of accomplishment far greater than his previous greatest accomplishment—finishing medical school—fill him. Men around him weep. With gratitude, Ejub slaps 500 Deutschemarks into the hand of his guide.

They proceed straight to Bosnian army headquarters in Kladanj. The first thing Ejub does is ask to use a telephone and call his beloved Mubina. When she picks up the phone, he flirts with her without identifying himself.

"Mr. Ejub is that you?" she asks. "Only you talk like that!"

It takes a while to convince her that he is calling from Kladanj. She bursts into tears. He tells her to prepare for a celebration.

"Buy lots of alcohol and lots of meat; I'm going to bring the guys with me to Tuzla!"

The men change their clothing and eat at the army headquarters. Then they undergo questioning about the situation in Srebrenica and their reasons for leaving. After two hours, the group is ordered to wait in Kladanj for the return of some officers. Ejub calls Mubina and tells her to cancel the party.

Most of the guys wait around headquarters, but Ejub heads into town to have a drink with one of the commanders. He's just met the man, but one drink turns into two, turns into four . . . Inhibitions lost, Ejub goes on his usual drunken riff about missing his wife. He tells the commander he can't wait to get to Tuzla to see her and his son.

"Oh, doctor, don't worry about it, you're with me," the commander says, and at 3 A.M. they slide into his chauffeur-driven car singing a Balkan pop song, "Love Is Where You Are." Two hours later, Ejub gathers his wife and his son in his arms.

24

OVERTURE

AFTER NEGOTIATIONS WITH NEDRET ENDED IN LATE 1993, life quieted down for the artful doctor, Boro Lazić. He worked with four other Serb physicians in the health center of his small town, Šekovići, in the Serb-held part of Bosnia, treating townspeople with typical illnesses, such as influenza, that were sometimes complicated by exhaustion, stress, and poor nutrition. Šekovići was a fairly safe location, but as time went on, fighting shifted closer to the town and his side had its share of hardships. Bosnian government forces near Kladanj clashed with Bosnian Serb forces near Šekovići, and grenades sometimes exploded in town. Occasionally, Boro treated someone injured by one of those grenades or by a mine. Electricity sometimes went out, and the phones usually didn't work; rumor had it that they'd been disconnected to prevent people from passing "secrets." Boro and other townspeople traveled from Serb-held Bosnia across the Drina River to Serbia to buy food. About once every month or so, Boro's commander recalled him to participate in field actions as chief of the medical services of Šekovići Brigade, typically in response to Muslim attempts to break the battle lines and retake certain areas near the frontiers of their territory.

Then, in spring 1995, Bosnian government forces in the capital, their leaders swearing not to endure another winter under siege, attempted to break southward out of Sarajevo. The area they attacked was a strategically important area for the Serbs, as it connected the central part of their self-declared republic to the geographical area known as Herzegovina.

Boro's unit was called to participate in the defense. Fighting was heavy and many of the infantry soldiers, teenaged inductees, were facing their first major battle. During a thunderstorm, Boro, along with an inexperienced sergeant and about fifty of these young men, found himself stranded without vehicles or other officers on a plateau called Umchani, cut off from two sides and under heavy attack. As grenades fell, so did the men, and it was hard for Boro to tell as they fell whether they'd been hit by shrapnel or, as often happened, had grown hysterical and fainted away from fear. The group retreated three to four miles under shellfire, first cautiously, then running for their lives down a winding road in the rain toward a dark forest to the sound of thunderclaps and explosions.

Boro's resourceful nature was a boon to his fellow medical workers. One evening he caught sight of a set of radios that an officer had carelessly left behind in a car. Boro snatched them for his medical teams, which lacked communications equipment. The heist was successful until it was discovered, and Boro was reprimanded for his mischief.

Times grew tougher as the Bosnian government grew more determined to break out of Sarajevo. Boro's unit was sent to rest, but was twice called back to the area around Sarajevo. In late June, Boro took charge of three teams of medical technicians providing aid to a unit responding to a Bosnian army offensive. Boro's unit took eighty casualties, injured and killed, in that action.

THE LAST WEEK OF JUNE, a few Bosnian Serb soldiers cross a mining tunnel and emerge inside Srebrenica enclave, on a hilltop community above the hospital. They set a house on fire, kill a man, and fire their M85 machine guns and *zolja* anti-tank rockets in the direction of the hospital, frightening everyone inside, before retreating.

Two days later, early in the morning of June 26, Srebrenica soldiers—urged by the Bosnian army headquarters to conduct a diversionary action to help draw even more Serb forces from the capital—raid the Serb village of Višnjica, three miles west of the enclave. They torch houses. They lead sheep away. They kill a few people.

It is not a major offensive. U.N. analysts assess that Srebrenica forces, although greater in number than the 1,000–2,000 Serb soldiers surrounding them, are so disorganized and poorly armed that they pose no real threat to the Serbs. Still, General Ratko Mladić, the commander of the Bosnian Serb army, uses the occasion to lodge a protest with the U.N. Protection Forces. Attacks from Srebrenica "brutally violate the status of the Safe Area," he says, and he issues a grim warning: "We will not tolerate such cases in the future."

—————

SIX DAYS LATER, the commander of the Bosnian Serb Army Drina Corps issues two orders laying out plans for an attack on the enclave of Srebrenica and ordering various units of the Bosnian Serb army to ready for combat. The plan, Krivaja '95, directs the Drina Corps to "split apart the enclaves of Žepa and Srebrenica and to reduce them to their urban areas" and "to create conditions for the elimination of the enclaves."

The commander of the Šekovići Brigade calls Boro and tells him to be ready to leave for an offensive on Srebrenica the following day. The goal, Boro assumes, is to take the city, which seems farfetched. He doesn't worry too much about his friends inside. He gathers medicines and food, and then joins his driver and a nurse to settle in a region south of the Srebrenica enclave borders, not far from Srebrenica's destroyed water treatment plant. There, his forces await orders to strike.

PART FOUR

"AN ATTACK ON THE
ENTIRE WORLD"

What greater grief than the loss

of one's native land.

—**Euripides**
Medea [431 B.C.], L. 650

25

"OUR SINCEREST APOLOGIES"

ON JULY 4, 1995, AN international humanitarian worker escorting a food convoy from Serbia into Serb-controlled Bosnia sends a coded message to a colleague in Srebrenica. Recently the worker aid heard that the Serbs were planning to shrink the enclave and promised the colleague that if he ever saw any evidence to substantiate this, he'd send the message, "Say hello to Ibrahim." While traveling south along the Drina River, the worker witnesses signs of military preparations: heavy weapons and tanks being moved along the route from Zvornik to Bratunac. He passes the message to his contact in Srebrenica, who passes it to the U.N. Dutch battalion.

"Say hello to Ibrahim."

FOR THE FIRST TIME IN OVER A YEAR, Ilijaz is the sole surgeon at Srebrenica Hospital. When a four-member MSF team rotated out of the enclave two weeks ago, Serb authorities permitted only two MSF staff members to replace them: a veteran MSF nurse from Germany, Christina Schmitz, and an Australian generalist on his first humanitarian mission, Dr. Daniel O'Brien. No surgeon. Ilijaz isn't pleased about the extra work this is causing him, but at least he's now competent to handle it.

Christina, a petite, freckle-faced thirty-one-year-old with red hair and blue eyes of an almost disturbing pallor, has taken charge of coordinating the mission—communicating with Belgrade headquarters by radio about the medical programs, telexing reports, and keeping up contacts with local authorities and the United Nations. She's been learning her way around with gusto, familiarizing herself with the security procedures, studying MSF's communications equipment (taking down the radio and checking what cable goes in what hole) and striking those around her as very efficient.

She takes extra care for a reason. Srebrenica, as a surrounded enclave in an active war zone—an open-air prison, she calls it—is something new for her. Over the past four years she has worked in hot spots from Kurdistan to Somalia, Croatia to Liberia, South Sudan to Chechnya, realizing a childhood vision of working with disadvantaged people. But two weeks ago, when she walked past the yellow bridge and the last Serb and United Nations checkpoints with Deutschemarks for the local staff stuffed in her shoes, she had the creepy feeling that a door was shutting behind her. She comforted herself with the thought that if thousands of Bosnians could live here, she could, too.

It also reassured her to meet the Dutch U.N. commander, Col. Ton Karremans, at a security meeting at Dutchbat headquarters later that first day. "The enclave will not fall," he told her. Karremans was sure that the Srebrenicans could hold their positions for at least seven days under attack and that they were strong enough to prevent the Serbs from taking Srebrenica.

Christina didn't know much about the safe area—learning about places before going to them has long struck her as rather useless—so when she traveled into town she paid attention to landmarks, including three important military points along the main road. Just inside the northern border of the enclave, in a converted factory complex in an area called Potočari, the Dutch U.N. battalion has its main headquarters and hospital. Dutchbat B Company, with its own medical team and the second largest encampment of Dutch soldiers in the enclave, is located about three miles south in a former textile factory, just before the entrance to the town proper and not far from Srebrenica Hospital. Finally, the headquarters for a team of U.N. military observers is located in the post office building directly across the street from the hospital. The three observers (down from a typical six after Serb authorities refused to permit replacements for outgoing personnel) spend their days visiting the fourteen observation posts manned by Dutch soldiers that ring the safe area: Alpha, Charlie, Delta, Echo, Foxtrot, Hotel, Kilo, Mike, November, Papa, Quebec, Romeo, Sierra, and Uniform.

The day after Christina's arrival, Dutch military doctors showed up to work at the hospital. This surprised and concerned her. MSF doesn't typically collaborate with soldiers.

"How come we accept their weapons in our house?" she asked MSF headquarters. She fears that getting too close to any military, even that of the United Nations, will threaten the hospital's neutral, protected status under international law.

THE SOUND OF AN EXPLOSION FILLS THE AIR and rattles the windows of the bedrooms in the Doctors Without Borders house behind the hospital. Christina's blue eyes snap open. It's dark outside, still early in the morning on July 6, 1995. She hears more thudding explosions and makes her way to the corridor, huddling with her MSF colleague, Daniel O'Brien, as they listen carefully.

"Yes, that's it," Christina tells him. She has experienced shelling just once before, in Chechnya, but is pretty sure she recognizes the sound. A few days ago she heard the same noises and was relieved to find it was only the Dutch soldiers detonating ammunition. This can't be the case now, not in the middle of the night. When the barrage fails to stop for forty-five minutes, she sends a satellite telex message to MSF headquarters in Belgrade.

"Sorry to wake you up," she writes, informing them of heavy shelling near the town and explaining that she's dismantling the radio and going with it into the shelter. She and Daniel run to the back of the adjacent medical clinic building, pulling open a cellar door and descending a staircase into a basement built by the Yugoslavs in case of war. The two stay there until daylight.

Throughout the morning, 200 shells, including tank bombs, artillery, and mortars, hit the enclave from all directions—ten of them landing in the city itself—and several of the U.N. observation posts along the perimeter of the enclave report seeing Bosnian Serb army troops and tanks. The Serbs fire on positions of Srebrenica soldiers, who return small-arms fire, and at U.N. soldiers in their observation posts, who don't. Rockets zoom over the Dutchbat compound in Potočari in an impressive show of the Serbs' twelve-tube Multiple Launch Rocket System.

The Serbs also lob shells into civilian areas, including a collective center for displaced people in Potočari. The hospital receives several lightly injured patients.

AROUND 1 P.M., the twenty-seven-year-old commander of a Dutch observation post in the south of the enclave, "OP-Foxtrot," radioes his commander that a Serb tank has fired a round into his defense wall. Less than a half hour later, another round tears into the watchtower, rendering the long-range, optically tracked TOW anti-tank missile atop the observation post inoperable, effectively taking away the observers' ability to view the Srebrenica-Skelani road, and showering those inside with sand. Two more rounds fired directly at the post narrowly miss it 20 minutes later.

At 1:50 P.M., the Dutchbat commander requests NATO close air support to protect his targeted observation post. Close air support—the use of air power for direct support of U.N. troops on the ground—is one of two official options for the use of NATO air power and can be requested by a commander on the ground, but must be approved at higher levels of U.N. command. Air strikes, the other option, mean large-scale bombing and must be initiated by those at the top level of U.N. Protection Force command.

The fact that the Serbs are directly attacking a U.N. observation post in Srebrenica satisfies the strict criteria for the use of NATO close air support. The Dutch commander's air power request begins its long quest for approval up the U.N. ladder of command—from Dutchbat in Srebrenica to U.N. Sector North East headquarters in Tuzla to Bosnia-Herzegovina command in Sarajevo to the force commander in Zagreb—French General Bernard Janvier—to the special representative of the U.N. Secretary-General, Yasushi Akashi, a famously weak-willed and force-shy official who holds the first air strike "key." The other is with NATO.

The humiliating hostage crisis following the last use of NATO air power two months ago helped shape this Byzantine structure and has dampened the already feeble enthusiasm that existed among many in the U.N. hierarchy for the use of targeted bombing. During hostage negotiations, the Serbs demanded an outright end to the future use of NATO power. The top commander of all U.N. forces in the former Yugoslavia, General Bernard Janvier, held an unpublicized meeting with Bosnian Serb General Mladić on June 4, after which the hostages were released. The Serbs then bragged that he had agreed to their condition. He denied the allegation, but stated publicly that from now on the United Nations would stick to a peacekeeping, rather than peace-enforcement, mission. U.N. Secretary-General Boutros Boutros-Ghali stripped the right to request air strikes from the man most interested in using them, British Lieutenant General Rupert Smith in Sarajevo. The secretary-general announced he would personally make all future decisions about air strikes from his headquarters in New York. Many analysts interpret these actions as a veiled promise of non-confrontation with the Serbs.

Janvier, usually based in Zagreb, is out of town at a meeting in Geneva. However, his wish that air power be used only as a "last resort" is clear to his subordinates. In Srebrenica, Serb firing and shelling fall off by mid-afternoon. The Dutchbat commander's request for air support hasn't ascended far along the chain of command before it's turned down on grounds that the direct assault on the U.N. observation post has ended. This relieves some Dutch soldiers, who fear that NATO strikes might incite the Serbs against them.

Yesterday U.N. military observers noted numerous new tanks and soldiers to the south and east of the enclave, but the Serb attack takes Dutchbat by surprise. The local U.N. military officers make their assessment. The Serbs are most likely attacking with a limited objective. They have long wished to move the southern boundary of the enclave north to gain access to a strategic crossroads on the main Srebrenica-Skelani asphalt road.

While this assessment may be somewhat reassuring to the internationals, giving the Serbs the crossroads is an unacceptable idea to the Srebrenicans. In the absence of Naser Orić, the commander of the Bosnian Army's Twenty-Eighth Division in Srebrenica, his chief of staff, a thirty-nine-year-old former Yugoslav Army officer named Ramiz Bečirović, takes charge. Badly injured in the helicopter crash in April, he has only recently emerged from his bedridden state.

Bečirović communicates with Orić by coded telex. He asks the Dutchbat battalion commander to return the weapons surrendered by the Srebrenicans in 1993 so that Srebrenica's decommissioned soldiers, who now occupy shadow positions near the U.N. observation posts, can defend against the Serb assault. Srebrenica has perhaps 5,000 potential soldiers, but, even with the recent furtive helicopter deliveries of small arms and supplies from Tuzla, not enough weapons to arm all of them. The Dutch have only 250 minimally equipped infantry soldiers on the ground. The Serbs, whatever their numbers, are likely to be well armed. The Dutch-bat officer consults with his superiors about the Bosnian commander's request, noting that the Serbs haven't breached the enclave borders. For now the answer is no.

AS A TRAINED NURSE, Christina Schmitz has an urge to help in a more practical way than sending updates to MSF headquarters. Yesterday, the Dutch medical team promised her that today she could pick up some blood to transfuse a girl with end-stage leukemia. Christina throws on a flak jacket and helmet and heads for the main U.N. compound in one of the "soft-skinned" Land Cruisers to keep her commitment to the girl and her family.

She arrives safely, but the Dutch disappoint her. A transfusion won't save the girl's life, and in light of a shortage of blood bags and the increased risk of injury the soldiers face now that Srebrenica is under attack, they've decided to reserve what supplies they have. They've inventoried their remaining medical supplies and concluded that if a few Dutch U.N. soldiers are heavily wounded, there will barely be enough to treat them. They've stored away an emergency "iron ration" of medicines and supplies, enough to operate on and treat thirty soldiers with varying types and degrees of injuries, in a bunker that can support an operating theater.

Christina returns to Srebrenica empty-handed. A few hours pass, and then she has to ask the Dutch for help again. A woman has arrived in the hospital with a penetrating chest wound. A collection of blood and air beneath the covering of her lungs is collapsing them, decreasing the oxygen level in her blood. Ilijaz tries to stabilize her condition by inserting a chest tube to drain the blood and air. But without the services of a full intensive care unit to keep careful track of her blood pressure and blood oxygen saturation, he fears that she could die. The Dutch have such an ICU, and Ilijaz asks Christina to request that they take the injured woman into their care.

This time, Christina sends the request by telex. She receives a reply from a Dutchbat surgeon who, like her, has just recently arrived in the enclave:

"With our sincerest apologies we are not able to treat your patient, because of lack of I.C. capacity and material."

Christina knows that Srebrenica Hospital, though it lacks the sophisticated monitoring equipment the patient requires, has plenty of supplies. She could send whatever the Dutch need with the patient. By the time the response comes in, though, other crises have hit, and she doesn't pursue the case. She is peeved, though. She lets MSF Belgrade headquarters know about the incident and comments that if the Dutch soldiers can't do anything to protect the population they're here to protect, they could at least take some patients. Keeping all their supplies for themselves and refusing to take patients is, in her opinion, unethical.

"That will mean also that if Daniel or myself are in need for urgent medical care, they will refuse. . . . For the time being their only aim is to protect themself."

A colleague from MSF Belgrade writes back to assure her.

"If either you or Daniel would be in (trouble) I do not think there will be a problem. I am sure they will help. It has always been the case in all the countries I have been to."

Christina manages to find a positive side to Dutchbat's suspension of its medical activities. She tells headquarters that it's an opportunity for MSF to reaffirm its neutrality by initiating a new, more distanced involvement with the U.N. military forces.

SREBRENICA AWAKENS FRIDAY, JULY 7, to a quiet, overcast morning. In the bunker beside the hospital, the MSF telex comes to life, spitting out a message from Dutch medical personnel stationed at the U.N. B Company compound near the soccer pitch. They ask for information about yesterday's civilian casualties. The death toll, at least among people who made it to the hospital, was four, and more than a dozen were treated for injuries.

Before noon, the phone in the MSF house rings. Christina stares at it, surprised. In the two weeks she's been here, she never even thought to pick it up and see if it worked. Apparently some sort of internal phone exchange exists for emergencies. The voice on the other end says there are wounded people close to Potočari who need help. Can she come? Again, it's dangerous to venture out in anything less than an armored vehicle given the recent military assault, but Christina can't imagine not trying to help people knowing they are hurt. If the shelling keeps up, she thinks, MSF will need an armored personnel carrier. She and one of the local drivers put their heavy flak jackets and helmets back on and set out in an MSF Land Cruiser to pick up the injured. She finds two casualties opposite the Dutchbat compound—one with minor injuries and the other with a life-threatening head wound—and drives with them back to the hospital.

Why didn't someone ask the Dutch to help them, given that it was an emergency and they were much closer to the Dutchbat hospital? Christina doesn't know.

Srebrenica remains quiet throughout the rainy day. Perhaps it's the weather, or maybe the Serb military has decided not to pursue whatever objectives it had in mind. Whatever the case, in spite of the recent shelling and the rain, Srebrenica's streets are full of people who cannot bring themselves to stay inside their hot, overcrowded dwellings. It surprises Christina that parents let their children play outside. The two MSF expatriates and the local doctors take advantage of the quiet moments, too, to finally sit down for lunch.

Around 6 P.M., the hospital shudders with the force of repeated explosions; sixteen artillery shells crash into the center of town. The injured come pouring into the hospital, among them one of Ilijaz's good friends, a big-boned twenty-six-year-old teacher, organizer of the schools in wartime Srebrenica and an original member of the ragtag troops Ilijaz helped put together to defend his village. The teacher's body is ravaged by shrapnel wounds. Holes as wide as two inches pepper his chest, abdomen, and buttocks, leaving nothing for a surgeon to open and everything for him to close.

Ilijaz has to leave another patient with chest wounds and puts his best friend, the instrument technician Naim, in charge of sewing the wounds closed. Then, he makes it his first priority to support his injured friend's breathing, relieving the tension on the man's damaged right lung by inserting a tube into his chest to drain it of air and blood. Ilijaz turns to the abdomen, which is bleeding heavily. Over the next several hours, he repairs an injury to a major vein, sews a rupture in the urinary bladder, and cuts out several lengths of damaged intestines, which will die if left in the abdomen. Then he painstakingly stitches the healthy ends of intestine back together, creating an anastemosis and leaving an opening to drain outside the skin in a colostomy.

One and a half liters of blood transfused, numerous liters of fluids infused, and nearly five hours later, at 10 P.M., Ilijaz finally completes the operation successfully. The moment he finishes, he goes weak-kneed and nearly faints. His friends in the operating room grab hold of him and help him to the doctors' lounge.

Christina tries to convince Ilijaz to get some sleep with her and Daniel in the cellar she calls "MSF's bunker." He refuses. Like a good captain, he won't abandon his ship. The 450-square-foot shelter, filled with a handful of canvas mattresses and the MSF desk, telex, and radio, has nowhere near enough room for all the hospital staff. If Ilijaz leaves them, he thinks, they might panic. He won't even use the bulletproof vest and helmet Christina gave him, because when he put them on once, everyone's eyes bugged out with fear.

The medical staff work until midnight, and Christina later reports the day's toll to headquarters: seven wounded, five of them severely, and one woman dead. Three of the injured die over the next twelve hours. Ilijaz is about to break down, she writes. Srebrenica "desperately" needs an MSF surgeon.

THE ATTACK HAS GONE ON FOR TWO DAYS NOW, and the Dutchbat commander again speculates on its possible goals in a report to his superiors in Bosnia. The Serbs' aim is to reduce the number of U.N. forces and/or either "eliminate" or "neutralize" Srebrenica's forces. With the Serb army's limited manpower, he predicts, it won't be able to conquer the enclave in the short term. However, the shelling of urban areas, attacks on the U.N. forces, and blockage of aid and resupply convoys concern him enough to conclude with an "appeal on behalf of the population of the enclave of Srebrenica." He asks for assistance by all means: ground and air. There is no response from U.N. Protection Force leadership.

SERB FORCES GREET SREBRENICANS the next morning, Saturday, July 8, with two shells sent crashing into the center of town. Over the next few hours, they score nearly three dozen more hits in town and many outside it. Shortly after 11 A.M., Serb forces in the south of the enclave begin firing a T-54/55 battle tank and howitzers in the vicinity of the U.N. Foxtrot observation post they targeted two days ago, hitting positions held by Srebrenica soldiers some 200 yards in front of the post. The terrorized Dutch soldiers inside the small, sandbagged structure are instructed by superiors that they may not evacuate.

Around 1 P.M. the Dutchbat commander at the U.N. base in Potočari contacts his superiors in Sarajevo to again request close NATO air support. Before there is any response, one tank round and three shells tear into the defense wall of the observation post, ripping out a hole a tank could drive through. Dutch soldiers watch as Srebrenica soldiers abandon a trench in front of the U.N. post and retreat 100 yards behind it. A Serb tank then crosses the trench and stops 100 yards in front of the U.N. post, firing to the west. A firefight ensues between the Serbs, who assault the new Srebrenican positions with small arms, grenades, and mortars, and the Srebrenicans, who respond with small-arms fire. The Dutch, caught in the middle with a non-functioning anti-tank missile atop their observation post, have an AT-4 shoulder-launched anti-tank rocket at their disposal. They do not fire it.

The Dutch company commander, fearing for the lives of his men, orders them to withdraw instead of responding militarily and increasing the tension. Serb soldiers waving white flags approach the post and jubilantly order the Dutch soldiers to leave without their weapons. The Dutch pile into an armored personnel carrier and speed downhill toward Srebrenica. Moments later, they brake to a halt. Several Srebrenicans stand before them at the foot of the hill, blocking the road to prevent their retreat.

By pulling out, the Dutch are violating tacit assurances that they would hold their observation posts for seventy-two hours under fire and collaborate with the Srebrenica soldiers to defend the safe area. What the Bosnians want is to prevent a repeat of last month, when the Dutch gave up observation post Echo and allowed the Serbs to occupy part of the enclave. But the Dutch soldiers suspect that the Srebrenicans blocking their route may wish to use them as a shield against the Serbs. They radio their company command post to report that the men barricading the road appear to be armed with rifles but not anti-tank weapons. The commander orders the unit to proceed. The driver rams through the barricade, and, as his soldiers duck for cover beneath the APC's armored plating, they hear a muffled explosion. The tall gunner on the turret above them, slow to withdraw, crumples into the APC, bleeding from the head below the rim of his now-displaced helmet. The soldiers apply first aid as the driver rushes toward the Dutchbat hospital in Potočari. When the injured soldier arrives, doctors cannot resuscitate him.

The killing stuns and angers the Dutch, and the consequences unfold quickly. A unit of about twenty Serb soldiers overtakes a second observation post—Uniform—close to the first, forcing its six Dutch soldiers to hand over their equipment. Faced with five Srebrenica soldiers when retreating, this time the U.N. personnel return to their post and give themselves up to the Serbs, who take them into custody in Bratunac.

Meanwhile, the chief of staff of the U.N. Protection Force in Sarajevo, who has received the Dutch commander's request for close air support, holds off from sending an application through to higher levels of command. He gives various reasons to various parties: peacekeepers' lives are not directly threatened; air strikes might disrupt sensitive, ongoing political negotiations between a European envoy and the Bosnian Serbs; technical problems are preventing identification of specific targets; and some of the criteria necessary for air strikes have not been fulfilled.

Throughout the afternoon, Serb forces fire artillery and mortar rounds at several locations and launch at least two rockets toward the city. Christina reports hearing more than one shell a minute. Around 4 P.M. she hears airplanes in the hazy sky above, and wonders whether NATO air strikes will follow. They don't. Two British Jaguar fighter jets have been sent by NATO to overfly the enclave. They stay about a half hour and fly away in advance of approaching bad weather and indications that Serb forces are setting up an SA-6 anti-aircraft battery. A Red Cross truck waiting at the northern border of the enclave, with 30,000 messages for those trapped inside, also turns around, returning to Belgrade.

THE NEXT MORNING, Sunday, July 9, 1995, Christina reports to her head-quarters that the townspeople, including the local MSF staff, are "quite tense and shocked, spreading a lot of horrifying rumors . . . it is not easy to calm them a bit down." She is struggling to keep the hospital a neutral zone, free of soldiers, uniforms, and weapons. Her colleague, Daniel, the Australian generalist on his first mission for the organization, has decided to leave if Dutchbat does, and Christina asks that headquarters prepare to replace him.

Three to four thousand refugees pour into town from dwellings in the south of the enclave near the overtaken observation posts. Srebrenica's municipal president asks Christina to inform the outside world that Srebrenica is in danger and needs to be saved. He requests that she formally end MSF's ongoing strike against non-essential work in order to assist some of the hundreds, possibly thousands, of displaced people who've sought shelter in the schoolhouse. She agrees, on the condition that MSF's logistician, who has been drafted by the Srebrenica military, is allowed to return to his job.

In the morning, Serb forces capture the last observation post in the southeast of the enclave, OP-Sierra. The Serbs now control an important part of the Srebrenica-Skelani road—the major route into Srebrenica from the south. The eight U.N. soldiers manning the observation post are disarmed, and they consent to being taken to Serb territory. On the way, one manages to use his radio to report seeing Serb mortars, anti-aircraft weapons, a tank, and artillery located on strategic hills just east of the enclave. These positions offer a shooting view straight into the heart of Srebrenica.

Although none of the Dutch commander's requests for close air support have been approved in Zagreb, NATO planes on a routine "air presence" mission appear overhead at 8:15 A.M. Forward air controllers on the ground, who mistakenly assume the pilots are on a bombing mission, warn them: "Get the hell out of here; they're holding some of our guys." The Dutch commander doesn't want to provoke the Serbs while his observation post crew is in Serb hands nearby.

Srebrenica soldiers fight furious Serb infantry assaults on their lines in the east and south. The Serbs appear to be pushing toward a strategic mountain in the south, Mt. Kak, and in the afternoon, they take an observation post on the way, OP-Kilo. Under pressure, the personnel of OP-Delta—between OP-Kilo and the strategic mountain—also abandon their post. The Dutch have now lost all observation posts in the south of the enclave. The Bravo Company commander sends five soldiers in an armored personnel carrier to check the situation of civilians stranded in a shelter project in the southeast. On the way, the driver stops to urinate. As he does his business out the vehicle's open hatch, Serb soldiers capture the Dutch crew.

Meanwhile, back at the hospital, the doctors and nurses treat eight casualties from the center of town with shrapnel and blast injuries, to the ceaseless accompaniment of explosions. Shelling prevents Christina from making her trip to assess the situation at the schoolhouse.

In the afternoon, the team of three U.N. military observers reports that Bosnian Serb army aims may be widening because of lack of opposition. The Serbs will continue until they achieve their goals, the observers predict, and they are in a position to overrun the enclave if they wish.

The observers are more right than they can know. In the evening, President Karadžić, apparently emboldened by the lack of a significant military response from the Bosnians or NATO, authorizes the Drina Corps of the Bosnian Serb Army to capture the town of Srebrenica.

WHENEVER ILIJAZ HAS A SPARE MOMENT, he walks across the street to join meetings at the post office, which serves as the local Bosnian army headquarters (the U.N. military observers stationed here have left for the relative safety of the Dutchbat base). He learns that Srebrenica's meager defenses to the south have evaporated. The Srebrenica forces are in disarray, with Serb tanks advancing to less than a half mile from the city before nightfall. Srebrenica soldiers try but fail to neutralize one of the tanks firing into the city. The untrained soldiers have difficulty firing the complicated "Red Arrow" rocket-driven missiles recently smuggled into the enclave and give up after three attempts go astray. Srebrenica's war president sends messages to the Bosnian president and the commander of Bosnia's armed forces, saying that the command structure of the Srebrenica division is collapsing and can no longer prevent Serb forces from entering the enclave. He proposes a meeting with military and political leaders of the Serbs to raise the possibility of opening a corridor for free passage of the population to Bosnian government–controlled territory. He receives no reply.

Ilijaz shivers with fear. The local commanders invite him to a gathering at the primary school to urge Srebrenica's soldiers to fight. By 11 P.M., the school gymnasium, darkened without electricity, is packed with what Ilijaz thinks must be hundreds or thousands of soldiers. The head of the municipality and the head of police speak. Ilijaz ponders what to say. Now is not the time to focus on the fact that everyone is failing them—the international community that promised to protect them, the Bosnian government, and even their own commanders. It's time to inject Srebrenica's Twenty-Eighth Bosnian Army Division, the last hope for Srebrenica's protection, with the will to fight.

"Knives have been put to our throats!" Ilijaz shouts with no microphone, and he hears his voice quaver. "Are we going to stand here and wait for them to come and cut our throats and massacre our wounded? No! We are not going to stand and wait. We'll fight, and we'll fight for the sake of our families, for the sake of our wounded, for the sake of the living and even for the sake of the dead who gave their lives defending us."

Applause erupts from the crowd. Ilijaz rounds out his speech with a promise.

"I will stay in the hospital. I won't betray a single patient. Everyone else who respects our poor, injured patients should stay and protect them, too!"

One after another men shout.

"We should go for a defense!"

"We should go and fight!"

"You should be our commander!"

"We want you for our commander!"

This time Ilijaz knows his place is not on the battlefield. He returns to the hospital feeling like a hero from this, his proudest hour of war. Then he stays awake all night treating the injured.

26

AN UNACCEPTABLE SITUATION

U.N. Force Commander Bernard Janvier and the special representative to the U.N. Secretary-General, Yasushi Akashi, return to Zagreb, Croatia, from Geneva and finally receive a detailed report on the situation in Srebrenica. On the evening of Sunday, July 9, they order Dutch U.N. forces to establish defensive blocking positions around the city and authorize them to use force to prevent further Serb advances toward the city. The blocking positions are also aimed to test the resolve and intentions of the Bosnian Serb military. Will it stop when faced with resistance or do its leaders aim to take the whole enclave?

When the order for the blocking positions comes down, Dutch commanders inside of Srebrenica wonder how, with their limited supply of functioning anti-tank weaponry and ammunition, they can effectively prevent the Serb advance. Clearly their efforts will have to be backed up by NATO close air support, and the blocking positions will facilitate those air strikes by establishing a zone between attacking and defending troops. For the first time, the acting U.N. forces commander in Sarajevo furnishes U.N. Force Commander Janvier with target information and a standing written request for close air support.

Top U.N. military officials based in Bosnia and Croatia lay out their demands and threats to Bosnian Serb military leaders in writing and over the phone. The offensive must stop. The Bosnian Serb army must withdraw within two hours to the Srebrenica enclave borders and release all Dutchbat personnel and equipment or face a response with all available means. If Bosnian Serb army forces attack the new U.N. blocking positions, they can expect to be bombed by NATO fighter jets.

The local Serb commander refuses to acknowledge that his forces are even attacking the U.N. soldiers and the enclave.

———

IN THE DARK EARLY MORNING HOURS of Monday, July 10, about 100 Srebrenica volunteers, armed mainly with Kalashnikov assault rifles and energized by last night's rally, creep through the woods toward the enclave's southern border. Some of the men situate themselves on a hill a half mile north of former OP-Foxtrot and send their only rocket-propelled grenade careening into a Serb T-54 tank 100 yards away. Sparks fly from the rear of the vehicle. The men fire their rifles at about thirty surprised Serb soldiers who have been sleeping outside. Serb survivors pick themselves up and run into the woods, beating a retreat from this, their northernmost position, and falling back to near the borders of the enclave in the south. The tank's driver starts his engine and backs up, then stalls and is towed away by another tank down a winding road. The Srebrenicans rush in to grab the weapons the Serbs leave behind.

Meanwhile, the roughly fifty Dutch soldiers that B Company can spare rumble through Srebrenica in six armored personnel carriers on their way to set up blocking positions in plain view of several routes leading into the town from the west, south, and east. Their four prearranged vantage points, Bravo 1-4, will help them determine which route the Serbs might be planning to use to enter the enclave. Forward air controllers take up two positions in preparation for directing air strikes. The Dutch have two "Dragon" medium-range anti-tank weapons and a number of AT-4 short-range anti-tank weapons, along with .50-caliber heavy machine guns mounted atop their armored personnel carriers. Although the order from above is to oppose a Serb advance "by all available means," the company commander, believing his forces to be insufficiently equipped and inadequate in number for the task, instructs each unit to respond only in the case of a direct attack. First fire warning shots, he tells them, and engage in direct combat only if strictly necessary.

On the way to its position, one vehicle is targeted by Serb tank fire and skids off the road, stopping at the edge of a precipice. At first, the Dutch mistakenly believe the detonation to have come from a hand grenade tossed by a Srebrenica soldier, and they report this misinformation to superiors. The position the APC was heading to take, the one closest to town, is left unmanned.

In the early morning, Christina shelters in the bunker as the cracks and booms of heavy machine gun fire and shelling fill the air outside. The telex prints a never-ending stream of messages: The Dutch agree to evacuate MSF in an armored personnel carrier should the team desire it; the B Company soldiers see smoke in the hospital area and ask for a report.

". . . we are unharmed in our shelter," Christina types back. She has her short-wave radio tuned to the British Broadcasting Company, and she listens, incredulous, as Bosnian Serb army representatives deny that they are conducting an offensive on Srebrenica.

Since the start of the attacks four days ago until yesterday, roughly fifty injured patients have been registered in the hospital, and ten have died of their wounds. Now, venturing upstairs and taking a few quick, adrenaline-laden steps into the hospital, Christina finds it filled beyond capacity with a mixture of civilians wounded in the shelling and fighters injured at the front lines. She passes soldiers crying beside wounded and bleeding comrades and finds a haggard Ilijaz upstairs in the operating room, struggling to concentrate on stitching together the delicate liver of a twenty-two-year-old man. Only moments ago, Ilijaz heard that yet another close friend was killed, one of his early war compatriots in the Kragljivoda Brigade.

Christina meets with Srebrenica's acting commander, Ramiz Bećirović, who promises to protect the hospital. Christina repeats her mantra. She wants the hospital to be a neutral zone so that it cannot be considered a military target. She pleads with hospital director Dr. Avdo Hasanović for armed soldiers to be kept out. As more and more injured fighters are carried in, though, she realizes that the request is unrealistic.

Outside, lines of relatives wait to donate blood. People arriving from the town center warn the hospital workers to prepare for more casualties. Around 7 A.M., Christina goes back down into the bunker to send a situation report to MSF headquarters and raise the possibility of again asking one of the Dutch surgeons for help. She's afraid that, with a big influx of wounded, the hospital might not be able to cope. She ends the update: "This offensive has to stop."

Local MSF staff members pick up the wounded in the MSF car and truck and drive them to the hospital. They circumvent Christina's admonitions not to transport wounded soldiers—MSF policy, she calls it— by stopping the vehicles fifty yards before the hospital and carrying the injured the rest of the way into the hospital. One of these drivers is surprised, from the moment he walks in the door, at the number of patients who've filled the hospital since his last run. They litter the floor of the entranceway, and he has to jump over people to get to the staircase. As he carries his charge up the stairs, the sight of more injured and their trails of blood disorient him. Frenzied medical staff brush past him, running up and down the stairs looking for supplies, and pricking fingers to test for blood groups. Patients cry for help. People who are not medically trained pitch in and bandage the wounded. Upstairs, he finds Fatima in the hallway bent over an injured patient. He peeks into the operating room where Ilijaz is working. Someone has moved an extra table inside. The sound of shooting has become so regular, like the patter of raindrops on a rooftop, that the hospital workers don't even seem to notice it.

Outside, under deafening fire from Serb forces, the westernmost Dutch blocking unit, Bravo 1, placed unwittingly just under a Srebrenica artillery position (an old-fashioned M-48 howitzer), repeatedly relocates to safe positions. Grenades explode, sending clouds of smoke and dust swirling and lightly wounding several Dutch soldiers. Serb shells also impact close to another blocking position, Bravo 3. The Dutch watch as howitzers and tanks pound Srebrenica from a high point just east of the enclave, blowing apart house after house.

The shelling of the blocking positions triggers a call for close air support. The Dutch commander sends his request with a list of fifteen Serb targets at 8:55 A.M. It never reaches higher levels. Around the same time, U.N. Force Commander Janvier—impressed by the misinformation that Bosnians are firing at Dutchbat—suggests at a meeting that the root of the problem in Srebrenica is the Bosnian army. The army is strong enough to defend its own territory, he says, and the Bosnian government may be trying to force the United Nations to take a position it doesn't want to take, to defend Srebrenica. Janvier fails to sign the request for close air support received from Sarajevo last night. The false rumors that Srebrenica soldiers are attacking Dutchbat lead some in

NATO and the United Nations to consider using close air support against the Srebrenicans.

At 9:15 A.M., the driver of the Doctors Without Borders truck blares his horn as he comes down the hill to drop off another six wounded at the hospital. The nurse in charge of registering patients looks overwhelmed. Upstairs, Ilijaz, with Dževad assisting, operates on a patient with explosive injuries to his arm and face and a rupture of his left upper arm's main artery. About 11 A.M., Ilijaz is focusing intently on repairing the delicate blood vessel. He finds the two parts of the artery and his fingers begin to make tiny, precise sewing movements with a needle attached to thread-like suture.

Just then, a strong artillery blast shakes the operating room violently and shatters the windows. The building shudders as if it is about to collapse. Smoke and dust billow into the room. A moment passes. Ilijaz becomes aware of himself. He's standing like a statue over the sleeping patient, hands in the wound, still holding the needle. He looks around. His colleague Dževad is under the table. The rest of the operating staff is nowhere to be seen. He calls for them. One of the anesthesia technicians enters and bursts out laughing when he sees Ilijaz standing in the exact same position at the operating table.

"Chief," he says, "you have the reflexes of a dead horse." Ilijaz laughs at the joke and continues the operation. He simply didn't have time to be afraid. But he can't remember, besides the time a shell hit near his parents' house in Gladovići at the start of the war, having ever come so close to being killed.

UNDERGROUND, in the bunker next to the hospital, Christina is doing anything but laughing. Stunned, she's frozen as stiffly and instantly as if she was dipped in liquid nitrogen. She'd left the cellar door open. The shell hit just across the street. It seems as if an hour passes before she can move and control her body again. She realizes with a cold fear, the first one she's felt all week, that the hospital is now a target. She types an "urgent appeal" to a Dutchbat captain for an update about security and war activities.

"We want to continue working in the hospital in order to offer assistance to the many severely wounded," she writes. "This is only possible if the shelling of the surrounding of the hospital stops."

A telex response arrives in under a half hour from the Dutchbat operations room. "In spite of some shelling the situation in the enclave is stable," it says. Christina finds this more than a little hard to believe.

The Dutch inquire about the numbers of wounded and offer Plexiglas to help fix the broken hospital and pharmacy windows. *What a sign of helplessness*, Christina thinks. In the early afternoon, the Dutch report that they are still trying to establish observation points in the south. They haven't succeeded yet, they say, because every time they try to move their blocking positions south of the town, the Serbs shower their soldiers with tank and mortar fire.

AROUND THE WORLD, the Serb offensive against Srebrenica begins to draw responses. The Brussels and Paris country sections of Doctors Without Borders release a press statement, which Christina receives in English translation from MSF Belgrade. It describes intensive shelling in the center of "the protected UN zone" and appeals, to no one in particular, for respect of the hospital's neutral status and the civilian population.

A discussion about Srebrenica also takes place at the U.N. Security Council in New York, which has received some inaccurate information about the Serb offensive and the role of the Bosnian army in attacking the Dutch. Delegates from the U.S. and Russia disagree over whether a NATO air strike is an appropriate response to the Serb military action. In the end, the council fails to issue any kind of resolution condemning the attack.

AROUND 4 P.M. THE SERBS SEND multiple eighty-inch-long rockets screaming into the center of Srebrenica. One plows into a line of mainly elderly civilians waiting for water in the area of the town bazaar near Ilijaz's apartment building and the linden trees, exploding into fragments and sending bodies and body parts flying.

Ten minutes later, nine wounded are already in the hospital. They are severely, grotesquely injured, some missing arms and legs, shrapnel holes dotting every part of their bodies. Those in the hospital hear heavy machine gun fire as the wounded are being transported—Christina can only guess that the front lines are moving closer to the town.

Patients now fill the hallways of the hospital and every able-bodied staff member works to assess them, start intravenous lines, and stabilize their conditions. Ilijaz examines a man whose arm has been ripped from his shoulder and whose abdomen has been blown open—he can't believe the man is still alive. About eleven people need urgent surgery. Ilijaz asks Christina to beg Dutchbat for help, knowing he cannot possibly perform all the needed operations in time to save lives. Let's transport some patients to the Dutchbat hospital, he suggests; we can send them with all the materials they need. If not, then at least have them send one of their surgeons here to help. It's a matter of life and death.

Christina sends a telex to Dutchbat. She has a feeling they'll refuse, so she requests that at the very least they send an armored personnel carrier to help transport the wounded to the hospital. This time the response comes not from the surgeon but the second-in-command of the battalion, Major Robert Franken, who answers without consulting the medical team.

UTC Time: 16:20:15, in 14:48:04 10 July, 1995
From: Maj Franken
To: MSF Christine

- Again with a troubled mind I must state that we are not able to support you in giving actual medical aid.
- Although really very willing I have a responsibility in securing medcare for my soldiers
- my medstocks are at the minimum
- in spite of the fuel situation the only help I can offer is an APC ambulance to help evacuating casualties
- I have to make one restriction and that is that the vehicle can only be used in town, due to the fact that in case of an emergency I need him for my own soldiers which have priority
- please inform me if you want this (little) help

THE ROCKET ATTACK MARKS A TURNING POINT for many of the operating room staff, and for Fatima and other doctors and nurses. With no or little medical experience at the war's beginning, they have come to feel competent and useful; they have come to love their work. But now, as the wounded again fill the corridors and blood again covers the clothes, hands, and hair of the doctors and nurses, many of them find themselves unable to function. Their work turns back into the nightmare it was before Srebrenica's demilitarization two years ago.

Since five days ago, when the attack started and he collapsed after surgery, Ilijaz has worked like an automaton in the operating theater. When he's stolen a few moments to rest his head on the doctors' room bed, merely the thought of things getting worse and worse, far worse than 1993, has kept him tossing and turning. He hasn't slept, showered, shaven, or changed. He hasn't gone home in days. His only comfort is the presence of his colleagues.

Ilijaz operates nonstop. The man with the arm and abdomen wounds dies on the operating table before Ilijaz even begins to treat him. Another patient with liver injuries doesn't make it through his operation. While Ilijaz works, five others die waiting in their rooms. One is a boy of about thirteen.

OVER THE DAY, with assaults and shelling of the Bosnian lines, the Serbs succeed in regaining the positions they lost in the early morning. The Srebrenica defense collapses. About 6:30 P.M., 150 Serb infantry soldiers appear on high ground overlooking the town, advancing across a ridgeline where the Dutch failed to establish their last blocking position. Dutch soldiers in another blocking position fire flares from their 3.2-inch mortar. Machine gun fire peppers the air above the Serbs' heads. The Dutchbat commander requests close air support, and his request is approved at lower U.N. levels in Tuzla and Sarajevo and passed all the way to Commander Bernard Janvier's U.N. Protection Force headquarters in Zagreb. Janvier orders that NATO planes be "cockpit ready" and convenes a meeting of his crisis staff in Zagreb.

After about an hour, the Serb soldiers regress in a southwesterly direction behind the ridgeline. The B Company commander orders the blocking positions to fall back closer to town to avoid being outflanked at night. Panicked Srebrenicans surround the Dutch APCs. At the same time, fearful crowds of people move north, away from the town center and from the south of the enclave, collecting outside of the hospital and breaking into the B Company base in Srebrenica.

Christina telexes Colonel Karremans "and everybody who is concerned" at Dutchbat, reporting that 10,000 people are massed before the hospital and that the mayor has requested the Dutchbat commander come to the post office building.

"We urge you to take some immediate action," Christina writes. "The population and the hospital are without protection and shelling is going on. . . . On behalf of MSF I request assistance for the population. This is a nonacceptable situation."

Medical staff and their families crowd into the small underground bunker. "We can hardly move anymore," Christina reports to MSF headquarters, "and it is difficult with the screaming children to keep the radio contact." She writes that the United Nations is failing to update her, and the population is relying on MSF to help them.

The Serb advance halts around 11 P.M. The enclave quiets. Srebrenica soldiers push most of the population back to their homes in the center, but the dozens of local medical workers, along with their spouses and children, refuse to leave the bunker, demanding some sort of a solution to the crisis. Christina senses that they're desperate and tired and that they want to leave their prison.

"We'd love to help you," she tells them, "but we can't." All she can do is contact MSF Belgrade again to report that the population wants to leave Srebrenica and that a solution must be found. She spends much time and energy trying to convince the locals that it won't be possible to sleep with eighty people crammed into the small bunker. She tells them to leave and go sleep in the hospital. She has sympathy for them, yes, but she has to keep her own mind together to be able to continue with her job. Finally they leave, and she settles down for a few hours of sleep.

Meanwhile, around midnight, Ilijaz breaks away from the hospital for a meeting of the high command—about fifteen military commanders and civilian authorities, including the mayor, deputy mayor, president of the executive council, and the Bosnian army chief of staff—in the post office building. Gathered by candlelight around a large table covered with maps, they discuss whether to launch another counteroffensive in the morning or plan a massive retreat from the enclave on foot through enemy territory toward Tuzla or elsewhere. The question is—if they retreat, what will become of the civilians? They can't possibly take along all of the children, the elderly, and the infirm for scores of miles, and neither can they abandon them to the Chetniks. The only option seems to be to stay and fight.

The command studies the maps and plans a counteroffensive. One brigade will attempt to defend the city while another, numbering about 1,000, will move to outflank the Serbs and attack their positions from the rear. The Srebrenicans have two factors in their favor: One, Serb tanks will be less effective at night. Two, the territory, since it falls inside the enclave boundaries, lacks land mines and is more familiar to the Srebrenicans than to their attackers.

At the end of the planning meeting, Dutchbat Commander Karremans appears at the door. Ilijaz has the creepy feeling of having been spied upon. The commander sits down at their table, looking at their maps as if he's been invited to join them.

The commander announces that if the Bosnian Serb army has not withdrawn to the boundaries of the safe area by 6 A.M., NATO will conduct a massive air strike against Serb positions throughout the enclave. He points to the Chetnik troop locations, referring to them as "killing fields." When the air strikes come, anyone in those regions will be incinerated, he says. Ilijaz infers that if the Srebrenicans are there, engaged in a counterattack, that would mean them, too.

Ramiz, the acting Bosnian army commander, expresses disbelief. He asks what his forces should do in preparation for the NATO air strike, if it is really to be delivered. Stay as far away as possible from the current confrontation line and take cover in your houses, the U.N. commander replies. The Srebrenicans decide to withdraw one and a quarter miles from Serb positions, and they give up their plans for a counteroffensive.

In his desperation, Ilijaz believes the Dutch commander's promise of air strikes. He returns to the hospital churning with anticipation for the sound of NATO jets and massive bomb explosions, which he expects to hear in just a few hours. For the moment, the night remains quiet, as if a ceasefire has already gone into effect. Not a single grenade lands in town.

About 1 A.M., a Dutch orderly arrives at the hospital carrying a critically injured forty-five-year-old woman found not far from the U.N. base in Potočari. The Dutch medical team refused to use any of its "essential rations" to provide her even the most basic emergency care. She has lain untreated for hours in the Dutch compound. No laparotomy, the opening of the abdomen, has been performed to repair her intestinal injuries. No chest tube has been placed to drain the blood in her chest and prevent her lungs from collapsing. Not even an IV has been started to replace the fluid she is losing from bleeding. All she has received are shots of morphine. A shelling "red alert," until it was lifted by the Dutch commander minutes ago, kept the compassionate orderly from leaving the U.N. base and bringing her to Srebrenica Hospital. The dozens of shrapnel wounds to the woman's chest, abdomen, and leg have gone untouched.

Ilijaz and Daniel O'Brien, the Australian generalist from Doctors Without Borders who is assisting Ilijaz in surgery, are shocked and furious. The neglect of the woman seems to defy all principles of medical ethics. Daniel thinks of Dutchbat's "amazing" medical facilities sitting unused just a few miles up the road, while here the doctors and nurses struggle to save a few of the many patients who need them, risking their own lives every time they walk up the staircase to the single, exposed, top-floor operating theater. Daniel, just as the others, now feels a sense of dread every time he climbs these stairs. Still, once he's in the operating theater surrounded by patients in need, like this woman, professional autopilot takes over. Ilijaz and Daniel stabilize the injured woman and then successfully perform the abdominal operation she needs.

27

KILLING FIELDS

THE BLACK-BLUE NIGHT DIFFUSES into damp slate gray as morning breaks on Tuesday, July 11, 1995. At 6 A.M., NATO fighter jets lift off from an airbase in Italy and circle, awaiting orders.

The yard of Srebrenica Hospital again fills with thousands of people. A creepy silence reigns. The sky presses down on the town with a thick, smoke-like fog that smells of gunpowder and makes the people whisper. Someone, they suppose, is marking targets for NATO. The people wait, eyes turned up the sky, ears perked for the sounds of the "killing fields."

North of the hospital in Potočari, Dutch soldiers sit in their bunkers wearing powder-blue U.N. hardhats and bulletproof vests, steeling themselves for massive air attacks and possible reprisals. Of the area held by the Bosnian Serbs: "No stone will be left on another stone," the soldiers' commander told them last night. In Tuzla, the next link up in the U.N. chain of command, officers also wait expectantly for air strikes.

In Zagreb, Croatia, the U.N. Force Commander, General Janvier, waits, too. But he waits for something different. He never approved last evening's request for close air support, let alone initiating the other NATO option, massive air strikes. He has no idea that everyone in Srebrenica is expecting them. Somewhere along the U.N. structure—from Zagreb to Sarajevo to Tuzla to Srebrenica—the message, like one passed along in a game of "telephone," has changed dramatically. What General Janvier awaits is another request for close air support from the Dutchbat commander—a target list with smoking guns, evidence that the Serbs are again attacking U.N. forces. The Dutchbat commander, expecting air strikes, not close air support, has no idea that he needs to make such a request.

In Srebrenica, a dazzling sun burns away the fog and heats the valley.

Ilijaz peels off the flak jacket that he agreed to wear at Christina's behest. He, too, waits.

The Dutchbat commander, finally alerted to the fact that NATO air power hinges on his issuing another request for close air support, in addition to the already standing order, tries to fax the necessary paperwork to his superiors at the U.N. office in Tuzla. The fax machine in Tuzla is broken. Eventually, after much back-and-forth, the request reaches the next level in the chain of command, in Sarajevo. The person who receives the request rejects it because it's on the wrong form. Further delays follow over the question of whether, since the Serbs have momentarily halted the attack, the criteria for close air support have been met. In a Catch-22, the rules for air support require an ongoing attack on a U.N. target, but by the time a request ambles through the bureaucracy to the top decisionmakers, the U.N. soldiers will have withdrawn from the positions under attack.

Finally, around midday, the air support request, resubmitted on the correct form, reaches U.N. command in Zagreb. General Janvier and the Special Representative of the U.N. Secretary-General, Yasushi Akashi, are pressured, at last, to sign it. Five days into the Serb assault on Srebrenica, the U.N.'s rusty air strike "key" has turned. Now only NATO is needed to unlock the force.

But the request arrives at the worst possible moment. NATO jets, airborne since 6 A.M., need to land for refueling. For various reasons, the option of in-air refueling is not available today. Considering that the Serbs have not attacked Srebrenica since last night, the planes are sent back to Italy, to be ready again by 2 P.M.

UNABLE TO SIT STILL, Ilijaz buzzes back and forth between the hospital, the bunker, and the post office building. Every minute that passes without air strikes leaves him more convinced that the Serbs will take the town. The fate of the roughly eighty patients in the hospital weighs heavily on his mind. He thinks of Vukovar—where in 1991 Yugoslav soldiers removed dozens of people from the hospital and massacred them in a nearby field. Vukovar was where Eric Dachy had arrived too late, the place that made him resolve to "interpose" somewhere else before such evil happened again. Vukovar was what led MSF to Srebrenica.

Ilijaz wants to evacuate patients to the U.N. military hospital in Poto-čari. The other physicians agree, and they meet with Christina to discuss the plan. She doesn't share their expectation that Srebrenica will soon be overtaken. In any case, she explains, the hospital is a protected, neutral location according to the Geneva Conventions, whereas the Dutch compound is a potential military target. She expresses her preference to keep the patients here.

Ilijaz likes Christina and admires the calm bravery she's shown these past few days. But Christina, because she's only been here a couple of weeks, doesn't know what he knows about the character of the war. How could she possibly know? Ilijaz reminds her about the Vukovar massacre, where the Geneva Conventions that Christina respects so much failed to protect the hospital. One after another, the other local medical workers express to Christina their fear that Bosnian Serbs will enter Srebrenica Hospital and murder those they find there.

Christina listens. She doesn't share the locals' pessimistic vision, but she sees their determination, and she respects and accepts their decision. She figures this evacuation, like most evacuations in MSF history, will be temporary. She gets on the HF radio and demands that those outside recognize and understand the extent of the locals' desperation.

"Is there another source who can confirm your information?" someone on the other side of the radio asks.

"Well, people," Christina replies. "I went there with my car. I was collecting injured people. And I saw the Serbs at the entrance of the city. What else do you need?"

Ilijaz and Commander Ramiz drive to the Dutch Bravo compound just north of the hospital. A large crowd mills outside the base, and Ilijaz has to push through it to reach the gate, which is locked and guarded by armed Dutch soldiers. Ilijaz and Ramiz identify themselves and ask to speak with the guards' superiors. An officer appears.

"What do you want?" he asks.

They explain in fractured English that they think the military situation is hopeless and that they want to evacuate their patients to the Dutch medical base so that at least the helpless, injured people can be saved. The officer categorically refuses, telling Ilijaz that the Dutchbat soldiers don't want to get involved in the conflict. Ilijaz boils.

"I'm going straight back to the hospital," he says. "I'm putting the in-jured people on properly marked trucks, and in a few minutes those trucks will go to your base. If you don't open this gate, we'll break through it with the truck. And your soldiers, if they don't move, we'll drive over them."

With that, Ilijaz turns around and starts to leave.

"Stop! Stop!" the officer yells after him. "Let's talk."

There's still plenty of time, he tells Ilijaz. Let's wait to see what hap-pens, and if it really becomes necessary then we can arrange proper med-ical transport to the base at Potočari.

Ilijaz believes the officer's playing for time Srebrenica doesn't have.

"We're coming," he says simply, and returns to the car.

In front of the hospital, medical workers prepare two trucks, covering their cabs with white sheets marked with a red cross. They pack patients inside like sardines, too quickly to count.

As they're working, explosions begin again, the familiar boom of Serb tank fire, not NATO bombs. One of the volunteer drivers flees in panic. A patient, half of whose foot Ilijaz amputated a few days ago, volunteers to take his place. The other driver is the cheerful drummer whose left arm Nedret and Ilijaz amputated without anesthesia in 1992. The trucks drive off to the Dutch compound.

As the day spins forward, the population fractionates on the weight of their expected fates. One MSF translator rushes down into the bunker to find Christina dressed in her bulletproof vest, hardhat, and the "MSF"-emblazoned clothing that distinguishes her from the local Srebrenicans. For several days now, the translator has asked Christina what will hap-pen to the thirteen MSF local staff members if the Serbs take the town. Will MSF provide protection for himself and his family? He hasn't felt as if she's given him a clear answer, and now he needs one.

"Christina," he begins, "I have a four-and-a-half-month old baby. . . . Can you give protection for myself and my wife?"

"No," she answers. "I can't guarantee your protection." She doesn't believe she has the power. In fact, in the entire history of MSF and most humanitarian organizations, it has been rare for internationals who choose to evacuate during times of insecurity to take along their local staff. In Rwanda in 1994, hundreds of the local hires from humanitarian aid and intergovernmental organizations were left to their killers as their employers fled. The MSF Srebrenica security plan discusses what equipment expatriates should take with them in case of an evacuation, but does not address the issue of what to do with locals. But even as the staff panics around her, Christina clings to the belief that any evacuation that might occur in Srebrenica will be only temporary.

Another local aid worker, the employee of another nongovermental organization, the Swedish Rescue Services Agency, which doesn't have an international presence in Srebrenica, jogs down the steps into the bunker to send a final message to his bosses that the town is falling. He has used the MSF telex twice to send messages to them, but now Christina tells him she doesn't want him to use it anymore. She is afraid to let locals use the machine out of fear that they will send military information in a telex that carries the MSF imprint.

The local aid worker is furious. Christina seems too cool to him. How can she be going about her job so calmly, asking for numbers of injured, numbers of dead, and smiling? And how can she refuse him now? Doesn't she realize that the town is about to fall?

The worker has seen so much death these past years that he is not afraid of it any more, but he is still afraid of pain. He has scoured the hospital for pain killers to take with him if Srebrenica falls, but the strongest he's found is pentazocine. He wants morphine. He turns to Daniel, the Australian, noticing that the young doctor has taken the time to comb his hair neatly, as if trying to convince himself that the situation is under control, but his body language belies fear and utter exhaustion. The local worker asks for some ampoules of the strong pain killer, thinking mistakenly that Daniel might have them. Daniel looks at him strangely. "Why do you need that?" he asks. The local worker looks back at him, speechless. That's when he realizes that MSF's Daniel and Christina have no idea what is about to happen, that thousands of people are about to flee across enemy territory in a desperate bid to reach safety that could last days or weeks.

ILIJAZ CROSSES THE STREET to the post office building, where he watches Srebrenica's acting commander and war president attempt—and fail—to reach the Bosnian president by ham radio to report that Srebrenica is falling. Ilijaz hears that two shells have fallen on Camp Bravo, where the patients were delivered, reinjuring some. He runs back across the street to the hospital and joins the nearly complete contingent of 125 local medical workers, who've gathered in the surgical department to decide what to do. Nurses are crying. The air fills with a cacophony of opinions.

"Let's all go to Potočari," someone suggests. "We're all medical staff; they won't hurt us." A person who agrees adds that they should find the Dutch surgeon who knows them and ask for his protection.

Someone else argues that only women should seek shelter with the Dutch and men should go through the forest and attempt to hike to other Bosnian government–held territory. But another person points out that the Serbs have shelled Camp Bravo, which suggests that the United Nations can't protect them and that everyone should go through the forest.

Fatima speaks up. "Nobody can protect anybody," she asserts, strident. She remembers being trapped in Bratunac in the early days of the war. If she goes to Potočari and the Chetniks come, she'll be in their hands and nobody will help her. "I would rather kill myself than be raped by Chetniks," she declares. She believes the Serbs consider doctors war criminals for treating their enemy's soldiers.

Outside the windows, below them on the main road before the hospital, a wave of humanity surges north ahead of the Serb advance into the town. The medical workers have not yet decided on a plan when they realize that whether they set their sights on free territory or on the Dutch compound in Potočari, it is clearly time for everyone to shove off from Srebrenica.

Ilijaz and the other surgical staff members tear off their bloody hospital scrubs, littering the floor. After seventy-two hours of working without stopping to wash or change, they are so filthy and sweaty they can smell themselves. Ilijaz pulls on a white T-shirt and the cheap imitation Levi's blue jeans that a Lithuanian anesthesiologist gave him two years ago. He throws a denim shirt over his shoulders and thrusts his feet into military boots. He ties together the laces of his Reebok athletic shoes, a gift from an MSF gynecologist, and slings them around his neck.

Into a large backpack, Fatima jams bandages, infusions, analgetics, a change of underwear, and tampons, because she's expecting her period. She packed some bags of belongings several days ago and stored them in the hospital. Now, faced with an imminent overland journey, most of the items seem unimportant to her. She keeps some gold and a few of her and Ilijaz's photographs, then goes next door to her apartment to drop off the other things and advise her mother to prepare to leave Srebrenica, too.

Naim Salkić, the dark-haired operating room instrument technician who has become Ilijaz's closest friend, crams anesthetics, first-aid kits, gauze, and bags of glucose solution into a medical bag. His cousin, the anesthetist nicknamed "the professor," packs other bags with analgetics, antibiotics, bandages, iodine, tourniquets, and infusions that can expand blood volume in case of hemorrhage.

Avdo, the hospital director, is one of the few medical workers who've not been constantly around the hospital these past few days. Now he appears wearing military trousers and a shirt. He carries his diploma, personal documents, three family photo albums, salt, and sugar. He stuffs his pockets with multivitamins. At forty-eight, he is one of the older men about to undertake the journey.

On Ilijaz's way back to the post office, he sees his lover, nurse Hajra outside. They kiss one another in silence, then part. At the post office Ilijaz asks around among the military leaders to find out the plan for breaking through to free territory. The first man he asks just shrugs. The next man he asks shrugs, too. A third. A fourth. Ilijaz feels like he's just been killed. There's obviously no plan. He doesn't know what to do.

At 1:30 P.M., Fatima and the professor treat a new patient whose buttock was injured by a tank round. They pour iodine on the wound and wrap it tightly with an abdominal bandage. He seems to be the last patient. They are the last to leave the hospital.

Other hospital workers and their families stand out front in the blaring July sun. As if in a dream, Ilijaz starts floating north on the main road with his two brothers, Fatima, and friends and colleagues beside him. Crowds of other Srebrenicans fill the road. An old woman, head covered with a scarf, walks bent beneath an overstuffed backpack. A young boy wears a winter coat in the July heat. Long hair streams down the backs of two girls and shimmers in the sun with each step. Thoughts reel through Ilijaz's head as he walks:

It's unreal. It's not really happening. We'll be back tomorrow . . .

After about 100 yards, they reach the town gas station, where a small road turns off from the main road, runs by an old graveyard, and continues southwest toward the only part of the enclave not within the vision of the Serb army, the only area still under control of Srebrenica's soldiers. Hundreds of men ahead of them are turning left onto this road. This is the decision point. The main road leads north to the U.N. base in Potočari.

Ilijaz's brother Hamid, forty-one years old with a wife and children announces, at this intersection, "I can't go to the forest." He has a stomachache and is "lost with fear."

"I'm going to Potočari," he says. He'll seek protection with the U.N. forces.

Please let's stick together.

Ilijaz thinks it, but does not say it. As when he was a little boy and he'd been truly upset, his words stick in his throat and he cannot speak.

Maybe the Dutch really will protect everybody. We have only a theoretical chance of survival if we go to the forest. Maybe my brother will survive to take care of the family.

Maybe going toward Potočari is a better choice for all of them . . .

A grenade explodes somewhere in the direction of Potočari. Ilijaz stands still. A century passes. His brother turns away without a word and joins the masses surging toward the U.N. base.

Dark-haired Naim grabs Ilijaz's arm and yanks him hard to the left toward the small road that heads southwest.

"Come on," he says. "We're going there and once it gets dark we'll think of what to do." Ilijaz lets himself be led.

"Yes," Ilijaz says dreamily, "when we get a little further from the city, when we find a relatively safe place, we'll sit down and discuss whether to continue walking through the night. If we judge that it's silly to continue on this road, we'll come back to Potočari, all of us." And so all of them turn left here—Ilijaz, Fatima, and the three other Srebrenica doctors; Naim, the professor, and most of the other male nurses and hospital technicians, including Boro's old friend Sadik; a female nurse named Ajka Avdic from Osmaće, with whom Ilijaz treated his first patients; a few other women who'd served as fighters; and, both before and after them, dozens of others from the hospital and thousands and thousands of fighters and civilians, most of them men and boys afraid of giving themselves up to the Chetniks.

ADVANCING SERB FORCES ENTER THE CITY from the south. At 2:07 P.M., one of the victorious soldiers hangs a flag over a bakery at the southern end of town. The entire remaining population of Srebrenica flees northward, U.N. blue helmets mingling among them, retreating from the blocking positions on foot and by armored personnel carrier. Srebrenica has fallen without a single bomb dropped by NATO, without a single shot fired by U.N. forces directly at Serb forces. The Dutchbat commander has issued multiple NATO air support requests, all turned down at various points in the U.N. labyrinth.

FOR MUCH OF THE OFFENSIVE, boyish, sandy-haired Dr. Boro Lazić, in his role as medical chief of the Šekovići Brigade of the Bosnian Serb Army, has been stationed in a village called Jasenova south of Srebrenica, near the site of the destroyed water treatment plant. Without much resistance from the Srebrenica forces and none from the Dutch U.N. battalion, there have been few casualties, and Boro has had an easy job. When victory comes for the Bosnian Serb army, his unit begins to follow the vanguard into Srebrenica. He rides in his ambulance, a passenger car, along the hilly, winding roads beneath a blue sky. He can't see too far ahead of him, but at times he catches sight of Srebrenica soldiers and civilians fleeing northward.

He's been warned to expect NATO air strikes, but so far the sky is quiet, at least as far as he can tell amidst the sound of rumbling trucks and whooping soldiers. In the early afternoon, just as his ambulance nears the main Srebrenica-Skelani road, the sound of jets rips the air. The convoy halts. The driver of a truck carrying a three-barrel grenade launcher in its bed, a perfect target, pulls up beside Boro's ambulance. *Stupid guy!* Boro thinks and he leaps out of the ambulance and runs for cover from the F-16s circling overhead.

Boro throws himself to the ground and clasps his hands over his head. Bombs explode with a terrifying force, bouncing his body and showering him with soil. He jumps to his feet. Smoke and dirt hang thick in the air all around him, and he makes out the crater of one bomb that burrowed into the sylvan hillside above him. The crescendo of an approaching jet spurs him to take cover again. He braces himself. More over-flights occur, each one heightening his fright. A Serb surface-to-air artillery battery thunders back. In only a few minutes, though, the air quiets and Boro takes stock. A few cars and a tank have been damaged. No one around him is injured.

ILIJAZ AND HIS GROUP are on a hillside when the planes streak over Srebrenica and circle. Grabbing a pair of binoculars, Ilijaz tries to get a view of the bombings.

Strong air strikes will change everything!

Several explosions thunder in the distance. Then silence. Smoke pours from a hillside, but as it clears, Ilijaz and the others see an untouched tank atop the hill and soldiers walking around it. Eventually Ilijaz's group resumes walking. They stop at a stream.

"Those were probably just scout planes, going to investigate the terrain," someone says. Any minute, the escadrille.

It never comes.

Somewhere to the south, a Serbian tank, intact, belches another shell, and then another, into Srebrenica.

THE VOICE OF GENERAL RATKO MLADIĆ, commander of the Bosnian Serb army, breaks into the U.N. radio frequency. Using equipment stolen from a captured Dutchbat observation post, he issues a stern warning: If NATO continues its use of air power, the Serb army will shell Srebrenica and the Dutch U.N. compound and will kill the thirty Dutchbat soldiers in Serb custody. Around the same time, the Netherlands minister of defense telephones the U.N. Special Representative of the Secretary-General, Yasushi Akashi, requesting that close air support be discontinued because of the proximity of the Serb soldiers to the Dutch troops. Akashi doesn't need to be persuaded—he passes the message to NATO and the air action is halted. The U.N. Protection Force commander, Janvier, agrees with the decision.

MSF STAFF MEMBERS Christina Schmitz and Dr. Daniel O'Brien are standing outside the bunker watching the sky as the fighter planes drop their bombs. When the strikes stop and Serb shelling resumes from the mountains, they run to Srebenica Hospital to see how many patients are left and whether any new ones have arrived. They see a long stream of people moving north on the main road.

Realizing the population is almost gone, they decide to leave, too. Christina still figures they'll be back by tomorrow. She locks the door to the bunker, gathers some of MSF's valuables, and then prepares to move twenty or so patients to U.N. Bravo base. She and Daniel have one pickup truck and two Land Cruisers at their disposal. Not everybody fits.

After dropping off the first load, Christina heads back toward the hospital for the last few elderly patients, driving slowly against the stream of villagers running northward carrying screaming babies and bags in their arms. Somewhere between the base and the hospital, she comes face to face with Dutch U.N. soldiers in vehicles and on foot, retreating from their blocking positions. They've been driving the population ahead of them like shepherds driving a flock of sheep away from a pack of wolves. Behind them are the encroaching Serbs. Christina can't see them, but she can feel them coming. The Dutch advise her not cross their line. Exhausted and hot, she agrees to give up temporarily on her plan to return to the hospital, turning her car instead toward Potočari. One U.N. truck stalls in front of her car, and she watches the flushed, overburdened Srebrenicans use the opportunity to scramble aboard from the hot, dusty road. They look as if they'd kill each other just to get on the truck and rest for the two-and-a-half mile trek.

Christina is tired, too, and incredibly tense. She feels her heart racing. *I'm going to die,* Christina thinks, *of exhaustion. Of the horror of all of this.*

When Christina arrives at the Dutch compound, a converted battery factory building, Daniel is already there, working at a makeshift care unit set up in a dark corridor by the Dutch.

Where are the local doctors? Christina wonders. She has no idea what's become of Ilijaz, Fatima, and the others. Around sixty-five patients have arrived, mostly war wounded, many untreated since being wounded again by shelling at the B Company. They lie on stretchers with closed fractures, open fractures, arm fractures, wrist fractures, concussions, and deep wounds.

The Dutch soldiers have gone on a shelling "red alert," ordered to their barracks wearing their helmets and vests. Because air strikes haven't taken out the Serb weapons on the north ridge of the enclave, near Potočari, the U.N. military observers fear that the U.N. compound is a "very easy target." Of the entire Dutch medical team, only one, surgeon Gerry Kramer, is ignoring the bunker alert and helping treat patients. Telling his superiors to "kiss my ass," he gathers supplies from the Dutch hospital and brings them into the factory building for the use of the population.

The building teems with roughly 5,000 people, and U.N. soldiers have stopped letting anyone else besides mothers with babies inside. Shafts of sunlight pour into the building, lighting up dust. A flush-cheeked woman in a red sweater ties up her hair, and a little boy holds tightly to his white stuffed animal. The place is hot, smelly, full of the odors of sweat, urine, and feces, the sounds of babies crying and people moaning. The clamor of hundreds, perhaps thousands, of voices mingle together. The air is visible, hazy. Dutch soldiers wearing powder-blue hard hats try to direct the crowds. People hold their belongings close and keep their jackets on them in spite of the heat.

Christina uses the car radio to request more supplies from Belgrade and then walks around the grounds near the U.N. compound. Crowds of people, perhaps 20,000–30,000, stretch as far as her eyes can see, hovering around the destroyed buildings and factories, on driveways, between trees and inside numerous discarded, skeletonized vehicles.

Babies cry. The elderly stand panting. People jostle back and forth, one foot to the other, looking beseechingly toward the U.N. base, shivering in spite of the beating sun at the continuous clamor of shelling.

MSF, alerted by Christina's updates, releases a public statement: "MSF appeals for an immediate ceasefire, respect for the immunity of civilian populations, and humanitarian access to populations in danger."

FOR AN HOUR OR SO AFTER THE AIR STRIKES, Dr. Boro Lazić waits with his medical team and two escorts in a line of Serb military vehicles just off the Srebrenica-Skelani road. Then burly, strapping Bosnian Serb General Mladić arrives, tough and dangerous, rumored to beat up soldiers and even officers if things aren't going the way he likes. Boro has met him before. He admires and respects the man for his bravery and his skills as an officer and commander. Mladić, wearing a dark camouflage shirt with matching pants stuffed into his combat boots, struts up to Boro's medical car and peers inside.

"Who's in charge of such a neat ambulance?" he asks. Boro identifies himself and the brigade to which he belongs.

"This is better than the Military Medical Academy in Belgrade," Mladić flatters him.

The general continues in a car on the main road toward Srebrenica. It is a fine day for him. A day of victory. A day of revenge against Bosnian Muslims, who symbolize the Turks who defeated the Serbs 600 years ago and established their empire on Serbian soil.

Mladić sits in the passenger seat, his Chetnik-style hat on the dashboard before him. The car curves along a dusty dirt road bordered by green grass and trees that throw long shadows. Reaching Srebrenica just after 4 P.M., the general gets out of his car and strides down a shaded city street to survey his fiefdom. Burnt-out buildings stretch along the road before him, the ones to his right lit by the afternoon sun. He stops beside a windowless building and looks around.

"Take down that Muslim street sign!" he orders the men near him, lifting a bare, meaty forearm and pointing across the street with his right hand. A .35 Heckler submachine gun extends from his left fist, below the rolled sleeves of his military shirt, and a set of large, black binoculars hangs around his thick neck.

"Selmanagić Reuf Street!" He reads the name of the World War II Partisan hero in a mocking tone. "Take it down! *Hajde.*" His brows furrow beneath his broad, hairless forehead and his voice turns into a fierce yell. "Climb up, man! Do I have to tell you ten times?"

Men ring him, some smoking cigarettes. They carry their hardhats in their hands and wear white bands around their upper left arms to identify themselves as Serbs.

The camera follows Mladić to a point near the town square. A smile opens up on his face as an officer walks up to shake his hand, embracing him by slinging his hand, holding a walkie-talkie, over his right shoulder, and kissing him in the Serb Orthodox manner, three times, like the trinity—left cheek, right cheek, left cheek.

"The eleventh of July," the man says, "Congratulations." This is not just any day. Mladić has taken his victory on the eve of *Petrovdan,* the day of St. Peter the Apostle, the patron saint of the ruling Bosnian Serb political party, the SDA. The holiday also marks the two-year anniversary of the Srebrenicans' humiliating attack on the Serb village of Zalazje.

Mladić poses in the shady square in front of Ilijaz's apartment building, which is lit in the background. Could he possibly have chosen this spot because it borders the site of yesterday's grisly rocket attack? Is his intelligence good enough to know that this is also where Srebrenica's intellectuals, Ilijaz's linden tree club, used to meet? He speaks to the camera.

"Here we are, on July 11, 1995 in Serbian Srebrenica, just before a great Serb holy day," he says, stiff-faced, barely moving his lips. He looks down and then slightly off to the distance through squinted eyelids. "We give this town to the Serb nation. Remember the uprising against the Turks. The time has come to take revenge against the Muslims."

———

NOT LONG AFTER, Boro rolls slowly through Srebrenica in his ambulance in a procession of army vehicles. He passes damaged buildings, burnt houses, and eerily abandoned streets littered with cast-off belongings, dead animals, and, here and there, human corpses. The city his troops have conquered looks horrible to Boro, but all around him, victorious soldiers are celebrating—singing, hugging, and carelessly discharging bursts of gunfire. The only wounded person Boro has to treat the whole day seems to be a victim of such friendly fire.

Boro, too, is excited, mainly because the offensive is finally over and he'll get to go home soon. When his ambulance draws near the hospital, so recently abandoned by Ilijaz and his colleagues, he gets out. The building appears undamaged by the recent shelling. He enters it with the ambulance driver and a few soldiers. A few elderly people cringe beside the entrance. Boro goes upstairs to look around, walking first to the surgical ward. It looks to him as if the Muslims, working hard, left in a great, panicked haste. The surgery table is covered with blood and bandages. Still, he's impressed at how much more well-equipped the operating theater appears now than when he saw it two years ago during the evacuations. He walks up and down the hallways of the two patient floors, peeking into every room. Closets are open. Sheets and blankets litter the floors.

His mind flashes back to his trip here in 1993, giving him an unexpected pang of nostalgia. He recalls, with pity, the doctors and nurses whom he met. They must be fleeing toward Tuzla, he figures, and the thought of their fear saddens him.

Boro takes nothing from the hospital except some bandages, which he uses to tie the door handles shut in an effort to protect the building from marauding, victorious soldiers. He continues northward in his ambulance on the main road, stopping at the abandoned U.N. Bravo Company base across from the soccer pitch an hour or so before nightfall.

Boro and his team find the base well stocked with modern medical supplies and equipment. Obviously these are of no use to the Dutch now, so Boro and his buddies decide to do a little "evacuating" themselves. They stay until dark, gathering supplies, medicines, food, boots, and uniforms and loading them into their truck. Boro even finds some sleeping bags to take for himself and his team.

They go back out. The streets are filled with joyful looters stuffing their cars and tractors. At a partially constructed church nearby, Boro ties a bandage to a bell and rings it in celebration of Serbian Srebrenica. He hears that a car is headed toward his hometown and decides to jump in and make a quick visit with his wife and children. As he heads north past Potočari, the site of the U.N. soldiers' base, Boro looks out the window and sees the thousands of Srebrenicans massed around both sides of the street. Muslims, mostly women and children. His car does not stop.

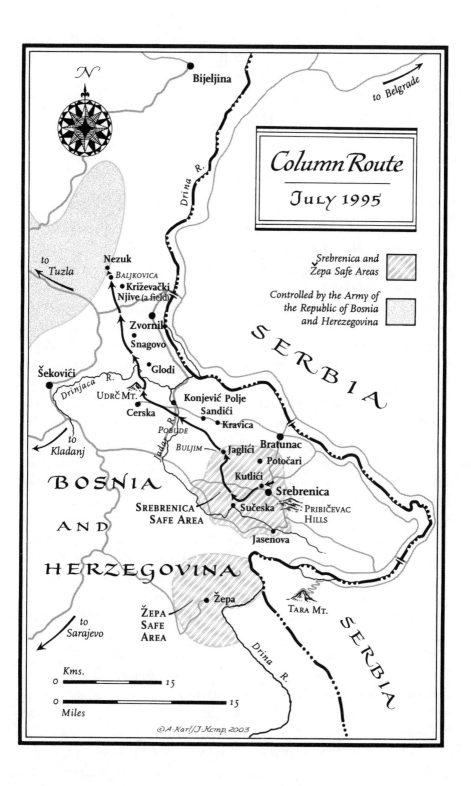

28

HEGIRA

AFTER WALKING A MILE OR TWO, Ilijaz's group catches up with Srebrenica's civilian authorities and military commanders, including
Ramiz, in the small village of Kutlić. Ilijaz, calmer now, suggests the
large group of about 10,000, mainly men, several thousand soldiers, head
toward Žepa. The distance through Serb territory is short and they
should be able to break through it relatively easily. Since the group left
Srebrenica completely unprepared for a long journey, nearby Žepa,
though also enclosed, will be a good place to get organized and plan next
steps.

Everyone seems to agree, but they set another meeting point a few
miles farther west, sending couriers to alert others. Ilijaz rejoins the
medical staff, explains the plan, and eventually they start walking west,
but must change direction at the sound of rocket fire. Fear deepens with
the darkness. Then, around 9 or 10 at night, word spreads that Žepa, too,
has fallen. The escape plan has to change.

Ilijaz's group arrives in Šušnjari, one of the last areas still under control
of the Srebrenica forces. A meeting of Srebrenica's brigade commanders
is under way. Major Ibro Dudić, a friend whom Ilijaz respects, explains
the latest plan. The thousands of Srebrenicans gathering here will form a
line and walk northwest roughly fifty miles through Serb territory toward Tuzla, passing Konjević Polje and Cerska, near Zvornik. Military
units, their commanders communicating by way of Motorola walkie-
talkies, will take various positions in the column, with civilians interspersed among them for protection. Scouts, some elite soldiers, and the
brigade from Cerska, most familiar with the terrain, will lead the line.

Major Dudić's brigade is slotted for somewhere near the middle of the
line, but he warns Ilijaz not to accompany him.

"If the Chetniks think strategically," he says, "they'll fire in the middle . . . I'd like you to be with me, but as a friend, I'm advising you to stick as much as possible toward the beginning of the line."

Ilijaz agrees and informs Ramiz, the overall commander, that the medical staff and their family members will join the line near its front. Ilijaz's core group of about fifteen close friends, colleagues, and family members—including all five hospital physicians and most of the operating room nurses and technicians—make a solemn pledge to stick together.

The night is chilly and clear with a full moon. Ilijaz's feet are already hurting, so he pulls off the military boots and puts on tennis shoes. While the other medical staff rest in the valley, he focuses on building his fighting unit.

If this huge group breaks up, we have to have people around us we can trust. Some strong guys, guys with weapons, guys who won't desert us.

Someone informs Ilijaz's group that they should form up into a line and that they will start moving at 1 A.M. on July 12. But 1 A.M. passes and 2 A.M. passes and still there is no signal to move.

I don't like this at all. A line has got to be the worst way of moving and this route must be the most dangerous, longest one imaginable. But there's no point in asking questions . . .

At last they start moving one by one through the forest on soggy ground, halting whenever someone ahead wearing poor shoes slips, or a cow or a provision-laden horse on the path refuses to budge. By the time they reach Buljim, a nearly treeless plateau that marks the enclave's northwest border and the beginning of their journey through enemy territory, day is breaking. Ilijaz thinks of all the patients he's treated who've been injured in the minefields they're about to cross, of all the amputations he's done, and all the people who've died here.

If I cross Buljim and nothing happens then I might have a chance . . .

For safety, each person steps in the tracks of the person ahead. They hold hands, Ilijaz, then Fatima, then her brother and the others, walking in silence except for an occasional message whispered down the line: "Careful here," "Please, absolute quiet."

The group passes into enemy territory, apparently unseen, descending a steep hill and entering a dense forest of thick, tall beech trees. As morning breaks, Ilijaz hears shooting behind their backs. At first it sounds far away, nothing to worry about. Then he hears grenade explosions.

Something's going on with the last part of the line.

Ilijaz's group continues away from the sounds as fast as they can on uneven ground, up and down hills, covering fewer than two miles in an hour. The pathless hills rise in endless undulations, blanketed with trees. Fatima looks up at a hill that seems to rise straight into the sky and wonders how they'll ever have the energy to get to Tuzla. Around 11 A.M. they reach a designated stopping point in a forest between a hill and a valley. They sit down, exhausted and feet swollen, near others who are already sleeping. A major asphalt road lies ahead, and they must wait until nightfall to cross it.

Ilijaz asks around and discovers they're between two Serb towns. *Between two fires*, he thinks. One is Kravica, where Srebrenica soldiers made their punishing Orthodox Christmas attack in January 1993. "This spot doesn't feel safe," Ilijaz tells the others and gets up to find Ramiz and suggest that armed units be placed around them while they rest here.

Before long, a breathless messenger arrives to announce that the back of the line has been shelled. Ilijaz watches Ramiz and another commander digest the news. They don't trust that it's anything serious. It sounds like an incident, they say, not a major attack. They tell the man to quiet down, to avoid panicking the population.

The messenger stares at them in disbelief. For a moment, Ilijaz is sure he's going to try to kill them. But when the man speaks again, it is in a quiet, deliberate voice.

"OK, you don't need to believe me," he says. "I'm going back to my people, my soldiers, to die with them. And you will be guilty for everything that's about to happen."

Ilijaz doesn't know whom to believe, but the sound of shelling in the distance and the sight of wounded people beginning to arrive sway him toward the messenger. This is war, not a game. From now on, he's going to be very suspicious of the commanders. He's going to look out for his own group rather than trusting that others have their best interest in mind.

Twenty or so injured appear, carried in the arms of others or on improvised stretchers made of uniforms stretched between two logs. Ilijaz and the other medical workers place bandages and give analgetics until the time, after sunset, that their turn comes to proceed.

They walk about a third of a mile, climbing to the top of a small, treeless hill covered with tall fern that rises above their heads. Then explosions begin around them, seeming to come from every direction. Ilijaz can't orient himself enough to figure out where the fire is coming from. He thinks he hears all kinds of weapons—grenades, *zolja* rockets, infantry weapons. Gunfire slices the tips of the ferns.

"I'm hit!" yells the hospital locksmith, holding a gushing water bottle.

"It's just the water bottle. Throw it away," someone tells him.

The line scatters. Ilijaz notices trenches running along the length of the hilltop. He scrambles into the shallow depression of an old Austro-Hungarian-style trench now overgrown with grass and thorns. He waits, but the storm of fire is unending.

It's not safe to stay here. We should get down the hill as soon as possible.

Ilijaz stands up and calls to his group.

"Go, whatever happens."

They run through the tall fern, then curl up and roll down the hill, falling into some bushes. The remains of a couple of burned houses nearby don't seem to offer much chance of protection. They keep moving until they reach a small riverbank that provides some cover. They look around. Five of the medical technicians who started out with them this evening are missing.

Somehow a messenger, a former postal worker, finds his way to Ilijaz with a walkie-talkie and a message from Major Ibro Dudić.

"He has a lot of dead and injured people, and he's asking if there's a way you could come help him."

Ibro is a friend. Many of Ilijaz's relatives are traveling in his group, including his brother-in-law.

"What should we do, Naim?" Ilijaz asks his best friend, the medical technician.

"We're going back," says Naim, whose father is behind.

Then the ear-splitting booms start up again. They stand and wait, not knowing what else to do. Amplified voices echo up the mountains, Serbs calling for their surrender. Ilijaz isn't going back to help. For the first time in the war, someone's asking for his assistance, and he isn't even able to try.

A Srebrenica soldier Ilijaz knows only as "Big Ears" appears above them on the hill.

"What are you doing here?" he asks. "Don't you know the Chetniks are right behind you?"

He guides them farther west to a path the first part of the line has taken that runs between some burned houses toward the asphalt road they have to cross. There, Ilijaz's group and some of the injured for whom they cared the previous day rest and wait out the shelling. Eventually, it seems safe enough to follow a trail toward the main road, but as they climb a hill in the moonlight, Serb forces aim anti-aircraft gunfire at them.

A hospital worker, Dževad Begić, takes hits to the fleshy part of both legs, but they can't stop to examine him until they reach the foot of the hill. They treat his minor wounds and carry on, taking turns helping him walk. They know that they are heading for a raised section of the road that runs over the Jadar River so that they can cross beneath it, but a walk that should take two hours stretches through the night.

We are not going straight, we are making half-circles, turns . . .

It is nearly light outside on Thursday, July 13, when they reach the main road. With no overpass in sight, they decide to sprint across the road rather than cross under it. Ilijaz makes it to the other side, runs about 100 yards farther, and barrels straight into the Jadar River, which he expects from experience to wet him to his knees. The familiar river emanates miles to the southeast, from beneath the hill of his childhood, Kragljivoda. But July has been rainy, and icy-cold water cuts him at his waist; his tennis shoes bob up from the bottom. He grabs hold of some ground on the riverbank to prevent himself from being swept away.

Even the river is trying to kill me.

Everywhere around him people are splashing into the water. Men carrying injured people lose their balance, their charges crashing into the river and screaming as the current takes them. Ilijaz scrambles back out.

"Hold on to each other's hands!" he tells his group.

They begin to cross.

"Hey, your pictures!" someone yells to Ilijaz, who turns back to see photographs of himself floating away. The man who'd offered to carry Fatima's heavy backpack must have dropped the bag into the river upstream.

The area after the river is quiet, and the worst seems to be behind them. After some time, they stumble into swampland. Ilijaz takes his turn supporting the injured medical technician, and as he does, the man's eyes bug out and a strange expression overtakes his face.

"Just leave me here," the technician pleads. "I want to lie down. I can't go on."

Ilijaz and the others talk to him, tease him, try to keep him conscious.

"Come on, you're just pulling our leg, making all this up," they jibe. "You're actually fine."

"*God* I wish Ramo was here with his truck," the injured man says, in a voice tinged with silliness, of the driver of Srebrenica's bread delivery truck. "It would go so fast. I wish he would come and pick me up!"

They make headway northwest toward Cerska. Infected with a terrible thirst, they bend to drink greedily from every stream they pass, not caring about the quality of the water. In the late morning, they climb their next goal, thickly forested Udrč Mountain, 3,419 feet high, where the head of the column has gathered since dawn. They stop to rest on a plateau.

Hunger gnaws at Ilijaz. This is his third day of walking without having had a proper meal, and he wishes he'd thought to take something with him. Fatima runs her finger around the edge of her tennis shoes, trying to make them more comfortable, afraid to take them off because it would take too long to put them back on. The lost backpack with her and Ilijaz's photographs also contained infusions, medications, and her clean socks. All she has now is the loaf of bread her mother packed into her brother's bag, thinking the trip would last two days, but it is saturated with spilled water and powdered juice mix. Thankfully, the others convinced her not to toss it away. Everyone shares small pieces of it, and they lighten the mood by calling it "cake."

Ilijaz asks some brigade commanders about last night's attack, but they seem unaware of it, having been out of communication with the back of the column. Their walkie-talkies weren't compatible. They rely on news coming from each new group to arrive on the mountain, and it grows more and more disturbing. The attack was a major one. Over time, the stream of arrivals peters to a trickle. Then it stops altogether.

The gathering on Udrč Mountain is noticeably smaller than the one the night before. Perhaps only 2,000–3,000 people of the original 10,000 are here. Ilijaz is afraid to try to count. For the first time, he and the others realize how many people have been left behind.

Ilijaz tries to sleep awhile, then gets up and walks around the groupings of people, gleaning information. It surprises him to come across many who seem to be hallucinating, eyes widening and fantasy overtaking them, possessed like pod people in *Invasion of the Body Snatchers*. It's a mystery. Ilijaz can't understand what could cause so many men to go out of their minds. Sure, they are exhausted, hungry and frightened, but perhaps there is something more. A group of men began hallucinating not long after a shell fell near them on the mountainside and discharged a thick, yellow smoke that slowly spread sideways. They're sure that the Serbs are firing at them with chemical weapons. Others insist that the water they drank with such gusto was poisoned.

Some of those hallucinating have become aggressive and confused, killing themselves or giving themselves up to Serbs; others remain passive, expressing things for which they seem to be wishing such as: "I'm going to my room to lie down"; "My child is outside and I need to call him in"; "My wife needs to come in for coffee." Ilijaz hands out Valium, vitamins, and lies to the frightened people, telling them the pills will calm them and take away their visions.

When Ilijaz gets back to his own group, they are gathered around one of the medical technicians. Upright, pale, and wide-eyed, he also appears to be hallucinating.

"Go into the next room and call Selma to come make coffee," he says, again and again. "I'm tired. I can't wait any longer. I'm going to fall asleep. Why did you take my bed to the other room? Why didn't you leave it here? I can't be bothered to go all the way to the other room. I just want to go to sleep here."

They call his name and splash his face with water. He shakes his head and for a moment appears more lucid and oriented. They get him to lie down and rest awhile.

Someone on the mountain has a working radio. The news from Sarajevo is that Srebrenica has fallen and the population is making its way through the forests toward Tuzla. To Ilijaz, it seems like the kind of information that should be kept secret, not publicly broadcast so that the enemy can hear it. And if the capital knows what's happened, then where is the Bosnian army? Why isn't anybody doing anything to help them?

The air is still and quiet, punctuated only by the sound of infantry weapons in the distance behind them. It gives Ilijaz hope that perhaps the Srebrenica soldiers are fighting back.

THE DUTCH U.N. HEADQUARTERS back in Potočari, where most Srebrenicans have gone seeking safety, is another chamber of hell this
Thursday afternoon. Through limpid eyes, nurse Christina Schmitz
watches Bosnian Serb soldiers beat up a crazy man. "Horror," she writes
simply to MSF headquarters.

Yesterday morning, after the Dutch surrendered and the shelling finally ceased, Serb soldiers descended on the Dutchbat compound from
several directions, setting haystacks and houses ablaze on their way.
Wearing strips of bullets across their chests, hefting assault rifles, and
dressed in various uniforms, including those taken from the United Nations, the Serbs were soon demanding weapons from Dutch U.N. soldiers. By afternoon, they roved freely through the crowds gathered in
the factory complexes around the compound, making threats and herd-
ing the increasingly terrified Srebrenicans onto a line of empty passenger
buses and trucks arriving from throughout Serb-held eastern Bosnia.
The vehicles, the soldiers announced, would safely "evacuate" civilians
toward Muslim-held territory. However, the soldiers picked men and
boys out of the waiting crowds, directing them into a separate van and
later to a nearby house guarded by soldiers with German shepherds—
for "questioning," they told the Dutch, and to compare their names to a
list of "war criminals." Christina heard gunshots nearby.

Christina found Serb General Mladić and tried to protest the proposed method of evacuation.

"Do your job," he told her, and walked away.

The operation lasted well into the evening, removing thousands from
Potočari in a matter of hours. The Dutch soldiers mainly watched,
dazed, some crying, and the troops managed to follow only one convoy
all the way to Tuzla.

Christina was traumatized. After spending the day shuttling back and
forth with water and rehydration fluid for the crowds sweltering outside
in the burning sun, without shelter or means of sanitation, she finally
reached the point of absolute exhaustion. Yesterday evening, for the first
time, in a moment of desperation she telexed MSF headquarters and
asked to be replaced.

Just an hour's nap downstairs in the Dutch medical bunker under the care of a Dutch surgeon restored her strength, and she returned to action. She assessed the situation again at 9 at night, walking outside to find a still-large, panicked crowd. Buses were still coming. Men were still being separated. Bosnian Serb soldiers were firing in the air.

"It's horrifying outside," she reported to MSF headquarters. "The world has failed here. A complete enclave has been wiped away. Srebrenica doesn't exist anymore."

The night cast terror on Potočari. Clutched with fear, people didn't sleep. The terrible sounds of gunshots, screams, and other awful noises caused waves of panic to roll through the crowds. Small groups of Serb soldiers, some wearing Dutchbat uniforms, infiltrated the groups of refugees and selected people to take away. A Dutchbat medical orderly came across two Serb soldiers raping, in view of other refugees, a bloodied young woman who seemed to be, as the orderly would later describe it, in "total shock . . . totally crazy." A few Srebrenica men committed suicide. By this morning, stories of rapes and killings abounded, and clusters of dead bodies had been discovered, including by a stream where many children went to fetch water.

Earlier in the evening, dozens of wounded patients were put on U.N. trucks bound for Tuzla, accompanied by a Dutch anesthesiologist. At 2 A.M., Christina was awakened to prepare for the return of three dozen of the patients. The news puzzled her. She was grateful, at least, that since the U.N. compound went off red alert, the rest of the Dutch medical team had come out of their bunkers to help and had opened their medical facilities and drugs to the population. Around the same time she was awakened, a fourth baby was delivered in the open, on a dirty stretcher in a dark, muddy, wet corridor with everyone watching.

Today, three more women went into labor and delivered, perhaps triggered by the stress. One baby was stillborn. The patients who were rumored to be on their way back this morning never showed up. Their convoy was stopped on its way to Tuzla—men of military age were removed, Bosnian nurses working for MSF were led away, and the rest of the patients, many immobile, were told they had to walk four miles to Bosnian government–held territory. The Dutch anesthesiologist protested, and the thirty-three patients remaining on the convoy were turned around and driven back in the direction of Potočari. The vehicles were stopped at the yellow bridge, the former front line, and the wounded were eventually taken to the health clinic in Bratunac.

For all the tribulations of yesterday, Christina could still believe it, at least enough to report it to headquarters, when the Dutch commander told her last night that the Bosnian Serbs weren't going to enter the U.N. building and they weren't killing any men. But today, another truth is asserting itself in prickly moments of half-realization, making it harder and harder to avoid a different conclusion. This morning, someone asked her to go behind the factory to check on rumors of bodies there. She refused—it was a job for the military observers, not MSF. But later, while she was standing outside, a local man in his mid-twenties, carrying a baby and escorted by a Serb soldier, approached Christina in tears. One of MSF's translators explained that the Serb soldiers were taking the man away and there was no one to care for his baby. His wife was dead. There were no grandparents. Christina took down his name and the baby's name.

Then, as the man sobbed, Christina had to gently separate him from his baby. The soldier immediately pulled the man away to a nearby house. It occurred to her that the man would never see his daughter again, but she chased the thought away. Hundreds of family members were getting separated from one another in this massive exodus from Srebrenica. She would make sure this baby's father was traced.

This afternoon, her third day here, Christina has distracted herself by finding about a dozen new patients outside to bring into the compound for treatment. She tells headquarters that most of them are either old and exhausted; old and crazy; or young, exhausted, and freaking out. Although people are being separated before her eyes, she is overwhelmed and unable to comprehend the totality of what is going on. Everything is happening in real time—there's no one here to interpret it. Christina wishes that everyone who had the power to stop this mass exodus could be standing beside her, seeing the violence on the faces of the Bosnian Serbs and feeling the panic and desperation of the population as they are herded, like animals, toward the buses, running for their lives, holding their screaming children to their breasts, and dropping and leaving behind the possessions they've managed to bring with them this far.

She receives a situation report from MSF headquarters saying that 20,000 detainees are being transported to Bratunac stadium. Christina realizes that the promise of protection the United Nations gave Srebrenica by designating it a safe area means nothing. She has never experienced anything more horrible in her life.

She's in constant contact with MSF Belgrade. MSF country sections are fielding dozens and dozens of media calls. Christina feeds them information. Some of her dispatches are carried in a French newspaper, *Liberation*. MSF headquarters staff make public calls for protection of the population and try to send in supplies and more expatriates.

By the late afternoon, the only remaining refugees are the 5,000 gathered inside the stinking, chaotic Dutch compound, where toilets overflow and new mothers have stopped lactating from the stress. Several hundred men remain here, 251 of whom allow their names to be recorded on a list for the Dutch. Others refuse out of fear the Serbs will see it. The Serbs demand that those inside leave the compound, too, and the Dutch agree, even helping to ensure their orderly removal through a corridor created by tape. The men, pleading not to be handed over to the Serbs, include family members of Dutchbat's local staff. The Dutch order all of them out of the compound.

The Dutch second-in-command reassures Christina that the Bosnian Serbs are not touching men who aren't soldiers. Her experiences these past few days convince her otherwise. She takes a step nearly unprecedented in MSF—she insists the local male medical staff members stay with her. The internationals should be evacuated tomorrow, and she'll make sure that all the male medical staff members and any female staff members who want to stay be evacuated along with MSF.

After everyone is gone except the patients, medical staff, and some of their family members, Serb soldiers come to inspect the building. They receive a list of the patients and spend only ten minutes inside, seemingly shocked and disgusted by the conditions in the compound—the smells, the shit, the bedraggled look of the patients. Christina takes the opportunity to ask for an escort to town to pick up the patients she had to leave behind in the hospital two days ago. She's driven quickly to Srebrenica with a U.N. military observer. She finds three elderly patients in good condition sitting where she left them. Someone has given them biscuits to eat. The Bosnian Serb escorts are afraid that Srebrenica soldiers might be hiding in the hospital rooms, so Christina and the U.N. military observer have to carry the patients to the pickup truck themselves. She spots three more elderly people in the social center and brings them to the truck, too.

Outside the windows, she sees Serb soldiers everywhere, looting. She watches TVs and washing machines being loaded up and livestock being herded north. Srebrenica, a city she'd started to love, feels strange and empty, a city populated by cast-off belongings instead of people.

———

AROUND FOUR THE SAME AFTERNOON, Thursday, July 13, a Belgrade television reporter rides with Serb soldiers along the asphalt roads northwest of Potočari, stopping at a meadow in Sandići where dozens of Srebrenica men who've surrendered to Serb soldiers are seated on the ground under guard. The soldiers, holding automatic rifles with rounds of ammunition slung across their necks, instruct the captives to call for their friends and family members still in the woods.

"Ay, Nermine!" a thin, bent graying man in a wet T-shirt yells through cupped hand for his son in the nearby woods, "Come here. Don't be afraid of the Serbs." Gunshots crackle in the distance.

The cameraman continues down the road in the car as joyful folk music plays on the radio. Along the roadside, posted every several yards, a Serb soldier stands or crouches by a guardrail or behind tall grasses that grow to his chin, looking out into the hills, thick with deciduous trees and blooming with flowers. He carries a set of binoculars or a powder-blue U.N. hardhat, and always a gun, frequently with his finger on the trigger. He wears camouflage clothing or a T-shirt and pants, or a black headband, or a grenade on his belt. He cups a free hand to his mouth and yells into the woods at the Srebrenicans still hiding there.

"Come on, guys!"

"Come on, hurry up!"

The cameraman stops on the road where gunners on two boxy armored vehicles take turns firing their top-mounted anti-aircraft guns into the lush, green hillside. *Rip* goes one gun, with a burst of smoke and a streak of light that heads for the hillside, lighting it up for a moment before it disappears into a cloud of smoke and dust. *Thump* goes the answering impact. *Rip, thump. Rip, thump.* Casings clatter to the ground; the gunmen whistle and aim their guns with steering wheels. A line of figures appears on the crest of a hillside. *Rip . . . rip . . .* the figures fall down, *thump . . . thump.*

MILES NORTHWEST OF THE FIRING and the asphalt road, Ilijaz's group lines up to walk again around 5 P.M. Just as they're about to depart, a lone shell explodes at the edge of the forest, at a safe distance from everyone.

It's almost as if it didn't want to hurt anyone, just to say, "Why aren't you on your way yet?"

They start down the north side of the mountain, slowly descending its steep, rough surface toward a river whose banks, they are warned, are mined. It's still light out when they near the river and turn right to follow a path along its course. Few can resist the siren call of the rushing river, and hundreds clamber down, Ilijaz among them, to gulp its clear, cold water. The water is so beautiful, so comforting and precious that they stop to splash around, heedless of the fact that the cool night is falling. It is the Drinjaca, the same river that flows, farther west, through Šekovići.

They come to an old, wooden bridge and cross it into the burnt Muslim village of Glodi. Daylight fades as they follow an old country road out of the village in silence.

I don't like this quiet. Something bad is going to happen.

A message whispered down the column beckons Ilijaz to come to the front.

Who's calling me? Why?

Thinking it is probably an emergency, Ilijaz puts his best friend Naim in charge of the group, takes another man with him, and starts out quickly alongside the column to catch up with the front. After more than two hours walking uphill at a brisk pace, they reach a bottleneck where the path diverges from the road, crosses a roadside ditch, and disappears into what looks, in the dim light of dusk, like a tall beech forest. Ilijaz hears some vague complaints from the people ahead, but ignores them until it is his turn to cross the ditch. Numb with exhaustion, Ilijaz can barely keep his eyes open.

He descends into the complete darkness of the forest and sees a wall of skyscrapers rising before him, squeezed around narrow staircases that lead downward. He tries to put his feet on the steps, but can't force them to work. It's like finding himself paralyzed in a vivid bad dream.

I must be starting to hallucinate.

He slaps both hands over his eyes.

I am in the forest on my way to Tuzla, I am in the forest on my way to Tuzla . . . Someone's calling me from the front of the column. Maybe someone's wounded.

He opens his eyes. He sees only forest.

"What are these buildings doing here?" he hears other men ask. Ilijaz turns around and slaps his companion to prevent him from experiencing a similar vision. Then he hustles back up to the edge of the forest to warn the others.

"Certain visual effects are possible when you walk down into the forest," he tells those waiting their turn to descend. "Don't be afraid."

For the next half hour, they feel their way through the forest. Then the column stops moving. Ilijaz and his companion continue alongside to its front.

"Who called for me?" Ilijaz asks. The men at the front don't have an answer.

"What unit are you in?" Ilijaz asks them.

"The 284th brigade."

That is right. That is the unit that is supposed to be leading the column.

When he asks, "Where's your commander?" they say he went ahead with a scouting unit of about 100 people.

This seems strange. Suspicious.

"Why are you standing here waiting?"

"We're waiting for couriers to come back with commands for us to proceed."

"Hey! My son's not feeling right!" a man calls from somewhere behind Ilijaz. Ilijaz walks fifty yards back to find a man lying on the ground with his father leaning over him.

"He's dying," the father says. Ilijaz bends down to examine the man and hears the rhythmic sound of snoring. He isn't dying; he's simply so exhausted that he went to sleep standing and then fell to the ground.

Ilijaz and his companion sit down to wait, deciding to nap in shifts. It will take at least two hours for the others to catch up with them.

"Wake me up in half an hour," Ilijaz says.

ILIJAZ OPENS HIS EYES. He looks around. His companion is on the ground beside him, fast asleep. Ilijaz doesn't see or hear anyone else nearby. Perhaps they've slept for hours. Ilijaz awakens his companion, who claps his hands to his head, upset at his lapse. They sit there for a while, unsure of what to do, all alone in the dark, unfamiliar forest. It seems they'll have to wait for daybreak to proceed.

Then they hear people yelling at one another. A man cussing at the top of his lungs runs past them.

"Fuck! I know this way really well," he says. "There are no Chetniks here. Someone is screwing with the column!"

Ilijaz turns to see the column coming up behind them. He and his companion scramble to their feet and join it.

Around dawn they reach an asphalt road beside a river and stop. The column falls apart as people wait and try to figure out where they are and where they should go next. There is no sign of the scouting group that went ahead.

The medical group catches up. During the wait, people panic again. A man rushes from the river tearing off his clothes and yelling, "Airplanes!" with his arms spread out like wings. "They're Chetniks!" he shouts, and then gunshots crack the air. He kills several of those unlucky enough to be standing nearby, then commits suicide.

If we stay here much longer, we'll all have psychological breakdowns.

Ilijaz gathers a group of leaders, and they discuss which way to go. Someone figures out that they're on an old, abandoned asphalt road that runs from northeast to southwest between Zvornik and Šekovići. Ilijaz figures that since they're coming from the south that means Zvornik is to the right. They must go left. Left is west. Left is toward Tuzla.

He borrows a gun and takes two young men on a scouting mission. At first unsuccessful, they eventually find a path that diverges from the main road into a forest with good cover. They return and form up into a column again, proceeding with the aim of getting off the road and into the forest before daybreak. Very soon, as the elevation climbs, they reach an area of open plains. Afraid of being seen and anxious to reach better cover, Ilijaz and other leaders prod the exhausted group onward at a brisk pace.

At last they encounter the scouting group. Ilijaz, furious, confronts them, accusing them of leaving the column behind.

"That's not true," they counter, insisting that they've just been scouting terrain and would have come back for the group. The scouts instruct everyone to rest in a valley surrounded by forests. They'll move again around 5 P.M. Some people lie down and go to sleep. Others search for fruit in the forest.

I won't let them out of my sight this time.

Ilijaz's vigilance keeps him from sleeping much during the day. Cracks of gunfire echo from the outskirts of the valley. Ilijaz wonders whether Srebrenica soldiers have been placed around their perimeter and are fighting the Chetniks. When he asks, he's shooed away.

"Take it easy, get some rest. We won't let another massacre happen."

Ilijaz prepares his group. Around 4 P.M. they hear a couple of gunshots.

"Those shots mean something," says his friend Naim, "some kind of warning."

Ilijaz and Naim walk to where the commander Ramiz is. Another scouting group has departed the valley and is heading over the hills. A Motorola held by Ramiz's young assistant crackles to life.

"Those who were supposed to leave have left," a voice says. "Make sure the right and left wings work together."

Ilijaz freezes. It sounds as if the Motorola's tapped into the Chetnik frequency and that the Chetniks are planning to catch them in a horseshoe. Ilijaz and Naim give each other a silent look that says, "What can we do?" Obviously their officers know where the Chetniks are.

Ilijaz and Naim agree not to tell their own group about the Chetnik plan, to avoid demoralizing them. When they return to the group they don't mention a thing, but they place armed men on the outside of the column.

All evening, as his part of the column inches over the hill and into the next valley, Ilijaz feels as if they're being watched by the Serbs. At any moment he expects shellfire to burst open the night. Beyond fear, he is numb.

Just before dark, the column comes to a stop and an order passes down the line for anyone armed to come to the front. The Srebrenicans successfully fight off an ambush. Some are killed, but not as many as before. A few soldiers have light wounds, and Ilijaz examines a dying man with a serious head wound.

The column breaks through to an area called Snagovo, crosses the main road leading west from Zvornik—the back part of the column encountering and shooting off a vehicle—and re-enters mountainous terrain, stopping to rest at a meadow called Križevački Neve in the morning.

The Serb officer who organized the ambush, a certain Captain Janković, has been captured in the fighting. Ilijaz and hundreds of others are eager to get a look at him. He sits, hands crossed and bound in front of him, looking at the ground. He appears unharmed, though Ilijaz hears that another Serb soldier who tried to fight back when captured was killed. From the officer, the Srebrenica forces learn that the Serb army is sparing no expense in the effort to capture as many of them as possible. The Srebrenicans hope to exchange the captain for free passage across the lines to Tuzla. However throughout the day, repeated attempts to negotiate fail. Ilijaz hears that the Serbs won't even discuss it.

Sitting in the field, the medical team members are down to their last sour breadcrumbs. Their shoes are in tatters. Avdo, the hospital director, has his shoeless feet bound up in bandages and carries a walking stick. Fatima has her period, and, with her tampons in her lost backpack, she uses the two dishtowels in which her mother had wrapped the bread. They chafe at her skin.

They're very close to the front lines—only two to two and a half miles as the bird flies—but a difficult forest lies ahead of them, Baljkovica, consisting of two hills with a valley in between. Rumor spreads that it's impassable. People are exhausted, jumpy, panicked. Ilijaz just feels hopeless. He grieves for himself.

I'm still so young and would have had so many beautiful things ahead of me.

They sit and wait. People around them hallucinate. Compared to the others, the medical group seems stronger. They've stuck together, shown each other kindness, and it seems to have protected them.

Hakija Meholjić, Nedret's former confidante, chief of the "Hotel Fresh Air," who became chief of police after demilitarization, has been walking in a group just behind Ilijaz's. During rest periods, the two men have frequently talked. Hakija has often thought of Nedret on this trip, remembering their old conversation at the "Hotel Fresh Air" about how long a man could survive without food if he had access to salt and sugar. When Hakija's grip on reality faded, he asked people for salt and sugar and found that they indeed renewed his strength.

Now he limps toward Ilijaz with a walking stick, his unshaven face looking haggard. He suspects the medical staff are taking drugs to keep strong.

"Doctor, it looks like the only normal people left are these few around you. Let's try and do something." They find two men with some knowledge of the region and make a back-up plan to split off from the main group if necessary. The sunny, warm day stretches toward evening. Around 4 or 5 P.M., they receive instructions to line up.

As they do so, clouds blow in and the sky turns dark. Icy-cold raindrops fall, drenching them to their skin within minutes. Then actual ice begins to fall. Pieces of hail as big as walnuts crack the ground, the trees, and Ilijaz's head, momentarily disorienting him as he runs for shelter beneath the trees.

Hail in the middle of the summer? This is the culmination of hell.

In a while the hail stops, but it continues to rain. They line up again, dripping.

An explosion about fifty yards away startles Ilijaz. The line scatters. People run up to Ilijaz.

"Kemo killed himself, and he wounded ten people around him."

Kemo, the head nurse's husband, had held strong throughout the trip. Ilijaz last saw him about an hour ago, giving water to his exhausted brother. Nobody can explain why he suddenly snapped, pulling out a hand grenade and activating it as they lined up. The hail saps the will of many men.

After bandaging the survivors, they set out northwest, wending their way for hours in the rain through pathless, mountainous terrain. Night falls, and clouds diffuse the light of the nearly full moon as it rises. Ilijaz hears explosions coming from the direction of the minefield they have to cross. When they enter it, he is exhausted, numb, wet, and cold, barely able to keep his legs moving, keep upright, keep from tripping, keep concentrating on the obscured footsteps of Naim, walking ahead of him.

Ilijaz grips the hand of Fatima, behind him.

If we survive this together, I will marry her.

He takes one careful step. Then another. Then another. Moans waft through the darkness of the minefield, distracting him. He hears a woman's voice nearby pleading for help.

"I'm going to at least try to help her," Ilijaz says.

Someone tells him it's too dangerous, and he knows it's true. Nobody can save these people. For the second time that he can ever remember, Ilijaz is being begged for help and can't even try to respond. This time is worse. He can hear the injured. The calls from the sides of the path continue, one fading, another starting up, over and over like the howls of ghosts.

When he had pledged the Oath of Hippocrates, becoming a physician, he had sworn himself to the service of others. Now, he does not even think he can save himself.

Ilijaz begins to shiver, then shudder with cold. His body shakes with every step. He can barely control his movements.

I wish this was over. If I have to die, then let me die. Just let my suffering stop, my exhaustion, hunger, cold, fear. Just let it stop.

The terrain flattens and they're told the mine danger has passed. Ilijaz falls asleep as he walks. He dreams he is tired and talks in his sleep.

"I hate walking, and when I buy a car, I'll never walk again."

Someone shakes him awake. Naim.

"Hey, what are you saying?"

Ilijaz smiles in the dark, because he remembers himself talking in his dream. Then he scowls, not wanting those around him to know he's so exhausted.

"I'm fine," he whispers, pretending to be angry. "Be quiet! Just shake me from time to time."

Around dawn they emerge from the wood into a valley echoing with shellfire. People who've arrived before them are sitting around campfires, some drying their clothes. Ilijaz flies to a campfire like a moth.

"Doctor, we made it!" a young man, some sort of officer, approaches him with enthusiasm. "We're fine. There's no more danger!"

"How come there's all that shooting?" Ilijaz asks him.

"It's a bit of fighting just to keep the corridor open. We'll stay here until we get orders to march to safe territory. You should gather some of your people and march up front. Take ten of your people and get up to the front right away!"

He has the delirious air of a man planning a victory parade. It seems odd that they haven't passed any trenches or signs of fighting. Ilijaz peers at the man and sees his eyes are bugged out. He's hallucinating.

A more oriented person explains that the Chetniks have a double front line and planned to trap the Srebrenicans inside. The hailstorm was a godsend, helping the armed Srebrenicans achieve an element of surprise. They are attacking the Serbs' first front line and have already captured two tanks, one of which is functional.

Ilijaz climbs a hill to catch a glimpse of the battle. The earth shakes and the air reverberates with the detonations of gunpowder, shells, and mortars. Machine guns rattle away. Tanks fire. The ground burns. Ilijaz has only seen it in the movies.

From time to time men arrive from the hot-fire areas to collect ammunition and grenades and lead newer arrivals to the front. Nobody appears afraid. Many men volunteer to fight, more than can be supplied with weapons. They head to the front, prepared to pick up the weapons of those who fall. Now everyone has hope. Nobody wants to stay back.

With the few supplies left in their bags, Ilijaz and the other medical staff try to give first aid to the masses of wounded who are dragged back to a sheltered area behind the front lines. People call for help. Soldiers offer their bandages. There is enough work for a hundred doctors and nurses, let alone their dozen. They try to prioritize the severely wounded and designate someone to carry each casualty once the lines are opened.

As the morning wears on, Ilijaz, impatient, decides to see for himself what's going on. He walks toward the battle with a group of soldiers, emerging from the woods at an unfinished one-story house. Three or four Srebrenica soldiers are lying beside it with their weapons. One waves him to approach. Ilijaz jogs over.

"There are some injured people inside."

Ilijaz gets busy providing first aid. The commander of the brigade has heavy wounds to his chest and legs. The others have only minor injuries. But the loudest moans of all come from the mouth of an uninjured man, bound foot and hand, tied up because of hallucinations and aggression.

"Free me, doctor," he pleads. "These guys want to kill me."

Ilijaz tries to calm him and persuade him to take an anti-anxiety tablet, but the man refuses.

"Now you want to kill me, too," he yells and continues screaming. "Untie me!"

"Keep him tied," Ilijaz says and steps back outside, bewitched by the sight of an apple tree a few yards away. He starts walking toward its beautiful orbs when he's knocked to the ground by one of three soldiers lying nearby.

"We're right in the line of fire!" cries the soldier, and a burst of rifle-fire underscores his remark. Ilijaz retreats to the sheltered area. Then a young man enters, saying that he needs a grenade.

"There's just one APC left," he declares. "When we destroy it, we're going through."

Someone hands him a grenade and tells him, "This is the last one. Don't miss."

SOMETIME AROUND 2 P.M. word reaches Ilijaz that the Serb lines are broken. The young man strode right through the line of fire with the grenade, right up close to the Serb armored personnel carrier, and threw it. Then the Chetniks started running away.

Ilijaz gives Naim the word to start moving out. On improvised stretchers made of uniforms and tree branches, the injured are carried past empty trenches.

Ilijaz, Fatima, and the other doctors, medical technicians, and nurses walk uphill through tall, yellowed grass toward a road. Some around them hobble, some around them run, some look dazed, others burst with newfound energy. At the top of the hill, people in camouflage uniforms with yellow arm bands greet them, offering a hand to help them to the road: Bosnian army.

"Guys, you're free!" they welcome them. "You're in free territory."

29

FREEDOM

A FEW DAYS AFTER ARRIVING IN TUZLA, Ilijaz, Fatima, and the other medical staff reunite at Tuzla Hospital. Ejub, though he left Srebrenica a month before its fall and in any other situation would have been considered a traitor, comes, too, forgiven in light of the catastrophe. Here, on July 21, 1995, they draw up a list of the medical workers of Srebrenica. The first column, "those who've arrived in Tuzla," begins with the names Dr. Ilijaz Pilav, Dr. Fatima Dautbašić, Dr. Branka Stanić, Dr. Avdo Hasanović, and Dr. Dževad Džananović and continues down the page and onto a second with the names of the medical students and nurses and student nurses, fifty-four in all, who've made it safely to Tuzla. The last name on this part of the list is Dr. Ejub Alić.

Next, the medical workers list those killed in Srebrenica. They begin with Dr. Nijaz Džanić, who died in the air bombing of his clinic. Next is Sulejman Pilav, Ilijaz's cousin the medical technician, who was mortally injured near his medical station in Kragljivoda. The names of two other nurses follow.

Next, under "those who started out by convoy, and haven't yet arrived," they write the names of the only four male medical staff members who sought protection with the Dutch in Potočari. Then they write the names of "those who started out in the column, and haven't yet arrived." Among the eleven men listed is Sadik Ahmetović. The well-liked twenty-six-year-old medical technician walked farther back in the column with friends and relatives, rather than up front with the rest of the medical staff. Nobody has seen him since the Serb attack.

The final category on the list is "killed doctors." It includes the names of the five men who tried to reach Srebrenica during the war and never arrived. Dr. Naser Siručić and Dr. Avdo Bakalović are listed first. They were the two who were lost, unarmed, in a snowstorm in the mountains west of Srebrenica in 1992 and ambushed by the Serbs. The staff end their list with Drs. Sead and Huso Halilović and Dr. Muharem Deljković, the three physicians who set out nervously on a helicopter from Tuzla one dark night just three months ago and died on a mountainside near Žepa.

AS THE DOCTORS ARE MAKING THEIR LIST IN TUZLA, Christina and the MSF staff members and Dutch soldiers are finally receiving permission from the Serbs to leave Potočari, eight long days after most of the rest of the population was removed. Christina refused to depart without official clearance for every one of the local MSF and UNHCR staff members, their family members who managed to stay, and a few elderly people whom the Serbs found in Srebrenica during the week.

She despised having to meet with a Bosnian Serb army colonel and listen to him talk about art, paintings, and Van Gogh. So cynical! She had to smile and play along. He even teased her once that she would be forced to stay behind.

Although she carefully prepared the remaining fifty-five injured patients, insisting the Serbs recognize and document that all were indeed wounded, when the Red Cross came to evacuate them, the Serbs still separated some men and took them away. She gave the unaccompanied baby to the Red Cross. She never saw its father again, but she telexed MSF headquarters to alert another nongovernmental organization to begin tracing him. As for the forty-five patients being held in Bratunac—it's been too risky for her to leave Potočari and attempt to see what is happening with them. She heard that a girl died of diabetic ketoacidosis and that several of the patients are in urgent need of surgery, which cannot be performed in Bratunac's small clinic. Christina has heard even more worrisome rumors—that hundreds of Srebrenica men are being held in the Bratunac stadium after having been captured on their way to Tuzla.

Those at MSF headquarters have backed Christina's plan to evacuate her local staff, and the Belgrade MSF staff fought hard for days for clearance from the Serbs. Finally today, after an approval process so complicated that someone at MSF Belgrade writes, "The whole thing could not have been imagined even by Kafka," Christina has all the permissions she needs to leave. Instead of proceeding directly to Tuzla through Serb territory, the evacuation route the Serbs have approved takes them through Serbia, Croatia, and back into Bosnia.

The three MSF cars are filled with eight local staff, five of whom are male, five of their family members, and two old people. They join a convoy of 163 U.N. Protection Force vehicles. The local Serb commander bids them farewell at the gate of the Potočari compound. When they reach the Bosnian side of the iron bridge to Serbia, Serb Military Commander Ratko Mladić meets them with the press. They cross the bridge and proceed to the Croatian border. Immigration officers keep them for two and a half hours, interviewing local staff, chiding the U.N. Protection Forces for not protecting civilians, and shouting at Christina. At 4 A.M. on July 22, they arrive at U.N. Camp Plešo in Croatia. The MSF local staff are lodged in a hotel and given their pay for July.

Christina has managed to evacuate many of her local staff. She is relieved about that and happy to be alive. Still, she feels that so much more could have been done, both medically and with advocacy, to help the people of Srebrenica. The magnitude of all she has witnessed is just beginning to hit her.

30

SADIK

THE DAY HIS COLLEAGUES LIST HIM AS MISSING, ten days after the fall of Srebrenica, Sadik Ahmetović is in fact very much alive, but his choice to walk farther back in the column has markedly changed the character of his as-yet-unfinished journey.

When the Serbs attacked the column, the large, dark-haired medical technician was cut off from the rest of the medical staff. His intense, intelligent eyes surveyed a scene of almost unimaginable carnage. Dozens of Srebrenicans lay dead and dying on the ground. He stopped to treat some of the injured, applying bandages with the help of anyone nearby. These past few days, as the front of the column made a beeline for Tuzla, he and the dwindling number of survivors from the back of the line have wandered through the woods. Every couple hundred yards he met someone else with a wound and stopped to help him. Sometimes wounded people lay everywhere, every step he took, in every direction he turned.

As the column was broken into smaller and smaller parts, with men being killed and thousands surrendering to the Serbs, the group of people Sadik traveled with shrank. Eventually he found himself in a group of fifty-two, and together they concluded it wasn't possible to make it to Tuzla. The Chetniks had cut off key points along the possible routes. They decided to turn back toward Srebrenica.

The paths on the way back were a ghoulish scene of littered bodies. Sadik turned them over, trying to find friends. He walked for days and days that blended together. None of the men in his group slept. They were exhausted beyond description. Afraid. Confused. Crazed. At one point, Sadik forgot his own name. He became convinced that the Chetniks were attacking them with poison gas.

The group, picking up a few others as it went, eventually made it to

Slatina, a small village near Srebrenica, and spent the night. Where could they go for safety? Srebrenica was taken. Žepa, too, from what they'd heard. But there was a famous saying about the woods near Žepa—"You can wander for ten years in Žepa's forests without bumping into another person." The next day, they decided to head there.

As they neared Žepa, they heard sounds of shooting from two sides. This made them realize the enclave hadn't yet fallen. The news that it had, which was heard on Serb radio and caused the entire column to head for Tuzla, might well have been willful misinformation.

After discovering this last night, most of Sadik's group went to stay in a nearby village. He continued into town, because he knew Žepa's doctor, Benjo, the one who had trained for a while in Srebrenica and treated the survivors of the helicopter crash with Ilijaz.

When Sadik awakens the morning after his arrival, he can't walk. The skin on the soles of his feet is swollen, cracked, and bleeding. He tells Benjo the horrible story of the exodus. The doctor warns him not to make people in Žepa, particularly the soldiers, afraid. "Keep quiet about it," he says.

When Benjo first heard that Srebrenica had fallen, he hadn't believed it. He'd been there just a month ago and experienced the "there but for the grace of God go I" sensation that haunts one who leaves a place by chance just before disaster strikes. His incredulity trickled away as he watched Mladić on Serb TV, standing before Ilijaz's apartment building, announcing Srebrenica's liberation from the Turks. But only now, hearing Sadik speak, does he get an inkling of the horror that has taken place.

During the day, Žepa comes under fierce attack. Serb forces pound grenades into the two-story medical building in the center of town where Sadik works, demolishing its rooftop. Several more shells carve craters into the side of the building. Within a half hour, the rooms Benjo has been using are destroyed. He moves his medical work, amputating a limb and giving first aid to patients, to the only place left that provides significant protection, a barn.

On July 25, the town of Žepa falls. General Mladić makes another triumphant arrival. Benjo, both doctor and mayor of the sparsely populated enclave, negotiates with him, and they reach an agreement to evacuate the wounded to a hospital in Sarajevo.

This is good news for the wounded, but medical technician Sadik Ahmetović, although he can barely walk five yards with his ravaged feet, isn't one of them, and this sends him spinning into a psychological crisis. With his feet this way, he can't possibly hike through the mountains again.

Sadik needs to be injured to qualify for the evacuation. In a panic, he asks Benjo to cut him, explaining that he's seen too many dead people on his journey and can't imagine making it through the woods again. "I just don't have the strength to go back there."

"I'm sorry, I can't," the doctor replies without explaining why. He takes all blades and other cutting implements away from Sadik's part of the barn. Sadik figures the doctor is scared that he is going to seriously harm himself, perhaps even kill himself. But Sadik's perspective has shifted. Compared with the dead bodies, the confusion, the whistling of rockets, the rat-tat-tat of heavy machine gun fire and worst of all the shells that landed with a thud and smoked, seeming to Sadik to be releasing poison gas that drove men to hallucinate and give themselves up to the Serbs—compared with all this, a small injury seems harmless.

Sadik begs a pistol from a soldier. He sets out bandages, gauze, an aspirin-like painkiller and penicillin antibiotic. Then he warns the doctor he's going to shoot himself. If Benjo wants to help, he can tell him the safest place to aim. The doctor points to the fleshy front of the upper leg, a place with no major blood vessels or bone. He turns away, unable to watch.

Sadik gathers the skin at the front of his left thigh and shoots a bullet through it. The doctor, with tears in his eyes, returns immediately to help him. They bandage the wound. In spite of the pain, Sadik isn't sorry for what he's done. He feels relief. By giving himself an injury, he's given himself a chance to survive.

AFTER RINGING THE BELL to herald the Serbianization of Srebrenica the night of its capture on July 11, Dr. Boro Lazić took advantage of the fact that some vehicles were going back to Šekovići. He went home that night for an hour to see his family and then returned to an army base a half mile south of the entrance to Srebrenica. He spent the next couple of days in relative peace with his medical team, gathering more medical supplies from the U.N. Bravo base and the Srebrenica pharmacy. His unit was not even on alert.

Then they received orders to proceed to Žepa and participate in the offensive. Only then did Boro hear of the large numbers of Muslim men from Srebrenica walking through the woods west of the enclave toward Tuzla.

Boro and his team went the other way, south, and arrived at the front lines on a hill about two and a half to three miles from the city of Žepa. The line proved much more difficult for the Serb soldiers to break than the line around Srebrenica, and Boro had much more work treating the injured and sending them to hospitals in larger Serb-held cities. Serb leaders publicly announced their plans to take the Žepa "safe area" before beginning their advance. The announcement drew no military response from the international community. Žepa's soldiers held out for day after day, but the fall of their town had been accepted as a fait accompli.

For ten days Boro stayed there, the only qualified doctor on his side of the front line, impressed by the best defenses he witnessed throughout the entire war. Finally, today, two weeks after the capture of Srebrenica, the line around Žepa broke. Žepa's soldiers fell back east of the town up another hill toward Serbia, and the Serbian soldiers Boro was with advanced down their hill to the river that ran before the west side of the town. They have been ordered to stop here and refrain from engaging in provocations. While he waits, Boro inspects the Muslim soldiers' trenches, struck by their professionalism.

Meanwhile, the Serb and Muslim commanders begin to negotiate a surrender agreement in the presence of the Ukrainian U.N. battalion that was stationed in Žepa. Unlike Srebrenica, there were no representatives of humanitarian organizations here, and Boro is invited to cross the river into the city and participate in talks about evacuation of children and the injured. He is tasked with drawing up lists of those to be evacuated, in what order and by what means. His first priority is to evacuate the seriously injured to Sarajevo by bus.

SEVERAL THOUSAND INHABITANTS of Žepa town and the remote hillside settlements around the enclave congregate in the town square, awaiting evacuation.

"Dr. Boro, Dr. Boro," someone shouts.

Next to the Žepa town square, inside the open U.N. barracks, Sadik Ahmetović lies with other injured and ill men and women, listening to the hubbub of thousands of people gathering for the evacuation. People walk in and out, calling to one another, issuing instructions. In the distance he hears someone shout, "Dr. Boro, Dr. Boro."

"Call that doctor," he tells a soldier.

A MUSLIM SOLDIER APPROACHES. "Are you Doctor Boro?" he asks.

"I am," Boro answers, surprised because he doesn't recognize the man. "That's my name."

"A young man is asking for you," he says, and beckons Boro to follow him toward the U.N. barracks.

Boro wonders who could know him here in Žepa, this out-of-the-way backwoods town that he's never before visited. He suspects, with some fear, that it could be a setup. The soldier leads him to an improvised medical station inside the barracks. Boro looks around and doesn't see anyone he knows. The man keeps walking, taking him deeper inside, into a second part of the barracks, to a young man lying on the ground. Boro immediately recognizes Sadik, a former nurse from Boro's days of medical training. They met two years ago at the stadium in Srebrenica, and, when Boro was frightened, Sadik had said, "No one will harm you here."

They greet one another warmly.

"I'm very sorry for you," Boro says, noting Sadik's wound. "How are you doing? How did it happen?"

Sadik lies. He tells Boro he was injured while fleeing from Srebrenica to Tuzla. That was why, he explains, he came back toward Žepa.

"Are you still bleeding?" Boro asks, offering to look at Sadik's wound and change his bandages. He unwraps the wound, cleans it, and places a fresh, clean dressing. Boro sees that the injury isn't serious. Still, he promises to evacuate Sadik by bus with the heavily injured to Sarajevo, even offering to make sure any family members he has can go with him. Sadik has none here. Boro asks if Sadik is in pain and gives him analgesics and a pack of cigarettes. When the buses line up in the late morning, Boro makes sure that Sadik is aboard one of the first to depart. Boro hops on the bus and speaks with the bus driver. Then he guarantees Sadik, once more, that he will make it through the front line.

The two men bid one another farewell. The buses begin to roll around noon.

IN THE MEANTIME, twenty other buses arrive to take non-injured women, children, and elderly civilians from Žepa to Kladanj. A nervous crowd of about 500 people stand around Boro—women, children, and some men he figures, he hopes, are unarmed. Boro is unarmed. He treats the lightly injured who are still here, changing bandages and giving medicines. One of the injured refuses his care. He looks at Boro with hatred, as if he doesn't believe the Serb could be a doctor and thinks his help would be some sort of a trick.

A woman looks toward the river where the Serb soldiers are waiting on the other side and begins to scream hysterically, "The Chetniks are coming!" Her words spark mass panic. Mothers and grandmothers and children start screaming, too.

Boro can't stand to hear the children crying. He grabs someone's plastic water bottle and pours it on the woman who started the hysteria, yelling at her to calm down.

"Don't scare the kids!" he shouts. "The kids don't need this kind of traumatizing. The soldiers won't come into the city. There's no need to be afraid!"

The crowd immediately falls silent. Then it strikes Boro that as an unarmed "enemy" soldier surrounded by 500 Muslims, he probably shouldn't be yelling at anyone.

Soon after, a middle-aged man approaches Boro in tears, explaining that he is a soldier worried about sending away his wife and five daughters.

"Is it true that the women and children being put onto these buses are being taken to Kladanj?" he asks.

"It's true and it's for sure," Boro answers. "It's a fact."

"My wife and five daughters are getting onto one of these buses," the man persists, "and I'm afraid something will happen to them."

"Nothing will happen, it's for sure. There's an agreement and there's no reason for you to be afraid. Everyone will stick to that."

The answer fails to reassure the man. Boro knows why he is afraid. The Muslims are telling wild stories about Serbs raping women and girls. He doesn't believe the rumors and wants to prove to the man that they aren't true.

"I'll go and personally escort the bus where your family is," Boro promises him. "And when I come back I'll bring you the message that they've arrived safely."

"I'd be grateful if you'd do that for me."

The requests for assistance don't end with this man. Žepa's other doctor, a young man about Boro's age, approaches Boro and begs him for help leaving Žepa because the agreement doesn't provide for the transport of a non-injured man like himself. Boro requests approval for the man to be evacuated, based on the concept of medical neutrality—that those serving medical functions in war are neutral noncombatants entitled to protection. His superiors grant it, and in the evening, he takes the doctor on a bus, and also the wife and five daughters of the man who beseeched him, planning to ride with them to the front lines. A Serb commander, surprised to see Boro on the bus, tries to talk him out of the trip. Boro goes anyway.

BORO RETURNS FROM THE JOURNEY to Kladanj at night and looks for the soldier to report that his wife and daughters have made it to safety. He does not find him. Most of Žepa's men of fighting age are melting into the hills.

Boro remains in Žepa for two more days, the only doctor to help with the evacuations and to treat the lightly injured. Almost all of the women, children, elderly, injured, and ill inhabitants of Žepa—about 5,000 in all—are safely evacuated to the main body of Bosnian government—held territory. When the evacuations are complete, the Muslim soldiers fail to keep their end of the bargain by surrendering, en masse, to the Serbs. Having regrouped in the hills, they skirmish with the Bosnian Serb army. Boro moves back into the field, but after just a few days, most of the Muslims exfiltrate themselves from the enclave and across the border into Serbia, where they give themselves up. They are imprisoned, but most are not killed.

Boro receives a military promotion to lieutenant. At the beginning of August 1995, he finally makes it home, where he has not been since the night after the capture of Srebrenica. It was his longest separation from his family in the entire war. He hugs his little girl and kisses his baby. He asks his wife to make some coffee and they sit and talk long into the night, remembering old times. He tells her nothing of what happened these past three weeks. It is his last field mission of the Bosnian war.

EPILOGUE

What though the radiance which was once so bright

Be now for ever taken from my sight,

Though nothing can bring back the hour

Of splendour in the grass, of glory in the flower;

We will grieve not, rather find

Strength in what remains behind;

In the primal sympathy

Which having been must ever be;

In the soothing thoughts that spring

Out of human suffering;

In the faith that looks through death,

In years that bring the philosophic mind.

—**William Wordsworth** (1770–1850)
Ode, Intimations of Immortality
from Recollections of Early Childhood

May justice be done lest the world perish.

—**Hegel**

THROUGHOUT JULY, the women of Srebrenica waited, mostly in vain, for their men to emerge from the woods or be released from Serb detention. Every now and then a man would struggle into Tuzla from the mountains to the east, appearing disheveled and emaciated and bearing a story that began with his surrender in the woods or his separation from the women and children in Potočari, and ended with his unlikely survival by jumping out of a moving truck or falling under the bodies of his friends, brothers, or neighbors during a mass execution that took place in a factory building or a house or a field. It became clear that thousands were missing.

The tide began to turn against the Serbs. The first week of August 1995, the Croatian Army launched Operation Storm, an offensive on the Serb forces controlling a third of Croatia. Over the next days, the Croatians swept eastward toward Bosnia, capturing all the land the Serbs had held. Thousands of Serb civilians fled the advance, and some of those who remained were killed.

The last week of August, the Bosnian Serb army sent another mortar bomb crashing into a Sarajevo marketplace and attacked the safe area Goražde. This time the international community responded, under the belated leadership of the United States whose president, Clinton, was under extraordinary pressure from the public, Congress, and his political rival in the upcoming presidential election, Senator Bob Dole. More than eighty peacekeepers were secretly removed from Goražde and NATO's Operation Deliberate Force was launched. Within a matter of days, the air attack, the largest in NATO history to that point, destroyed bridges, communications equipment, anti-aircraft systems, and other strategic targets of the supposedly invincible Bosnian Serb military, including the barracks at Lukavica, which Eric Dachy had seen the United Nations sharing with Serb forces in the war's early days. After two weeks, the Serb military finally pulled its heavy weapons back from around Sarajevo, and NATO ended the campaign. Meanwhile, though, the Croatian army had joined forces with the Bosnian army and moved into Bosnia from the northwest. By the time that international leaders, citing the growing numbers of Serb civilians fleeing the ground advance, pressured the Croatians and Bosnians into halting their offensive, Serb forces' control of Bosnian territory had dropped from 70 percent to 50 percent. All sides agreed to a ceasefire, then peace negotiations in Dayton, Ohio. On December 14, 1995, in Paris, with a flourish of pens and staged handshakes for the cameras, the war was declared officially over. On paper, at least, Bosnia remained a unitary state with all of its citizens enjoying freedom of movement and the right of return to their pre-war homes, but the state comprised two constituent parts, the so-called Muslim-Croat Federation and *Republika Srpska,* the Serb Republic. Many Bosnia analysts and even Richard Holbrooke, the top U.S. Dayton negotiator, believed that recognizing *Republika Srpska* inappropriately rewarded the atrocity-filled war strategies that were used to create it. The final agreement had something each side had wanted all along—the Bosnians had their unified state; the nationalist Serbs had their separate entity. All had what they wanted and none had what they wanted. And meanwhile hundreds of thousands of people had died.

When the map was drawn, as Srebrenicans had feared, Srebrenica and Žepa were left to the Serbs.

THE WOMEN AND CHILDREN AND ELDERLY of the Drina Valley remained huddled in displaced persons tents on the Tuzla airbase, still waiting for their husbands and fathers and sons, the ones whom Christina had seen being separated into columns by Serb soldiers and the ones who'd fallen behind Ilijaz's group in the hills and given themselves up, surrendering to the Serbs. Where were these thousands of missing? The International Committee of the Red Cross demanded the right to visit them. Serb authorities did not reply. The United States dispatched Assistant Secretary of State John Shattuck to Bosnia to speak with refugees. Stories of massacres convinced the C.I.A. to review satellite photographs of the areas where mass killings were rumored to have occurred. The U.S. ambassador to the United Nations, Madeleine Albright, showed these satellite photographs at a closed session of the U.N. Security Council on August 10, 1995, a month after Srebrenica fell. They revealed large land disturbances in areas where Dutch soldiers had seen prisoners being held: evidence of mass graves.

With a faxed copy of one of the photographs in hand, David Rohde, an intrepid American reporter for the *Christian Science Monitor,* slipped into a Serb-held field in eastern Bosnia where a survivor had alleged that a massacre took place. Rohde saw bones protruding from the ground and found the personal effects of several men. Noticed by a shepherd, arrested, and threatened with death, Rohde was released after ten days of high-level pressure. His findings were published and his work led to forensic, journalistic, and legal investigations to determine what had happened to Srebrenica's missing.

Estimates of the missing range from 7,500 to 10,000. Although many bodies were dug up and reburied in October 1995, presumably by Serb military attempting to hide evidence, more than 7,500 body bags of commingled remains had been exhumed from mass graves by May 2003. By the same month, 2,600 unique DNA profiles, each representing one individual, had been obtained using DNA analysis techniques introduced a year-and-a-half previously, and the family members of 1,355 of those missing individuals had been matched with loved ones and informed, after years of uncertainty, of their deaths. On March 31, 2003, 600 Srebrenicans were reburied by family members at a ceremony in Potočari.

Forensic studies have demonstrated that the majority of the dead were massacred, not killed in combat. These studies, combined with the testimony of survivors and participants in the events, have revealed a story of organized massacres at farms and abandoned factory buildings, where unarmed captives, blindfolded, hands tied behind their backs, were shot with automatic weapons or killed by hand grenades, and then buried in mass graves. Torture preceded some of the killings. Most of the victims were men and boys; a few were women.

On the basis of this evidence, the leaders of the army corps in which Dr. Boro Lazić served are accused of having engaged in widespread and organized killings and mass executions of thousands of people fleeing Srebrenica between July 11 and 18. They are accused by the International Criminal Tribunal for the former Yugoslavia of having committed the most heinous crime against humanity—genocide, the intent to destroy, in whole or in part, a national, ethnic or religious group.

In 1999, the successor to Boutros Boutros-Ghali as U.N. Secretary-General, Kofi Annan, who had been undersecretary for peacekeeping affairs at the time of Srebrenica's fall, delivered a report on the United Nations' role in the fall of Srebrenica:

> Srebrenica crystallized a truth understood only too late by the United Nations and the world at large: that Bosnia was as much a moral cause as a military conflict. The tragedy of Srebrenica will haunt our history forever.
> . . . the provision of humanitarian assistance could never have been a

solution to the problem in that country. The problem, which cried out for a political/military solution, was that a Member State of the United Nations, left largely defenceless as a result of an arms embargo imposed upon it *by the United Nations*, was being dismembered by forces committed to its destruction. This was not a problem with a humanitarian solution.

It was what Eric Dachy had believed all along.

WHO BEARS THE BLAME FOR THE TRAGEDY OF SREBRENICA? Clearly, it lies principally with the individuals who committed the massacres or had command responsibility over them. In August 2001, the International Criminal Tribunal for the Former Yugoslavia found General Radislav Krstić, deputy commander of the Drina Corps of the Bosnian Serb Army, guilty of the crime of genocide in Srebrenica. As of May 2003, the tribunal had indicted thirteen of Mladić's soldiers for crimes against humanity committed exclusively in Srebrenica in 1995, and one civilian authority for crimes committed in the area in 1992. More than seven years after the end of the war, fewer than half of these men had appeared before the tribunal, a result of the unwillingness of Bosnian Serb and Serbian authorities to turn over many of the suspects sheltered in their territories. The Bosnian Serbs' military leader, General Ratko Mladić, and civilian president, Dr. Radovan Karadžić (the first physician to be indicted for war crimes since the 1946 Nuremberg Doctors' Trial), as well as Boro Lazić's hated commander, tall, redheaded Vinko Pandurević (the same officer who delayed Eric Dachy's aid deliveries to Srebrenica, watching aid workers buzz around him as if they were flies hitting glass walls), remained at large. Mladić was sighted from time to time dining comfortably in Belgrade, reportedly under the protection of Yugoslav army forces. The governments contributing to Bosnia's international stabilization force, including the United States, have been reluctant to put their troops at risk by arresting indicted war criminals as they are authorized, and in fact in certain circumstances required, to do by the 1995 Dayton Peace Accords.

Serbia's governmental corruption and international isolation spurred a popular movement to vote out Serbian President Slobodan Milošević and then, when he refused to leave office, to depose him. Under international pressure, his replacements handed him over to the tribunal, where he faces, among other charges, the charge of genocide for his command responsibility in Srebrenica. At last, Ilijaz and the other villagers from Gladovići —who watched bombers fly and tanks fire at them from Serbia long after Milošević insisted his troops were no longer involved in the Bosnian war—may be vindicated in court.

However, many Bosnian Serbs, including those involved in the attack on Srebrenica—Dr. Boro Lazić among them—still refuse to accept that a massacre of more than 7,000 Srebrenica residents actually took place. In September 2002, just before Bosnian elections that threatened Serb nationalists' hold on power, the *Republika Srpska* government bureau responsible for relations with the International Criminal Tribunal released a report arguing that the only deaths in Srebrenica were those of 2,000 Muslim soldiers who were killed, or killed one another, while fighting their way out of the enclave. The absolute preponderance of evidence, both forensic and testimonial, of mass killings of civilians and surrendered soldiers renders such statements as ridiculous as the claims of Holocaust deniers. And yet a large proportion of Bosnian Serbs and their political leaders—perhaps unwilling to believe their own people were capable of committing such crimes—appear to accept this revisionist history. This radical vision of "historical truth" may prepare the ground for future conflict, just as manipulation of history cultivated the previous war.

Some Bosnian Serbs also assert that any executions that may have been committed by Mladić's forces at Srebrenica were acts of vengeance, understandable responses to atrocities committed by Naser Orić, his troops, and the Srebrenica *hapsi* in the course of military actions undertaken by the Muslims in the early part of the war. The Orthodox Christmas attack on Kravica, described in this book, is cited as one example. On April 10, 2003, Naser Orić was arrested by NATO-led forces and brought before the International Criminal Tribunal in the Hague where he faced charges of having violated the laws or customs of war through acts committed by forces and individuals under his control. These included murder and cruel treatment of several Serb detainees, and wanton destruction and plunder of at least fifty villages and hamlets, including Bjelovac, Kravica and Jezestica, between June 1992 and March 1993.

While some Srebrenicans almost certainly committed atrocities against Serbs in 1992 and early 1993, there exists no earthly excuse for the genocide Mladić's forces committed against thousands of Srebrenica's

Muslims two years later. The victims of Europe's worst massacre in fifty years cannot justly be blamed for the crime committed against them. Many of the soldiers who participated in the killings, including Drazen Erdemović, a Bosnian Croat conscript in the Bosnian Serb army who turned himself in to the tribunal and admitted his role in shooting hundreds of unarmed prisoners, had nothing to do with eastern Bosnia, and no family members or friends killed there. In any case, nothing, not even vengeance, justifies genocide.

Although Bosnian Serb forces are responsible for committing genocide, others bear responsibility for having failed to prevent it. The United States, Great Britain, and France among others, had ratified the 1948 Convention on the Prevention and Punishment of Genocide. The leaders of these countries certainly had the power to prevent genocide in Srebrenica. They failed. As the events in this book showed, for three years they lacked the will.

In November 2002, lawyers representing survivors of Srebrenica filed a case in Dutch court seeking damages from the United Nations and the Dutch government. Similar suits may follow in other countries. Perhaps fearing such liability, most countries involved in the Balkans have failed to investigate the role of their governments in Srebrenica's fall, in spite of the fact that U.N. Secretary-General Kofi Annan requested they do so in his 1999 U.N. report on Srebrenica. Stressing that U.N. member states, by imposing an arms embargo on Bosnia-Herzegovina, had assumed the duty to protect it, he called on members of the Contact Group (the United States, Britain, France, Germany, and the Russian Federation), the Security Council, and "other Governments which contributed to the delay in the use of force" to accept their share of responsibility for allowing the tragedy to occur. A key question left unanswered in the U.N. report, because of the unwillingness of member states, including the United States, to turn over intelligence reports, is whether any states had prior knowledge of the Serb attack on Srebrenica and the massacre that followed.

Thus far, only France and the Netherlands have heeded Annan's call and convened public parliamentary inquiries to investigate their roles in and responsibilities for the fall of Srebrenica. The French inquiry came at the persistent instigation of none other than the French section of Doctors Without Borders, several of whose local staff members were executed in Srebrenica. MSF demanded that the government establish political and military responsibility for the events and "determine how far France's political and military authorities were responsible for the paralysis of the United Nations and NATO in the face of the Bosnian Serb attack on Srebrenica." MSF challenged the government to investigate rumors that it had interfered from outside the U.N. chain of command to prevent the launching of air strikes during the Serb offensive on Srebrenica and that it had concluded an agreement with Serbs to release 300 peacekeeping forces taken hostage in May 1995, in exchange for a guarantee not to launch future air strikes.

The French inquiry failed to answer MSF's questions. It acknowledged that France deserved a share of the blame, but diluted that share by fingering other blameworthy parties. It accused the United States for having failed to engage meaningfully in the Balkans, Dutch UNPROFOR soldiers for failing to fight back against the Serb attack on Srebrenica, and even the Bosnian government for having accepted the seizure of Srebrenica as a fait accompli. However, the French parliamentarians concluded definitively that Srebrenica could have been saved with massive air strikes along the southern road and criticized themselves, along with the United Kingdom, the United States, and the Bosnian government, for the "lack of political will to intervene in Srebrenica." Finally, the report showed that the French government had at last recognized, just as the United Nations did, but much too late, that the very approach of the international community to the war in Bosnia was faulty. Asking the United Nations "to maintain a non-existent peace [in Bosnia] using strictly humanitarian logic" rather than "opposing one of the parties or stopping the conflict" was what led, inexorably, to the genocide.

The Dutch government has made three notable attempts at soul-searching. In 1999, it published a debriefing report of its U.N. peacekeeping troops deployed in Srebrenica. Then, in April 2002, the government-appointed Netherlands Institute for War Documentation (NIOD) released the results of an extensive inquiry into Srebrenica. The NIOD's 7,600-page report laid part of the blame for the fall of Srebrenica at the feet of the Dutch government. Days later, the government resigned in recognition of its political responsibility for the failure to protect the Srebrenica population and prevent the massacre. Srebrenica survivors, viewing the resignation as a token gesture, demanded a more specific assignment of responsibility and guilt among Dutch soldiers and officials. A leader of the Association of Victims' Families demanded to know why

Dutchbat members, having observed men and boys being separated and killed, nonetheless handed the last men sheltering inside the U.N. base to the Serbs rather than protecting them.

Subsequently, in January 2003, the Dutch government released the results of a parliamentary inquiry into its own actions before, during, and after the fall of Srebrenica. It concluded that the attack on Srebrenica met all conditions for the use of air support and blamed U.N. Force Commander General Bernard Janvier for delaying its implementation. Further, it suggested that better protection could have been offered to Srebrenica men after the town fell, but concluded that Dutchbat was not in a position to "conclusively prevent the evacuation" carried out by Serb forces.

Dutch officers argued that the responsibility for preventing the massacre lay with NATO. "The air strikes should have been massive, without regard for possible victims in the Dutch battalion or civilians," former Dutch Commander Ton Karremans testified before the inquiry committee on November 19, 2002. "Then we could have turned the tables. Those chances were just thrown away."

And what of NATO's powerhouse, the United States? There has been shockingly little public examination of the responsibility of the 1990s' sole superpower for the genocide committed in Srebrenica. As detailed in this book, the United States abdicated primary responsibility for dealing with the war in Bosnia to Europe until after the fall of Srebrenica. Still, the U.S. government kept close tabs on the war. I reviewed thousands of pages of internal communications about Srebrenica released by the U.S. Departments of State and Defense, the CIA, and the National Security Agency in response to Freedom of Information Act requests. These reveal that the U.S. government had vast knowledge of the atrocities taking place in Bosnia since 1992.

As just one example, in January 1993, a secret State Department report reviewing such atrocities concluded, "An extensive review of embassy cables and intelligence reports . . . strongly suggests that the magnitude and egregiousness of atrocities committed by Serbs in Bosnia amount to a program of attempted genocide." In spite of the qualification of genocide with the word "attempted," this suggests that U.S. officials could easily predict the intentions of General Mladić's military forces upon capturing Srebrenica. They would attempt genocide. I interviewed army intelligence officer Lt. Col. Rex Dudley (now retired, then major), who traveled to Srebrenica in April 1993. He says he warned high-ranking individuals upon his return from Srebrenica that a Serb takeover of the town would result in genocide.

The fact that the United States, knowing the pattern of Serb atrocities, failed to intervene during the five-day attack on the safe area arguably puts the United States in violation of its Genocide Convention commitment to prevent genocide.

When it comes to the events of July 1995, in and around Srebrenica, what exactly did the United States know and when? The exhaustive Netherlands Institute of War Documentation investigation revealed several points. U.S. officials received daily confidential briefings from Dutch governmental officials whose troops were inside of Srebrenica. The chairman of the American Joint Chiefs of Staff, General John Shalikashvili, was briefed by the Supreme Allied Commander Europe, General George Joulwan. Two days before Srebrenica's fall, Bosnian President Alija Izetbegović appealed to President Clinton, among other leaders, to use his influence to prevent the genocide of Srebrenica's citizens.

The United States also had surveillance drones and observation satellites focused on eastern Bosnia, as the release of several before and after satellite photographs of mass graves reveals. Soon after the massacre, a diverse coalition of activist groups, prominent citizens, and congressional representatives applied for the release of other surveillance photographs and reports under the U.S. Freedom of Information Act, with the aim of ascertaining whether the United States had information about the massacres during the several-day period they were being committed.

The Department of Defense, CIA, and State Department, citing concerns about national security and the divulgement of sources and intelligence-gathering techniques, refused to provide the specific information sought. The group filed a lawsuit for release of the information, "Students Against Genocide et al. vs. State Department," but was denied in District Court and on appeal. The question of how much the United States knew and when remains unanswered. Many of the groups that initiated the lawsuit, including the named plaintiff, the group I led as a medical student, are now defunct. It remains for others to renew the campaign for release of this information, as well as the results of an investigation, rumored to have been conducted by the United States, of the use of chemical weapons in the attack on Srebrenica. On January 31, 2003, Doctors

Without Borders called upon the United States and Great Britain to heed the U.N.'s request and conduct public investigations into the fall of Srebrenica.

FINALLY, WHAT TO MAKE OF THE ROLE of the individual humanitarians and doctors in this story? Without in any way minimizing the major issue, genocide, and the blame belonging to those who committed the massacre, I would like to examine a few other moral questions related to aid and medical assistance.

Many MSF staff members involved with Srebrenica believe that international political leaders used them and their work as a cover for states' unwillingness to intervene decisively to end the war. Some feel that they themselves bear part of the responsibility for the deaths that occurred as an unintended consequence of their work. The question is, what can humanitarians possibly do to prevent being used this way in the future?

One idea is that aid workers should refuse to participate in missions that lend populations a false sense of security. In August 2000, MSF pulled its medical teams out of parts of Kosovo. The statement announcing the pull-out reads as if it could have been written about Srebrenica seven years earlier:

"MSF questions the appropriateness of humanitarian medical and psychological assistance when, in the presence of internationally mandated protection forces, the fundamental rights of people are being denied."

Not surprisingly, Dr. Eric Dachy helped draft the statement.

But would Srebrenicans have been better off had MSF launched a major publicity campaign to get them out of the jail-like enclave before it fell, and in so doing risked losing MSF's permission from Serb authorities to work there? Eric Dachy thinks so now. While some staff members rang alarm bells within MSF about the situation in Srebrenica in 1994 and 1995, overall MSF was lulled over months and years of routine into accepting Srebrenica as a normal work place. Eric regrets having dismissed the U.N. refugee agency's idea of evacuating Srebrenica in 1993. At the time, it was an odious idea to assist the Serb military in "ethnic cleansing," but it would have been the lesser of two evils (although it must be pointed out that it is very far from sure that Serb forces would have permitted Srebrenica's menfolk to be evacuated even in 1993). In retrospect, Eric compares Srebrenica to a dying patient who MSF, along with General Morillon and others, put on artificial life support.

"I think we made a strategic mistake," says Eric. "If people wanted to leave they should have been given a chance to leave."

On another topic, many of the doctors involved in these events found they could not remain neutral in the face of atrocities. The revered principle of medical neutrality, a construct drawing on international humanitarian and human rights law, in combination with medical ethics, begs wider examination. Whenever doctors shot guns or engaged in military planning, they effectively forfeited their special protected status under international law. (Doctors are allowed to carry guns in wartime, but only for their personal protection—medical neutrality simply requires they treat any patient who needs their care, without regard to factors besides medical need, and that they don't participate in the fighting.) Certain humanitarian groups, traditionally bound by the related principle of humanitarian neutrality (which includes the demand that they not ally themselves with one or another side in a conflict), seemingly renounced their neutrality when they called publicly for military action against forces violating international humanitarian and human rights law. A notable example was MSF President Rony Brauman's call for military intervention in Bosnia in 1992.

I would argue that there is nothing inherently unethical about doctors engaging in or calling for military activity against forces committing atrocities. In fact, quite the opposite. This is not about taking sides in a territorial conflict—it is about taking the side of the almost universally recognized humanitarian and human rights principles. Neutrality in the face of genocide amounts to complicity.

There are times when the higher moral duty to oppose attacks on civilians should outrank the doctor's loyalty to medical principles or the aid worker's loyalty to humanitarian principles. Of course, because doctors have no particular expertise in military matters, diplomacy, or conflict resolution, there is a limit to how far to go with this. But military intervention or advocating military intervention must remain an option for those who would act to prevent crimes against humanity. This remains a highly controversial topic in medical circles.

On a related note, even strict adherence to the concept of humanitarian neutrality should not prevent international aid workers from assisting wounded combatants who are, by definition, hors de combat. So many aid groups, MSF included (as described in this book), shy from such activity, demanding that soldiers be kept out of the hospitals where the aid groups operate and focusing their efforts instead on the civilian victims of war. I have witnessed this on the ground in all of the war-torn regions I have visited—aid workers don't want to touch soldiers. However, refusing to treat soldiers who have no other medical options is a breach of a fundamental medical tenet: Physicians must provide emergency care unless assured that others are willing and able to give such care (incidentally, by the same principle, Dutch military doctors were wrong to deny emergency care to Srebrenica civilians in July 1995, based on their military order to keep an "iron ration" for themselves; and any medical workers who went on strike, left, or otherwise refused to treat patients from Srebrenica could rightly do so only to the extent that there was someone else available to treat patients or—I would argue— in cases where their own safety would have been put at grave risk for doing so). It should not be forgotten that the Red Cross itself, the bastion of humanitarian neutrality, had its genesis with the wounded soldiers on the battlefields of Solferino.

On the other side, what is it worth to maintain one's neutrality these days? Taking the example of Srebrenica, combatants, particularly Bosnian Serb forces (who fired on Srebrenica Hospital and the grounds of the 1993 medical evacuation, detained and killed patients and medical workers, and repeatedly denied access to humanitarian assistance) but also Srebrenica's soldiers (who killed a Serb nurse in the war's early days) and the Bosnian government (which included military supplies on helicopters bound for Srebrenica that were marked with a red cross—thus abrogating their neutral status and making them legitimate military targets) failed from the very beginning of the war to respect the neutrality and protected status of medical workers and medical objects.

This begs another question: How can doctors and humanitarians who *are* observing medical neutrality and humanitarian impartiality assure their own protection? From the first MSF workers to be injured in Vukovar, experiences in the former Yugoslavia throughout the 1990s have left many aid workers questioning how to go about assuring their own safety when respect of the Geneva Conventions can no longer be counted upon for their protection. Many humanitarians were and are unwilling to accept armed protection from militaries: Independence from military authorities is a fundamental concept of humanitarian work, and one over which MSF in Srebrenica was even willing to go on strike.

In the case of Bosnia, however, humanitarians, including Eric Dachy, wouldn't have been able to function in places like Srebrenica without at times accepting military escorts. It was simply the only way for him to get access to the people who needed him and to perform his humanitarian work. The humanitarian-military cooperation and military involvement in humanitarian assistance that Eric and other aid workers first witnessed in northern Iraq in 1991 has only expanded since Bosnia; there are many examples, including Kosovo in 1999 and, in the post-9/11 world, Afghanistan. In the latter, it was feared that a blurring of the distinction between military and humanitarian actors was leading to the targeting of neutral aid workers. In the spring of 2003, the controversy reached its highest pitch in Iraq. Aid groups split over whether and how much to cooperate with coalition (U.S., Great Britain, Australia) military to gain access to populations in a highly insecure environment; whether to "boycott" a major funding source—the U.S. government—if the U.S. Department of Defense, rather than the U.S. State Department, maintained control of relief efforts; and whether to work at all in post-war Iraq, given the capability and legal responsibility of the "occupying powers" to assure adequate health service delivery.

In theory, traditional humanitarianism requires independence from governments and militaries (impartiality—providing aid based on need alone—is the fundamental precept of humanitarians, and adherence to the principles of independence and neutrality help to ensure it); in reality, most NGOs require government funding (inevitably meted out according to political priorities) to function and military intervention or protection to reach certain target populations. The humanitarian community, with its "classicist" versus its "political humanitarians," still struggles with these contradictions. A search for other options is under way, from private funding of NGOs and the U.N.'s Central Emergency Trust Fund to the European Rapid Reaction Force and the creation of a capable U.N. intervention force. For now, the coexistence of orthodoxy and pragmatic reform related to humanitarian independence, neutrality, and speaking out about human rights violations allows some humanitarian organizations to operate more effectively in some situations, and others in other situations. The fact that the international order and the nature of conflicts have continued to change in the years since Srebrenica fell, with no let up in human suffering, shows that humanitarians must remain flexible and open to constant reexamination of their work in order to remain effective.

Finally, the shining example of a doctor who observed medical neutrality in this book was Boro Lazić, who repeatedly demonstrated his willingness to treat all who requested his assistance, regardless of their ethnicity, and never took part in the fighting. How ironic that he ended up serving the forces that committed the greatest act of genocide on European soil in fifty years.

There is a burgeoning idea among medical leaders and ethicists, such as the renowned Arthur Caplan of the University of Pennsylvania, that "medical neutrality is not enough." It is a doctor's special duty, as someone dedicated to healing and the preservation of health, to protest atrocities. By this principle, it would have been incumbent upon all of the doctors in this story to speak out and try to stop human rights violations being conducted by the military forces with whom they had contact. Of course, this would not have been an easy task. In the case of the Bosnian doctors—both Serb and Muslim—it could have put them in significant danger. So, too, with the Doctors Without Borders internationals, who had to balance condemning those authorities who violated human rights (like Radovan Karadžić) and working with them to gain access to people in need.

That tension—between carrying out their duties as doctors and humanitarians and ensuring their own safety and survival—was one that every health professional in this book was forced to face. Each of them, as a result of their individual personalities and belief systems, made different decisions about how to react to the war zone, when to practice medicine, when to refuse to do so, when to speak out about moral issues, when to keep silent, when to participate in military actions, when to enter dangerous areas, and when to leave their patients behind. A great deal can be learned from the dignity and humanity every one of them showed in the outrageous situations in which they found themselves.

It is my great, albeit unrealistic, hope that no doctors or nurses will ever again have to face such decisions.

———

YOU MAY BE INTERESTED in knowing the fates of the main characters and their reflections on the events described in this book.

—Dr. Boro Lazić opened his own psychiatry clinic in Belgrade, Serbia, the Special Hospital for Addiction Medicine, in March 2003. After returning home from the offensives on Srebrenica and Žepa, he tuned into Bosnian television and saw a hospital bedside interview with Sadik Ahmetović, learning that the medical technician he helped save was indeed alive. (Sadik later went on to become vice president of the Srebrenica municipal assembly in the Serb Republic, elected because thousands of displaced Srebrenicans voted for government representatives in absentia.) War followed Boro and Boro followed war. After the peace settlement in Bosnia, his sense of adventure and desire to earn money led him to enlist as a mercenary with Mobutu Sese Seko's troops in Zaire. Seko's regime was overthrown and Zaire became Congo. Boro returned to Bosnia, gave up on the idea of training in surgery, and moved to Belgrade, Serbia, to do a residency in psychiatry. There, he found himself caught in yet another war, NATO's 1999 bombing of Serbia over Kosovo. He is hopeful that his war days are over.

Boro has visited Dr. Nedret Mujkanović several times in Tuzla, where they attended medical school together. The doctors of Srebrenica Hospital maintain the highest regard for Boro and what he did for them.

Boro looks back on his war years as a "painful, dirty, torturous" experience, and he considers himself one of the many "ordinary, little people" who suffered in a war led by politicians and soldiers. However, he remains proud of having helped others and carries with him one enduring lesson: "Good should be done regardless of the difficulty of the times and regardless of the level of power or importance that one possesses."

—Dr. Nedret Mujkanović won the Golden Lily, the highest medal of the Bosnian army, for his year of volunteer service in Srebrenica. After his whirlwind trip to Croatia and France with Bianca Jagger, he returned to Bosnia and completed training in plastic surgery, finding himself much more capable of handling difficult moments in the operating theater than his colleague trainees who hadn't worked in Srebrenica. In July 1995, he stood at the edge of the battlefield and watched as the surviving Srebrenicans broke through the front line and entered free territory near Tuzla. In 1999, he returned for the first time to the abandoned hospital in the Serb-held town of Srebrenica with the author, posing as her driver. The Serb doctors leading a tour of the empty hospital must have thought it strange that this "driver" asked to take a copy of a medical book, *Sudski Medicine*, that he found lying on a chair on the second floor. It had been his book in Srebrenica.

For several years, Nedret served as minister of health of the Tuzla Canton. He often intervened to assist friends from Srebrenica. They speak of him fondly as their champion.

—**Dr. Ejub Alić** works as an internist in a town called Srebrenik outside of the city of Tuzla. Every afternoon he returns home to the top floor of a split-level house (built after the war with monetary assistance from the guilt-stricken Dutch government) and to his bright son, Denis, and his beloved wife, Mubina. They sat, arm in arm, throughout the hours-long interviews for this book. In the fall of 2001, Ejub returned to Srebrenica as a physician, volunteering once a week to staff a clinic where both Serbs and the small but growing number of returning Muslims seek care.

—**Dr. Eric Dachy** learned of Srebrenica's fall one morning in July 1995, when reading the French newspaper *Liberation*.

"It really slashed me," he recalls. "I thought: Shit, Ilijaz and the others, they might be dead. Suddenly I realized all we did during these two years not only was canceled, but maybe made it worse! And that the evil forces that were working there had not been stopped at all. Never. They simply went to the end of what they intended to do. And no one ever changed, no one ever helped anybody. And then of course my philosophy became questions, and I realized that to help did not work. Not in such circumstances. There is no justice without power and humanitarian compassion is not power." He sat and thought a long time of Ilijaz and the others and wondered if they would survive.

Srebrenica's fall cast Eric's entire personal philosophy into doubt. As part of his subsequent soul-searching, he began writing a memoir of his time in the former Yugoslavia, and he concluded an early draft with this reflection:

Injustice, which I loath so strongly, which I fight against, is in fact a part of reality. My rebellion was vain because, in a way, I wanted to eradicate the evil. I must tell this story, but not cast blame or foment fear. I no longer want to strike others with the weight of the world's suffering. As for the violence and evil that I brushed up against, I no longer want to oppose such things with anger, but rather with intelligence.

... My destiny has returned to its own place, at home, with a broader vision of my past. ... In this rediscovered peace, liberated from any mad idealism as well as of any bitter resignation, I view the world differently. A game of good and evil. Everyone chooses a side. With more or less determination. The future is open and belongs to us.

Less idealistic, perhaps, but still passionate, Eric overcame his disillusionment and returned to aid work. He went on to serve as a research director for MSF's headquarters in Brussels, Belgium. Several years ago, he fell in love with the smart, beautiful banker who handled his finances. The couple now has a son. Eric has a motorbike now, too, and when he takes it out for a ride he throws on his black leather jacket from Belgrade, sturdy as ever.

—Months after the fall of Srebrenica, Eric Dachy reached out to nurse **Christina Schmitz,** who he felt completed the job he started in Srebrenica. The two became close friends.

Christina and her colleague Dr. Daniel O'Brien testified about Srebrenica at a French parliamentary hearing and provided written testimony to the International Criminal Tribunal. Christina is glad that she was there to witness the events and testify about them; she believes MSF made a difference. She also struggles to come to terms with what she experienced.

It has been until today incredibly difficult to cope with the memory, to cope with what happened. But ... I believe we have to continue to fight, to speak, to argue, to talk on behalf of people in danger.

Srebrenica has only strengthened my resolve and my motivation to stay with this organization," she said in an interview several months after Srebrenica fell. "It may sound strange, but I wouldn't have wanted to miss the experience of Srebrenica, however sad it was. I still fully embrace MSF's approach: to go to or stay in places where others leave.

Christina has kept in touch with Srebrenicans, including Ilijaz. She and Daniel are considered heroes by many Srebrenicans. One of the male staff members whose life Christina helped save said of her: "She fought for us like a lion."

—**Dr. Fatima Klempić-Dautbašić** completed her training after the war and is now an obstetrician/gynecologist in Tuzla. In the days and weeks after Srebrenica's fall, she and Ilijaz, hand in hand and looking tired and worn, testified before numerous television cameras and investigators about the events of the fall of Srebrenica. Several months later, the two parted ways for a final time.

Fatima feels that the war, which took so much away from so many, gave her several things. For one, the suffering she witnessed instilled in her an empathy for people's pain that has made her a better doctor. Working without diagnostic equipment also honed her medical intuition, and that also serves her patients well. But for Fatima, the primary lesson is that life's most important gifts are family and friends.

Fatima married Smail Klempić, the gentle lawyer she'd first noticed at Srebrenica Hospital caring for his injured brother. She calls Smail her "smile." They have two young children, a boy and a girl.

—The love for surgery that **Dr. Ilijaz Pilav** discovered in Srebrenica led him to undertake years of formal training, which he successfully completed in 2001. In the meantime, he fell in love with and married a woman from Sarajevo. They have two young children. Ilijaz helped found a humanitarian organization, "Drina," which provides computer training and English language courses for Srebrenica survivors. As for Ilijaz's patients: The drummer whose arm he helped amputate in 1992 disappeared after helping drive Srebrenica's patients to safety on July 11, 1995. The patient he miraculously saved after the helicopter crash by performing a brain craniotomy recovered well from his injury. When Srebrenica fell, he took to the woods and is credited with saving the lives of several dozen men. The school teacher whose surgery brought Ilijaz to the point of fainting on July 7, 1995, survived the fall of Srebrenica. Ilijaz's protective older brother, Hamid, who went to Potočari with his family, never arrived in Tuzla.

In spite of the highest recommendations from his professors and the glowing reports of nearly a dozen international surgeons with whom he worked in Srebrenica, Ilijaz has been unable to secure a job as a surgeon in Bosnia. He has slipped into increasing depression over his, his family's, and his country's uncertain future. Often at night, he is started awake by nightmares of the minefield and its victims who begged for help.

"The war ended a long time ago," he wrote in a letter to me in November 2002, "but I still carry it in me; I live with all the consequences it brought and I live through it again and again. The war ended, but time hasn't made the pain go away; it hasn't even lessened it. The war is over but its effects live on, persisting and accumulating and growing ever stronger."

NOTES

This narrative account was reconstructed from hundreds of hours of interviews with doctors, nurses, patients, and others involved in the events, and informed by visits to the region and the use of existing videotapes, photographs, hospital records, and diaries as well as books, maps, temperature records, testimony at war crimes trials, and documents produced by militaries, humanitarian agencies, governments, and other sources listed below. Believing that work labeled nonfiction should not knowingly incorporate fiction, even to fill in details that are hard to find, I tried hard to ensure that what is printed on these pages is true. "Truth" is a charged word in any war, especially in a place like the Balkans, and people's memories aren't always accurate and don't always dovetail with those of others. When significant differences arose that could not be clarified using existing records, I tried to indicate the discrepancies in the text or in the endnotes that follow.

I wish to explain my choice to use two techniques somewhat less typical for the written genre known as narrative nonfiction. First, the use of present tense to relate events from the summer of 1992 forward: Some of the main characters spoke in the present tense when deeply immersed in telling their stories. Replicating this in the book, while trying to provide only information that was available to the characters at the times being depicted, seemed like natural ways to convey the progress of the story and an appreciation of the difficult-to-imagine situations confronting the main characters.

Secondly, inclusion of characters' thoughts and feelings, which are nearly impossible to document: Psychologists have shown that people are often poor at divining what motivations underlie their actions. On the other hand, to not include what interviewees said was going on in their minds at the time of the events would have been to leave out valuable insight into their personalities. When thoughts or feelings were attributed to a character, that person either shared them with me in a plausible way, recorded them close to the time of the events, or expressed them to someone else, whom I then interviewed. Their presentation in italics or paraphrase, rather than in quotation marks, was meant to reflect their unsubstantiated nature.

Any errors that have wormed their way into this book are mine alone. None of those acknowledged here are responsible.

SOURCES

CHAPTER I: FIRST DO NO HARM

Interviews
Dr. Ejub Alić, Dr. Eric Dachy, Dr. Avdo Hasanović, Dr. Fatima Klempić-Dautbašić, Hakija Meholjić, Dr. Nedret Mujkanović, Dr. Ilijaz Pilav

Published Literature
Bellamy, Ronald, and Zajtchuk, Russ (eds.) *Conventional Warfare: Ballistic, Blast and Burn Injuries* (used throughout this book as reference); *Bosnia Country Handbook*, p. 10–3; *Columbia Encyclopedia*, Sixth Edition, 2002, Columbia University Press. As cited in http://www.bartleby.com/people/Lister-J.html, accessed 12/1/02; Coupland, *Amputation for War Wounds*, pp. 1–26; *Emergency War Surgery*, pp. 5, 273–279; Hoffer, *The True Believer*, p. 11; Médecins sans Frontières, *Techniques Chirurgicales de Base*, pp. 115–140; Naythons, *The Face of Mercy*, pp. 39–69; Orić, *Srebrenica*, p. 224; Silber and Little, *Yugoslavia*, p. 256; Zajtchuk and Grande (eds.), *Anesthesia and Perioperative Care of the Combat Casualty*, pp. 2–42 (excellent overview of history of military medicine).

Other Materials
Amateur videotape of this operation was made at Srebrenica Hospital, imprinted with date and time. Begins July 17, 1992, 2:50 P.M., video recorder was reportedly powered by a car battery. Another videotape, taken by Dr. Ejub Alić (date unknown), depicts the line of burnt houses and is narrated with the names of their pre-war owners.

Notes
Based on the name given on the videotape, the patient whose surgery is described in this chapter was first treated by Dr. Fatima Klempić-Dautbašić in an area near the village of Sase. She reports that he later died of his wounds. However, his death is listed in Orić, *Srebrenica*, as having taken place July 14, 1992, three days before the video imprint. This was most likely the date of his injury, not death.

CHAPTER 2: ERIC

Interviews
Françoise Bouchet-Saulnier, Dr. Eric Dachy, Senator Alain Destexhe (Belguim), Glenn Hodgson, Dr. Bernard Kouchner, Dr. Jean-Pierre Luxen, Martin Zogg

Published Literature
Aeberhard, "A Historical Survey of Humanitarian Action," pp. 30–45; Agence France-Presse October 25, 1991 ("Truce in battle for Dubrovnik but no letup on other fronts"); Associated Press, October 19, 28, 1991; Berger, *The Humanitarian Diplomacy of the ICRC and the Conflict in Croatia,* pp. 22, 66; Bouchet-Saulnier, *The Practical Guide to Humanitarian Law,* pp. 359–360; Brauman, "When Suffering Makes a Good Story," pp. 153–154; Council of the International Institute of Humanitarian Law, "Guiding Principles on the Right to Humanitarian Assistance," pp. 519–525; d'Atorg, Bernard (writing in Espirit); Destexhe, "From Solferino to Sarajevo," pp. 46–59; Eknes, "Blue Helmets in a Blown Mission?"; Groenewold, *World in Crisis,* p. xxi; Hermet, "Humanitarian Aid Versus Politics," p. 110; Holbrooke, *To End a War,* pp. 27–28, 32; *Le Soir,* December 21–22, 1991 (p. 2, interview with Dr. Vesna Bosanac; Van Velthem, Edouard, "Sur le siège de Vukovar et la guerre en Croatie: Dr. Vesna Bosanac"); Jelavic, *History of the Balkans,* pp. 267–269 (history of "Chetnik," Tito), 295–297 (creation of Yugoslavia after World War II); Malcolm, *Bosnia,* pp. 229–230; Moreillon, "The Promotion of Peace and Humanity in the Twenty-First Century," pp. 595–610; Pollack, *The Threatening Storm,* p. 51; Rieff, "The Humanitarian Trap," p. 3; Russbach, "Humanitarian Action in Current Armed Conflicts"; Sandoz, "'Droit' or 'devoir d'ingérence' and the right to assistance," pp. 215–227; Silber and Little, *Yugoslavia,* pp. 58–69 (rise of Slobodan Milošević), 204 (deployment of U.N. peacekeepers in Croatia); UNHCR, *The State of the World's Refugees: In Search of Solutions,* pp. 117–118; UNHCR, *The State of the World's Refugees: The Challenge of Protection,* pp. 84–85, p. 182; Vincent, "The French Doctors' Movement and Beyond," pp. 25–29.

Documents
Belgrade Tourist Map, Tourist information Center; Protocol Additional to the Geneva Conventions of 12 August 1949, and Relating to the Protection of Victims of Non-International Armed Conflicts, June 8, 1977; UN Doc. S/RES/688(1991), April 5, 1991 (the text of UN Security Council Resolution 688). UN Doc. S/RES/743(1992), February 21, 1992 (text of UN Security Council Resolution 743 establishing UNPROFOR). Information on Kalemegdan fortress from http://copernico.dm.unipi.it/~milani/belgrado/node7.html accessed 1/20/03, and an example of Kalemegdan's continuing influence can be found in Radovan Karadžić's poem, "Kalemegdan," an English translation of which is in Post and DeKleva, "The Odyssey of Dr. Radovan Karadžić"; Eric Dachy's unpublished chronicle of his experiences in the former Yugoslavia; International Criminal Tribunal for the Former Yugoslavia, Case IT-95-13a-I, amended indictment December 2, 1997, "The Prosecutor of the Tribunal against Mile Mrkšić, Miroslav Radić, Veselin Šljivančanin, Slavko Dokmanović." Information on the history of the ICRC in Biafra and in Vukovar, Croatia, from the International Committee

of the Red Cross's yearly reports 1967–1971; 1991–1992. The information on Eric Dachy's activities in late 1991/early 1992 is taken from "Ex-Yugoslavia, Summary of MSF activities," a seven-page fax document about the activity of the Belgrade and Zagreb offices on letterhead of the MSF international office in Brussels, Belgium. "The Referendum on Independence in Bosnia-Hercegovina, February 29–March 1, 1992," a report by the Commission on Security and Cooperation in Europe, Washington, D.C., March 12, 1992.

Other Materials
Visnews, Vukovar rushes (videotape footage), November 20, 1991

Notes
PAGE 13   *Although some came to consider* ... Vincent, Anne. "The 'French Doctors' Movement and Beyond." *Health and Human Rights.* Vol. 2, No. 1. 1996, pp. 25–29.
PAGE 13   *"The age of the 'French doctors'* ... " Brauman, Rony. "When Suffering Makes a Good Story." In *Life, Death and Aid: The Médecins Sans Frontières Report on World Crisis Intervention.* New York: Routledge, 1993, pp. 153–154.
PAGE 18   *He closed his eyes and thought of Vukovar* ... From Eric Dachy's unpublished chronicle of his experiences in the former Yugoslavia.

CHAPTER 3: ILIJAZ

Interviews
Dr. Ejub Alić, Dr. Sabit Begić, Muhamed Duraković, Dr. Avdo Hasanović, Dr. Fatima Klempić-Dautbašić, Dr. Petar Lončarević, Dr. Irfanka Pašagić, Dr. Radomir Pavlović, Dr. Ilijaz Pilav, Ibrahim Purković

Published Literature
Anić, *Sanitetska Služba u Narodno Oslobodinaćkom Ratu Jugoslavije 1941–1945*; Duizings, *History, Memory and Politics in Eastern Bosnia* (extensive history of the Srebrenica enclave), chapters: 1 (ethno-religious geography of the region), 3 (Srebrenica and its surrounding villages in World War II; Duizings relates stories of atrocities against Serbs in places such as Bjelovac, Podravanje, Rašića Gaj, Zalazje, and Kravica, and against Muslims in places such as Sebiočina and Srebrenica, but he also provides examples of neighbors of various ethnicities protecting one another and conveys the impression of elderly townspeople and villagers that World War II was "not as brutal and inhumane" as the conflict in the 1990s), 4 (pre-war economy and ethnic migrations), 5 (elections, provocative use of nationalist symbols), 6 (one of several sources for the story of the Muslim driving patients from the spa who was killed on April 11, 1992; an accompanying Serb

staff member was released in Serbia and survived); Golemović, *Narodna Muzika Podrinja,* pp. 534, 587–90; Jelavic, *History of the Balkans,* pp. 62–273 (Yugoslavia during World War II); Kreševljaković, "Stari Bosanski Gradovi," pp. 12–13; Magaš, Branka, *The Destruction of Yugoslavia,* pp. 48–73 (rise of nationalism); Malcolm, Noel, *Bosnia,* pp. 24–25, 249; Maletić, Mihailo, *Znamenitosti i Lepote,* pp. 51–52; *Medecinska Encikopedija,* pp. 89–90; *Bosnia: Echoes from an Endangered World—Music and Chant of the Bosnian Muslims* (liner notes); *Treasures of Yugoslavia,* pp. 273–274 (Bratunac), 321–322 (Srebrenica). Netherlands Institute for War Documentation, *Srebrenica A 'Safe' Area* (the 7600-page document is henceforth referred to as "NIOD report"), Part II/Chapter 2/Section 3 concerns the April 1992 negotiations to divide Srebrenica into Serb and Muslim parts. Sudetic, *Blood and Vengeance,* pp. 149–150.

Documents
Population figures for Gladovići, Srebrenica, and all other Bosnian towns and villages mentioned in the book are from the March 31, 1991, census, "Statistićki bilten" No. 234, DZS BiH, Sarajevo, as presented by the Bosnian Congress USA, http://www.hdmagazine.com/bosnia/census.html (accessed 3/4/03) and Den Krieg Uberleben (Bonn, Germany) http://refugees.atvirtual.net/de/1991/buh_1991.html (accessed 3/4/03).

Ilijaz's recollections in our interviews were checked against a transcript of his fall 1995 interview with Laurence de Barros-Duchêne (parts published in de Barros-Duchêne, *Srebrenica*). Pre-war promotional flyer for the Banja Guber spa. "Florističko-faunističko-turističke ljepote Srebrenice," by Jakov Sucic.

Other Materials
NIMA 1:50,000 topographic maps of the relevant areas of Bosnia and Serbia (used for reference throughout the book). Information on Tara Mountain can be found on www.uzice.net/tara. Accessed 1/22/03. E-mail exchange (1/22/03) with the site administrator, Predrag Supurović, confirmed details about Tara, the Drina River dam and hydroelectric power plant. Descriptions of the pre-war town were based partly on a home videotape (exact origins unknown) of Srebrenica imprinted July 17 and 18, 1990, and a remarkable, sugary promotional film for the Banja Guber spa (*Banja Guber Centar za Lijecinje,* produced by Jadra, Zagreb, year unknown) presenting Srebrenica as a "prosperous, modern town," and showing footage from the 1990 Srebrenica cultural festival.

Notes
PAGE 29   *"Comrade Tito"* . . . Front page of a special issue of *Srebreničke novine* 3(24), at the event of Tito's death, May 1980, as quoted in Duizings, *History, Memory and Politics in Eastern Bosnia.*

CHAPTER 4: EJUB

Interviews
Dr. Ejub Alić, Mubina Alić

Published Literature
Duizings, *History, Memory and Politics in Eastern Bosnia,* Chapter 4 (economic and so-
cial changes in eastern Bosnia), 5 (confirms story of two killed just outside of
Srebrenica in early April 1992).

CHAPTER 5: WAR

Interviews
Ajka Avdić, Dr. Sabit Begić, Mirsad Dudić, Muhamed Duraković, Samira
Hodžić, Dr. Fatima Klempić-Dautbašić, Dr. Ilijaz Pilav, Ibrahim Purković,
Naim Salkić, Ahmedan, Hikmeta and Nedžla Ustić

Published Literature
Duizings, *History, Memory and Politics in Eastern Bosnia,* Chapter 5 (story of Osmaće);
Ivanišević, *Hronika Našeg Groblja,* p. 41, 59, 71 (for Serb version of the May 7, 1992,
ambushes including names and birth dates of those killed), 74, 168 (Shpat offensive); Ivanišević, "Fate of the Serbs," p. 83 (Shpat); Mašić, *Srebrenica,* p. 46 (for Srebrenica version of May 7, 1992, ambushes); "NIOD Report," I/10/7 (atrocities in
Bratunac); Orić, *Srebrenica,* p. 143 (for Srebrenica version of May 7, 1992, ambushes); Selimović, *The Fortress,* p. 4; van Laerhoven, *Srebrenica,* Chapter 5 (Ilijaz's
thoughts in the woods).

Documents
Transcript of interview with Dr. Ilijaz Pilav conducted by Laurence de Barros-
Duchêne in the autumn of 1995.

Other Materials
Videotape footage of Srebrenica imprinted June 1, 1992, showing burnt houses
with no rooftops and a damaged minaret.

Notes
PAGE 45   *They witnessed lines of villagers* ... NIOD Report II/2/3 and 4 describes
    "large-scale ethnic cleansing" of the Muslims in late April (in several towns
    including Bratunac) and beginning on May 1 when certain Muslim villages
    refused to give up their weapons and surrender: "Paramilitary units and lo-
    cal SDS militias were sent to the villages; they chased the Muslim popula-
    tion out of their villages, killed them, plundered their houses and set them

in flames. In Bratunac, the Bosnian-Serbian authorities began to pick up Muslims, political leaders and intellectuals primarily, also from Srebrenica, a large number of whom were killed."

PAGE 45   *If this was war . . .* Duizings, *History, Memory and Politics in Eastern Bosnia,* chapter 5, reports that a year before the war, in spring 1991, Serb paramilitary leaders began recruiting in eastern Bosnia. After withdrawing units from Croatia, the Yugoslav army reinforced its positions along the Drina River, with artillery on the mountains across the border in Serbia directed toward Srebrenica. When Muslim villages in Bosnia first came under fire from gunmen in Serbia, on September 5, 1991, local leaders of the Muslim nationalist party, the SDA, that controlled Srebrenica suggested the establishment of crisis staffs to arm local Muslims. Most of the promised arms were never delivered. Ilijaz denied knowledge of such a crisis staff. He and others interviewed for this chapter recalled only that automatic guns were given to members of the police reserves (consisting of both Serbs and Muslims) some months prior to the war.

PAGE 46   *Ilijaz might have been a doctor . . .* Ilijaz's group had three former policemen who had submachine guns. These were likely the weapons that had been distributed to the police reserves before the war.

PAGE 54   *Out of Srebrenica's original forty-five doctors . . .* This figure is from Dr. Sabit Begić, the pre-war director of Srebrenica's health clinic.

CHAPTER 6:
A BLUE FEAR

Interviews
Dr. Rony Brauman, Dr. Eric Dachy, Guy Hermet, Dr. Bernard Kouchner, Dr. Jean-Pierre Luxen

Published Literature
Agence France-Presse, May 29, 1992 ("Relief chief castigates EC 'cowardice' over Bosnia"), June 5, 1992; Bouchet-Saulnier, "Peacekeeping Operations Above Humanitarian Law," pp. 125–130; Donini, "Beyond Neutrality," pp. 31–45; Eknes, "Blue Helmets in a Blown Mission?" p. 58; Hermet, "The Human Rights Challenge to Sovereignty," pp. 131–137; Holbrooke, *To End a War,* p. 48; ICRC, *Saving Lives,* p. 8 (details of the May 22, 1992, agreement by all conflicting parties to respect International Humanitarian Law); Jean, "Refugees and Displaced Persons"; Oberreit and Salignon, "Bosnia"; Rieff, *Slaughterhouse,* pp. 164, 196–198; Rufin, "The Paradoxes of Armed Protection," pp. 111–123; Sandoz, "'Droit' or 'devoir d'ingérence' and the right to assistance," pp. 215–227; Silber and Little, *Yugoslavia,* pp.254–256 (Sarajevo airlift).

Documents

"Sarajevo Declaration on the Humanitarian Treatment of Displaced Persons," April 11, 1992, signed by Alija Izetbegović, president of the Party of Democratic Action; Radovan Karadžić, president of the Serbian Democratic Party; Miljenko Brkić, president of the Croatian Democratic Community; and Jose Maria Mendiluce, special envoy of the United Nations High Commissioner for Refugees.

Press releases of the International Committee of the Red Cross: #1715 May 18, 1992 (attack on ICRC), #1716 May 19, 1992 (killing of ICRC workers), and #1719 May 27, 1992 (withdrawal of ICRC).

Logistics report of MSF Belgrade covering the period 4/29/92–6/30/92; MSF report entitled "ex-Youg resumé d'activities" dated 1/11/93.

Eric Dachy's unpublished chronicle of his experiences in the former Yugoslavia.

UN documents: UNSC Resolutions 758 and 764 (1992), concerned airlift to Sarajevo and extended mandate for U.N. Protection Force to work in Bosnia, 770 (1992) called on member states to take necessary steps to deliver humanitarian aid, and 777 (1992) authorized UNPROFOR to protect relief convoys and assist the International Committee of the Red Cross in escorting released detainees (an unprecedented step for the ICRC).

Notes

PAGES 55–56   *Just days after Bosnia's recognition* . . . Egnes, "Blue Helmets in a Blown Mission."

PAGE 56   *The headquarters of Doctors Without Borders* . . . "Relief chief castigates EC 'cowardice' over Bosnia," Agence France-Presse, May 29, 1992.

PAGE 60   *The plan split the aid community.* Sandoz, Yves. "'Droit' or 'devoir d'ingérence' and the right to assistance: the issues involved." *International Review of the Red Cross.* May-June 1992, No. 288, pp. 215–227.

CHAPTER 7: INGRESS

Interviews

Dr. Ejub Alić, Mubina Alić, Dr. Fatima Klempić-Dautbašić, Dr. Ilijaz Pilav, Naim Salkić

Published Literature

Duizings, *History, Memory and Politics in Eastern Bosnia,* Chapter 7 (attack on Sase); Ivanisević, *Hronika,* p. 77–79 (Serbs killed in *Petrovdan* attacks), 286–8; Mašić, *Srebrenica,* p. 80, 86 (Shpat, Zalazje attacks on *Petrovdan*); Sudetic, *Blood and Vengeance,* p. 155.

Other Materials

Srebrenica Hospital Maternity Record Book showing the dates of deliveries and the names of physicians and nurses who assisted with them. The first delivery after the start of the war took place on July 14 1992 (the last recorded delivery before the war was on April 17, 1992).

Notes
PAGE 66   *The month after the war started* ... Suljice was the village beside Alići that was burned.

CHAPTER 8: WAR OPERATIONS

Interviews
Dr. Ejub Alić, Dr. Avdo Hasanović, Damir Ibrahimović, Dr. Fatima Klempić-Dautbašić, Hakija Meholjić, Sabahudin Muhić, Dr. Nedret Mujkanović, Naser Orić, Dr. Ilijaz Pilav, Ibrahim Purković, Rahima Tursunović-Ibrahimović

Other Materials
Transcript of interviews with Srebrenica health care workers performed by Laurence de Barros-Duchêne in fall, 1995.

Notes
PAGE 68   *"Sarajevo"* English translation in DeKleva and Post, "Genocide in Bosnia."

CHAPTER 9: NEDRET

Interviews
Dr. Sead Ahmetagić, Hadžo Gadžo, Mensur Gadžo, Dr. Besim Hajdarović, Dr. Ibrahim Huskić, Dr. Senad and Jasmina Kasumović, Azra Mujkanović, Dr. Nedret Mujkanović, Dr. Miroslav Oprić (Nedret's mentor in pathology), Dr. Božina Radević (director of surgery at Tuzla Hospital), Dr. Adi Rifatbegović, General Hazim Šadić

Published Literature
The Socialist Republic of Bosnia and Hercegovina, pp. 154–160, 168

Documents
Delic, Sead, "Privremena Ratna Formacija 2 Sanitetskog Bataljona," *Armija Republike Bosne i Hercegovine Komanda 2 Korpusa, Sektor za Popunu i Personalne Poslove 2 Korpusa,* Tuzla, February, 1995; Gavrilović, Radivoj, "Osnovi Taktike i Organizacije Sanitetskob Snabdevanja Oružanih Snaga," *Vojnomedicinska Akademija JNA, Katedra taktike i organizacije sanitetske službe,* 1971, pp. 43–44; Letter to Dr. Asim Kurjak from the health administration of the Second Corps, dated November 10, 1992,

describing the structure of the health system and war hospitals in southeast Bosnia; "Nivoi Zdravstvene Zastite 2 Korpus, Šema 2," from the archives of the Second Corps Sanitary Service, Tuzla.

Other Materials
Photographs of the early medical stations where Nedret worked. Notes taken on visit to the sites. Photograph of Sava Kovačević.

Notes
PAGE 78   *"It can't wait."* Both Nedret and the chairman (Dr. Božina Radović) recalled having the conversation, but Nedret alone of the two remembered details of the dialogue, and so this exchange is based solely on his recollection.

CHAPTER 10: PROFESSIONAL DUTY

Interviews
Dr. Avdo Hasanović, Rifet Ibišević, Damir Ibrahimović, Dr. Fatima Klempić-Dautbašić, Hakija Meholjić, Dr. Nedret Mujkanović, Dr. Ilijaz Pilav, Rahima Tursunović-Ibrahimović

Published Literature
Emergency War Surgery, p. 87; Ivanišević, *Chronicle of an Announced Death,* p. 76 (statement of Rajko Jovanović, a Serb survivor of August 8 Srebrenica offensive on Ježestica).

Documents
International Criminal Tribunal for the Former Yugoslavia, Case IT-02-61-I, indictment July 3, 2002, "The Prosecutor of the Tribunal against Miroslav Deronjić" (details about killings of Muslims and destruction of Glogova); Human Rights Watch report: "Chemical Warfare in Bosnia? The Strange Experiences of the Srebrenica Survivors," Human Rights Watch, November 1998, Volume 10, Number 9 (D) (Yugoslav army had weaponized sarin and experimented with soman, tabun, and VX).

Other Materials
Videotape footage from Srebrenica Hospital imprinted August 8, 1992, depicting several of the operations described in this chapter.

Notes
The events in the hospital on August 8 were reconstructed using a combination of videotape footage and the memories of the doctors and soldiers who partici-

pated in them. No existing medical records could be found to confirm the sequence of the operations.

CHAPTER 11: "DEAR DOCTOR"

Interviews
Dr. Rony Brauman, Dr. Eric Dachy, Guy Hermet, Dr. Vesna Ivančić, Laurens Jolles, Dr. Slavica Jovanović, Judith Kumin, Dr. Jean-Pierre Luxen, Fahreta Omić, Dr. Lazer Prodanović, Gerard van Driessche

Published Literature
Associated Press, November 27, 1992; *BBC Summary of World Broadcasts (Radio Bosnia-Hercegovina),* December 7, 1992; *Christian Science Monitor,* November 30, 1992 ("UN convoy relieves siege on Bosnia town," by Jonathan Landay); DeKleva and Post, "Genocide in Bosnia," pp. 485–496; Duizings, *History, Memory and Politics in Eastern Bosnia; The Economist,* December 5, 1992; *Financial Times,* November 25, 26, 28, 30 ("Aid for Srebrenica after seven-month siege: Laura Silber arrives with the UN convoy bringing relief to a Moslem stronghold in Bosnia," by Laura Silber), 1992; *The Guardian,* November 30, 1992; *The Independent* (London), November 7, 27, 28, 1992; Ivanišević, "Fate of the Serbs," pp. 76–77 (testimony of Slavoljub Rankić, Serb survivor of December 14, 1992 attack on Bjelovac); *The New York Times,* November 29, 1992; Post and DeKleva, "The Odyssey of Dr. Radovan Karadžić"; Nelan, "Seeds of Evil"; Rieff, *Slaughterhouse,* p. 210; Silove, "The Psychiatrist as a Political Leader in War," pp. 125–126; The *Times* (London), September 22, November 17, 27, 30, 1992; *United Press International.*

Documents
Eric Dachy's unpublished chronicle of his experiences in the former Yugoslavia.
"UNHCR Update on Ex-Yugoslavia," November 25 and December 1, 1992; MSF unpublished documents: Faxes from Eric Dachy to MSF Belgium Headquarters and MSF Yugoslavia task force December 6 and 12, 1992, reporting on the trip to Srebrenica and containing drafts of his letters to UNHCR and to Radovan Karadžić; Letter from Eric Dachy to Nedret Mujkanović, undated, delivered on December 10, 1992. UN document S/1994/674/Add.2 28 December 1994, *Report of the UN Commission of Experts on the former Yugoslavia, Established Pursuant to Security Council Resolution 780 (1992),* Annex 4, Part 6 (the "ethnic cleansing" campaign). World Medical Organization "Resolution concerning Dr. Radovan Karadžić," adopted October 1996 (denounces Karadžić for failing to have turned himself in to the ICTY: ". . . as a physician he is bringing our profession into disrepute").

Other Materials
The film *Serbian Epics* (1993, BBC TV, UK), directed by Paul Pawlikowski contains

interviews with Radovan Karadžić and information on his family history. The physical descriptions of Karadžić are based on viewing this film.

Notebook found in Srebrenica Hospital labeled "Protokol Bolesnika," containing a list of medicines provided to outpatients, was used to confirm doctors' memories of the supplies they had in winter 1993. These included predominantly antibiotics, antiparasitics, painkillers, blood pressure and heart medications, diuretics, anti-nausea drugs, vitamins, and anti-anxiety drugs as would be expected after having received basic drug kits from MSF.

Notes

PAGE 89   *Just before dying in 1992 . . .* This quote is from Armstrong and Forestier, "Ending the Balkan Nightmare" (Forestier's study of Rašković and this quote are also discussed in Annex 4 of the U.N. Commission of Experts final report). Rašković is said to have spoken these words on Belgrade's "Yutel" television station. I could find no other reference to confirm this information.

PAGE 90   *"Dear doctor . . . "* The hypocrisy of Karadžić's greeting outraged Eric Dachy, but in an interview he offered a different analysis, using his own knowledge of psychology. "Literally he was saying, 'I would like to meet you in other circumstances.' And he said it and addressed me as a doctor. Maybe he was expressing a deep wish, an unconscious wish, to be in better circumstances. I didn't feel so at the time, but this occurred to me later. He was old. I was young. The whole world saw him as evil. I was representing good and he was representing evil and he must have felt it. This made me feel he had a soul, but he was simply hiding it. It was under a layer of brutality."

PAGE 95   *Patients have died . . .* Srebrenica doctors recalled at least one diabetic patient having died for lack of insulin. Several patients with need for more sophisticated treatments also died early in the war, including those dependent on kidney dialysis.

PAGE 97   *He sends the letter.* The attack on December 14, 1992, took place in the towns of Bjelova and Loznička Rijeka.

PAGE 97   *During the attack . . .* Dr. Vesna Ivančić of the Bratunac health clinic, interviewed by the author in 1999, estimated one hundred and six wounded and seventy-six dead, including two medics.

CHAPTER 12: SPECIAL K

Interviews
Mensur Gadžo, Hakija Meholjić, Dr. Nedret Mujkanović, Naser Orić, Dr. Simon Mardel, Dr. Ilijaz Pilav, Ibrahim Purković

Published Literature
Bosnia Country Handbook, p. 16–1 (anti-aircraft gun specifications); *Mosby's GenRx*

(entry for Ketamine Hydrochloride); Miller, *Anesthesia*, pp. 240–245; Naythons, *The Face of Mercy*, pp. 39–69; Orić, *Srebrenica*, p. 167; Mašić, *Srebrenica*, p. 65; Sudetic, *Blood and Vengeance*, p. 154, 157–161.

Documents
Unpublished World Health Organization documents: "Clinical Uses of Ketamine and Contraindications to Its Use," and "The Use of Ketamine in Hospital Anaesthesia," by Dr. Simon Mardel; the latter essay is contained in "Final Report of Dr. Simon Mardel W.H.O. Sarajevo, 1/28–6/1, 1993."

CHAPTER 13:
HOLIDAYS IN HELL

Interviews
Sabera Alić, Dr. Ejub Alić, Dr. Eric Dachy, Elvira Duraković, Muhamed Duraković, Samira Duraković, Hadžo Gadžo, Mensur Gadžo, Dr. Avdo Hasanović, Samira Hodžic, Dr. Vesna Ivančić, Dr. Fatima Klempić-Dautbašić, Hakija Meholjić, Dr. Nedret Mujkanović, Dr. Radomir Pavlović, Dr. Ilijaz Pilav, Ibrahim Purković, Naim Salkić, Emira Selimović, Rahima Tursunović-Ibrahimović, Philipp von Recklinghausen

Published Literature
Duizings, *History, Memory and Politics in Eastern Bosnia*, Chapter 1 (section on Kravica); Holbrooke, *To End a War*, p. 51; *New York Times*, February 11, 1993; Ivanišević, *Hronika* (pp. 55–56, 88–89, 160, 172–173, 323–329 Kravica; pp. 56–57; 161 Skelani); Malcolm, *Bosnia*, pp. 247–250 (Vance-Owen plan); Masić, *Srebrenica* (pp. 72, 112–113 Kravica; pp. 72–73 death of Nijaz Džanić; 114–115 Skelani); Orić, *Srebrenica* (p. 219 death of Sulejman Pilav; p. 164 death of Nijaz Džanić; p. 169 Kravica); Sudetic, *Blood and Vengeance* (pp. 161–164 Kravica offensive; pp. 171–172 Skelani offensive and killing of Serbs in Srebrenica).

Documents
UN document S/1994/548 (Serb casualties in vicinity of Srebrenica); copy of a Bosnian Army Second Corps document listing all wartime medical workers and information on doctors killed (title, date unknown). Data on U.S. healthcare workforce statistics for the early 1990s is from the U.S. Health Resources and Services Administration, Bureau of Health Professions. Data on Bosnia healthcare workforce statistics is from the WHO Regional Office for Europe.

Notes
PAGE 109 *With Kravica . . .* This figure, 350 miles, is based on information in Naser Orić, *Srebrenica*, map section, p. 253, and is quoted in other sources, for exam-

ple, Sudetic, *Blood and Vengeance,* and Report of the Secretary-General Pursuant to General Assembly Resolution 53/35 (1998), "Srebrenica Report."

PAGE 114   *Kicking machine gun casings out of the way...* According to the photographer, Philipp von Recklinghausen, Orić took the injuries as a sign and abandoned the idea of poisoning the Drina River.

CHAPTER 14:
THE ROAD TO SREBRENICA

Interviews
Muriel Cornelis, Dr. Eric Dachy, Senator Georges Dallemagne (Belgium), Rex Dudley, Larry Hollingworth, Dr. Simon Mardel, Dr. Nedret Mujkanović, Dr. Ilijaz Pilav, Hans Ulens, Martin Zogg

Published Literature
Agence France-Presse, March 10, 1993 ("Le général Morillon à Mali Zvornik mercredi et à Srebrenica jeudi," by David Daure); *BBC,* March 11, 1993; *CNN,* March 20, 1993; *Daily Telegraph,* March 8, 1993 ("Rescue hope for refugees fades in the chaos of war Aid officials suspect UN commander fell for Serbian cover-up of butchery in Cerska," by Patrick Bishop), March 12, 1993 ("British patrol held hostage in Bosnia," by Robert Fox), March 16, 1993 ("The general who refused to go away: Has General Morillon, the UN commander in Bosnia, experienced a dramatic conversion?" By Robert Fox and Michael Montgomery); de Barros-Duchêne, *Srebrenica,* pp. 77–81; Hollingworth, *Merry Christmas Mr. Larry,* p. 184; Honig and Both, *Srebrenica;* Morillon, *Croire et Oser,* pp. 161, 165, 167–169; *Los Angeles Times,* March 10, 1993 ("Serbs block evacuation of wounded civilians," by Carol J. Williams); *New York Times,* January 12, 1993 ("U.N. to ask NATO to airdrop supplies," by John F. Burns), January 13, 1993 ("U.S. Finds Serbs Skimming 23% of Bosnian Aid," by Michael R. Gordon), February 13, 1993 ("Bosnians tell U.N. they'll refuse relief aid shipments to Sarajevo," by John F. Burns), February 14, 1993 ("UN halts flights to Bosnia capital in dispute over aid," by John F. Burns), February 19, 1993 ("Halt in aid leaves Bosnians stunned, and hungry," by John F. Burns), February 23, 1993 ("U.N. General warns against an airdrop for Bosnia," by John F. Burns), March 1, 1993 ("U.S. planes start dropping relief supplies to Bosnians," by Stephen Kinzer), March 4, 1993 ("UN Report sees massacre by Serbs," by Paul Lewis), March 7, 1993 ("UN General visits besieged Bosnians," by Chuck Sudetic), March 17, 1993 ("U.N. General to stay in Bosnian town," by John F. Burns), Sudetic, *Blood and Vengeance,* pp. 178–181.

Documents
UN document S/25353 March 3, 1993 has details of the emergency session of the

Security Council. International Criminal Tribunal for the Former Yugoslavia, Case IT-98-33, indictment October 27, 1999, "The Prosecutor of the Tribunal against Vinko Pandurević." Unpublished reports from UNPROFOR and U.N. military observers; Unpublished communique from UNHCR Tuzla to other UNHCR offices February 19, 1993; UNHCR Update March 18, 1993; Climatological data for western Serbia during dates of Eric Dachy's trip to Srebrenica (data kindly provided by the Federal Hydrometeorological Institute of Yugoslavia, Belgrade); Eric Dachy's unpublished chronicle.

Other Materials
Photographs of main characters and areas featured at this time taken by Simon Mardel and Muriel Cornelis. Web site: www.sunrisesunset.com/calendar for daylight, sunset and moon information.

Notes
PAGE 119   *The winter passes.* "UN Report sees massacre by Serbs," Paul Lewis, *New York Times,* March 4, 1993.
PAGE 131   *Of course the United Nations . . .* "U.N. General warns against an airdrop for Bosnia," John F. Burns, *New York Times,* February 23, 1993, p. A8.

CHAPTER 15: THE VELVET GLOVE

Interviews
Tony Birtley, Muriel Cornelis, Dr. Eric Dachy, Senator Georges Dallemagne, Rex Dudley, Larry Hollingworth, Dr. Fatima Klempić-Dautbašić, Dr. Simon Mardel, Dr. Nedret Mujkanović, Dr. Ilijaz Pilav, Philipp von Recklinghausen, Dr. Thierry Pontus

Published Literature
De Barros-Duchêne, *Srebrenica,* pp. 81–86; Hollingworth, *Merry Christmas Mr. Larry,* pp. 184–197; Morillon, *Croire et Oser,* pp. 175, Sudetic, *Blood and Vengeance,* pp. 182–185.

Documents
Eric Dachy's unpublished chronicle. Unpublished U.N. Protection Force document describing the retrieval of the medical supplies.

Other Materials
Raw video footage of Morillon's announcements and Srebrenica and surroundings taken by ABC journalist Tony Birtley. Other footage included in the video-recording, *Yugoslavia: Death of a Nation.* Photographs of main characters and areas featured at this time taken by Simon Mardel and Muriel Cornelis.

Notes

PAGE 143   *Is the general sincere?* These are some of the thoughts that Eric Dachy recorded in an unpublished chronicle of his experiences and that he shared in interviews with the author.

CHAPTER 16:
"THE TIME FOR TALKING IS NOW FINISHED"

Interviews

Tony Birtley, Daniela Cerović, Muriel Cornelis, Dr. Eric Dachy, Senator Georges Dallemagne, Rex Dudley, Larry Hollingworth, Laurens Jolles, Dr. Fatima Klempić-Dautbašić, Judith Kumin, Dr. Nedret Mujkanović, Dr. Ilijaz Pilav, Philipp von Recklinghausen, Dr. Thierry Pontus, Hans Ulens

Published Literature

Hollingworth, *Merry Christmas Mr. Larry,* pp. 211–215; *The New York Times,* March 19, 1993 ("UN moving to toughen Yugoslav flight ban," by Paul Lewis), March 22, 1993 ("UN Aide Seeks Deal on Stranded Serbs," by John F. Burns), March 25, 1993 ("Shelling grounds Bosnia evacuation," by John F. Burns); Sudetic, *Blood and Vengeance,* p. 175.

Documents

U.N. Military Observer report (undated); unpublished cable from Annan to Wahlgren, March 23, 1993; U.N. Documents: S/24900add.27 "Note verbale dated 16 March 1993 from the Secretary-General addressed to the President of the Security Council." S/25426 March 17, 1993, "Note by the President of the Security Council" condemns the flight ban violations, demands that they cease and that the Bosnian Serbs provide "an immediate explanation." It also requests an investigation of the use of Yugoslav territory to launch attacks on Bosnia and includes the quote, "the above flights are the first violations of Security Council resolution 781 (1992) observed by UNPROFOR which involved combat activity." S/25444 "Letter dated 16 March 1993 from the Secretary General addressed to the President of the Security Council," includes details of the banned flights. UNSC Resolution 781 (August 1992), the text of the flight ban resolution. S/25440 March 31, 1993 contains the text of the draft resolution to authorize military action against those violating the flight ban.

Cable from the U.S. Embassy in Zagreb to the U.S. Secretary of State, January 11, 1993, entitled "CGY001—Zagreb Update Jan 11, 1993," cites reports of Serb air attack on Srebrenica.

Personal diary of Thierry Pontus recording impressions of Srebrenica, such as number and types of patients and his activities there.

Situation report by Simon Mardel, WHO, March 17, 1993.

UNHCR internal communication March 24, 1993, from Albert Alain Peters, director UNHCR liaison office New York, to Kofi Annan with details of the aborted helicopter evacuation.

Transcript of radio communication with UNHCR Srebrenica March 24, 1993.

Other Materials

The events of the aborted evacuation are based partly on a video recording of the evacuation, shelling of the airfield and the scene inside Srebrenica Hospital on March 24, 1993, made by ABC journalist Tony Birtley, and partly on photographs taken by Philipp von Recklinghausen.

Notes

PAGES 147–148 *"In brief . . . "* U.N. document S/25457, "Letter dated 22 March 1993 from the Secretary General addressed to the President of the Security Council." March 22, 1993.

PAGES 148–149 *The day after Eric returns to Belgrade . . .* Letter to Mrs. Joanne Edwards, senior project officer of the Soros Humanitarian Fund, office of the charge de mission for Bosnia-Herzegovina, sent to her attention at UNHCR Zagreb. From Dr. Alain Devaux (program responsable) and Anne Simon (task force ex-Yu) on behalf of MSF task force ex-Yugoslavia faxed from MSF office in Brussels, Belgium. March 15, 1993. "Soros-funding budget revision," MSF reference TFY 170. Original in English. Activities had not yet acquired funding, but MSF received $1 million on December 18, 1992, as part of a larger Soros grant to UNHCR.

PAGE 149 *However, Eric finds the attitude . . .* Internal UNHCR report entitled "Urgent Negotiation Items and Strategy—Suggestions" sent by UNHCR Belgrade head Judith Kumin to UNHCR Zagreb and Geneva and copied to the other UNHCRs in Bosnia. She says that Larry Hollingworth is reporting that Srebrenica is under heavy attack with multiple rockets, some landing near him at PTT. She writes: "Strongest possible pressure needs to be placed on the Bosnian Serbs for unconditional and regular access to Srebrenica. However, with latest attack on Srebrenica, this seems overtaken by events." And later: "Given the latest development in Srebrenica, we strongly believe that it is too late to prevent Srebrenica from falling. We feel that we should now take our fall back position, i.e., to negotiate for the safe passage of civilian population from Srebrenica towards west to Tuzla. This would include negotiations with both Bosnian government and Serbian sides. All available resources, including UNPROFOR, ICRC and others, should be mobilized to guarantee the safe passage."

PAGE 153 *The next day . . .* Annan later became U.N. Secretary-General.

PAGE 157   *"John."* The name of the guard has been changed to protect his privacy.

PAGE 159   *Fear engulfs Srebrenica.* The injured in fact arrive safely in Bosnian government-held territory and are transferred to a hospital in Tuzla.

PAGE 160   *The next day, General Morillon and the UNHCR Belgrade team . . .* This meeting
is described in an internal cable to Kofi Annan from General Wahlgren on
March 25, 1993. Wahlgren was not at the meeting.

CHAPTER 17: INTERLUDE

Interviews
Tony Birtley, Muriel Cornelis, Dr. Eric Dachy, Dr. Martin De Smet,
Laurens Jolles, Hakija Meholjić, Dr. Nedret Mujkanović, Dr. Thierry Pontus,
Philipp von Recklinghausen, Hans Ulens, Dr. Piet Willems

Published Literature
The Atlanta Journal and Constitution, January 22, 1993 ("Serbs bomb Bosnian city despite pact," news services); *The Herald (Glasgow),* January 22, 1993 ("Muslims claim
advances in Bosnian battles," by Joel Brand); *The Independent,* April 8, 1993 ("Morillon takes road back to besieged town," by Marcus Tanner); *The New York Times,*
March 30, 1993 ("Thousands jam U.N. trucks to flee Bosnian town," by Chuck
Sudetic), April 1, 1993 (article by Chuck Sudetic), April 16, 1993 ("Bosnia yielding
town to Serbs, U.N. Aides Say," by John F. Burns); *The Times (London),* March 30,
1993 ("UN rescues 2,000 refugees from Srebrenica," by Joel Brand).

Documents
*Report of the Secretary-General Pursuant to General Assembly Resolution 53/35 (1998), "UN Sre-
brenica Report,"* (hereafter referred to as "UN Srebrenica Report"), Section 40 describes overcrowding and death on UN convoys. Unpublished internal UNHCR
report by Laurens Jolles, "Confidential report on fifth convoy to Srebrenica and
evacuation to Tuzla 28–29 March, 1993." The discussion over the adoption of Resolution 816 is detailed in United Nations Security Council document S/PV.3191,
"Provisional Verbatim Record of the Three Thousand One Hundred and
Ninety-First Meeting," March 31, 1993. Diary of Philipp von Recklinghausen with
details of April 3, 1993, incidents. Transcript of MSF interview with Dr. Martin De
Smet in late 1995 conducted by Laurens de Barros-Duchêne. Unpublished internal UNHCR situation report by Louis Gentile April 13, 1993, describing the calm
in Srebrenica between April 6–11.

Other Materials
Videotaped footage of events of April 3, 1993, by Tony Birtley. Photographs of
Srebrenica taken by Philipp von Recklinghausen and MSF staff members.

Notes

PAGE 161 *"Srebrenica is safe . . . "* The *New York Times,* "Food convoy arrives in Bosnian town," by John F. Burns. March 29, 1993.

PAGE 163 *"As time is running out . . . "* Ogata's letter is included in U.N. document S/25519 "Letter dated 2 April, 1993 from the Secretary-General addressed to the President of the Security Council," April 3, 1993.

PAGE 163 *The Security Council responds . . .* U.N. document S/25520 "Note by the President of the Security Council," April 3, 1993.

PAGE 164 *"We don't even transport livestock that way . . . "* Statement made by Hazim Šadić on March 29, 1993 quoted in the *New York Times,* "Thousands Jam U.N. Trucks to Flee Bosnian Town," by Chuck Sudetic, March 30, 1993.

PAGE 165 *The UNHCR special representative for the former Yugoslavia . . .* "U.N. plans to evacuate 20,000 trapped Muslims," John F. Burns, *New York Times,* April 6, 1993.

CHAPTER 18: THE HOTTEST PART OF HELL

Interviews
Dr. Ejub Alić, Dr. Sabit Begić, Muriel Cornelis, Dr. Eric Dachy, Dr. Fatima Dautbašić, Muhamed Duraković, Dr. Avdo Hasanović, Larry Hollingworth, Dr. Simon Mardel, Hakija Meholjić, Dr. Nedret Mujkanović, Dr. Ilijaz Pilav, Nijaz Salkić, Dr. Martin De Smet, Hans Ulens, Dr. Piet Willems

Published Literature
de Barros-Duchêne, *Srebrenica,* pp. 90–92; Holbrooke, *To End a War,* p. 56; Honig and Both, *Srebrenica,* p. 96; Mašić, *Srebrenica,* p. 63; *The Los Angeles Times,* April 14, 1993 ("U.N. officials outraged over Serb shelling of civilians; Balkans: Death toll in Srebrenica nears 60. Convoys evacuate almost 1,000 refugees," By Carol J. Williams); *The New York Times,* April 14, 1993 ("Ending restraint, UN aides denounce Serbs for shellings," by John F. Burns); Orić, *Srebrenica,* p. 193; Sudetic, *Blood and Vengeance,* pp. 202–207; *The Times,* April 16, 1993 ("Muslims stop evacuation until soldiers get help," by Tim Judah and Dessa Trevisan).

Documents
Bosnian Army Second Corps document listing all wartime medical workers and information on doctors killed (title, date unknown) includes information on Dr. Hamdija Halilović's death. Diary of a displaced person from Konjević Polje (requests anonymity). MSF unpublished documents: Radio reports made by MSF staff member Hans Ulens on April 12, 1993, transcribed by Muriel Cornelis. Unpublished final mission report of Dr. Norbert Scholtzen (MSF anesthesiologist) including a detailed listing of the injuries suffered by patients undergoing surgery after the April 12, 1993, attack. Transcript of MSF interview

with Dr. Martin De Smet in late 1995 conducted by Laurens de Barros-Duchêne. Unpublished notes of the MSF Yugoslavia Task Force April 16, 1993. U.N. Srebrenica report Section 40 (describes UN convoys).

Other Materials
Photographs taken by MSF staff members in aftermath of April 12, 1993, shelling attack.

Notes
PAGE 168 *"I will never be able to convey the sheer horror . . . "* Unpublished internal UNHCR situation report by Louis Gentile, April 14, 1993.
PAGE 171 *I then thought about my Serb friends . . .* Hollingworth, *Merry Christmas Mr. Larry,* pp. 215–216.
PAGE 172 *Fierce condemnation rings from many corners.* "U.N. officials outraged over Serb shelling of civilians; Balkans: Death toll in Srebrenica nears 60. Convoys evacuate almost 1,000 refugees," Carol J. Williams, *Los Angeles Times,* April 14, 1993.
PAGE 174 *In the United States . . .* "'The CNN effect': TV playing extraordinary role in setting national agenda," Matthew C. Vita, Cox News Service, *Houston Chronicle,* May 7, 1993. The article cites data of the Center for Media and Public Affairs, also comparing Bosnia coverage with that of the Clinton economic policy, Middle East, crisis in Russia, Waco (Waco crisis lasted from February 28–April 19), and the U.S. bombing in Iraq. Includes U.N. Secretary-General Boutros Boutros-Ghali's criticism that the media are being selective, ignoring such places as Afghanistan.

CHAPTER 19:
THROUGH THE LOOKING GLASS

Interviews
Dr. Sead Ahmetagić, Sadik Ahmetović, Dr. Louisa Chan-Boegli, Dr. Eric Dachy, Dr. Radomir Davidović, Larry Hollingworth, Fatima Klempić-Dautbašić, Dr. Boro Lazić, Sanja Lazić, Dr. Mehdin Hadžiselimović, Danijela Lazić, Hakija Meholjić, Dr. Nedret Mujkanović, Dr. Miroslav Oprić, Dr. Lazer Prodanović, General Hazim Šadić, Chuck Sudetic, Hans Ulens

Published Literature
Agence France-Presse, November 3, 1991 ("At least 25 dead in new violence in Croatia"), November 21, 1993, November 28, 1993 ("Bosnian Serbs attack on several fronts : radio"); *BBC Summary of World Broadcasts,* January 10, 1992 ("Bosnia-Hercegovina in brief; Fifth Serbian autonomous region set up in Bosnia-Hercegovina," Yugoslav News Agency), April 30, 1993 ("Bodies of 19 reportedly massacred Serbs exhumed in Bosanski Brod," Yugoslav Telegraph Service); Duizings, *History,*

Memory and Politics in Eastern Bosnia, Chapter 3 (for history of Šekovići); *The Economist,* April 4, 1992 ("Bosnia and Hercegovina; All mixed up"); *Glasgow Herald,* April 20, 1993 (article by Laura Pitter); *The Guardian,* April 19, 1993 (article by Ian Traynor); Ivanisevic, *Hronika,* pp. 51–52, 82–83, 172–173, 179–180, 294–305; Maass, *Love Thy Neighbor,* pp. 242–247; *Newsday,* May 10, 1993 ("From Bosnia to Bianca, Jagger saves dying child from war zone," by Gale Scott); *New York Times,* April 21, 1993 (article by Chuck Sudetic), April 24, 1993 ("Conflict in the Balkans; a view of the Bosnia war from the Srebrenica Hospital's O.R.," by Chuck Sudetic); Orić, *Srebrenica,* p. 165 (final battle for Srebrenica before safe area declared); Mašić, *Srebrenica,* pp. 63, 100, 124, 138; Sudetic, *Blood and Vengeance,* p. 157; *Washington Post,* April 23, 1993. ("Binding Up the Wounds; Bosnian Surgeon Recounts Life Under Siege" by Peter Maass).

Documents
International Criminal Tribunal for the Former Yugoslavia, "The Prosecutor of the Tribunal Against Dragan Nikolić," Case IT-94-2-PT. Second amended indictment, January 2, 2002 (Commander of the Sušica camp in Vlasenica, arrested April 20, 2000, original indictment was November 4, 1994). International Criminal Tribunal for the Former Yugoslavia, Case IT-01-51-I, Bosnia and Herzegovina initial indictment," November 22, 2001, "The Prosecutor of the Tribunal Against Slobodan Milošević"; International Criminal Tribunal for the Former Yugoslavia, Case IT-98-33, indictment October 27, 1999, "The Prosecutor of the Tribunal against Vinko Pandurević"; UN document UN-S/1994/548 (details of September 1992 Podravanje offensive from Serb side). Census figures for Šekovići and Vlasenica are from the March 31, 1991, census, "Statistički bilten" No. 234, DZS BiH, Sarajevo, as presented by the Bosnian Congress USA, http://www.hdmagazine.com/bosnia/census.html (accessed 3/4/03) and Den Krieg Uberleben (Bonn, Germany) http://refugees.atvirtual.net/de/1991/buh_1991.html (accessed 3/4/03). UN document S/1994/674/Add.2 (Vol. IV) 28 December 1994: Final Report of the UN Commission of Experts on the former Yugoslavia, Established Pursuant to Security Council Resolution 780 (1992), Volume 4, Annex 8, Section 85 (Vlasenica).

Other Materials
The film *Death of Yugoslavia,* Part V (footage of Elie Wiesel at Holocaust Memorial opening, April 22, 1993).

Notes
PAGE 182   *Slowly, the barrage of media stories about atrocities against Serbs . . .* An independent Serbian journalist, Miloš Vasić, wrote in the March 15, 1993, *New Yorker* that it was as if all television in the United States had been taken over by the Ku Klux Klan. "You too would have war in five years."

PAGE 197   *Boro and Nedret continue to plan meetings . . .* The date that the negotiations ended is remembered inexactly and somewhat differently by Nedret and Boro, and I have no supporting documentation on the negotiations. There was a major Serb offensive in the area (Teočak) that began about November 18, 1993. A smaller offensive had been rebuffed on June 16, 1993.

CHAPTER 20: TO INTERPOSE

Interviews
Danijela Cerović, Muriel Cornelis, Dr. Eric Dachy, Dr. Martin De Smet, Judith Kumin, Hans Ulens

Published Literature
Atlanta Constitution, July 1, 1993 (about sanitation situation in Srebrenica); Malcolm, *Bosnia,* pp. 250–1 (the end to the air strike threat in 1993); *The New York Times,* April 26, 1993 ("U.N. visitors say Srebrenica is 'an open jail'," by Paul Lewis)

Documents
Eric Dachy's unpublished recollections.

Unpublished memo of the MSF Yugoslavia Task Force dated April 16, 1993, details what Eric's colleagues believed he was thinking in the days before Srebrenica's demilitarization agreement.

U.N. Security Council Resolutions pertaining to Srebrenica: SRES 819, April 16, 1993 (text of U.N. Security Council Resolution designated Srebrenica a "safe area"), SRES 824 May 6, 1993 (established six "safe areas" in Bosnia), SRES 836, June 4, 1993 (invoked Chapter 7 of U.N. charter to extend UNPROFOR's mandate to peace enforcement, giving it qualified authorization to use force to "deter attacks" and authorizing U.N. member states to support U.N. forces militarily), SRES 844, June 18, 1993 (authorized additional 7,600 troops for UNPROFOR). Also, text of the discussions prior to adoption of these Resolutions. Other U.N. documents: S/25800 May 19, 1993 (text of French report to the Security Council about safe areas).

MSF documents: Unpublished report of MSF anesthesiologist Dr. Norbert Scholzen. Copy of letter dated May 1, 1993, from Eric Dachy to Diego Arria. Copy of a draft of letter dated May 1, 1993, from Eric Dachy to Radovan Karadžić.

Unpublished internal MSF situation reports of Hans Ulens, June 16 and 27, 1993 (about water situation). Urgent message from Hans Ulens to Eric Dachy May 26, 1993 (warning that Srebrenica may fall without water). Other internal unpublished MSF reports and cables about water situation including MSF Srebrenica activity report covering July–October 1993. Unpublished MSF mission report by Stefaan Maddens. Unpublished internal communications (faxes) between Eric Dachy and representatives of MSF Holland about Goražde and other coordination issues dated June 17, 18, and 22, 1993.

Anesthesia records found in Srebrenica Hospital were used to confirm dates that MSF surgeons and anesthesiologists were in Srebrenica.

Report of the Secretary-General Pursuant to General Assembly Resolution 53/35 (1998), "UN Srebrenica Report," Sections 29–32 (Vance-Owen Peace Plan), III (interpretation of the criteria for NATO air power)

Other Materials
The film *Death of Yugoslavia,* showing Karadžić signing the Vance-Owen peace plan.

Notes
PAGE 201 *Eric's storm cloud of anger needs a release.* Eric Dachy fax message to Alain Devaux, April 20, 1993.
PAGE 201 *As for the "demilitarization of Srebrenica"* ... The ceasefire agreement, signed by the two Bosnian generals and witnessed by General Wahlgren on April 18, 1993, includes the clause: "... All weapons, ammunition, mines, explosives and combat supplies (except medicines) inside Srebrenica will be submitted/handed over to UNPROFOR under the supervision of three officers from each side with control carried out by UNPROFOR. No armed person or units except UNPROFOR will remain within the city once the demilitarization process is complete. ..."
PAGE 202 *The next week, ceasefire violations send more wounded into the hospital* ... Reported in the *Ottawa Citizen,* April 29, 1993 ("War in the Balkans; 56 Canadians make it into Srebrenica; Bosnian Serbs insist town has not yet been completely disarmed," AP/Reuters).
PAGE 202 *The fact that five Serbian soldiers were able to defy* ... U.N. Document S/25700, "UN Security Council Mission Report to Srebrenica," April 30, 1993.
PAGE 204 *The leader of the Canadian House* ... "Canadians not ordered to defend Muslim town; Tory minister sees no immediate threat to 150 troops in Srebrenica," Terrance Wills, (Montreal) *Gazette,* April 24, 1993.
PAGE 205 *"While this option cannot, in itself, completely guarantee the defence of the safe areas* ... " UN Document S/25939, Secretary-General's Report to the UN Security Council, which was adopted.
PAGE 208 *In June, a reporter catches up with Eric* ... "Aid workers also find themselves on front lines," Elizabeth Sullivan, *Plain Dealer,* June 13, 1993.

CHAPTER 21: LIFE IN THE TOMB

Interviews
Dr. Ejub Alić, Dr. Neak Duong, Dr. Martin De Smet, Graziella Godain, Dr. Mehdin Hadžiselimović ("Mad Max"), Dr. Avdo Hasanović, Damir Ibrahimovic, Dr. Fatima Klempić-Dautbašić, Judith Kumin, Isabel Ollieuz,

Fahreta Omić, Dr. Ilijaz Pilav, Naim Salkić, Nijaz Salkić, Rahima Tursunović-Ibrahimović, Hans Ulens

Published Literature
Celebije, *Putopis;* Malcolm, *Bosnia,* pp. 121–2 (about the "Dragon of Bosnia"); Sudetic, *Blood and Vengeance,* p. 243–245.

Documents
The original Srebrenica Hospital anesthesia record forms for this period (found in the hospital in 1999) show the date and time of operations, patient information, and a list of physicians involved in each surgery. These were used to confirm the nature of Ilijaz's surgical experiences. Srebrenica's delivery record notebook was used to confirm details of deliveries. Srebrenica's obstetrics nursing notebook from this period was used to confirm details of the premature baby's birth and care.

MSF unpublished internal documents: Letter from Hans Ulens to Col. Angstrom December 19, 1993, about generator and fuel needs. Debriefing report of Jean-Paul Taziaux (surgeon) and Eric Coppie from June 6, 1993, stating that Dr. Mehdin Hadžiselimović wishes to return to Tuzla. Report of activities of MSF Srebrenica team July 12–August 12 by Martin De Smet crediting Mehdin with reorganizing the hospital. Letter asking that Mehdin be allowed to leave Srebrenica written August 3, 1993, by Dr. Genevieve Begkoyian (Eric's replacement) and sent to Rick Garlock of UNHCR Belgrade with an attached letter written August 2, 1993, and signed by Dr. Martin De Smet (medical coordinator of MSF Srebrenica), Ruth Huber (ICRC Delegate Srebrenica), and Jose Luis Loera (UNHCR field officer Srebrenica). Mission reports of Dr. Sergei Zotikov, dated December 14 and 24, 1993, detail the surgical activity in Srebrenica throughout the summer and fall of 1993. MSF reports dated January 10 and 25, 1994, discuss Ilijaz's growing abilities and stress the continued need for an MSF expatriate surgeon. Report of Paul Lavollee contains a note about problems with obstetrical care in the enclave in December 1993–January 1994. Report by Dr. Simon Moore, January 1994, details the medical work being performed in Srebrenica's hospital and clinics and mentions the psychiatric problems in the enclave. MSF report on August 1, 1993, states that no salt has been delivered since May. Problems with Medevacs are discussed in: MSF Srebrenica situation report #7 (dated January 8, 1994), Srebrenica monthly report October 1994, letter from MSF Belgrade to MSF Srebrenica team June 26, 1995, and the UNHCR Srebrenica weekly situation report January 4, 1994. There were no Medevacs from October 1993 to July 1994, when approximately 19 people were evacuated. MSF Srebrenica April and June 1994 monthly reports and May 1994 population study as well as the Dutchbat surgical activity report of June 1994 discuss abortions, botched abortions, and birth control. A July 9, 1995, situation report discusses the need for IUDs and reports five "criminal abortions" for the week at a cost of 100 Deutschemarks each. End of mission report of Neak Duong covers period of January 26 to July 9, 1994.

UNPROFOR Civil Affairs, Sector NE, report on a trip to Srebrenica September 21–24, 1994, relates the work of the Joint Demilitarization Commission and failure to set exact boundaries for the Srebrenica safe area, and also discusses the 'mafia' situation and tensions between original Srebrenica inhabitants and displaced villagers.

Web sites consulted about the linden tree: (accessed 5/10/02): www.magdalin.com/herbal/plants-page, butler.edu/herbarium/linden.htm (Butler University Friesner Herbarium web site), and enature.com.

Other Materials
Videotape footage of the operation on July 6, 1994 (given as a going-away gift to Dr. Neak Duong).

Notes
PAGE 213 *A raucous outdoor party is held* ... "Mad Max" (Dr. Mehdin Hadžiselimović) asserts that he was coerced into going to Srebrenica by the Bosnian army under pressure from the United Nations and ICRC. According to a letter supporting his departure signed by representatives of MSF, UNHCR, and ICRC in Srebrenica on August 2, 1993, he was brought from Tuzla to Srebrenica by helicopter because of the urgent need for a surgeon and was promised that everything would be done to effect his evacuation whenever he expressed his desire to return to his family, with the hopes that he'd be replaced by one or more other Bosnian doctors. At this point, he had been asking to leave for over a month and had a five-months-pregnant wife and three-year-old son at home.

PAGE 220 *"Thus," the report says* ... Sudetic, *Blood and Vengeance*, p. 243, quoting from Bosnian government's copy of a Yugoslav army document written March 3, 1992, by General Kukanjac, "Odbrambene snage," SFRJ, pov. Br. 546.

PAGE 222 *Since then, Ilijaz has found himself* ... Ironically, Ilijaz was the only one of Srebrenica's doctors to oppose abortions and refuse to perform them—on account of personal (rather than religious) beliefs about the sanctity of life.

PAGE 222 *The women bring him offerings of cigarettes, coffee, and plum brandy.* Payment for abortions was the norm before the war, and during the war, other Srebrenica doctors besides Avdo Hasanović accepted money and gifts in exchange for performing them and also for circumcising babies.

PAGE 228 *Going-away parties for MSF staff are fancy affairs* ... The description of the party in this section is based partly on photographs taken the summer of 1994. It's not clear if it was Dr. Neak's going-away party or a party celebrating some other occasion.

PAGE 230   *Lindens are blooming* ... Translation of *Lipe Cvatu,* by Goran Bregović 1984. www.bisonmusic.com/zabe/brumovinotes.

PAGE 232   *"Why are you expelling my guys from the hospital?"* This exchange is based entirely on the recollection of Dr. Ilijaz Pilav.

CHAPTER 22: ANOTHER WORLD

Interviews
Dr. Sead Ahmetagić, Dr. Ejub Alić, Dr. Neak Duong, Elvira Duraković,
Samira Duraković, Dr. Dževad Džananović, Hadžo Gadžo, Mensur Gadžo,
Dr. Avdo Hasanović, Damir Ibrahimović, Dr. Gerry Kremer, Dr. Benjamin
Kulovac, Dr. Irfanka Pašagić, Dr. Ilijaz Pilav, Dr. Wim Wertheim

Published Literature
NIOD Report: III/6/24 discusses military purpose of Bosnian helicopter flights
and the shortage of weapons and military knowledge in Srebrenica; III/6/7 discusses NATO air strikes and UNPROFOR hostages used as human shields in
May, 1995; III/2/4 and 5 describe the targeting of Captain Scott O'Grady's F-16
with an SA-6 system; III/1 covers the debate over whether UNPROFOR should
pull out of Bosnia.

Westmoreland et al., *Medical Neurosciences,* pp. 116–118 (about increased intracranial pressure). Mašić, *Srebrenica,* pp. 187–188 (covers the helicopter crash), 177
(story of the ambush near Srebrenica, which Mašić says occured on May 31,
rather than June 1 as other sources have it). Honig and Both, *Srebrenica,* pp. 118–137
(history of Dutchbat in Srebrenica and its increasing difficulties in 1995). Kremer,
"Medical neutrality in crisis control areas," *Medisch Contact,* #45, November 8, 1996
(reviews Dutchbat medical work in Srebrenica and the case of the comatose
woman). Holbrooke, *To End a War,* pp. 65–67, describes the U.S.'s major military
commitment in the event that UNPROFOR pulled out of Bosnia.

Documents
Diary of a local (who wishes to remain anonymous) describing the helicopter
crash. Anesthesia records of Srebrenica Hospital on day of Fatima's injury. *Report
of the Secretary-General Pursuant to General Assembly Resolution 53/35 (1998), "UN Srebrenica
Report"*: Section 43 (describes how troop-contributing countries opposed robust
military action resulting in a "lowest common denominator" response to atrocities), Sections 114–116 (the proposals to exchange Srebrenica and Žepa for Serb-
held territory around Sarajevo), Section 222 (describes movements between
Srebrenica and Žepa), Section 223 (June 1, 1995, Serb ambush and taking of the
southern tip of the enclave, including Dutch surrender of OP Echo), Section 125
(difficulty of finding U.N. troops for safe areas), Section 233 (worsening humani-

tarian situation in Srebrenica by June 1995 and inability of Dutchbat to respond). MSF internal documents: MSF Srebrenica monthly report for October 1994 reports that Ilijaz is increasingly depressed, and he made and aborted plans to leave the enclave; July 7, 1994, Srebrenica interagency meeting agenda discusses goods and people being smuggled in and out of the enclave; May 13, 1994, MSF report about helicopter crash; MSF Srebrenica weekly situation report #21, May 27, 1995, describes Fatima's wounding and military activity in and around Srebrenica.

European Community Monitoring Mission (ECMM) Weekly Report for May 4–11, 1995, tells of Bosnian Serb army shelling of Bosnian government military facility outside of Sarajevo.

Report of the Dutch Parliamentary Inquiry into Srebrenica, January 2003, describes the Dutch decision to send troops to Srebrenica.

International Criminal Tribunal for former Yugoslavia, case IT-98-33, "Prosecutor v. Radislav Krstić," text of the August 2, 2001 judgement (from here on referred to as "Krstić judgment") describes Dutchbat's shrinking forces in early 1995 and the Dutchbat decision to allow Srebrenica forces to occupy shadow positions around observation posts.

Other Materials
Photograph of helicopter crash site (Mašić, *Srebrenica*, p. 167); Videotape footage taken by Dutchbat's Dr. Gerry Kremer of the comatose patient in spring 1995 and of Fatima performing procedures at the Dutchbat hospital in Potočari, making good on her internal promise to do more surgery.

Notes
PAGES 233–234 *International tension over Bosnia is high. Report of the Secretary-General Pursuant to General Assembly Resolution 53/35 (1998), "UN Srebrenica Report,"* Section 124. Refers to the commander of UNPROFOR Bosnia-Herzegovina Command, who departed in December 1993.

PAGE 240 *Inside, boxes fly.* The account of the helicopter flight was based on the recollections of four witnesses who were either on the helicopter (Dževad), on the ground awaiting it (nurses Elvira and Samira Duraković), or at a Bosnian army base in radio contact with the pilots (Hadžo Gadžo).

CHAPTER 23: EGRESS

Interviews
Dr. Ejub Alić, Mubina Alić, Dr. Mehdin Hadžiselimović, Dr. Ilijaz Pilav

Documents
Red Cross messages sent by Ejub Alić to Mubina Alić in 1994 dated January 6

("I'm sending you a photograph . . . "), July 12 ("I'm very hopeful . . . "), and July 17 ("Here love has become very cheap . . . "). Letter sent to Mubina Alić via "Mad Max" dated July 26, 1993 ("People are evil . . . "). These letters are among a group of several dozen kindly made available by the Alić's to the author.

Other Materials
Home videotape of Srebrenica taken by Dr. Ejub Alić.

Notes
PAGE 252   *The ugliness he saw led him to read his favorite author* . . . Selimović, *The Fortress,* p. 7.
PAGE 256   *On June 8* . . . No other supporting documentation could be found to confirm the exact date of Ejub's departure, which he estimates was June 8 or 9, 1995.

CHAPTER 24: OVERTURE

Interviews
Dr. Boro Lazić, Sanja Lazić, Damir Ibrahimović, Dr. Ilijaz Pilav

Published Literature
Agence France-Presse, June 12, 1995, describes military activity around Sarajevo and Bosnian government forces' capture of Mt. Treskavica; Mašić, *Srebrenica,* p. 178 covers the June 24, 1995, attack on Vidikovac above Srebrenica hospital; NIOD III/5/11 provides details on the military plan, *Krivaja 95,* including axes of attack (only one, from the southeast, was actually used) and command structure.

Documents
European Commission Monitoring Mission weekly reports provide details about the military activities around Sarajevo described in this chapter, in particular: April 21–27, May 4–11, May 11–18, and June 16–22, 1995.
    Report of the Secretary-General Pursuant to General Assembly Resolution 53/35 (1998), "UN Srebrenica Report": Sections 211–212 are about the attempts of Bosnian government forces to break the siege of Sarajevo; Section 225 describes Srebrenica soldiers' June 26, 1995, attack on Višnjica, arguing that it was a diversionary offensive to draw Serb forces away from the Sarajevo attack, and providing details of Mladić's response.
    Krstić judgment describes the Srebrenica soldiers' June 26, 1995, attack on Višnjica, arguing that it was a response to the Serbs' capture of OP-Echo; it also details the Bosnian Serb army plan, *Krivaja 95,* stressing that the original objective was not, as Boro Lazić assumed, to capture the town, but to split Sre-

brenica and Žepa and possibly to reduce each enclave to its "urban core," triggering a humanitarian crisis that would lead to an abandoning of the "safe area" concept.

Notes
PAGES 261–262 *It is not a major offensive. Report of the Secretary-General Pursuant to General Assembly Resolution 53/35 (1998), "UN Srebrenica Report,"* Section 225.

CHAPTER 25:
"OUR SINCEREST APOLOGIES"

Note
A great deal is now known about the attack on the Srebrenica enclave and the responses of Dutch U.N. forces. In addition to interviews, this account relies heavily on two secondary sources, both of which are based on original communications of the Dutch forces: the U.N. Srebrenica Report and the 7,600-page NIOD report. The excellent accounts by Chuck Sudetic (*Blood and Vengeance*) and David Rohde (*Endgame*) were also extremely valuable, as was the text of the ICTY judgment against General Krstić. I doublechecked these secondary sources against primary source material from MSF (frequent satellite telex reports sent by Christina Schmitz at MSF Srebrenica to MSF Belgrade headquarters) and interviews with those on the ground, including one Dutch soldier, Dr. Gerry Kremer, who, having been relieved of his medical duties by his surgeon replacement a few days before the attack on Srebrenica, spent much of his time with Dutch officers and on the rooftop of the Dutchbat compound viewing the offensive. I've done my best to reconcile conflicting accounts and have noted any important outstanding questions in footnotes.

Interviews
Dr. Fatima Klempić-Dautbašić, Dr. Gerry Kremer, Dr. Daniel O'Brien, Dr. Ilijaz Pilav, Naim Salkić, Pierre Salignon, Nijaz Salkić, Christina Schmitz

Published Literature
Holbrooke, *To End a War,* p. 64–65 (Janvier's secret hostage negotiations with Mladic and the subsequent change in UN air power approval policy), Rohde, *Endgame,* p. 11; "NIOD report:" III/5/12 (advance indicators of the attack); III/6/5 (Serb attacks on July 6); IV/4 (explains that the UNMO team had dropped from six to three when, during a rotation on June 24, Serbs had refused entry to the replacements); III/6/5 and III/6/6 (events on sixth, also discusses tacit pledge of Dutchbat to Srebrenicans that they would resist a Serb attack and who knew and didn't know about this promise); III/6/4 (explanation of the detailed appli-

cation procedure required for Close Air Support); III/6/24 (Ramiz Bečirović); III/6/8 (denial of Bečirović's request for arms held by UNPROFOR); III/6/6 (events of the seventh); III/6/7 (events of the eighth including the killing of a Dutchbat soldier, Van Renssen, and failure to transmit air power request); III/6/8 (July 9 including flight of Swedish shelter project residents, Karadžić decision to authorize capture of Srebrenica, Srebrenica War President Osman Suljić's letter to Bosnian President Izetbegović); III/6/9 (Srebrenicans' inability to use "Red Arrow" missiles); III/6/13 (July 10 discord between U.S. and Russian Federation in Security Council, debate over calling in a NATO air strike, failure to decide on a resolution, declaration by Security Council chairman calling on the parties to respect the safe area).

Kremer, "Medical neutrality in crisis control areas," *Medisch Contact, #45*, November 8, 1996, reviews Dutchbat's refusals to provide medical care to the local population

Documents
Report of the Secretary-General Pursuant to General Assembly Resolution 53/35 (1998), "UN Srebrenica Report": Section 480 (asserts that the attack on the OPs warranted the use of Close Air Support "even in the most restrictive interpretation of the mandate"); Section 249 (Karremans' July 7 "appeal on behalf of the population"); 250–251 (attacks on morning of the eighth); 252–254 (afternoon of the eighth and takeover of OP-Foxtrot)

Srebrenica hospital anesthesia records: details of surgery performed on the schoolteacher; records from July 6–11 have some gaps (e.g., no records for July 8 and 9) and appear possibly incomplete; the low number of surgeries represented is inconsistent with recollections of the doctors and nurses involved. They say they were too busy to document all of their work. It is also possible that some of these records were taken or destroyed before I found them in Srebrenica Hospital in 1999.

Unpublished internal MSF reports: situation report from Christina June 26, 1995 ("How come we accept their weapons ... "); Christina's final situation report covering July 6–22, 1995 (describes being awoken by the shelling on the July 6, agreement to end MSF's strike on July 9); telex MSF Sreb to Belgrade (hereafter "Bg") July 6 10:35 (indicators of the attack); telex MSF Sreb to Bg July 7 12:23:27 (Dutchbat refusal to give blood or treat patients, comment "they could at least take some patients"); telex MSF Bg to Sreb July 9 11:49 ("I am sure they will help"); weekly MSF Srebrenica report ending July 7 ("new, more distanced involvement"); telex UN B Company to MSF Sreb July 7 02:11:45 (requests casualty information); telex MSF Sreb to MSF Bg July 8 11:19:59 (casualties opposite Dutchbat compound, July 7's casualties, Ilijaz close to breakdown); telex July 8 [no time on my copy] MSF Sreb to Bg (Christina hears more than one shell a minute); telex July 9 [no time] MSF Sreb to Bg ("quite tense and shocked");

telex July 9 MSF Sreb to Bg "News from 10:30AM" (Christina requests soldiers and weapons be kept out of hospital complex); telex July 10 MSF Sreb to Bg, 7:00AM (events in hospital overnight July 9–10 confirming Ilijaz worked all night); telex July 10 Dutchbat to MSF Sreb, 12:16 UTC describes the APCs coming under tank and mortar fire whenever the APCs attempt to move south; telex July 10 UTC Dutchbat logs offers Perspex windows to MSF.

Krstić judgment relates Karadžić's decision to authorize the capture of Srebrenica.

Notes

PAGE 265   *"Say hello to Ibrahim."* This combines information from two sources, which may or may not be describing the same event: The U.N. Srebrenica Report (Section 238) says the "Say Hello to Ibrahim" message was conveyed by an "international humanitarian worker" who saw military preparations, including heavy weapons and tanks, along the Bosnian Serb side of the Drina River on July 4 from near Zvornik down to Bratunac. The NIOD report (III/5/12) describes a similar event, that a U.N. interpreter said on July 5 that a "large column of armoured and mechanized units were moving from the direction of Zvornik to Bratunac . . . A passing UNHCR convoy only noticed these transports by coincidence."

PAGE 266   *It also reassured her . . .* Karremans was not interviewed. His quote was recalled by Christina Schmitz. His assertion in June that the Bosnian army could hold its positions is also unverified. It is taken from the NIOD Report (section III/5/12) based on the recollections of the commander of the British Joint Commission Observers that Karremans had made this statement to an MSF doctor in June.

PAGE 267   *Throughout the morning . . .* The figure comes from a satellite telex message sent from MSF Belgrade to MSF Srebrenica citing information from U.N. military observers based on reports from the observation posts. NIOD III/6/5 says the Bosnian Second Corps in Tuzla reported to UNPROFOR Sector North East that a thousand projectiles hit the city over the day.

PAGE 267   *The Serbs fire on positions of Srebrenica soldiers . . .* NIOD III/6/6.

PAGE 267   *The Serbs also lob shells into civilian areas . . .* According to capsat 7/7/95, 12:23:27 from MSF Srebrenica to MSF Belgrade.

PAGE 268   *Around 1 P.M. . . .* Rohde, *Endgame*, p. 11, reports the 1 P.M. attack on the defense wall and the "UN Srebrenica Report" describes the 1:20 P.M. hit to the watchtower. Sudetic, *Blood and Vengeance*, reports a hit to the watchtower, p. 267. These might all have been the same event.

PAGE 268   *At 1:50 P.M. . . .* NIOD III/6/5 says that only Karremans viewed this as a formal request.

PAGE 269   *Janvier, usually based in Zagreb . . .* NIOD III/6/5.

PAGES 269–270   *Bečirović communicates with Naser by coded telex.* The numbers of troops quoted in this chapter should be taken as inexact, as various sources ("UN Srebrenica Report," NIOD Report, etc.) quote different and wide-ranging estimates.

PAGE 271 *"With our sincerest apologies . . . "* The message is signed, "Greetings, H. G. J. Hegge, surgeon" (the new surgeon who'd arrived in the enclave to replace the departing surgeon, Dr. Gerry Kremer, who was still inside but off active duty). The message is entitled, "Your message concerning patient time 20.17 hrs" and is marked with a UTC time of 20:49.

PAGE 271 *Srebrenica awakens Friday . . .* Death toll according to NIOD III/6/6.

PAGE 272 *Around 6 P.M. . . .* "UN Srebrenica Report" section 248.

PAGE 274 *Around 1 P.M. . . .* For some events occurring over the days of the attack, the local times cited in the NIOD report differ by approximately one hour from the times cited by the U.N. Srebrenica Report. As the sequence of the events is more important than the exact time at which they occurred, I have attempted to at least ensure consistency.

PAGES 274–275 *By pulling out . . .* According to U.N. Srebrenica Report (section 254), however the NIOD Report says the unit proceeded through the checkpoint "with permission."

PAGE 276 *Although none of the Dutch commander's requests . . .* NIOD III/6/8.

PAGE 278 *"We want you for our commander!"* The quotes are based upon Ilijaz's recollections several years after the events, and this account was confirmed by Naim Salkić, who was there, and Fatima Dautbašić, with whom he shared the story just after it occurred.

CHAPTER 26:
AN UNACCEPTABLE SITUATION

Interviews
Dr. Daniel O'Brien, Damir Ibrahimović, Dr. Fatima Klempić-Dautbašić, Dr. Gerry Kremer, Dr. Ilijaz Pilav, Naim Salkić, Nijaz Salkić, Pierre Salignon, Christina Schmitz

Published Literature
NIOD Report: III/6/9 (events of July 9, UNPROFOR decision to take blocking positions and exact orders given to Dutchbat soldiers, warnings to Bosnian Serb army); III/6/10 (events of July 10, including Srebrenicans' counterattack, Dutchbat creation of blocking positions, subsequent wounding of the Dutch, Janvier's assertion that the Bosnian army is capable of defending the enclave; the collapse of the Srebrenica lines); III/6/11 (attack of blocking positions and failure to deploy Close Air Support on the tenth); III/6/13 (Janvier's fear that UNPROFOR may be manipulated by the Bosnian government); III/6/16 (Srebrenica soldiers'

plans for another counterattack the night of July 10); Medical chapter of the NIOD report details the Dutch refusal to treat the wounded local woman on the night of the tenth.

Rohde, *Endgame*, pp. 95–97 (describes Srebrenica forces' July 10 AM counter-attack based on interviews with the participants).

Interview with Christina Schmitz published in MSF's magazine, *Ins and Outs*, Volume 7 number 9, November/December, 1995 (describes her experience when area near hospital was shelled on the morning of July 10). Kremer, "Medical neutrality in crisis control areas," *Medisch Contact*, #45, November 8, 1996 (reviews the Dutchbat refusals to provide medical care to the local population)

Documents

U.N. Srebrenica Report: Sections 273–275 (Bosnian Serb army warned and Dutchbat ordered to take blocking positions); 277–278 (attack on Dutchbat APC attempting to take blocking position), 281 (impact in front of hospital morning of July 10), 284 (Serb infantry movements on evening of July 10 and request for Close Air Support), 288 (panic of population), 295 (Karremans' promise of air strikes at meeting of Srebrenica soldiers).

Dutch Parliamentary Debriefing Report of January 31, 2003, speculates on the differing interpretations at different U.N. Protection Force command levels of the order for Dutchbat to take blocking positions; the report also asserts that taking blocking positions contributed to fulfilling Janvier's terms for granting air support.

MSF unpublished communications: July 10 04:17 UTC from Christina to UNPROFOR Srebrenica asking whether Dutch would provide an APC to evac-uate MSF. July 10 05:09 UTC from Dutchbat OPs room to Christina answering in the affirmative. July 10 05:47 UTC B-Company to MSF asking for report after see-ing smoke in their area. July 10 05:56 UTC MSF to B-Company "we are un-harmed . . ." July 10 telex MSF Sreb to Bg describes events in the overcrowded hospital at 7:00 A.M. including news that Ilijaz's good friend has just been killed, Christina's meeting with acting Commander Ramiz Bečirović, and the BBC re-porting that Serb forces are denying an offensive (no indication of exactly when she heard this). July 10 telex MSF Sreb to Bg 10:56 UTC describes events in hospi-tal at 9:15 A.M., that hospital is full of armed soldiers, and that Dutchbat liaison has come to Srebrenica and accused the Bosnian soldiers of throwing grenades at the APCs. July 10 telex MSF Sreb to UNPROFOR Dutchbat Captain Schreijen 10:55 UTC reports on shelling in front of the hospital, "We want to continue working . . ." July 10 telex Opsroom Dutchbat to MSF Sreb 11:34 UTC, ". . . the enclave is stable." July 10 telex UTC 16:26 from MSF Sreb to MSF Bg and Pale with details of the injuries suffered in the rocket attack and decision to request Dutchbat medical assistance. July 10 telex UTC 19:27 from Christina to "Major

Karremans and everybody who is concerned." July 10 telex UTC 21:08 from Christina to MSF Bg describing panic of population. July 11 telex UTC 06:51 from Christina to MSF Bg describes conditions overnight.

Anesthesia records found in Srebrenica Hospital: details of the liver surgery performed from 6:10–7:40 A.M. on July 10, the facial and vascular surgery performed from 9–11:30 A.M., several surgeries performed after the rocket attack, the woman Dutchbat refused to treat (as identified by Dr. Ilijaz Pilav) whose surgery began at 2 A.M. on July 11. As mentioned earlier, a number of records appeared to be missing.

Krstić judgment describes the panic of the population as evening fell on July 10.

Transcript of interview with Dr. Ilijaz Pilav conducted in the autumn of 1995 in which he describes his response to the meeting where Karremans promised air strikes, included in "Eyewitness accounts of the evacuation from Srebrenica and the fate of missing colleagues," An MSF report, February 1996.

Notes

PAGE 282 *Local MSF staff members pick up the wounded . . .* This account is from Damir Ibrahimović, one of the drivers. Christina Schmitz confirmed that MSF's standing policy was not to transport people in uniform, particularly those with guns, although exceptions could be made for those without, but she couldn't recall any special requests being made to the drivers on July 10.

PAGE 284 *A response arrives in under a half hour . . .* At that point, the Serb army advance toward the town may have seemed for the moment to have been halted, with no attacks on blocking positions, but this quickly changed. Christina described her disbelief in her final situation report to MSF covering the period July 6–22.

CHAPTER 27: KILLING FIELDS

Interviews
Ajka Avdić, Dr. Daniel O'Brien, Muhamed Duraković, Dr. Avdo Hasanović, Damir Ibrahimović, Dr. Fatima Klempić-Dautbašić, Dr. Gerry Kremer, Dr. Boro Lazić, Dr. Ilijaz Pilav, Naim Salkić, Nijaz Salkić, Christina Schmitz, Emira Selimović

Published Literature
NIOD Report: III/6/17 (events of July 11); III/5/11 (describes of the structure of the Serb forces participating in the attack on Srebrenica); III/7/3 (decision to call off air strikes—appears to be a combination of factors. Akashi may have already decided before receiving the message from the Netherlands Ministry of Defense).

Interview with Christina Schmitz published in MSF's magazine, *Ins and Outs*, Volume 7 number 9, November/December, 1995 (reports that MSF had thirteen local staff and collaborated with about 130 local medical staff; describes how she locked the shelter door assuming they'd be back the next day).

Rohde, *Endgame*, pp. 137–169, covers the events of July 11; Sudetic, *Blood and Vengeance*, p. 288, provides a beautiful and chilling description of the NATO air strikes.

van Laerhoven, Bob, *Srebrenica*, Chapter 5 (transcript of interview with Ilijaz not long after the time of the attacks).

Documents
U.N. Srebrenica Report, sections: 297–301 (confusion over air support requests morning of July 11), 302–303 (resumption of attack on Srebrenica on July 11 and shelling of Dutchbat B Company), 304 (Serb forces enter Srebrenica), 305–306 (NATO air strikes and the decision to halt them), 308 ("very easy target")

MSF unpublished documents: MSF Srebrenica final situation report covering July 6–21, 1995 (decision to evacuate hospital, locals invoke Vukovar; MSF's evacuation from Srebrenica); MSF security plans (e.g., 1994 plan by Isabel Ollieuz); MSF telexes on July 11 with information on number of patients and people (65/30,000) in Potočari.

Hospital documents: Hospital staff list, "Spisak radnike u Opštoj bolnici u Srebrenici," March 7, 1994, lists 125 local hospital workers.

Krstić judgment describes panic in Potočari.

Other Materials
Film, *The Fall of Srebrenica*, 1996 with footage of people fleeing was used to describe the scene. Video taken by Belgrade TV journalist Zoran Petrović (including missing pieces broadcast on Dutch IKON TV April 11, 2002, and viewable on the Website domovina.net).

Notes
PAGE 290 *The yard of Srebrenica Hospital* . . . The mysterious fog in the sky and the inhabitants' widespread belief that it was the work of NATO were described by
   several of the inhabitants interviewed and mentioned in the situation report
   Christina sent to MSF Belgrade at 06:51 UTC. The NIOD (III/6/18) asserts that
   the phenomenon was in fact caused by Bosnian Serbs, ordered by Gen.
   Ratko Mladić to set fire to haystacks, creating a smokescreen to to obscure
   potential targets.
PAGE 290 *In Zagreb, Croatia* . . . It is also notable that while Karremans expected air
   strikes (one of two air options; it had to be initiated by higher levels of the
   U.N. command structure and would not have been as dependent on mo-

ment-to-moment action on the ground), only close air support was ever on the table. Close air support required a target list with smoking guns. To this day, there is confusion over why Karremans apparently believed that air strikes were coming, when no such option had been decided upon at higher levels (Zagreb, Sarajevo) of UNPROFOR command.

PAGE 292   *"What do you want?"* This exchange is presented as Ilijaz recalled it.

PAGE 293   *"Christina," he begins ...* This interchange is presented as it was recounted by the translator, Damir Ibrahimović, who later survived the fall of Srebrenica by walking through the woods to Tuzla. Christina did not recall the specific conversation, but agreed that she wouldn't have guaranteed anyone's protection.

PAGE 293   *"No," she answers.* In some security crises, local staff members of humanitarian agencies have preferred to remain in their homes with their families.

PAGE 294   *Another local aid worker ...* These interchanges were recalled in detail by the local aid worker (Muhamed Duraković), but only in general terms by Christina, who said that she feared misuse of the telex for military purposes. Interviewed years after the incident, Dr. Daniel O'Brien also could not recall having been asked for morphine, but was almost certain that nothing but pentazocine remained in the medical stocks.

PAGES 294–295   *Ilijaz crosses the street ...* Roughly a half dozen hospital staff were interviewed about the meeting and recalled it, but each had different memories of when it occurred and what was said by whom. Ilijaz insists that he advised men to go through the woods and women who hadn't been part of the military to seek refuge at the Dutchbat compound. Someone else recalls him advocating a different position. This telling reflects the various opinions that were expressed.

PAGE 297   *"Come on," he says.* This is Ilijaz's version of the exchange. Naim recalls telling Ilijaz, "We have a 1 percent chance if we go to the forest, but if we go to Potočari, we haven't got any chance."

PAGE 304   *They go back out.* The account of Boro's entry into Srebrenica is based entirely on his recollections.

CHAPTER 28: HEGIRA

Note

The account of the doctors' exodus through the woods took Ilijaz Pilav's personal recollections as a base, related in dozens of interviews. Interviews with others who traveled with him, including Naim, Fatima, Ajka, Nijaz, Avdo, Dževad, Hadžo, Asim and Hakija, confirmed many of the details. Their memories were checked against other accounts, and the timing of certain events had to be estimated. People's recollections of a time when they were suffering from extreme stress and prolonged sleep deprivation will undoubtedly have many errors, particularly in terms of the sequence of events, so this chapter must be viewed as a best approximation of what actually happened.

Interviews
Ajka Avdić, Dr. Dževad Džananović, Hadžo Gadžo, Dr. Avdo Hasanović, Dr. Fatima Klempić-Dautbašić, Dr. Gerry Kremer, Asim Lučanin, Stephane Oberreit, Dr. Daniel O'Brien, Hakija Meholjić, Dr. Ilijaz Pilav, Naim Salkić, Nijaz Salkić, Christina Schmitz.

Published Literature
de Barros-Duchêne, *Srebrenica,* pp. 111–124; NIOD Report: (Rumors of the fall of Žepa, panic the night of July 11, details of the deportations and separation of men in Potočari on July 12 and 13; the story of the Dutchbat medical orderly who found the woman being raped; story by MSF worker Emira Selimović that bodies were found and Christina was asked to go see them; the story of the first group of wounded and medical staff that were supposed to be evacuated, but were forced back to Bratunac instead and some taken away).

van Laerhoven, *Srebrenica,* Chapter 6 (Serb megaphone calls during the group's rest by the river on July 12; lining up to walk again on July 13; Ilijaz's view of the final battle). Rohde, *Endgame,* p. 194, describes the appearance of Serb troops who barged into Potočari on July 12.

Documents
U.N. Srebrenica Report section 394 (Serb radio reports the imminent fall of Žepa).

Krstić judgment (decision to inform the column on the evening of July 11 that they are going to Tuzla; information on the artillery attack that split the line near the main road on the twelfth and the tactics, including the use of megaphones and stolen Dutch uniforms, used to draw men to surrender; details of the atrocities that took place in Potočari, the deportations, the forced evacuation of the Dutchbat compound; the men on the list remain missing.)

MSF: Christina's situation reports to Belgrade about July 12 in Potočari, e.g., 6:12 P.M. (reporting that thirty-five men are being guarded in a nearby house); 9 P.M. ("It's horrifying outside . . . "), and July 13, e.g., 11:30 A.M. (being asked to look at dead bodies, situation of patients, zero hospital mortality); a note back from Belgrade advising her not to investigate the dead bodies; 4:25 P.M. (she's going back to Srebrenica); 5 P.M. (she insists the male medical staff stay with her).

Transcript of interviews with MSF local staff members and doctors in late 1995, including Emira Selimović (story about the man giving the baby to Christina).

Other Materials
Zoran Petrović footage showing men in Sandići field being forced to call for their relatives; shooting anti-aircraft guns into the hillsides. Film entitled *Fall of Srebrenica* (Tuzla, 1996), shows the medical staff members entering free territory.

Notes
PAGE 307 *Ilijaz agrees and informs Ramiz . . .* There is not complete agreement among interviewees as to where in the column the medical staff members were. Ilijaz Pilav says they were always in the front, whereas others recall they were in the middle until the first ambush near Kravica, and after that in the front. The same goes for Dudić's brigade. Ilijaz believes that Dudić was in the middle, but the NIOD report says that his brigade was the last.

PAGE 308 *Ilijaz's group continues away from the sounds . . .* The part of the Zvornik-Vlasenica road that runs between Nova Kasaba and Konjevići.

PAGE 309 *They run through the tall fern . . .* Jusef Sulejmanović, Senahid Salihović, Redžo Babić, Mehmedalia Dedić, and Rešid Bektić. Sadik Ahmetović stayed in the back in the first shelling during the day.

PAGE 309 *"What are you doing here?"* One Srebrenica soldier interviewed for this book (Mensur Gadžo) said that he was part of a detail of soldiers assigned by military authorities to keep an eye out for the doctors and protect them, in gratitude for their work (there was a similar protection unit for commanders). Ilijaz denies knowing of such a unit and believes the medical group fended for themselves.

PAGE 310 *"Hey, your pictures!"* Ilijaz later heard that the man carrying his and Fatima's photographs was shot and killed by the river. Some of those who crossed the river after Ilijaz and saw his photographs assumed that Ilijaz had been killed.

PAGE 311 *Ilijaz asks some brigade commanders . . .* This information is from the NIOD report, which says that the front and back weren't in direct communication because of a problem with walkie-talkie frequency mismatch.

PAGE 311 *They rely on news coming from each new group . . .* The NIOD report contends that the reason the Serb attack was not launched immediately was that the Serb army did not know about the existence of the column until midday on the twelfth, and only then deployed all available units to attack it. This (rather than a deliberate choice to attack the middle of the column, which is also a possibility) could explain why groups toward the front of the column crossed the road with ease.

PAGES 311–312 *Ilijaz tries to sleep awhile . . .* This particular incident, not specifically recalled by Ilijaz, is noted in the Human Rights Watch report *Chemical Warfare in Bosnia? The Strange Experiences of the Srebrenica Survivors*, Human Rights Watch, November, 1998, Volume 10, Number 9 (D). The report speculated on use of BZ or other psychochemical incapacitant by the Serbs. Testimonial evidence was compelling but hard evidence was lacking, in part because of lack of funding to do chemical testing. HRW called for more investigation and making public the results of an investigation rumored to have been carried out by the U.S. government.

PAGE 312   *The air is still and quiet* . . . One of the Srebrenica military, Mensur Gadžo, claims that on Mt. Udrč he suggested taking the doctors by another route. The doctors were undecided until Branka Stanić (the young Croat physician) had the last word: "I was there for the whole war, and I want to be with them now." The NIOD report suggests that all civilians on the journey were taken under the wing of one of the military units.

PAGE 314   *Earlier in the evening* . . . Naval captain Andre Schouten.

PAGE 319   *"What are these buildings doing here?"* Naim tells another version of this story in which Ilijaz had the hallucination while the medical group was together and Fatima slapped him awake.

PAGE 323   *"Doctor, it looks like the only normal people left* . . . *"* The conversation was recalled by both of them, but Hakija thought it took place at night. Hakija Meholjić insists that he saw the medical staff members take pills, refuse to share them with others, and fail to treat the injured. The medical staff members deny this.

PAGE 323   *If we survive this together* . . . Ilijaz didn't specify exactly when in their journey he had this thought.

PAGE 326   *Sometime around 2 P.M.* . . . According to the Krstić decision: "On 16 July 1995, Lieutenant Colonel Vinko Pandurević, the Commander of the Zvornik Brigade, reported that, in view of the enormous pressure on his Brigade, he had taken a unilateral decision to open up a corridor to allow about 5,000 unarmed members of the Bosnian Muslim column to pass through." The NIOD reports that other elements of the Bosnian army attacked the Serb lines from behind, which explains the confusing appearance of the battle to Ilijaz and the amount of firepower displayed.

CHAPTER 29: FREEDOM

Interviews
Dr. Ejub Alić, Dr. Dževad Džananović, Dr. Avdo Hasanović, Stephane Oberreit, Dr. Fatima Klempić-Dautbašić, Dr. Ilijaz Pilav, Christina Schmitz

Documents
List of Srebrenica hospital workers, "Spisak: Medicinski radnika—prognanika iz Srebrenice," July 21, 1995, Ministry of Health, Tuzla-Podrinja Canton, Bosnia-Herzegovina.

MSF documents: Christina's situation reports to MSF Belgrade from Potočari, July 14–21. MSF Srebrenica final situation report covering July 6–21, 1995.

CHAPTER 30: SADIK

Interviews
Sadik Ahmetović, Dr. Benjamin Kulovac, Dr. Boro Lazić, Sanja Lazić

Published Literature
Physicians for Human Rights, *Medicine Under Siege in the Former Yugoslavia 1991–1995*, pp. 58–61.

Documents
Transcript of interview with Sadik Ahmetović performed in the fall of 1995 by Laurence de Barros-Duchêne.
  Krstić judgment describing the offensive on Žepa.
  U.N. Srebrenica Report sections 415–431 (the capture of Žepa)

EPILOGUE

Interviews
Dr. Ejub Alić, Mubina Alić, Francis Boyle, Arthur Caplan, Dr. Eric Dachy, Rex Dudley, Kris Janowski, Dr. Boro Lazić, Sanja Lazic, Dr. Fatima Klempić-Dautbašić, Dr. Bernard Kouchner, Dr. Nedret Mujkanović, Stephane Oberreit, Dr. Ilijaz Pilav, Pierre Salignon, Christina Schmitz, Dr. Ernlie Young

Published Literature
Barry, "A bridge too far"; Coady, "The ethics of armed humanitarian interventions," p. 34; Fink, "Physician groups and the war in Kosovo"; Holbrooke, *To End a War*, p. 102; Marmon et al., "The diplomat/physician in the emerging international system"; Power, *A Problem from Hell*, p. 419. NIOD report III/6/6 (U.S. officials received daily briefings from Dutch officials); *RFE/RL* December 20, 2002 ("Bosnian Muslims seek UN compensation for Srebrenica"); Physicians for Human Rights, *War Crimes in Kosovo*, pp. 95–97 (summary of medical neutrality concept); *TimeEurope*, September 11, 2002 ("A Bosnian Serb official investigation claims "exhaustion," not massacre, killed thousands in Srebrenica," by Anis Alić and Dragan Stanimirović), *Voice of America*, September 4, 2002 ("International officials denounce Serb Srebrenica report," by Stefan Bos).

Documents
Krstić judgment.
  MSF unpublished documents: Press Release, Doctors Without Borders, New York/Paris, January 31, 2003: "Dutch inquiry fails to answer key questions into Srebrenica Massacre: MSF calls for the US and the UK to carry out investigations." Doctors Without Borders, November 11, 2000, "Why MSF is calling for a parliamentary commission on Srebrenica." Doctors Without Borders briefing

document, November 2001, "Parliamentary hearings on Srebrenica: the arguments, omissions and contradictions."

U.N. Srebrenica Report, sections: 486 (question of countries possessing advance knowledge about the attack on Srebrenica), 501 (call for U.N. member states to examine their responsibility for Srebrenica by their "prolonged refusal to use force in the early stages of the war").

Asemblée Nationale (France), November 22, 2001, "Report by the Parliamentary Committee on the events in Srebrenica: Conclusion."

Asemblée Nationale (France), November 22, 2001, #3413, "Rapport d'information dépose en application de l'article 145 du Règlement: Par la mission d'information commune sur les événements de Srebrenica," pp. 183–192.

Dutch Parliament, January 27, 2003, the Hague, "Introduction by the Chairman of the Committee of Inquiry into Srebrenica at the presentation of the final report, 'Missie Zonder Vrede'—'A Mission Without Peace.'"

Other Materials

Information on those indicted and arrested comes from the International Criminal Tribunal for the former Yugoslavia website: www.un.org/icty accessed April 30, 2003.

Photographs released by the United States government showing land disturbances near Srebrenica in July 1995 suggestive of mass graves.

Notes

PAGE 340 *The last week of August* ... After more than a year of lobbying by the American Committee to Save Bosnia (a coalition of grassroots and national organizations) and the Action Council for Peace in the Balkans (composed of prominent citizens) led by State Department resignees Stephen Walker and Marshall Harris, both houses of the U.S. Congress passed, by veto-proof margins, legislation to lift the arms embargo on Bosnia. The Senate vote immediately followed the fall of Srebrenica, and several previously undecided Senators cited it as a major reason for their affirmative votes. According to Walker, "If lifting the embargo worked, Clinton's responsibility for facilitating genocide—and (Senate majority leader Bob) Dole's leadership in ending it—would stand in stark contrast in the election."

PAGE 340 *By the time that international leaders* ... Some analysts suggest that it was Clinton's election-year political need to conclude a quick peace deal with Serbian President Slobodan Milošević that led him to halt the Croatians and Bosnians at the moment they had command of roughly the amount of territory allotted to them in the latest "Contact Group" peace plan.

PAGE 347 *Dutch officers argued* ... *Radio Netherlands*, November 19, 2002, by Marina Brouwer. www.nrw.nl/hotspots/html/sreo21119.html (accessed November 20, 2002).

PAGE 347   *As just one example . . .* This is a four-page document marked "secret" to P-Mr. Kantor from INR-Douglas P. Mulholland. Subject: Bosnia: Actions contributing to genocide. United States Department of State. January 11, 1993.

PAGE 350   *On another topic . . .* Even the International Committee of the Red Cross, which guards its humanitarian neutrality extremely closely out of a belief that this allows it to function on all sides of every war, broke its characteristic silence and repeatedly denounced violations of humanitarian law in Bosnia—condemning such violations should in no way be considered a violation of humanitarian neutrality.

PAGE 350   *There are times when the higher moral duty . . .* Some analysts have called for the creation of "physician-diplomats," trained in both medicine and international relations.

PAGES 351–352   *In the case of Bosnia, however . . .* Military involvement in humanitarian action is itself a controversial subject, and events in Srebrenica illustrate some of its problems as well as its benefits. Dutchbat medical teams became involved in medical assistance to the Srebrenica population out of a genuine desire to help at a time when they had abundant resources and helping the population improved the standing of Dutchbat. However, because provision of humanitarian assistance wasn't Dutchbat's main aim, it withdrew that assistance when other priorities took precedence. In the meantime Srebrenicans and even MSF in Srebrenica had become dependent on this medical assistance. In the spring of 2003, the fear of dependence on temporary military medical aid was raised in Iraq when U.S. marines set up temporary field hospitals in parallel with the regular health system as part, according to several of those involved, of a "hearts and minds" campaign to improve their standing with the local population.

PAGE 352   *In the spring of 2003 . . .* However, it could be argued that the "occupying powers" were trying to meet that responsibility, in part, by funding nongovernmental humanitarian aid agencies to do the work in which they, not the military, excel.

PAGE 352   *Finally, the shining example of a doctor . . .* This must be said of many of the Srebrenica doctors, too, including Ejub Alić, Fatima Dautbašić, and Nijaz Džanić among others. Eric Dachy, though he held passionate beliefs about the war, consistently acted as a neutral humanitarian, bringing assistance to all who needed it, regardless of their nationality.

PAGE 356   *"Srebrenica has only strengthened my resolve and my motivation . . ."* Ins and Outs, November/December 1995, by Malou Nozemann. Volume 9, #7. Interview with Christina Schmitz entitled "We can't remain silent and just do our medical work."

BIBLIOGRAPHY

Aeberhard, Patrick. "A Historical Survey of Humanitarian Action." *Health and Human Rights.* Vol. 2 No. 1, 1996, pp. 30–45.

Anić, Nikola, et al. *Sanitetska Služba u Narodno Oslobodinačkom Ratu Jugoslavije 1941–1945.* Belgrade: Vojnoizdavački i novinski centar, 1989.

Armstrong, Gail, and Patricia Forestier. "Ending the Balkan Nightmare." *Freedom,* Volume 31, Issue 2 (year unknown).

Barry, Jane, with Anna Jefferys. "A Bridge Too Far: Aid Agencies and the Military in Humanitarian Response." *Humanitarian Practice Network Paper,* Number 37, 2002.

Beauchamp, Tom, and James F. Childress. *Principles of Biomedical Ethics, Fourth Edition.* New York: Oxford University Press, 1994.

Bellamy, Ronald, and Russ Zajtchuk (eds.). *Conventional Warfare: Ballistic, Blast and Burn Injuries.* Washington, D.C.: Office of the Surgeon General, 1991.

Berger, Jean-François. *The Humanitarian Diplomacy of the ICRC and the Conflict in Croatia (1991–1992).* Geneva: International Committee of the Red Cross, 1995.

Bosnia Country Handbook. Washington, D.C.: United States Department of Defense and Peace Stabilization Force (SFOR), 1997.

Bosnia: Echoes from an Endangered World—Music and Chant of the Bosnian Muslims. Compact disc. Smithsonian Folkways, SF-40407, 1993.

Bouchet-Saulnier, Françoise. "Peacekeeping Operations Above Humanitarian Law." In François Jean, ed., *Life, Death and Aid: The Médecins Sans Frontières Report on World Crisis Intervention.* New York: Routledge, 1993, pp. 125–130.

———. *The Practical Guide to Humanitarian Law.* Lanham, Md.: Rowman and Littlefield, 2002.

Brauman, Rony. "When Suffering Makes a Good Story." In François Jean, ed., *Life, Death and Aid: The Médecins Sans Frontières Report on World Crisis Intervention.* New York : Routledge, 1993, pp. 149–158.

Celebije, Evlije. *Putopis—Odlomcia Jugoslavenskim Zemljama.* Sarajevo: Svjetlost, 1967.

Coady, C. A. J. "The Ethics of Armed Humanitarian Intervention." *Peaceworks,* #45, United States Institute of Peace, July 2002.

Columbia Encyclopedia, Sixth Edition. New York: Columbia University Press, 2002. As cited in http://www.bartleby.com/people/Lister-J.html. Accessed 12/1/02.

Council of the International Institute of Humanitarian Law. "Guiding Principles on the Right to Humanitarian Assistance." *International Review of the Red Cross.* November–December, No. 297, 1993, pp. 519–525.

Coupland, Robin M. *Amputation for War Wounds.* Geneva: International Committee of the Red Cross, 1992.

D'Atorg, Bernard. "La Peste." *Esprit* (Paris), 1947.

de Barros-Duchêne, Laurence. *Srebrenica: Histoire d'un crime international.* Paris: L'Harmattan, 1996.

Dekleva, Kenneth B., and Jerrold M. Post. "Genocide in Bosnia: The Case of Dr. Radovan Karadžić." *Journal of the American Academy of Psychiatry and the Law.* 25 (4), 1997, pp. 485–496.

Destexhe, Alain. "From Solferino to Sarajevo." *Health and Human Rights.* Vol. 2, No. 1, 1996, pp. 46–59.

Donini, Antonio. "Beyond Neutrality: On the Compatibility of Military Intervention and Humanitarian Assistance." *The Fletcher Forum.* Summer/Fall, 1995. pp. 31–45.

Duizings, Ger. *History, Memory and Politics in Eastern Bosnia.* Original English language version graciously provided by the Duizings to the author. Published in Dutch as: *Geschiedenis en herinnering. De achtergronden van de val van Srebrenica.* Amsterdam: Boom.

Eknes, Åge. "Blue Helmets in a Blown Mission? UNPROFOR in Former Yugoslavia." *Research Report: Norwegian Institute of International Affairs.* No. 174, December. (Oslo, Norway), 1993.

Emergency War Surgery: Second United States Revision Emergency War Surgery NATO Handbook. El Dorado, Ariz.: Desert Publications, 1992.

Fink, Sheri. "Physician groups and the war in Kosovo: Ethics, neutrality and interventionism." *JAMA* 283 (March, 2000), p. 1200.

Golemović, Dimitrije O. *Narodna Muzika Podrinja.* Sarajevo: Drugari, 1987.

Groenewold, Julia, and Eve Porter (eds.). *World in Crisis: The Politics of Survival at the End of the Twentieth Century.* New York: Routledge, 1997.

Kreševljaković, Hamdija. "Stari Bosanski Gradovi." *Godišnjak Zemalskog Zavoda za Zaštitu Spomenika Kulture i Prirodnih Rijetkosti N. R. Bosne i Hercegovine* SV (I), 1953.

Hermet, Guy. "The Human Rights Challenge to Sovereignty." In François Jean, ed., *Life, Death and Aid: The Médecins Sans Frontières Report on World Crisis Intervention.* New York: Routledge, 1993, pp. 131–137.

———. "Humanitarian Aid Versus Politics." In François Jean, ed., *Populations in Danger.* London: John Libbey & Company Ltd., 1992, pp. 107–111.

Hoffer, Eric. *The True Believer: Thoughts on the Nature of Mass Movements.* New York: Harper and Row, 1989.

Holbrooke, Richard. *To End a War.* New York: Random House, 1998.

Hollingworth, Larry. *Merry Christmas Mr. Larry.* London: Mandarin, 1996.

Honig, Jan Willem, and Norbert Both. *Srebrenica: Record of a War Crime.* London: Penguin Books, Ltd., 1996.

International Committee of the Red Cross. *Saving Lives: The ICRC's Mandate to Pro-*

tect Civilians and Detainees in Bosnia-Herzegovina. ICRC Special Brochure. Geneva: ICRC Publications, April, 1995.

Ivanišević, Milivoje. "Fate of the Serbs of the Bratunac, Srebrenica, Skelani Region, Eastern Bosnia 1992–1993," in V. Hadživuković, M. Ivanišević and D. Tanasković (eds.), *Bosnia and Herzegovina: Chronicle of an Announced Death.* Belgrade/Milići: Ed. Center for Geopolitical Studies, 1993, pp. 74–91.

————. *Hronika Našeg Groblja: Ili slovo o stradanju srpskog naroda Bratunca, Milića, Skelana i Srebrenice.* Belgrade/Bratunac: Komitet za prikupljanje podataka o izvršenim zločinima protiv covecnosti i medžunarodnog prava, 1994.

Jean, François. "Refugees and Displaced Persons: A New Deal." In François Jean, ed., *Populations in Danger.* London: John Libbey & Company Ltd., 1992.

Jelavic, Barbara. *History of the Balkans: Twentieth Century.* Cambridge: Cambridge University Press, 1983.

Levi, Primo. *The Drowned and the Saved.* New York: Vintage International, 1989.

Maass, Peter. *Love Thy Neighbor: A History of War.* New York: Alfred A. Knopf, 1996.

Magaš, Branka. *The Destruction of Yugoslavia.* New York: Verso, 1993.

Malcolm, Noel. *Bosnia: A Short History.* New York: New York University Press, 1994.

Maletić, Mihailo. *Znamenitosti i Lepote.* Belgrade: Književne Novine, 1965.

Marmon, Louis, Christopher Seniw, and Allan Goodman. "The Diplomat/ Physician in the Emerging International System." *Medicine and Global Survival.* Volume 1, No. 4, 1994.

Mašić, Nijaz. *Srebrenica: Agresija, Otpor, Izdaja i Genocid.* Srebrenica: Općina, 1999.

Médecins Sans Frontières. *Techniques Chirurgicales de Base.* Paris: Hatier, 1989.

Medicinska Enciklopedija. Volume 6. Zagreb: Jugoslavenski Leksikografski Zavod, 1970.

Miller, Ronald D. (ed.). *Anesthesia, Fifth Edition.* New York: Churchill Livingstone, Inc., 2000.

Moreillon, Jacques. "The Promotion of Peace and Humanity in the Twenty-First Century." *International Review of the Red Cross.* November–December, No. 303, 1994, pp. 595–610.

Morillon, Général Philippe. *Croire et Oser: Chronique de Sarajevo.* Paris: Bernard Grasset, 1993.

Mosby's GenRx, Eleventh Edition. St. Louis: Mosby, Inc., 2001.

Naythons, Matthew. *The Face of Mercy: A Photographic History of Medicine at War.* New York: Random House, 1993.

Nelan, Bruce W. "Seeds of Evil: The opportunistic and allegedly criminal career of Radovan Karadžić may be coming to an end." *Time.* July 29, 1996.

Netherlands Institute for War Documentation (NIOD). *Srebrenica A 'Safe' Area: Reconstruction, Background, Consequences and Analyses of the Fall of a Safe Area.* The Hague: Boom Publishers (Dutch version) or online (English version) at www.srebrenica.nl (accessed 3/5/03).

Oberreit, Stephan, and Pierre Salignon. "Bosnia: In Search of a Lasting Peace."

In Groenewold, Julia, and Eve Porter (eds.). *World in Crisis: The Politics of Survival at the End of the Twentieth Century.* New York: Routledge, 1997.

Orić, Naser. *Srebrenica Svjedoći i Optužuje: Genocid nad Bosnjacima u istoćnoj Bosni (srednje Podrinje), April 1992–Septembar 1994.* Srebrenica: Općina, 1995.

Physicians for Human Rights. *Medicine Under Siege in the Former Yugoslavia 1991–1995.* Boston: Physicians for Human Rights, 1996.

Physicians for Human Rights and the Program on Forced Migration and Health, Columbia University. *War Crimes in Kosovo: A Population-Based Assessment of Human Rights Violations Against Kosovar Albanians.* Boston: Physicians for Human Rights, 1999.

Pollack, Kenneth M. *The Threatening Storm: The Case for Invading Iraq.* New York: Random House, 2002.

Post, Jerrold M., and Kenneth B. Dekleva. "The Odyssey of Dr. Radovan Karadžić." 1997. Unpublished manuscript.

Power, Samantha. *A Problem from Hell: America and the Age of Genocide.* New York: Basic Books, 2002.

Rieff, David. "The Humanitarian Trap." *World Policy Journal.* 12 (4) Winter 1995–1996. p. 3.

———. *Slaughterhouse: Bosnia and the Failure of the West.* New York: Simon and Schuster, 1995.

Rufin, Jean-Christophe. "The Paradoxes of Armed Protection." In François Jean, ed., *Life, Death and Aid: The Médecins Sans Frontières Report on World Crisis Intervention.* New York: Routledge, 1993, pp. 111–123.

Russbach, Remi, and Daniel Fink. "Humanitarian Action in Current Armed Conflicts: Opportunities and Obstacles." *Medicine and Global Survival*, Vol. 1, No. 4, December 1994.

Sandoz, Yves. "'Droit' or 'devoir d'ingérence' and the right to assistance: the issues involved." *International Review of the Red Cross.* May–June, No. 288, pp. 215–227, 1992.

Selimović, Meša. *The Fortress* (translated by E. D. Goy and Jasna Levinger). Evanston, Ill.: Northwestern University Press, 1999.

Silber, Laura, and Allan Little. *Yugoslavia: Death of a Nation.* New York: TV Books, Inc., 1996.

Silove, Derrick. "The Psychiatrist as a Political Leader in War: Does the Medical Profesion Have a Monitoring Role?" *The Journal of Nervous and Mental Disease.* Vol. 183, No. 3, March, 1995. pp. 125–126.

The Socialist Republic of Bosnia and Hercegovina: An Offprint from the Second Edition of Enciklopedija Jugoslavije. Zagreb: Jugoslavenski Leksikografski Zavod, 1983.

Treasures of Yugoslavia: An encyclopedic touring guide. Belgrade: Yugoslaviapublic, [undated].

UNHCR. *The State of the World's Refugees: In Search of Solutions*. Oxford: Oxford University Press, 1995.

————. *The State of the World's Refugees: The Challenge of Protection*. New York: Penguin Books, 1993.

van Laerhoven, Bob. *Srebrenica: Getuigen van een massamoord*. Antwerp: Icarus (Standaard Uitgeverij NV), 1996.

Vincent, Anne. "The 'French Doctors' Movement' and Beyond." *Health and Human Rights*. Vol. 2 No. 1. 1996. pp. 25–29.

Westmoreland, Barbara, Eduardo Benarroch, Jasper Daube, Thomas Reagan, and Burton Sandok. *Medical Neurosciences: An Approach to Anatomy, Pathology, and Physiology by Systems and Levels, Third Edition*. Boston: Little, Brown and Company, 1994.

Yugoslavia: Death of a Nation [Videorecording]. Brian Lapping Associates for Discovery Channel, BBC, and ORF; series producer Norma Percy; producer, Angus Macqueen; director, Paul Mitchell. New York: Discovery Channel Video, 1995.

Zajtchuk, Russ, and Christopher M. Grande (eds.). *Anesthesia and Perioperative Care of the Combat Casualty*. Washington, D.C.: Office of the Surgeon General, 1995.

PHOTO CREDITS

The town Srebrenica, Photo Institute for Military History RNLA; *The Srebrenica Hospital,* Sheri Fink; *The main road leading north,* Rene Caravielhe/MSF; *General Philippe Morillon,* Philipp von Recklinghausen; *Dr. Eric Dachy,* Courtesy of Dr. Eric Dachy; *In the pharmacy,* Courtesy of Dr. Thierry Pontus; *First attempted helicopter medical evacuation,* Philipp von Recklinghausen; *A young child mortally injured,* Philipp von Recklinghausen; *In the Srebrenica Hospital "emergency room,"* Philipp von Recklinghausen; *Srebrenica was flooded with displaced villagers,* Philipp von Recklinghausen; *Srebrenica's amputees march through town,* Philipp von Recklinghausen; *Local soldiers shoot into the air,* Philipp von Recklinghausen; *Injured patients lie on the floor,* Hans Ulens; *Dr. Nedret Mujkanović,* Suzanne Keating; *Because of a severe paper shortage, doctors wrote prescriptions,* Samples collected by Sheri Fink; *In the Srebrenica Hospital operating theater,* Laurence de Barros-Duchêne; *MSF party with hospital staff,* Courtesy of Dr. Ilijaz Pilav; *The "Ljiljanijade" sports competition,* Courtesy of Dr. Ilijaz Pilav; *Bosnian Serb army physician Boro Lazić,* Courtesy of Dr. Boro Lazić.

ACKNOWLEDGMENTS

This book owes its greatest debt to two physicians—Dr. Ilijaz Pilav and Dr. Eric Dachy—without whose stories and extensive cooperation it would not exist. I will never underestimate how difficult it was for all of those I interviewed to recall the most trying days of their lives. Dr. Boro Lazić, Dr. Nedret Mujkanović, Dr. Fatima Dautbašić, Dr. Ejub Alić, and nurses Ajka Avdić and Christina Schmitz also bore with me for dozens of hours. Thank you from the bottom of my heart for your openness and for learning to laugh knowingly every time I said, "Just one more question." In addition, I would like to extend my gratitude to all others whose names are listed in the chapter sections under interviews.

Thank you to the very many people who provided information, materials, encouragement, and other forms of support during the research and writing of this book. The most special thanks are due to two of the finest and most brilliant journalists I know, and to whom my work owes its greatest debt. Chuck Sudetic, the gifted author of *Blood and Vengeance*, was immensely generous and encouraging throughout this project. (And thanks to his parents, Kris and Al, for letting me rummage through their attic!) David Rohde, author of *Endgame: The Betrayal and Fall of Srebrenica,* was always supportive, and the sterling example he sets of journalistic integrity, hard work, and guts is one of my greatest inspirations. I'd also like to thank Dr. Sead Ahmetagić, Mubina Alić, Dr. Sabit Begić, Mayor Selim Bešlagić, Tony Birtley, Sonja Biserko, Urs Boegli, Norbert Both, Rony Brauman, Dr. Smail Čekić, Richard Claude, Dr. Louisa Chan-Boegli, Muriel Cornelis, Dr. Georges Dallemagne, Laurence de Barros-Duchêne, Dr. Martin De Smet, Alain Destexhe, Rex Dudley, Dr. Neak Duong, Muhamed Duraković, Dr. Dževad Džananović, Hadžo and Mensur Gadžo, Dr. Besim Hajdarović, Dr. Mehdin Hadžiselimović, Dr. Avdo Hasanović, Guy Hermet, Glenn Hodgson, Samira Hodžic, Larry Hollingworth, Dr. Ibrahim Huskić, Nedim Jaganjac, Kris Janowski, Laurens Jolles, U.S. Army Captain Omar Jones, Dr. Gerry Kremer, Dr. Benjamin Kulovac, Judith Kumin, Dr. Petar Lončarević, Sanja Lazić,

Asim Lučanin, Dr. Jean-Pierre Luxen, Hakija Meholjić, Dr. Milomir Mi-lošević, and the current staff of the Srebrenica and Bratunac Health Centers, Hasan Nuhanović, Azra Mujkanović, Bart Nijples, Daniel O'Brien, Isabel Ollieuz, Fahreta Omić, Dr. Miroslav Oprić, Dr. Irfanka Pašagić, Senad Pečanin, Dr. Radomir Pavlović, Ibrahim Purković, Dr. Božina Radević, David Rieff, Dr. Adi Rifatbegović, Gen. Hazim Šadić, Pierre Salignon, Naim Salkić, Nijaz Salkić, Dr. Mirha Saračević, Emira Se-limović, Rahima and Damir Tursunović-Ibrahimović, the Ustić family, Gerard van Driessche, Philipp von Recklinghausen, Dr. Piet Willems, and Dr. Wim Wertheim.

This would have been a far less informed book if not for the remark-able openness of the Doctors Without Borders organization. Its leaders' inclination to look critically at their own work and allow others to do the same is the key, I believe, to the organization's impressive history of growth and vitality. I have the utmost respect for the group and its members, who approach their work with a rare sense of purpose, in-tegrity, creativity, and intellectual curiosity. For their help in locating archival materials and connecting with former aid workers, thanks to the many staff members of Doctors Without Borders Belgium; to Cecile Guthmann, Anne Fouchard, and others at Doctors Without Borders France; and to the brave and compassionate Kenny Gluck, Malou Noze-man, and others at Doctors Without Borders the Netherlands.

The following institutions and their former and current representa-tives also provided a valuable font of materials: Anne Harringer, Pippa Scott, Svjetlana Tevapčić and the International Monitor Institute; Ger Duijzings, Paul Koedijk, Peter Romijn, Dijk Schoonoord, and the Netherlands Institute for War Documentation; Sead and Nihad Kreševl-jakovića and the Hamdija Kreševljakovića library in Sarajevo; Šefket Ib-rišević and the Archives of the Bosnian Army Second Corps in Tuzla; the New York and Boston Public Libraries; New York University Library and U.N. repository; libraries of the University of California at Berkeley, Har-vard University, Stanford University, Hoover Institution, and University of Michigan; Narodna Biblioteka Bratunac; Ministry of Public Health Tu-zla; University of Sarajevo Medical School; Bosnia-Herzegovina Institute of Public Health in Sarajevo; Federal Hydrometeorological Institute of Yugoslavia, Belgrade; Kris Janowski, Trudy Huskamp Peterson and the archives of the United Nations High Commissioner for Refugees; Dr.

Gillian Biddulph and the International Committee of the Red Cross archives, photo, video, and print libraries; Massaoutis Panayiotis and the World Health Organization archives; and Gregory Hess and the World Health Organization.

Hvala puno to those who helped with translation, context, and more in Bosnia, Serbia, and the United States including Izabella Gavrić, Iskra Čucković, Sanel Hadžiahmetović, Nermin Zukić, Melika Horozić, Dr. Anja Tomić, Ulvija Tanović, Damir Arsenijević, Rijad Hasić, Naida Begeta, Vedad Lihovac, Neven Luledvija, Senada Krešo, Boris Knežević, Zoran Ivančić, Darko Radošević, Elvira Jašarević, Besmir Fidahić, and Vanja Savanić.

Thanks to those friends and acquaintances who provided places to rest my head and suitcase along with valuable conversation and encouragement while working on this book, including: Adila and Jasmina Viteškić, Bisera and Mesud Imamović and Anna Husarska in Sarajevo; Čevala and Himzo Hasić, Doug Ford, Mary Ellen Keough, Catriona Palmer, Laurie Vollen and Physicians for Human Rights in Tuzla; Brian Ruane and the OSCE in Srebrenica; the Lazić family in Šekovići; Dr. Lazar Prodanović in Zvornik; Maja Vrhovac in Banja Luka; Sanja Ilić and Zoran, Stefan, and Oki in Belgrade; Pakize Kaleci (with Eric Dachy) for her great cooking in Brussels; Brad Blitz in London; Sharon Silber, David Weiss, George Musser, Talia Schaffer, and Douglas Rothschild in New York; Glenn Ruga, Barbara Ayotte, and Nan Fornal in Boston; Brent Phillips and Anna for a brief, welcome respite in the Algarve; Fokko De Vries, Sanja Percela, Yannick Du Pont, Gaby Post, and Natascha Jerkovic in Amsterdam; Margaret Samuels and Tom Parker in the Hague; the Ulens family in the Netherlands; Gil and Judy Kulick in Maryland; Vladimir and Svatava Mach in Prague; Dr. Simon Mardel and his wife in Barrow in Furness; Thierry Pontus and his wife in Belgium; and Lee and Irv Zelitsky in San Francisco.

A huge thanks to my best friend in Bosnia, Alma Šahbaz, and my best Bosnian friends in the United States, Amna, Memin, Anesa, and Fatih Tokmo, for their incredible support and for making me fall even more in love with their country.

I'm deeply indebted to those who supported this work with grants, beginning with Dr. Tom Raffin and the Center for Bioethics at Stanford University, which supported my first trip to Bosnia. Dr. Harvey Weinstein, Eric Stover, and Gilles Perress of the University of California at Berkeley Human Rights Center helped me develop the initial idea for a book on Bosnian war medicine and provided the means, with a generous grant from the Herbert and Marion Sandler Family Foundation, to spend a year in the Balkans (you were right, guys, it *did* take more than a year to research and write this book). If it were not for their initial interest and willingness to gamble their resources on an untested writer, this book would not exist. Thank you from the bottom of my heart. A grant from the U.S.-Mexico writer's exchange program (supported by the Writer's Room of New York, U.S. Embassy in Mexico, Fondo Nacional para la Cultura y las Artes, and Sociedad General de Escritores de Mexico) provided two months of very helpful semi-isolation at La Casa del Escritor in Mexico City, where the first draft of this manuscript was completed. Thanks to the staff of La Casa as well as to staff members, colleagues, and backers of the Writer's Room of New York and the (unaffiliated) Writer's Room of Boston, where I wrote at all hours without distraction.

I'm deeply grateful for the generous time and constructive criticism of those who read and commented on early drafts of this manuscript: Jack Hart, editor of the *Oregonian*, Harriet Washington of Harvard's Department of Medical Ethics, Herschel Fink (thanks Dad!), Christopher Hitchens, Krim Delko, Linda Pollack, and Steve Walker. Thanks, too, to John and Lynn Franklin for providing years of WriterL, no matter where in the world I was, and for brainstorming with me in a "stuck" moment at the 2002 Nieman narrative journalism conference, graciously hosted by Mark Kramer.

To my buddies from the U.S. army base in Sarajevo, Tony Castillo, Andy Fishman, and Jeffrey Abramowitz, thanks for looking out for me, taking me to the PX, and defusing the "mine" we found on Mjedenica. Thanks to Mirza Muminović and other student members of BoHeMSA at the University of Sarajevo Medical School for organizing the conference that inspired my interest in this subject.

The support and encouragement of friends, fellow writers, and other colleagues has been enormous. Thanks to Fred Abrahams, Patrick Ball, Marc Bartolini, Hamida and Ken Begović, Dino Besić, Vicky Bruce (a.k.a. fairy godmother), Darcy Cosper, Thomas Cushman, Susie Devenyi, Manuela Dobos, Nathaniel Eaton, Leslie Fratkin, Lisa Gervin, Rita Giglio for always believing in me, Tom Gjelton, Daniel Hoffman, Paul Keegan, Ken Kim, Sara Kurlich, Chris Momenee, Katie Orenstein, Barry Reese, Mike Rothenberg, Joe Sacco, James Sanders, Lee and Pip Sanders, Robert Sapolsky, Cindy Scharf, Bob Silk, Ulrike Sujansky, Stacy Sullivan, Kate Tedesco, Teun Voeten, and Sharon Webb. Thanks to Dr. Michael Thaler and Dr. Eliott Wolfe for being wonderful mentors and to leaders of International Medical Corps (Nancy Aossey, Kevin Noone, Martin Zogg, Stephen Tomlin) and Physicians for Human Rights (Len Rubenstein, Susannah Sirkin, Holly Burkhalter) for the opportunity to work and share ideas with you.

I'm indebted to several excellent past editors, including Sally Cheriel at the *Oregonian*, Pete Gavrilovich at the *Detroit Free Press*, and writing teachers Marc Niesyn at the University of Iowa and Carl Djerassi at Stanford.

Finally, I have been blessed with a perfect editor in Kate Darnton at PublicAffairs. Her sharp insights have strengthened this book tremendously, and I'm forever appreciative of her patience. She, and PublicAffairs' generous and supportive publisher, Peter Osnos, have repeatedly touched me with their enthusiasm for and belief in the importance of the Srebrenica doctors' story. I am deeply grateful to them and to the many other editors and staff members of PublicAffairs, and to my wonderful agent, Peter McGuigan, who worked very hard to make this book a reality.

INDEX

PUBLICAFFAIRS is a publishing house founded in 1997. It is a tribute to the standards, values, and flair of three persons who have served as mentors to countless reporters, writers, editors, and book people of all kinds, including me.

I. F. STONE, proprietor of *I. F. Stone's Weekly,* combined a commitment to the First Amendment with entrepreneurial zeal and reporting skill and became one of the great independent journalists in American history. At the age of eighty, Izzy published *The Trial of Socrates,* which was a national bestseller. He wrote the book after he taught himself ancient Greek.

BENJAMIN C. BRADLEE was for nearly thirty years the charismatic editorial leader of *The Washington Post.* It was Ben who gave the *Post* the range and courage to pursue such historic issues as Watergate. He supported his reporters with a tenacity that made them fearless, and it is no accident that so many became authors of influential, best-selling books.

ROBERT L. BERNSTEIN, the chief executive of Random House for more than a quarter century, guided one of the nation's premier publishing houses. Bob was personally responsible for many books of political dissent and argument that challenged tyranny around the globe. He is also the founder and was the longtime chair of Human Rights Watch, one of the most respected human rights organizations in the world.

———

For fifty years, the banner of Public Affairs Press was carried by its owner, Morris B. Schnapper, who published Gandhi, Nasser, Toynbee, Truman, and about 1,500 other authors. In 1983 Schnapper was described by *The Washington Post* as "a redoubtable gadfly." His legacy will endure in the books to come.

Peter Osnos, *Publisher*